CW00432567

HARRAP'S

English Spelling

Editors

BUD WILEMAN
ROBIN WILEMAN

HARRAP

London Paris

First published in this edition in 1989
by HARRAP BOOKS Ltd
Chelsea House, 26 Market Square,
Bromley, Kent BR1 1NA

© *Wileman Publications* 1988

ISBN 0 245-54832-7

Reprinted 1990 (twice)

**In gratitude to all those children and adults who helped with
the spelling in this dictionary.**

Typeset in Australia by
Abb-typesetting Pty Ltd
126 Oxford Street
Collingwood, Victoria

Printed and bound in Singapore by
Intellectual Publishing Co.

FOREWORD

This is a book that deals with an age old problem.

> "Please, how do you spell 'inconceivable'?"
> "Why don't you look it up in the dictionary?"
> "I did, but it's not there!"

Of course it was there, but not in the form sought by the puzzled inquirer, who was trying to find "inconseavable".

In English, there is no simple relationship between speech sounds and their graphic representation: a single sound may be written in a number of different ways. However, far from being a haphazard arrangement, English spelling is based on a complex system of rules which govern the interrelationship of a word's visual appearance, sound and meaning. Sometimes, as in the K sound in *skip* (Scandinavian) and *schizoid* (Greek), the word's origin determines the spelling. On other occasions it is the grammatical function, as in "there" and "their", which both derive from Old English.

The visual patterns also impose limitations on meaning, and they may give readers significant clues. For example, the homonyms "to", "too", and "two" have differing syntactic and semantic functions; "night" and "knight" are both nouns, but mean different things.

For struggling readers and writers, the whole system can be bewildering, and the rules difficult to learn. What can be done to help? One possibility is to reform spelling so that it becomes phonetically regular. G. B. Shaw left a legacy to that end, and some beginning reading and writing schemes such as the Initial Teaching Alphabet have attempted the task. However, such alleged reforms would result in considerable problems for those who have already learnt to read and write, and would deprive all readers of the valuable clues to meaning inherent in the present system.

The alternatives are, firstly, to find more efficient ways of teaching spelling in context as a system of auditory and visual patterns that contribute to our understanding of the printed word and, secondly, to provide writers with a key to correct spellings of incidental words as they need them.

Harrap's English Spelling provides such a key. It consists of a lexicon of commonly used words, containing not only their correct spelling but also common misspellings, so that the reader can look up "inconseavable" or "inconceivable" and find the accepted form of the word. The incorrect spellings are easily identified both by the indention and a pale blue lettering.

The misspellings have been drawn from a range of spelling tests, lists of commonly misspelt words, and the editors' own experience. An additional advantage is the provision of a set of simple guidelines to help inexperienced or erratic spellers to improve their mastery of written language.

Harrap's English Spelling is designed to help those people who, although their oral conversation is adequate, may not be able to spell all the words they know. It will be an invaluable reference for the many children and adults with problems in this area, as well as for teachers who are endeavouring to help them.

Dr. Patricia Long,
Chairperson
Special Education Department,
Melbourne College of Advanced Education

INTRODUCTION

How to Find a Word

If possible, write down what you think is the spelling of the word you wish to find. Decide which are the first two or three letters.

Find these in the dictionary by looking at the left hand column. If you have the correct spelling you will find the word printed in **black**.

If you have the incorrect spelling you will find the word printed in **blue**, in the second left hand column. You will then find the correct spelling in black in the right hand column. If you do not find the word, check any directions that may be given e.g.

Look under **de-** if the
word is not under **di**.

Then proceed as above. Check how close you were to the correct spelling and if necessary learn the correct spelling.

How to Learn the Correct Spelling

Say the words and letters.
Look at the word carefully.
Write the word three times.
Close your eyes and think of the word. **Write it down** with your eyes closed.
Check to see if you are correct.
Write the word in a sentence so that you will remember its meaning as well as its spelling.
Consult a standard dictionary if you are unsure of the meaning.

About the Dictionary

You will see that all the words, correct spellings and incorrect spellings are listed in alphabetical order.

Nouns

To form the plural of most nouns add "s" to the word.
  e.g. rabbit, rabbits.

Where the plural may be difficult, you are given help.

  e.g. injury, -ries (for 'injuries')
     goose, geese
     piano, pianos.

You will find hints to help you with plurals on page viii.

Verbs

Verbs listed in the dictionary give the endings for the past tense, the past participle and the present participle. Most verbs have the same word for the past tense and the past participle.

  e.g. reach, -ed, -ing for reach, reached, reaching.

Where difficulty could occur with the spelling, you are given further help.

  e.g. collide, -lided, -liding for collide, collided, colliding.
     erase, erased, erasing.

Where the past tense and the past participle are different, the words are given in full.

  e.g. sing, sang, sung, singing.

Adjectives

Where there may be difficulty in spelling the comparative and superlative forms, further help in given.

  e.g. dizzy, dizzier, dizziest.

Adverbs

Where the ending **-ly** is given, it is added to the word.

  e.g. mythical, -ly for 'mythically.'

Where there is a change in spelling, further help is given.

  e.g. haste, -tily for 'hastily.'
     palpable, -bly for 'palpably.'

SOME SPELLING HINTS

1. For short sounding words (one syllable words) *that do not end in* **e**, double the last letter when adding -ed, -er or -ing, e.g. ban, banned; jog, jogger; fit, fitting.

2. In short words that end in **e** where the central vowel sound is said the same way as the letter name − e.g. make − drop the **e** when -ed, -er or -ing are added, e.g. cope, coped; make, maker; bite, biting.

   Short words keep the **e** when -ly is added, e.g. tame, tamely; time, timely.

3. Short words (one syllable) ending in **y**, preceded by a vowel, keep the **y** when -ed, -er or -ing are added, e.g. key, keyed; buy, buyer; toy, toying. If the **y** is preceded by a consonant, when -ed or -er are added, the **y** is changed to **i**, e.g. try, tried; fly, flier.

   The **y** is kept when adding -ing, e.g. try, trying.

4. Longer words ending in **y**, change the **y** to **i** when adding other parts, e.g. berry, berries; marry, marriage; happy, happiness; hurry, hurried; funny, funnily; heavy, heavier and heaviest.

   However when adding **-ing**, the **y** is kept, e.g. hurry, hurrying; bury, burying.

5. Vowels that can be doubled are **e** (been) and **o** (moon) and sometimes **u** (vacuum); **a** and **i** are not doubled in English words.

6. Letters that can be doubled in the middle of a word are **b, d, f, g, m, n, r, s, t** and **z**.

7. In short words, **f, l, s** and **z** at the end of a word are doubled, e.g. cuff, doll, pass, buzz.

8. If **full** is added to the end of a word, one l is dropped, e.g. helpful, until.

9. When **all-** or **well-** are added to the front of a word, one l is dropped, e.g. already, welcome.

10. When **dis-** and **mis-**, meaning 'not' are placed in front of a word, the s is not doubled — e.g. disable, misbehave — unless the main word begins with s, e.g. disservice, misspell.

   Also when **un-** is placed in front of a word, the n is not doubled — e.g. unmade — unless the main word begins with n, e.g. unnecessary.

   Similarly, when **in-** is placed in front of a word, the n is not doubled — e.g. insane — unless the main word begins with n, e.g. innumerable.

PLURALS

1. Most words add **s** to form the plural — e.g. cat, cats, but words that end in a sibilant sound (-s, -sh, -ss, -tch, -x) add **es**, e.g. gases, wishes, masses, catches, foxes.

2. Most words ending in **f** change the f to v and add **es**, e.g. thief, thieves. There are sometimes exceptions, so check the word.

3. Most words ending in **o** add **es**, e.g. potato, potatoes. Exceptions are foreign words, so check the word if you are unsure.

4. Words ending in **y**, *preceded by a consonant*, change the y to i and add **es** — e.g. ferry, ferries, but words ending in **y**, *preceded by a vowel*, add **s**, e.g. day, days; monkey, monkeys.

5. Words ending in **ful** usually put the **s** after the stem word, e.g. cupful, cupsful. However the placement of s at the end of the word is now becoming acceptable, e.g. cupful, cupfuls.

6. Some words add **en** or **ren** to the stem word, e.g. ox, oxen; child, children.

7. Some foreign words change the ending and add **a**, **ae**, **i**, e.g. compendium, compendia; formula, formulae; bacillus, bacilli.

POSITION OF LETTERS

1. In **'ee'** sound words, **c** is always followed by **ei**, e.g. receive, ceiling. Most others have **ie**, e.g. believe, priest. However, there are many exceptions so check the word if you are unsure.

2. **q** is always followed by **u** in English words.

3. No English words end in **j** or **v**.

4. If **g** or **h** come together, **g** is always before **h**, e.g. eight, enough.

5. **ck** never starts a word.

SOUNDS

1. If a long word (more than one syllable) ends in the sound **'shun'**, it could be spelt -tion, -sion, -cion.

2. **ti**, **si** and **ci** make the **'sh'** sound, but not at the beginning of a word.

3. A long word ending in the **'j'** sound could be -age, -ige, -dge. Check the word if you are not sure.

4. A long word ending in the **'ree'** sound could be -ary, -ery, -ory or -ry. Check if you are not sure.

5. Very short words (one syllable) ending in **y** make the **'i'** sound as in sly, pry, sky.

6. Words ending in the **'ul'** sound could be spelt -ble, -al, -il, -ol, -le. Check if your are not sure.

7. Most words ending in the **'ize'** sound are usually spelt **-ise**, e.g. analyse, paralyse. Some exceptions are capsize, prize.

Aa

aback
abacus, abaci, abacuses
  abait   abate
  abakus   abacus
abalone
  abalonie   abalone
abandon, -ed, -ing
abandonment
abase, abased, abasing
abasement
abashed
abate, abated, abating
abatement
  abators   abattoirs
abattoirs
  abatwaz   abattoirs
  abayance   abeyance
abbess (nun)
  abbess   abyss (hole)
abbey, -beys
  abbie   abbey
abbot
abbreviate, -ated, -ating
abbreviation
  abcence   absence
  abdacate   abdicate
abdicate, -cated, -cating
abdication
abdomen
  abduckshun   abduction
abduct
abduction
abductor
  abel   able
  aberation   aberration
aberrant
aberration
abet, abetted, abetting

abeyance
  abeyense   abeyance
abhor, abhorred, abhorring
  abhore   abhor
  abhorent   abhorrent
abhorrent, -ly
abidance
  abidanse   abidance
abide, abode, abided, abiding
  abilitee   ability
  abilitey   ability
ability, -ties
  abismal   abysmal
  abiss   abyss
abject, -ly
  abjective   objective
  abjekt   abject
abjure, -jured, -juring
ablaze
able, abler, ablest
able-bodied
  ablushun   ablution
ablution
  abnegashun   abnegation
abnegate, -gated, -gating
abnegation
abnormal, -ly
abnormality, -ties
aboard
abode
abolish
abolishment
  abolishun   abolition
abolitionary
abolitionist
  abollish   abolish
A-bomb
  abominabel   abominable
abominable
abominably
abominate, -nated, -nating
abomination
  abord   aboard
aboriginal
Aborigine
  aborshun   abortion
abort, -ed, -ing

abortion
abortive, -ly
abound, -ed, -ing
about
above
aboveboard
  abowt   about
abracadabra
abradant
abrade, abraded, abrading
abrasion
abrasive
abreast
  abrest   abreast
abridge, abridged, abridging
abridgment
  abrige   abridge
abroad
abrogate, -gated, -gating
abrupt, -ly
abruptness
  absail   abseil
abscess
abscond, -ed, -ing
absconder
abseil, -ed, -ing
absence
  absense   absence
absent, -ed, -ing
absentee
absenteeism
absent-minded
  absess   abscess
absinth
  absolushun   absolution
absolute, -ly
absolution
absolutism
absolutist
absolve, -solved, -solving
absorb, -ed, -ing
absorbency
  absorbensy   absorbency
absorbent
  absorbshun   absorption
absorption
absorptive

abstain, -ed, -ing
  abstane   abstain
abstemious, -ly
  abstemius   abstemious
  abstenshun   abstention
abstention
abstinence
  abstinense   abstinence
abstinent, -ly
abstract, -ed, -ing
abstraction
  abstrakshun   abstraction
  abstrakt   abstract
abstruse, -ly
absurd, -ly
absurdity
abundance
abundant, -ly
  abundence   abundance
  abundent   abundant
  abusave   abusive
abuse, abused, abusing
abusive, -ly
abut, abutted, abutting
abuttal
abysmal, -ly
abyss (hole)
acacia
academic
academician
  academishun   academician
academy, -mies
  accacia   acacia
  accademic   academic
  accademy   academy
accede, -ceded, -ceding (agree)
  accede   exceed
             (surpass)
accelerate, -rated, -rating
acceleration
accelerator
accent, -ed, -ing
accentual, -ly
accentuate, -ated, -ating
accept, -ed, -ing
  acceptabel   acceptable
acceptability

acceptable, -bly
acceptance
acceptense   acceptance
access
accessable   accessible
accessary, -ries (crime)
accessibel   accessible
accessibility
accessible, -bly
accessibul   accessible
accession
accessory, -ries (extra)
accident
accidental, -ly
acclaim, -ed, -ing
acclamation
acclimatise, -tised, -tising
accolade
accommodate, -dated, -dating
accommodation
accomodation   accommodation
accompaniment
accompanist
accompany, -nied, -nying
accompanyment   accompaniment
accomplice
accomplish, -ed, -ing
accomplishment
accompliss   accomplice
accord, -ed, -ing
accordance
accordanse   accordance
accordant, -ly
accordingly
accordion
accordionist
accost, -ed, -ing
account, -ed, -ing
accountabel   accountable
accountability
accountable
accountably
accountabul   accountable
accountancy
accountant
accoustic   acoustic
accredit, -ed, -ing

accreditation
accreshun   accretion
accretion
accrew   accrue
accross   across
accrual
accrue, -crued, -cruing
accult   occult
accumen   acumen
accumulate, -lated, -lating
accumulation
accumulative
accumulator
accuracy
accurasy   accuracy
accurate, -ly
accurateness
accursed
accusation
accuse, -cused, -cusing
accuser
accustom, -ed, -ing
accute   acute
ace
acelerate   accelerate
acerage   acreage
acerbait   acerbate
acerbate, -bated, -bating
acerbic
acerbity
acerige   acreage
acetate
acetic (acid)
acetic   ascetic (hermit)
acetilene   acetylene
acetylene
ache, ached, aching
acheivable   achievable
acheive   achieve
achievabel   achievable
achievable
achievabul   achievable
achieve, achieved, achieving
achievement
achiever
acid
acidic

acidify, -fied, -fying

acidity

ackers

acknowledge, -edged, -edging

acknowledgment

For other ack-words,
look under ac- or acc-.

---

aclaim	acclaim
aclamation	acclamation

acme

acne

acolade	accolade
acommodate	accommodate
acommodation	accommodation
acompanist	accompanist
acompany	accompany
acomplice	accomplice
acomplish	accomplish
acord	accord
acordion	accordion

acorn

acost	accost
acount	account

acoustic

acoustical, -ly

acoustics

acquaint, -ed, -ing

acquaintance

acquaintanse	acquaintance

acquiesce, -esced, -escing

acquiescence

acquiescent, -ly

acquiess	acquiesce

acquire, -quired, -quiring

acquisition

acquisitive, -ly

acquit, -quitted, -quitting

acquittal

acre

acreage

acredit	accredit

acrid, -ly

acrimonious, -ly

acrimony, -nies

acrobat

acrobatic

acrobatically

acrobatics

acrofobia	acrophobia

acrophobia

acropolis

across

acrylic

acryllic	acrylic

act, -ed, -ing

acter	actor

acting

action

actionabel	actionable

actionable

actionabul	actionable

activate, -vated, -vating

active

activism

activist

activity, -ties

actor

actress

actual, -ly

actuality, -ties

actually

actuarial, -ly

actuary, -ries

actuate, -ated, -ating

acuity

acumen

acupuncture

acupuncturist

acupunshur	acupuncture

acute, -ly

acuteness

adage

adagio

adajio	adagio

adamant

adament	adamant

adapt, -ed, -ing

adaptabel	adaptable

adaptability

adaptable

adaptabul	adaptable

adaptation

adaption

adaptive, -ly
adaptor
  adda | adder
addendum, -da
adder
  addicshun | addiction
addict, -ed, -ing
addiction
addictive
  addishun | addition
addition (add)
  addition | edition (book)
additional, -ly
additive
addled
address, -ed, -ing
adduce, -duced, -ducing
  adducibel | adducible
adducible

> For other **add-** words,
> look under **ad-**.

adenoid
adept, -ly
adeptness
adequacy
  adequasy | adequacy
adequate, -ly
  adherant | adherent
adhere, -hered, -hering
adherence
  adherense | adherence
adherent, -ly
  adheshun | adhesion
adhesion
adhesive, -ly
adjacent, -ly
  adjasent | adjacent
adjectival, -ly
adjective
  adjetival | adjectival
  adjetive | adjective
adjoin, -ed, -ing
adjourn, -ed, -ing
adjournment
adjudicate, -cated, -cating
adjudication

adjudicative, -ly
adjudicator
adjunct
adjure, -jured, -juring
  adjurn | adjourn
  adjurnment | adjournment
adjust, -ed, -ing
  adjustabel | adjustable
adjustable, -bly
  adjustabul | adjustable
adjustment
  admeral | admiral
administer, -ed, -ing
  administrabel | administrable
administrable
  administrabul | administrable
administrate, -trated, -trating
  administrater | administrator
administration
administrative, -ly
administrator
admirable, -bly
admiral
admiralty, -ties
admiration
admire, -mired, -miring
admirer
  admishun | admission
  admissable | admissible
  admissibel | admissible
admissible, -ly
  admissibul | admissible
admission
admit, -mitted, -mitting
admittance
  admittanse | admittance
admittedly
admonish, -ed, -ing
  admonishun | admonition
admonition
ad nauseam
ado
adobe
adolescence
adolescent
  adolesense | adolescence
  adolesent | adolescent

adopshun	adoption
adopt, -ed, -ing	
adoption	
adoptive, -ly	
adorabel	adorable
adorable	
adorably	
adorabul	adorable
adoration	
adore, adored, adoring	
adorn, -ed, -ing	
adornment	
adorrable	adorable
adorre	adore
adrenalin	
adress	address
adrift	
adroit, -ly	
adroyt	adroit
adulate, -lated, -lating	
adulation	
adulatory	
adult	
adulterate, -rated, -rating	
adulteration	
adulterer	
adulteress	
adulterous	
adultery, -teries	
adulthood	
adultry	adultery
advacate	advocate
advance, -vanced, -vancing	
advancement	
advanse	advance
advansement	advancement
advantage, -taged, -taging	
advantageous, -ly	
advantaje	advantage
advenscher	adventure
advenshur	adventure
advent	
adventure, -tured, -turing	
adventureous	adventurous
adventurer	
adventuresome	
adventurous, -ly	

adverb	
adverbial, -ly	
adversary, -saries	
adverse, -ly	
adversery	adversary
adversity, -ties	
advert, -ed, -ing	
advertise, -tised, -tising	
advertisement	
advertiser	
advertisment	advertisement
advice (opinion)	
advice	advise (give advice)
advisabel	advisable
advisability	
advisable, -bly	
advisabul	advisable
advise, -vised, -vising (give advice)	
advise	advice (opinion)
advised, -ly	
adviser	
advisery	advisory
advisory	
advocacy	
advocasy	advocacy
advocate, -cated, -cating	
advokate	advocate
adze	
aegis	
aeon	
aerate, -rated, -rating	
aerator	
aerial, -ly	
aerobatics	
aerobics	
aerodrome	
aerodynamics	
aeronautical, -ly	
aeronautics	
aeronortics	aeronautics
aeroplain	aeroplane
aeroplane	
aerosol	
aerospace	
aesthetic	

aetiologist

aetiology

afable	affable
afadavit	affadavit
afair	affair

afar

afasia	aphasia
afect	affect (pretend)
afect	effect (result)
afectation	affectation
afected	affected
afected	effected
afection	affection
afectionate	affectionate
afective	affective
afeild	afield
affabel	affable

affability

affable

affableness

affably

affabul	affable
affadavit	affidavit

affair

affare	affair
affecshun	affection

affect, -ed, -ing (pretend)

affectation

affection

affectionate, -ly

affective, -ly (emotion)

affective	effective (actual)

affidavit

affiliate, -ated, -ating

affiliation

affilliation	affiliation

affinity, -ties

affirm, -ed, -ing

affirmation

affirmative, -ly

affix, -ed, -ing

afflicshun	affliction

afflict, -ed, -ing

affliction

afflictive, -ly

affluence

affluense	affluence

affluent, -ly

afford, -ed, -ing

affordable

affordabul	affordable
affraid	afraid

affray

affresh	afresh
affro	afro

affront, -ed, -ing

afield

afinity	affinity
afirm	affirm
afirmative	affirmative
afix	affix
aflict	afflict
afliction	affliction

afloat

afluent	affluent
aford	afford

afraid

afray	affray

afresh

afro

afront	affront

aft

after

afterbirth

afterglow

afterlife

aftermath

afternoon

afters

afterthought

afterwards

again

against

agape

agate

age, aged, ageing or aging

agency, -cies

agenda, -das

agensy	agency

agent

agghast	aghast

aggrandise, -dised, -dising

aggrandisement

aggrandiser
aggravate, -vated, -vating
aggravation
aggravator
aggreeved — aggrieved
aggregate, -gated, -gating
aggregation
aggregative
aggreived — aggrieved
aggreshun — aggression
aggression
aggressive, -ly
aggressor
aggreved — aggrieved
aggrieved
aggro
agground — aground
aghast
agile, -ly
agility
agis — aegis
agist, -ed, -ing
agistment
agitate, -tated, -tating
agitater — agitator
agitation
agitative
agitator
agnostic
agnosticism
ago
agog
agonise, -nised, -nising
agonisingly
agony, -nies
agorafobia — agoraphobia
agoraphobia
agraculture — agriculture
agrarian
agravate — aggravate
agravation — aggravation
agree, agreed, agreeing
agreeabel — agreeable
agreeable, -bly
agreeableness
agreeabul — agreeable
agreement

agregate — aggregate
agression — aggression
agressive — aggressive
agressor — aggressor
agricultural, -ly
agriculturalist
agriculture
agrieved — aggrieved
agronomist
agronomy
aground
ahead
ahed — ahead
ahoy
aid (help)
aide (assistant)
ail, -ed, -ing
ail — ale (beer)
aileron
ailias — alias
ailment
aim, -ed, -ing
aimless, -ly
aimlessness
ain't (am not)
aint — ain't
air, -ed, -ing
air — hair
airate — aerate
airborn — airborne
airborne
air-brake
air-break — air-brake
airbus
air condishun — air-condition
air-condition, -ed, -ing
aircraft, -craft
airfeild — airfield
airfield
airforce
airgun
air hostess
aireal — aerial
airial — aerial
airily
airlift
airline

airliner		albino, -nos	
airlock		albinism	
airmail		album	
airman, -men		albumen (egg white)	
airobatics	aerobatics	albumin (protein)	
airobics	aerobics	albuminous	
airodrome	aerodrome	albuminus	albuminous
airodynamics	aerodynamics	alcali	alkali
airoplane	aeroplane	alcaline	alkaline
airosol	aerosol	alchemist	
air-pocket		alchemy	
airport		alcohol	
air-pressure		alcoholic	
airship		alcoholism	
airspace		alcove	
airspeed		alderman, -men	
airstream		ale (beer)	
airstrip		ale	ail (ill)
air terminal		alege	allege
airtight		alert, -ed, -ing	
airtite	airtight	alfa	alpha
airwaves		alfabet	alphabet
airy, airier, airiest		alfalfa	
airy-fairy		alfresco	
aisle (path)		alga, -gae	
aitch		algebra	
ajar		algebraic, -ally	
ajis	aegis	alias, aliases	
akimbo		alibi, -bis	
akin		alien	
alabaster		alienate, -nated, -nating	
alabi	alibi	alienation	
alacart	à la carte	alienator	
à la carte		alight, alighted, alighting	
alackrity	alacrity	align, -ed, -ing	
alacritous		alignment	
alacritus	alacritous	alike	
alacrity		aliment (food)	
Alah	Allah	aliment	element (part)
alarm, -ed, -ing		alimentary (food)	
alarmist		alimentary	elementary (basic)
alas			
Alaska		alimony	
albatros	albatross	alive	
albatross, albatrosses		alkaholic	alcoholic
albeeit	albeit	alkali, -lis, -lies	
albeit		alkaline	

alkalinity	
alkeline	alkaline
alkohol	alcohol
alkoholic	alcoholic
alkoholism	alcoholism
alkove	alcove
all (every)	
all	awl (tool)
allabaster	alabaster
Allah	
allay, -layed, -laying	
allbatross	albatross
alledge	allege
allegation	
allege, -leged, -leging	
allegiance	
allegianse	allegiance
allegorical, -ly	
allegory, -ries	
allegro	
alleluia	
allergic	
allergy, -gies	
allert	alert
alleviate, -ated, -ating	
alleviation	
alleviator	
alley, alleys	
alliance	
allied	
alliense	alliance
allies	
alligator	
all-in	
alliteration	
alliterative, -ly	
allmanac	almanac
allmost	almost
allocate, -cated, -cating	
allocation	
alloft	aloft
allone	alone
allot, -lotted, -lotting	
allotment	
all-out	
allow, -ed, -ing	
allowabel	allowable

allowable	
allowabul	allowable
allowance	
allowense	allowance
alloy	
all right	
allrite	all right
all-rounder	
allso	also
allude, -luded, -luding (refer)	
allude	elude (avoid)
allure, -lured, -luring	
allushun	allusion
allusion (mention)	
allusion	illusion (trick)
allusive, -ly (mentioned)	
allusive	elusive (avoid)
alluvial	
ally, -lies	
ally, -lied, -lying	
ally	alley
almanac	
almanack	
almightily	
almightiness	
almighty	
almond	
almoner	
almost	
alms (gifts)	
alocate	allocate
aloe	
aloft	
alone	
along	
alongside	
alood	allude
aloof	
alot	a lot (of)
alot	allot (give)
aloud (speak)	
aloud	allowed (permit)
alow	allow
alowable	allowable
alowance	allowance
aloy	alloy

alp		amaize	amaze	
alpaca		amalgam		
alpacka	alpaca	amalgamate, -mated, -mating		
alpha		amalgamation		
alphabet		amalgum	amalgam	
alphabetical, -ly		amass, -ed, -ing		
alphebet	alphabet	amassabel	amassable	
alpine		amassable		
already		amassabul	amassable	
alredy	already	amatcher	amateur	
Alsatian		amatchur	amateur	
also		amater	amateur	
altar (church)		amateur		
altatude	altitude	amatory		
altenate	alternate	amaze, -mazed, -mazing		
alter (change)		amazement		
alterable, -bly		Amazon		
alteration		ambaguity	ambiguity	
altercation		ambassader	ambassador	
altercative		ambassador, -ial		
alter ego		ambel	amble	
alternate, -nated, -nating		amber		
alternately		ambiance	ambience	
alternation		ambiant	ambient	
alternative, -ly		ambidexterity		
alternator		ambidextrous, -ly		
alterration	alteration	ambience		
although		ambiense	ambience	
altimeter		ambient		
altitude		ambiguity, -ties		
alto, -tos		ambiguous, -ly		
altogether		ambiguus	ambiguous	
altrooism	altruism	ambishen	ambition	
altrueism	altruism	ambishus	ambitious	
altruism		ambit		
altruistic, -ally		ambition		
alturnate	alternate	ambitious, -ly		
alude	allude	ambivalence		
alumina		ambivalense	ambivalence	
aluminium		ambivalent		
aluminum	aluminium	amble, -bled, -bling		
alumminum	aluminium	ambul	amble	
alure	allure	ambulance		
alurt	alert	ambulanse	ambulance	
alushun	allusion	ambush, -ed, -ing		
alusive	allusive	ame	aim	
always		ameanable	amenable	

ameba	amoeba
ameliorate, -rated, -rating	
amelioration	
amen	
amenabel	amenable
amenable, -bly	
amenabul	amenable
amend, -ed, -ing	
amendment	
amends	
amenity, -ties	
America	
ameter	ammeter
amethist	amethyst
amethyst	

For amf- words, look under **amph-**.

amiabel	amiable
amiability	
amiable, -bly	
amiabul	amiable
amicabel	amicable
amicability	
amicable, -bly	
amicabul	amicable
amid	
amidst	
amigo	
amiss	
amity, -ties	
ammeter	
ammonia	
ammunition	

For other amm- words, look under **am-**.

amnesia, -iac	
amnesty, -ties	
amnesty, -tied, -tying	
amoeba, -bae, -bas	
amoebic	
amok	
among	
amongst	
amoral, -ly	
amorfous	amorphous

amorous, -ly	
amorphism	
amorphous, -ly	
amorphus	amorphous
amortise, -tised, -tising	
amount, -ed, -ing	
amownt	amount
ampair	ampere
ampel	ample
amperage	
ampere	
amphetamine	
amphibian	
amphibious, -ly	
amphitheatre	
ample, -pler, -plest (enough)	
amplefy	amplify
amplification	
amplifier	
amplify, -fied, -fying	
amplitude	
amply	
ampoule (bottle)	
ampul	ample (enough)
ampul	ampoule (bottle)
amputate, -tated, -tating	
amputation	
amuck	
amuk	amok
amuk	amuck
amulet	
amung	among
amungst	amongst
amunition	ammunition
amuse, amused, amusing	
amusement	
anachronism	
anachronistic	
anackronism	anachronism
anackronistic	anachronistic
anaconda	
anaemia	
anaesthesia	
anaesthetic	
anaesthetisation	
anaesthetise, -tised, -tising	

anaesthetist
anagram
  anaky   anarchy
anal
analgesia
analgesic
  analise   analyse
  analisis   analysis
  analist   analyst
analog (electric)
  analog   analogue
                  (similar)
analogous, -ly
analogue (similar)
  analogue   analog
                  (electric)
analogy, -gies
analyse, -lysed, -lysing
analysis, -ses
analyst
analytical, -ly
anarchical, -ly
anarchism
anarchist
anarchy
anathema, -mas
anatomical, -ly
anatomist
anatomy, -mies
ancestor
ancestral, -ly
ancestry, -tries
anchor, -ed, -ing
anchorage
anchorman, -men
anchovy, -vies
ancient
ancillary, -aries
anecdotal
anecdote
  anemia   anaemia
  anemic   anaemic
  anesthesia   anaesthesia
  anesthetic   anaesthetic
  anesthetise   anaesthetise
  anesthetist   anaesthetist
aneurism

anew
  anewity   annuity
angel (spirit)
  angel   angle (fishing)
angelic
  angellic   angelic
anger, -ed, -ing
angina
angle, angled, angling (fishing)
  angle   angel (spirit)
angler
Anglican
Anglicanism
Anglo-Catholic
  Anglo-Sacksen Anglo-Saxon
Anglo-Saxon
angora
  angree   angry
  angrie   angry
angrily
angry, angrier, angriest
  angsiety   anxiety
anguish, -ed, -ing
angular, -ity
  anguler   angular
  angwish   anguish
  anigma   enigma
animal
animate, -mated, -mating
animatedly
animation
  animel   animal
animosity, -ties
aniseed
  aniversary   anniversary
  anjel   angel
  anjelic   angelic
  anjina   angina
  anker   anchor
  ankerage   anchorage
  ankeridge   anchorage
  ankerije   anchorage
ankle
anklet
annals
anneal, -ed, -ing
annex, -ed, -ing (join)

annexation
annexe (building)
   annialate   annihilate
annihilate, -lated, -lating
anniversary, -ries
Anno Domini
annotate, -tated, -tating
annotation
announce, announced, announcing
announcement
annoy, annoyed, annoying
annual, -ly
annuity, -ties
annul, annulled, annulling
annulment
annulus, -li, or -luses
annunciate, -ated, -ating
annunciation

> For other **ann**-words,
> look under **an-**.

anode
   anodine   anodyne
anodyne
anoint, -ed, -ing
   anomaley   anomaly
anomaly, -lies
anon
   anonimity   anonymity
   anonimous   anonymous
anonymity
anonymous, -ly
anorak
   anorecksia   anorexia
anorexia
another
   anoynt   anoint
   anser   answer
   anserable   answerable
   anserabul   answerable
   ansestor   ancestor
   ansestral   ancestral
   ansestrul   ancestral
   ansestry   ancestry
   ansilary   ancillary
answer, -ed, -ing
   answerabel   answerable

answerable, -bly
   answerabul   answerable
antacid
antagonise, -nised, -nising
antagonism
antagonist
antagonistic, -ally
Antarctic
   antasid   antacid
   anteak   antique
anteater
antecedent
antechamber
   anteclimax   anticlimax
   antecyclone   anticyclone
antedate, -dated, -dating
   antediloovian   antediluvian
antediluvian
   anteek   antique
antelope, antelopes
   antena   antenna
antenatal
   antenatel   antenatal
   antenatul   antenatal
antenna, -tennae, -tennas
anterior
anteroom
anthem
anthill
anthology, -gies
anthracite
   anthracks   anthrax
   anthrasite   anthracite
anthrax, -thraces
anthropoid
   anthropologey   anthropology
anthropologist
anthropology
antibiotic
antibody, -bodies
antic
   anticeptic   antiseptic
   antichamber   antechamber
Antichrist
   anticiclone   anticyclone
anticipate, -pated, -pating
anticipation

anticipatory		antonim	antonym
anticlimacks	anticlimax	antonym	
anticlimactic		anus	
anticlimax		anuther	another
anticlockwise		anvil	
anticyclone		anvul	anvil
anticyclonic		anxiety, -ties	
antidate	antedate	anxious, -ly	
antidepressant		any	
antidotal		anybody	
antidote		anyhow	
antifon	antiphon	anyone	
antifreeze		anything	
antigen		anyway	
antihisstamine	antihistamine	anywear	anywhere
antihistamine		anywere	anywhere
antikwarian	antiquarian	anywhere	
antikwated	antiquated	Anzac	
antikwitey	antiquity	aorta, -tas, -tae	
antilope	antelope	apace	
antimony		apart	
antinatal	antenatal	apartheid	
antinatul	antenatal	apartied	apartheid
antinewklear	antinuclear	apartite	apartheid
antinuclear		apartment	
antipathy, -pathies		apase	apace
antiperspirant		apathetic, -ally	
antiphon		apathy	
antipodes		ape, aped, aping	
antipodies	antipodes	apeace	apiece
antiquarian		apease	apiece
antiquary, -quaries		apeice	apiece
antiquated		apeks	apex
antique		apercher	aperture
antiquity, -quities		apergee	apogee
antiroom	anteroom	apergey	apogee
anti-Semitic		aperitif	
anti-Semitism		aperture	
antiseptic, -ally		apex, apexes, apices	
antisiclone	anticyclone	aphasia	
antisipation	anticipation	aphid	
antisocial, -ly		aphorism	
antithesis, -theses		aphrodisiac	
antithisis	antithesis	apiary, apiaries	
antitoksic	antitoxic	apiece	
antitoksin	antitoxin	apissul	epistle
antler		apistle	epistle

aplom	aplomb
aplomb	
aply	apply
apocalipse	apocalypse
apocalypse	
apocalyptic	
apocrifal	apocryphal
apocryphal, -ly	
apogee	
apologetic, -ally	
apologey	apology
apologise, -gised, -gising	
apologist	
apology, -gies	
apoplectic	
apoplexy	
aposle	apostle
apostasy, -sies	
apostel	apostle
apostle	
apostolate	
apostolic	
apostrofy	apostrophe
apostrophe	
aposul	apostle
apothecary, -ries	
apoynt	appoint

> For other ap- words,
> look under **app-**.

appal, -palled, -palling	
apparatus, -tus, -tuses	
apparel	
apparent, -ly	
apparishun	apparition
apparition	
appart	apart
appeal, -ed, -ing	
appealing, -ly	
appear, -ed, -ing	
appearance	
appearense	appearance
appease, -peased, -peasing	
appeasement	
appelant	appellant
appellant	
appellate	

appellation	
append, -ed, -ing	
appendacitis	appendicitis
appendage	
appendectomy, -mies	
appendicitis	
appendige	appendage
appendiks	appendix
apperatus	apparatus
appertain, -ed, -ing	
apperture	aperture
appetiser	
appetite	
applaud, -ed, -ing	
applause	
applawd	applaud
applaws	applause
apple	
appliance	
applianse	appliance
applicability	
applicable, -bly	
applicant	
application	
applie	apply
applied	
applique	
apply, -plied, -plying	
appoint, -ed, -ing	
appointment	
apporshun	apportion
apportion, -ed, -ing	
apportionment	
apposishun	apposition
apposite, -ly	
apposition	
appraisal	
appraise, -praised, -praising	
appraysal	appraisal
apprayse	appraise
appreciabel	appreciable
appreciable, -bly	
appreciabul	appreciable
appreciate, -ated, -ating	
appreciation	
appreciative, -ly	
apprehend, -ed, -ing	

apprehenshun	apprehension	arable	
apprehensibel	apprehensible	arabul	arable
apprehensible		araign	arraign
apprehensibul	apprehensible	arain	arraign
apprehension		arange	arrange
apprehensive, -ly		aray	array
apprentice		arber	arbour
apprenticeship		arbiter	
apprentise	apprentice	arbitrary	
appricot	apricot	arbitrate, -trated, -trating	
apprise, -prised, -prising		arbitration	
approach, -ed, -ing		arbor (axis)	
approachabel	approachable	abor	arbour (shade)
approachable		arboreal	
approbation		arboricultural	
approch	approach	arboriculture	
approchabul	approachable	arbour (shade)	
approove	approve	arbour	arbor (axis)
appropos	appropos	arc, arced, arcing (curve)	
appropriate, -ated, -ating		arc	ark (boat)
appropriation		arcade	
approval		arcane	
approve, -proved, -proving		arch	
approvel	approval	archaeological, -ly	
approximate, -mated, -mating		archaeologist	
approximately		archaeology	
approximation		archaic	
apricot		archaism	
April		archangel	
apron		archary	archery
appropos		archbishop	
apt, -ly		archer	
aptitude		archerfish	
aptley	aptly	archery	
aqualung		archetypal	
aquamarine		archetype	
aquaplane		archipelago, -gos, -goes	
aquarium		architect	
Aquarius		architectural, -ly	
aquatic		architecture	
aqueduct		architrave	
aqueous		archival	
aquiline		archives	
arabel	arable	archivist	
arabesk	arabesque	arcipelago	archipelago
arabesque		arcipeligo	archipelago
Arabic numerals		arcitect	architect

arcitectural	architectural	arival	arrival
arcitecture	architecture	arive	arrive
arcives	archives	ark (boat)	
arc light		ark	arc (curve)
arctic			
Arctic Circle			
ardent, -ly			

> For other ark-words,
> look under **arc-**.

arder	ardour	arm	
ardour		armacher	armature
arduous, -ly		armachur	armature
arduus	arduous	armada	
are		armadillo, -los	
area		Armageddon	
arears	arrears	armament	
arena		armature	
aren't		armchair	
arent	aren't	armed	
arest	arrest	armer	armour
argent		armey	army
argew	argue	armistice	
argon		armistise	armistice
arguabel	arguable	armoner	almoner
arguable, -bly		armour	
arguabul	arguable	armoured	
argue, -gued, -guing		armourer	
arguement	argument	armoury, -ries	
argument		armpit	
argumentation		arms (weapons)	
argumentative, -ly		arms	alms (gifts)
argus		army, -mies	
arguw	argue	arogance	arrogance
argy-bargy, -bargies		aroganse	arrogance
aria (melody)		arogant	arrogant
aria	area (piece)	aroma	
arial	aerial	aromatic	
arid, -ly		arora	aurora
aridity		arose	
Aries		around	
arina	arena	arousal	
arise, arose, arisen, arising		arouse, aroused, arousing	
aristocracy, -cies		arow	arrow
aristocrasy	aristocracy	arownd	around
aristocrat		arowroot	arrowroot
aristocratic		arowse	arouse
arithmetic		arpeggio	
arithmetical, -ly		arpejio	arpeggio
arithmetician		arraign, -ed, -ing	

arraignment	artiste (actor)
arrange, -ranged, -ranging	artistic
arrangement	artistry
arrant, -ly	artizan — artisan
arras	artless, -ly
array, -ed, -ing	arvo (afternoon)
arrears	arwry — awry
arrest, -ed, -ing	asbestos
arrival	ascend, -ed, -ing
arrive, -rived, -riving	ascendancy
arrogance	ascendant
arroganse — arrogance	ascenshun — ascension
arrogant, -ly	ascension
arrogate, -gated, -gating	ascent (upward)
arrouse — arouse	ascent — assent (agree)
arrow	ascertain, -ed, -ing
arrowroot	ascertainabel — ascertainable
arsenal	ascertainable, -bly
arsenic	ascertainabul — ascertainable
arsenical	ascertainment
arsnic — arsenic	ascetic, -ally
arson	asceticism
art	ascribe, ascribed, ascribing
artachoke — artichoke	ase — ace
artefact	asend — ascend
arterial	asendancy — ascendancy
artery, -teries	asendansy — ascendancy
artesian bore	asendant — ascendant
artful, -ly	asenshun — ascension
arthritic	asent — ascent (upwards)
arthritis	asent — assent (agree)
articel — article	aseptic, -ally
artichoke	asershun — assertion
article, -cled, -cling	asertain — ascertain
articul — article	asertane — ascertain
articulate, -lated, -lating	asertayne — ascertain
articulation	asetic — ascetic
artifact	aseticism — asceticism
artifice	asexual, -ly
artificer	asfalt — asphalt
artificial, -ly	asfelt — asphalt
artificiality	asfixia — asphyxia
artifise — artifice	asfixiate — asphyxiate
artifishial — artificial	ash
artillery	ashamed, -ly
artisan	ashaymed — ashamed
artist (painter)	

ashfelt	asphalt	assault	
ashore (beach)		assaulter	
ashore	assure (certain)	assay, -ed, -ing (analyse)	
aside		assay	essay (try)
asidity	acidity	assayer	
asign	assign	assemblage	
asilum	asylum	assemble, -bled, -bling	
asimetrical	asymmetrical	assembly, assemblies	
asimetry	asymmetry	assembul	assemble
asine	assign	assend	ascend
asinement	assignment	assendancy	ascendancy
asinine, -ly		assendansy	ascendancy
asininity		assendant	ascendant
asitic	ascetic	assenshun	ascension
ask, -ed, -ing		assension	ascension
askance		assent (agree)	
askanse	askance	assent	ascent (upward)
askew			
askue	askew	assention	ascension
asleep		assershun	assertion
asma	asthma	assert, -ed, -ing	
asmatic	asthmatic	assertion	
asp		assertive, -ly	
asparagus		assess, -ed, -ing	
aspect		assessabel	assessable
aspen		assessable	
aspershun	aspersion	assessabul	assessable
aspersion		assessment	
asphalt		assessor	
asphyxia		asset, assets	
asphyxiate, -ated, -ating		assiduous, -ly	
asphyxiation		assign, -ed, -ing	
aspic		assignable, -bly	
aspirant		assignation	
aspirate, -rated, -rating		assignee	
aspiration		assignment	
aspirator		assine	assign
aspirayte	aspirate	assinment	assignment
aspire, aspired, aspiring		assist, -ed, -ing	
aspirin		assistance	
asprin	aspirin	assistant	
ass, asses		associate, -ated, -ating	
assail, -ed, -ing		associashun	association
assailant		association	
assassin		associayte	associate
assassinate, -nated, -nating		assonance	
assassination		assonanse	assonance

assonant

assort, -ed, -ing

assortment

    assoshiate   associate

assuage, -suaged, -suaging

assume, -sumed, -suming

assumption

    assumshun   assumption

assurance

    assuranse   assurance

assure, -sured, -suring (certain)

    assure   ashore (beach)

aster

asterisk

astern

asteroid

asthma

asthmatic

astigmatism

astir

astonish, -ed, -ing

astonishment

astound, -ed, -ing

    astownd   astound

astral

astray

astride

astringency

astringent, -ly

astrologer

astrological, -ly

astrology

    astronaught   astronaut

astronaut

astronautics

    astronort   astronaut

    astrul   astral

    astur   astir

    asturn   astern

astute, -ly

astuteness

asunder

asylum

    asymetry   asymmetry

asymmetric

asymmetrical, -ly

asymmetry

ate (food)

    ate   eight (number)

    ateen   eighteen

    atey   eighty

atheism

atheist

atheistic

    athiesm   atheism

    athiest   atheist

    athiestic   atheistic

    athleet   athlete

athlete

athletic

atlas

    atmosfear   atmosphere

    atmosfere   atmosphere

    atmosferic   atmospheric

atmosphere

atmospheric

    atol   atoll

atoll

atom

atomic

atomiser

atone, atoned, atoning

atonement

atrocious, -ly

atrocity, -ties

atrophy, -phied, -phying

    atroshus   atrocious

attach, -ed, -ing

attaché

attachment

attack, -ed, -ing

attain, -ed, -ing

attainable

attainment

attempt, -ed, -ing

attend, -ed, -ing

attendance

attendant

attention

attentive, -ly

attenuate, -ated, -ating

attest, -ed, -ing

attic

attire, -tired, -tiring

attitude
attorney
attract, -ed, -ing
attraction
attractive, -ly
attribute, -uted, -uting
attrishun   attrition
attrition
attune, -tuned, -tuning
atune   attune
aturney   attorney

For other at- words,
look under **att-**.

atypical, -ly
aubergine
auburn
aucshun   auction
auction, -ed, -ing
auctioneer
audacious, -ly
audacity
audasity   audacity
audeo   audio
audibel   audible
audibility
audible
audibly
audibul   audible
audience
audiense   audience
audio
audiometer
audiometric
audiometry
audiovisual
audishun   audition
audit, -ed, -ing
audition
auditor
auditorium, -toriums, -toria
auditory
auditree   auditory
auditry   auditory
auger (tool)
auger   augur (foretell)
aught (any part)

aught   ought (should)
augment, -ed, -ing
augmentation
augur (foretell)
augur   auger (tool)
augural
august (majestic)
August
aukward   awkward
aunt
auntie
aunt sally
aunty
aura
aural, -ly (hearing)
aural   oral (spoken)
aureole
auricle
auricular
auriferous
auriole   aureole
aurora
auspice, auspices
auspicious, -ly
auspise   auspice
Aussie
austeer   austere
austere, -ly
austerity, -ties
austral
Australasia
Australia
Australian
Australiana
Australien   Australian
australight   australite
australite
Australorp
autamatic   automatic
autamobile   automobile
authentic
authenticate, -cated, -cating
authentication
authenticity
authentisity   authenticity
author
authoress

authorisation

authorise, -rised, -rising

authoritarian

authoritative, -ly

authority, -ties

autism

auto

autobiographical, -ly

autobiography, -phies

autocracy

autocrasy — autocracy

autocrat

autocratic

autocue

autograf — autograph

autograph

automatic

automation

automative

automobile

automotive

autonomee — autonomy

autonomous, -ly

autonomus — autonomous

autonomy

autopilot

autopsy, -sies

autum — autumn

autumn

autumnal, -ly

auxiliary, -ries

avail, -ed, -ing

availabel — available

availability

available

availabul — available

avalable — available

avalanch — avalanche

avalanche

avale — avail

avaliable — available

avant-garde

avarey — aviary

avarice

avaricious, -ly

avaris — avarice

avarishus — avaricious

avenew — avenue

avenge, avenged, avenging

avenger

avenue

aver, averred, averring

average, -raged, -raging

avericious — avaricious

averidge — average

averige — average

averishus — avaricious

averiss — avarice

averse, -ly

avershun — aversion

aversion

avert, -ed, -ing

avery — aviary

avgas

aviary, aviaries

aviater — aviator

aviation

aviator

avid, -ly

avinue — avenue

avlanch — avalanche

avocado, avocados

avoid, -ed, -ing (evade)

avoid — ovoid (egg)

avoidable, -ably

avow, -ed, -ing

avowal

avoyd — avoid

avridge — average

avrije — average

avud — avid

avur — aver

avurse — averse

avurshun — aversion

avursion — aversion

avurt — avert

await, -ed, -ing

awake, awoke, awaking

awaken, -ed, -ing

award, -ed, -ing

aware

awareness

away

awayte — await

awb	orb	azalia	azalea
awe, awed, awing (fear)		azure	
awe	oar (boat)	azury	
awear	aware		
awesome, -ly			
awful, -ly			
awgy	orgy		
awksilary	auxiliary		
awkward, -ly			
awkwud	awkward		
awl (tool)			
awl	all (every)		
awning			
awoke			
awry			
axe, axes			
axe, axed, axing			
axel	axle		
axial, -ly			
axident	accident		
axidental	accidental		
axiom			
axiomatic			
axis, axes			
axle			
axsede	accede		
axseed	accede		
axsel	axle		
axsellerate	accelerate		
axsent	accent		
axsentuate	accentuate		
axsept	accept		
axseptable	acceptable		
axseptabul	acceptable		
axseptance	acceptance		
axsesary	accessary		
axsesory	accessory		
axsess	access		
axsessable	accessible		
axsessabul	accessible		
axsessible	accessible		
axsessibul	accessible		
ay, ayes (yes)			
ayatollah			
aye (ever)			
aysure	azure		
azalea			

Bb

babbel	babble (chatter)
babble, -led, -ling (chatter)	
babboon	baboon
babbul	babble (chatter)
babe	
babel (confusion)	
babel	babble (chatter)
babey	baby
babie	baby
baboon	
babul	babble (chatter)
baby, babies	
baby-sitter	
baccarat	
bach	batch
bacheler	bachelor
bachelor	
bacillus, bacilli	
back, -ed, -ing	
backbencher	
backblocks	
backbone	
back-burn	
backer	
backfire, -fired, -firing	
backgammon	
background	
backhand	
backing	
backlash	
back-pedal, -alled, -alling	
backroom	
back-seat driver	
backstage	

backstitch, -ed, -ing	
backstop, -stopped, -stopping	
backstroke, -stroked, -stroking	
back-to-back	
backwards	
backwash	
backyard	
bacon	
bacteria	
bad, worse, worst (not good)	
bade (ask)	
badge	
badger	
badly	
badminton	
baffel	baffle
baffle, -fled, -fling	
bag, bagged, bagging	
bagatelle	
baggage	
baggidge	baggage
baggy, baggier, baggiest	
bagman, -men	
bagpipes	
baige	beige
bail (court)	
bail	bale (bundle)
bailif	bailiff
bailiff	
bairn	
bait (fishing)	
bait	bate (hold)
baize, baized, baizing	
baje	badge
bake, baked, baking	
bakelite	
baker	
bakery	
bakshee	
balaclava	
balad	ballad
balalaika	
balance, -anced, -ancing	
balanse	balance
balast	ballast
balay	ballet
balcony, -conies	

bald (hairless)
bald   bawled (cried)
balderdash
balding
baldness
bale, baled, baling (bundle)
bale   bail (court)
baleful, -ly
balefull   baleful
balerina   ballerina
balero   bolero
balet   ballet
baliff   bailiff
ball (round)
ball   bawl (cry)
ballad
ballast
ball-bearing
ballerina
ballet
ballistics
balloon
balloonist
ballot, balloted, balloting
ballpoint
ballsa   balsa
ballsam   balsam
ballyhoo
balm
balmy, balmier, balmiest (good)
balmy   barmy (stupid)
balonee   baloney
baloney
baloon   balloon
balot   ballot
balsa
balsam
balustrade
balyhoo   ballyhoo
bamboo
bamboozle, -zled, -zling
ban, banned, banning
banal, -ly
banana
banana republic
band, banded, banding (strip)
band (group)

band   banned
       (forbidden)
bandage, -daged, -daging
bandanna
bandey   bandy
bandicoot
bandige   bandage
bandit
bandoleer   bandolier
bandolier
bandsaw
bandwagon
bandy, -died, -dying
bandy-legged
baner   banner
bangalow
bangel   bangle
banger
bangle
bang-on
banish, -ed, -ing
banishment
banister
banjo, banjos
bank, -ed, -ing
bankbook
banker
banknote
bankrupcy   bankruptcy
bankrupsy   bankruptcy
bankrupt
bankruptcy
banksia
bankwet   banquet
banned (forbidden)
banned   band (strip)
banner
banns (notices)
banquet, -queted, -queting
bans (forbids)
bans   banns (notices)
bantam
bantamweight
banter, -ed, -ing
bantum   bantam
banyan
baonet   bayonet

bap
baptise, -tised, -tising
baptism
baptismal
Baptist
bar, barred, barring
  barack — barrack
  baracouta — baracouta
  barage — barrage
barb
barbarian
barbaric
barbarism
barbarous, -ly
  barbarus — barbarous
barbecue, -cued, -cuing
barbed wire
barbell
barbeque, -qued, -quing
barber
barbiturate
bard (poet)
  bard — barred (stopped)
bare, bared, baring (uncover)
bare, barer, barest
  bare — bear (animal)
bareback
barefaced
barefoot
bareheaded
  barel — barrel
barely
  baren — baron (noble)
  baren — barren (sterile)
  bareskin — bearskin
bargain, -ed, -ing
bargainer
  bargan — bargain
barge, barged, barging
bargee
  bargen — bargain
  baricade — barricade
  barier — barrier
baring (uncovering)
  baring — barring (stop)
  baring — bearing (hold)

  barister — barrister
baritone
barium
bark, -ed, -ing
barley
  barlie — barley
  barm — balm
  barmade — barmaid
barmaid
barman, -men
barmy, barmier, barmiest (stupid)
  barmy — balmy (good)
barn
  barn — bairn
  barnacel — barnacle
barnacle
barnacled
  barnacul — barnacle
barney
  barnicul — barnacle
barnstorm
barometer
barometric
baron (noble)
  baron — barren (sterile)
baronet
baronial
baroque
  barow — barrow
barrack, -ed, -ing
barracker
barracouta
barracuda
barrage, -raged, -raging
barramundi
barrel, -relled, -relling
barren (sterile)
  barren — baron (noble)
barrenness
barricade, -caded, -cading
barrier
barring (stop)
  barring — baring (uncovering)
barrister
barrow
  barrul — barrel

barter, -ed, -ing
   barul   barrel
basal, -ly
basalt
base, based, basing (support)
base, baser, basest
   base   bass (low tone)
baseball
basement
   baset   basset
bash, -ed, -ing
bashful, -ly
basic
basilica
   basillus   bacillus
basin
   basinette   bassinette
basis, bases
   basit   basset
bask, -ed, -ing (enjoy warmth)
   bask   basque (garb)
basketball
   baskit   basket
   basoon   bassoon
basque (garb)
bas-relief
bass (low tone)
   bass   base (support)
bass clef
basset
bassinette
bassoon
bastard
   bastardisashun   bastardisation
bastardisation
bastardry
baste, basted, basting
   basterd   bastard
bastion
bat, batted, batting
batch
bate, bated, bating (hold breath)
   bate   bait (fishing)
   baten   baton (stick)
   baten   batten (timber)
   bater   batter
   baterey   battery

bath
bathe, bathed, bathing
bathers
bathroom
batik
   batle   battle
   batler   battler
batman, -men
baton (stick)
   baton   batten (timber)
batsman, -men
batt (insulating)
   batt   bat (cricket)
battalion
   battaliun   battalion
   battel   battle
batten (timber)
batter
battering ram
battery, -ries
battle, battled, battling
battleaxe
battledress
battler
battleship
batty, battier, battiest
   batul   battle
   baty   batty
   baubel   bauble
bauble
   baubul   bauble
baulk, -ed, -ing
bauxite
   bawble   bauble
   bawdie   bawdy
bawdiness
bawdy, -dier, -diest
bawl, -ed, -ing (cry)
   bawl   ball (round)
   bawlsa   balsa
bay
   bayliff   bailiff
   baynet   bayonet
bayonet
   baythe   bathe
bazaar (market)
   bazaar   bizarre (odd)

bazar	bazaar
bazooka	
be, been, being (exist)	
be	bee (insect)
beach, -ches (shore)	
beach	beech (tree)
beachcomber	
beachcomer	beachcomber
beacon	
bead, -ed, -ing	
beady, beadier, beadiest	
beaf	beef
beafeater	beefeater
beafy	beefy
beagel	beagle
beagle	
beak	
beaker	
beam, -ed, -ing	
bean (vegetable)	
bean	been (be)
beanie	
beano	
bear (animal)	
bear, borne, bearing (carry)	
bear	bare (uncover)
bearback	bareback
beard	
bearer	
bearfaced	barefaced
bearfoot	barefoot
bearheaded	bareheaded
bearing (hold)	
bearing	baring (uncovering)
bearskin	
beast	
beastliness	
beastly, beastlier, beastliest	
beat, beaten, beating (strike)	
beat	beet (food)
beatel	beetle
beater	
beatific	
beatify, -fied, -fying	
beatitude	
beatle	beetle

beatnik	
beatroot	beetroot
beatul	beetle
beau, beaus, beaux (suitor)	
beaut	
beauteous, -ly	
beautician	
beautie	beauty
beautiful, -ly	
beautify, -fied, -fying	
beautishun	beautician
beauty, beauties	
beaver	
becalmed	
became	
becarmed	becalmed
because	
beck	
beckon, -ed, -ing	
become, became, becoming	
becon	beacon
becos	because
bed, bedded, bedding	
bedeck, -ed, -ing	
bedevel	bedevil
bedevil, -illed, -illing	
bedevul	bedevil
bedlam	
bedouin	
bedowin	bedouin
bedpan	
bedraggled	
bedraguled	bedraggled
bedridden	
bedriden	bedridden
bedrock	
bedside	
bed-sitting room	
bedspread	
bedspred	bedspread
bedstead	
bedsted	bedstead
bed-wetting	
bee (insect)	
bee	be (exist)
beech (tree)	
beech	beach (shore)

beechcomber	beachcomber
beechcomer	beachcomber
beecon	beacon
beed	bead
beef	
beefeater	
beefy, beefier, beefiest	
beegel	beagle
beegle	beagle
beehive	
beeline	
beem	beam
been (be)	
been	bean (food)
beenie	beanie
beep	
beer (ale)	
beer	bier (coffin)
beerd	beard
beest	beast
beeswaks	beeswax
beeswax	
beet (food)	
beet	beat (strike)
beetel	beetle
beetle	
beetle off	
beetroot	
beetul	beetle
beever	beaver
befall, -fell, -fallen, -falling	
befit, -fitted, -fitting	
befor	before
before	
beforehand	
befuddle, -dled, -dling	
befudul	befuddle
beg, begged, begging	
began	
begar	beggar
beger	beggar
beggar	
beggarly	
begger	beggar
begile	beguile
begin, began, begun, beginning	
beginner	

begone	
begonia	
begrudge, -grudged, -grudging	
begruge	begrudge
beguile, -guiled, -guiling	
begun	
behalf	
beharf	behalf
behave, -haved, -having	
behavior	behaviour
behaviour	
behavioural	
behead, -ed, -ing	
behed	behead
beheld	
behest	
behind	
behive	beehive
beige	
beije	beige
being	
bekos	because
bekweath	bequeath
bekwest	bequest
bel	bell (ring)
bel	belle (girl)
belabor	belabour
belabour, -ed, -ing	
belated, -ly	
belay, -layed, -laying	
belbird	bellbird
belch, -ed, -ing	
beleaf	belief
beleavabul	believable
beleave	believe
beleif	belief
beleive	believe
belfrey	belfry
belfry, -fries	
Belgian	
beli	belie
belicose	bellicose
belie, -lied, -lying	
belief	
believable, -bly	
believe, -lieved, -lieving	
beligerence	belligerence

beligerency	belligerency
beligerense	belligerence
beligerent	belligerent
beline	beeline
belittel	belittle

belittle, -tled, -tling
bell (ring)
bellbird
belle (girl)
bellicose, -ly
belligerence
belligerency
belligerent, -ly
bellow, -ed, -ing (roar)

bellow	below (under)

bellows
belly, bellies
belly, bellied, bellying
bellyache
belong, -ed, -ing
belongings

belose	bellows

beloved

belovid	beloved

below (under)

below	bellow (roar)
belows	bellows

belt, -ed, -ing
belt-up, belted-up, belting-up

bely	belly

bemoan, -ed, -ing
bemused
bench, benches
benchmark
bend, bent, bending
bender
beneath
benediction
benefactor
benefactress
benefice
beneficence
beneficent, -ly
beneficial, -ly
beneficiary, -aries

benefis	benefice
benefisense	beneficence

benefisent	beneficent
benefishal	beneficial
benefisharey	beneficiary

benefit, -fited, -fiting
benevolence

benevolense	benevolence

benevolent, -ly
benign, -ly

benine	benign

bent

benum	benumb

benumb
benzene (coal tar)
benzine (petroleum)
bequeath

bequeeth	bequeath

bequest
berate, -rated, -rating

beray	beret

bereave, -reaved, -reaving

bereeve	bereave

bereft
beret

bereve	bereave
berglar	burglar
beri	berry (fruit)
beri	bury (in earth)
berial	burial

beri-beri

berie	berry (fruit)

berley (bait)

berley	burly (large)
berli	berley (bait)
berli	burly (large)

berry, berries (fruit)

berry	bury (in earth)

berserk
berth (ship)

berth	birth (born)
bery	berry (fruit)
bery	bury (in earth)
beseach	beseech

beseech, -seeched, -seeching

beseige	besiege

beset, -set, -setting
beside
besides

besiege, -sieged, -sieging		biass	bias
besotted		biassed	biased
best		Bibel	Bible
bestial, -ly		Bible	
bestiality		bibliografy	bibliography
bestir, -stirred, -stirring		bibliographer	
bestow, -ed, -ing		bibliography, -phies	
bestowal		Bibul	Bible
bet, bet, betting		bicame	became
beta		bicameral	
beta particle		bicarbonate	
betel nut		bicarmed	becalmed
betel	beetle	bicentenary	
betle	beetle	bicentennial	
betoken, -ed, -ing		biceps	
betray, -ed, -ing		bich	bitch
betrayal		bicicle	bicycle
betrayer		bicker, -ed, -ing	
betrothal		bicycle	
better		bid, bade, bidding	
betterment		biday	bidet
betul	beetle	biddy, -dies	
between		bide, bided, biding	
betwixt		bidet	
bevel, -elled, -elling		bidevil	bedevil
beverage		biennial, -ly (every two years)	
beveridge	beverage	biennial	biannual (twice a year)
bevarije	beverage		
bevie	bevy	bier (coffin)	
bevy, bevies		bier	beer (ale)
bewail		bifell	befell
beware		bifocal	
bewayl	bewail	bifurcate, -cated, -cating	
bewear	beware	big, bigger, biggest	
bewhere	beware	bigamist	
bewhich	bewitch	bigamy	
bewilder, -ed, -ing		bigan	began
bewilderment		biggot	bigot
bewitch		bight (bay)	
bewty	beauty	bight	bite (cut)
beyond		bight	byte (computer)
bezerk	berserk		
biannual, -ly (twice a year)		bigile	beguile
biannual	biennial (every two years)	bigin	begin
		biginer	beginner
bias, biased, biasing		bigining	beginning
bias binding		bigon	begone

bigone	bygone
bigot	
bigoted, -ly	
bigotry	
bigrudge	begrudge
bigun	begun

For bih- words, look under
beh-.

bikameral	bicameral
bike	
bikini	
bikweath	bequeath
bikwest	bequest
bil	bill
bilaber	belabour
bilated	belated
bilateral, -ly	
bilaw	by-law
bilay	belay
bild	build
bilding	building
bile	
bileavabul	believable
bileave	believe
bileif	belief
bilet	billet
bilge	
biliards	billiards
bilief	belief
bilingual, -ly	
bilingwal	bilingual
bilion	billion
bilious, -ly	
biliousness	
bilittul	belittle
bilius	bilious
bilk, -ed, -ing	
bill, -ed, -ing	
billabong	
billet, -eted, -eting	
billiards	
Billingsgate	
billion	
billit	billet
billow (wave)	
billy, billies	

billycan	
billygoat	
bilong	belong
bilow	below (under)
bilow	billow (wave)
bilyards	billiards
bilyon	billion
bilyus	billious
bimoan	bemoan
bimuse	bemuse
bin, binned, binning	
bin	been
binary	
bind, bound, binding	
binder	
bineath	beneath
binevolent	benevolent
binge	
bingo	
binine	benign
binoculars	
binomial, -ly	
binumb	benumb
biochemist	
biochemistry	
biodegradable	
biografer	biographer
biografical	biographical
biografy	biography
biographer	
biographical, -ly	
biography, -phies	
biokemist	biochemist
biologey	biology
biological, -ly	
biologist	
biology	
biopsey	biopsy
biopsy	
biorhythm	
bipartisan	
bipartite	
bipartizen	bipartisan
bipass	by-pass
biped	
biplane	
biproduct	by-product

birate	berate	bisy	busy
birch		bit	
bird		bitch, -ches	
birdie		bitchiness	
bird's-eye		bitchumen	bitumen
bireave	bereave	bitchy	
bireft	bereft	bite, bitten, bit, biting (cut)	
biro		bite	bight (bay)
birth (born)		bite	byte
birth	berth (ship)		(computer)
birthday		biter	bitter
birthrate		bitoken	betoken
biscet	biscuit	bitray	betray
biscuit		bitrayal	betrayal
biscut	biscuit	bitrothal	betrothal
bisecshun	bisection	bitser	
bisect, -ed, -ing		bitten (bite)	
bisection		bitten	bittern (bird)
bisector		bitter, -ly	
biseech	beseech	bittern (bird)	
biseege	besiege	bitterness	
biseige	besiege	bitters	
biseksual	bisexual	bitumen	
bisen	bison	bituminous	
bisentenary	bicentenary	between	between
bisentenyal	bicentennial	bitwixt	betwixt
biseps	biceps	biuld	build
biset	beset	bivalve	
bisexual, -ly		bivouac, -acked, -acking	
bisexuality		bivuac	bivouac
bishop		biwail	bewail
bishopric		biway	byway
bisicle	bicycle	biwear	beware
biside	beside	biwich	bewitch
bisier	busier	biwilder	bewilder
bisily	busily	biwitch	bewitch
biskit	biscuit	biword	byword
bismuth		bizar	bazaar (fair)
bisness	business	bizar	bizarre (odd)
bison, -son		bizarre, -ly (odd)	
bisotted	besotted	bizier	busier
bistander	bystander	bizily	busily
bistir	bestir	bizmuth	bismuth
bistow	bestow	bizness	business
bistowal	bestowal	bizy	busy
bistro		blab, blabbed, blabbing	
bisun	bison	blabber, blabbered, blabbering	

blabbermouth
  blaber   blabber
black
blackberry, -ries
blackbirding
blackboard
  blackbord   blackboard
blackbutt
blackcurrant
  blackcurrent   blackcurrant
blacken, -ed, -ing
blackfellow
blackguard
blackhead
blackjack
blackleg
blackmail
  blackmale   blackmail
blackout
blackshirt
blacksmith
blacktracker
bladder
blade
  blader   bladder
  blaggard   blackguard
  blaid   blade
  blaim   blame
  blaimless   blameless
  blair   blare
  blaise   blaze
  blaiser   blazer
blame, blamed, blaming
blameless, -ly
blameworthy
  blamonge   blancmange
blanch, -ed, -ing
blancmange
bland, -ly
blandish
blandishment
blank
blanket
blare, blared, blaring
blarney, -neyed, -neying
  blarny   blarney
  blasay   blasé

blasé
  blasfeem   blaspheme
  blasfemus   blasphemous
  blasfemy   blasphemy
blaspheme, -phemed, -pheming
blasphemous, -ly
blasphemy, -mies
blast, -ed, -ing
blast-off
blatancy
blatant, -ly
blather
blaze, blazed, blazing
blazer
blazon
bleach, -ed, -ing
bleachers
  blead   bleed
bleak, -ly
bleakness
blear, -ed, -ing
blearily
bleary, blearier, blearist
bleat, -ed, -ing
  bleech   bleach
bleed, bled, bleeding
bleeder
  bleek   bleak
bleep
  bleer   blear
  bleet   bleat
blemish, -ed, -ing
blench, -ed, -ing
blend, -ed, -ing
blender
  blert   blurt
bless, blessed, blessing
blew (to blow)
  blew   blue (colour)

> For other blew- words, look
> under **blue-**.

blight, -ed, -ing
blighter
Blighty
blimey
blimp

blind, -ed, -ing
blind, -ly
blindfold
blindman's buff
blindness
blink, -ed, -ing
blinker
blip
bliss
blissful, -ly
blister, -ed, -ing
blistery
   blite   blight
   bliter   blighter
blithe, -ly
blithering
   blits   blitz
blitz, -ed, -ing
   blizard   blizzard
blizzard
   blo   blow
bloat, -ed, -ing
bloater
blob
bloc (group)
block, -ed, -ing (stop)
blockade, -kaded, -kading
blockage
   blockaid   blockade
blockbuster
   blockidge   blockage
   blok   bloke
bloke
blond, blonde
   blone   blown
blood
bloodbath
bloodcurdling
blooded
bloodless
blood-poisoning
blood pressure
bloodshed
bloodshot
bloodstream
bloodthirsty
bloody, bloodied, bloodying

bloody, bloodier, bloodiest
bloom, -ed, -ing
bloomers
   blosom   blossom
blossom
blot, blotted, blotting
   blot   bloat
blotch, -ed, -ing
blotchy
   bloting   blotting
blouse
blow, blew, blown, blowing
blower
blowfly
blowhole
blowlamp
blow-out
blowpipe
   blowse   blouse
blow-up
   blu   blue (colour)
   blu   blew (to blow)
blubber
blubbery
   bluber   blubber
bludge, bludged, bludging
bludger
bludgeon

> For all other blud- words, look
> under **blood-**.

blue (colour)
   blue   blew (to blow)
blue, bluer, bluest
bluebird
bluebottle
blue-collar
blueprint
blue-ribbon
blues
blue-tongue
bluey
   bluf   bluff
bluff, -ed, -ing
bluish
   blummers   bloomers
blunder, -ed, -ing

blunt, -ed, -ing
blur, blurred, blurring
blurb
blurt, -ed, -ing
blush, -ed, -ing
bluster, -ed, -ing
blustery
| blustry | blustery |
boa
boa constrictor
boar (pig)
| boar | boor (rude) |
| boar | bore (drill) |
board, -ed, -ing
board (wood)
| board | bored (drill) |
boarder (lodger)
| boarder | border (edge) |
boast, -ed, -ing
boastful, -ly
boat
boater
boat-house
boating
boat people
boat-race
boatswain
bob, bobbed, bobbing
| bobbel | bobble |
| bobbie | bobby |
bobbin
bobble
| bobbul | bobble |
bobby, -bies
bobby-dazzler
bobby pin, bobby pins
bobcat
bobie	bobby
bobin	bobbin
boble	bobble
bobslay	bobsleigh
bobsled
bobsleigh
boby	bobby
boch	botch
boddy	body
bodgie

bodice
bodie	body
bodigard	bodyguard
bodiley	bodily
bodily
bodis	bodice
body, bodies
body, bodied, bodied, bodying
body corporate
bodyguard
body language
bodywork
boffin
bog, bogged, bogging
bogey, bogies (golf)
bogey	bogy (evil)
boggel	boggle
boggle, -gled, -gling
bogul	boggle
bogus
bogy, bogies (evil)
bogy	bogey (golf)
bohemian
boi	boy (male)
boi	buoy (afloat)
boiancy	buoyancy
boiant	buoyant
boicot	boycott
boil, -ed, -ing
boiler
boilermaker
boilersuit
boisterous, -ly
boisterus	boisterous
boks	box
bolairo	bolero
bolard	bollard
bolaro	bolero
bold, -ly (brave)
bold	bowled (ball)
bolder (braver)
bolder	boulder (rock)
bole (trunk)
bole	bowl (ball)
bolero
bollard
Bolshevik

Bolshevism
bolshie
bolster, -ed, -ing
bolt
  bom — bomb
bomb, -ed, -ing
bombardier
bombardment
bombastic
bomber
  bomberdeer — bombardier
bombora
bombshell
  bomer — bomber
bona fide
bonanza
bonbon
bonce
bond, -ed, -ing
bondage
bone, boned, boning
  bonet — bonnet
bonfire
  bonie — boney
  bonie — bonny
  bonit — bonnet
bonk, -ed, -ing
bonny, bonnier, bonniest
bonsai
bonus
bony, bonier, boniest
bonzer
boo, booed, booing
boob
  boobie — booby
boo-boo
booby, -bies
  boodwar — boudoir
  boofant — bouffant
boogie-woogie
book, -ed, -ing
  bookay — bouquet
bookcase
  bookeeping — bookkeeping
bookie
bookish, -ly
bookkeeping

bookmaker
bookstall
bookworm
  boolevard — boulevard
boom, -ed, -ing
boomer
boomerang
boon
boor (rude)
  boor — boar (pig)
  boor — bore (drill)
  boorjwah — bourgeois
  boorjwahzey — bourgeoisie
boost, -ed, -ing
booster
boot
bootee (shoe)
  bootee — booty (plunder)
  booteek — boutique
booth
  bootie — bootee (shoe)
  bootie — booty (plunder)
  bootik — boutique
bootleg, -legged, -legging
bootlegger
bootstrap
booty, -ties (plunder)
  booty — bootee (shoe)
booze, boozed, boozing
boozer
bora
boracic
  boraks — borax
  borasic — boracic
borax
  borbon — bourbon
  bord — board (plank)
  bord — bored (tired)
border (edge)
  border — boarder (lodger)
border, -ed, -ing
borderline
  bording — boarding
  bordom — boredom
  bordy — bawdy
bore, bored, boring (drill)

bore	boar (pig)		bottom -ed, -ing	
bore	boor (rude)		bottomless	
boredom			botul	bottle
boree			botulism	
borer			boudoir	
born (birth)			bouffant	
born	borne (carry)		bougainvillea	
born	bourn (limit)		bough (branch)	
borne (carry)			bough	bow (bend)
borne	born (birth)		bought	
borne	bourn (limit)		bouillon	
boronia			boukay	bouquet
borough (town)			boulder (rock)	
borough	burrow (hole)		boulder	bolder (braver)
borow	borrow		boulevard	
borrow, -ed, -ing			bounce, bounced, bouncing	
borrower			bouncer	
Borstal			bound, -ed, -ing	
bort	bought		boundary, -ries	
bos	boss		boundry	boundary
bosie	bossy		bounteous, -ly	
bosily	bossily		bountiful, -ly	
bosn	bosun		bountious	bounteous
bosom			bounty, -ties	
boss, -ed, -ing			bouquet	
bossom	bosom		bourbon	
bossy, bossier, bossiest			bourgeois	
bosun			bourgeoisie	
bosy	bossy		bourgwah	bourgeois
bot	boat		bourgwahzey	bourgeoisie
botaney	botany		bourn (limit)	
botanical, -ly			bourn	born (birth)
botanist			bourn	borne (carry)
botany			bout	
botch, -ed, -ing			bouteek	boutique
botchy			boutique	
boter	boater		bovine	
both			bow, -ed, -ing (bend)	
bother			bow	bough (branch)
bothersome			bow	beau (dandy)
bothersum	bothersome		bowel	
botom	bottom		bower	
bottel	bottle		bowerbird	
bottle, -tled, -tling			bowie knife	
bottlebrush			bowl (ball)	
bottleneck			bowl	bole (trunk)
bottler			bowleg	

bowler	
bowline	
bownce	bounce
bownd	bound
bowndary	boundary
bownse	bounce
bouwnser	bouncer
bownteous	bounteous
bowntiful	bountiful
bowt	bout
bowyang	
box, -ed, -ing	
boxer	
box-frame	
boy (child)	
boy	buoy (float)
boyansy	buoyancy
boyant	buoyant
boycot	boycott
boycott, -ed, -ing	
boykot	boycott
boyle	boil
boysterus	boisterous
bra, bras (brassiere)	
brace, braced, bracing (clamp)	
bracelet	
bracken	
bracket, -ed, -ing	
brackish	
brackit	bracket
braclete	bracelet
brade	braid
brag, bragged, bragging	
bragart	braggart
braggart	
bragger	
Brahma	
Brahman, -mans	
braid	
brail	braille
braille	
brain	
brainstorm	
brainwash, -ed, -ing	
brainy, brainier, brainiest	
braise, braised, braising (cook)	
braise	braze (solder)

braisen	brazen
brakage	breakage
brakaway	breakaway
brakdown	breakdown
brake, braked, braking (stop)	
brake	break (divide)
braken	bracken
brakeneck	breakneck
braker	breaker
brakewater	breakwater
brakidge	breakage
braking	breaking
brakish	brackish
brale	braille
brambel	bramble
bramble	
brambly	
brambul	bramble
bramin	Brahman
bran	
branch, -ches	
branch, -ed, -ing	
brand, -ed, -ing	
brandish, -ed, -ing	
brand-new	
brandy, -dies	
brane	brain
braney	brainy
bras (brassieres)	
bras	brass (metal)
brase	brace (clamp)
brash	
brasier	brassiere (bra)
brasier	brazier (burner)
braslet	bracelet
brass	
brassiere (bra)	
brassy, brassier, brassiest	
brasy	brassy
brat	
bravado, -does, -dos	
brave, braver, bravest	
bravely	
bravery, -ries	
bravly	bravely
bravo, -voes, -vos	
bravrey	bravery

brawd   broad

brawl, -ed, -ing

brawn

brawny, brawnier, brawniest

bray, -ed, -ing

  brayd   braid

  brayn   brain

braze, brazed, brazing (solder)

  braze   braise (cook)

brazen, -ly

brazenness

brazier (burner)

  brazier   brassiere (bra)

brazil nut

breach, -ed, -ing (break)

  breach   breech (gun)

bread (food)

  bread   bred (produced)

breadline

breadth

breadwinner

break, broke, broken, breaking (divide)

  break   brake (stop)

  breakabel   breakable

breakable

  breakabul   breakable

breakage

breakaway

breakdown

breaker

breakfast

break-in

breakthrough

breakwater

bream (fish)

breast

breastbone

breastfeed, -fed, -feeding

breastplate

breast stroke

breath (air)

  breath   breadth (wide)

  breathaliser   breathalyser

breathalyser

breathe, breathed, breathing

breather

breathless, -ly

breathtaking

bred (produced)

  bred   bread (food)

  bredth   breadth

  bree   brie

breech, -ches (gun)

  breech   breach (break)

breed, bred, breeding

breeder

breeding

  breef   brief

breeze, breezed, breezing

breezily

breezy, breezier, breeziest

  breif   brief

  brest   breast

  brest stroke   breast stroke

  breth   breath (air)

  breth   breadth (wide)

  brethalyser   breathalyser

  brethless   breathless

brethren

  brethtaking   breathtaking

breve

brevity, -ties

brew, -ed, -ing (beer)

  brewed   brood (worry)

brewer

brewery, -ries

  brews   bruise (hurt)

  breze   breeze

  brezy   breezy

briar

bribe, bribed, bribing

bribery, -ies

bric-a-brac

brick, -ed, -ing

brickbat

  brickette   briquette

bricklayer

brick veneer

brickyard

bridal (marry)

  bridal   bridle (horse)

bride

bridegroom

bridel — bridal (marry)

bridel — bridle (horse)

bridesmade — bridesmaid

bridesmaid

bridge, bridged, bridging

bridle, -dled, -dling (horse)

bridle — bridal (marry)

brie

brief, -ly

briefcase

briefs

brig

brigade, -gaded, -gading

brigadeer — brigadier

brigadier

brigalow

brigand

brige — bridge

bright, -ly

brighten, -ed, -ing

brightness

brilliance

brilliant, -ly

brilliantine

brilyanse — brilliance

brilyansy — brilliancy

brilyant — brilliant

brim, brimmed, brimming (edge)

brim — bream (fish)

brimstone

brindled

brine, brined, brining

briney — briny

bring, brought, bringing

brink

brinkmanship

briny, brinier, briniest

bri-nylon

briquette

brisel — bristle

brisk, -ly

brisket

brisle — bristle

bristle, -tled, -tling

bristly

Britain

brite — bright

briten — brighten

British

britle — brittle

brittle, brittler, brittlest

brittleness

broach, -ed, -ing (mention)

broach — brooch (pin)

broad, -ly

broadcast, -cast, -casting

broadcaster

broaden, -ed, -ing

broad-minded

broadsheet

brocade, -caded

broccoli

broch — broach (mention)

broch — brooch (pin)

brochure

brocoli — broccoli

brog — brogue

brogue

broil, -ed, -ing

broken, -ly

broken-hearted

broker

brokerage

brokeridge — brokerage

brolly, -lies

bromide

bromine

bronchial

bronchitis

bronco, -cos

bronkial — bronchial

bronkitis — bronchitis

bronze, bronzed, bronzing

brooch, -ches (pin)

brood (worry)

brood — brewed (beer)

broody, broodier, broodiest

brook, -ed, -ing

broom

broonette — brunette

broose — bruise

broot — brute

brootal	brutal	bubul	bubble
brootality	brutality	bucaneer	buccaneer
brootish	brutish	buccaneer	
brorn	brawn	buccaneering	
brort	brought	bucher	butcher
broshure	brochure	buck, -ed, -ing	
brosure	brochure	buckaneer	buccaneer
broth		buckel	buckle
brothel		bucket, -ed, -ing	
brother		bucketful, bucketfuls	
brotherhood		buckjump, -ed, -ing	
brother-in-law, brothers-in-law		buckjumper	
brotherliness		buckle, -led, -ling	
brotherly		buckshot	
brow, brows (eyebrow)		buckskin	
browbeat, -beat, -beaten, -beating		bucktooth, -teeth	
brown		buckul	buckle
brownee	brownie	bucolic	
brownie		bud, budded, budding	
brows	browse (read)	Buddhism	
browse, browsed, browsing		Buddhist	
browser		buddy, -dies	
bruise, bruised, bruising (hurt)		budge, budged, budging	
bruise	brews (beer)	budgereegar	budgerigar
bruiser		budgerigar	
brumby, brumbies		budget, -eted, -eting	
brunch		budgetary	
brunet	brunette	budgie	
brunette		budgrigar	budgerigar
bruse	brews (beer)	Budhism	Buddhism
bruse	bruise (hurt)	Budhist	Buddhist
brush, -ed, -ing		buf	buff
brushwood		bufalo	buffalo
brushwork		bufay	buffet
brusk	brusque	bufer	buffer
brusque, -ly		buff	
brusqueness		buffalo, -loes, -los	
brutal, -ly		buffay	buffet
brutality, -ties		buffer	
brute		buffet (food)	
brutish		buffet, -ed, -ing (hit)	
bubbel	bubble	buffoon	
bubble, -bled, -bling		buffoonery, -eries	
bubble-and-squeak		bufit	buffet
buble	bubble	bufoon	buffoon
bubly	bubbly	bufoonery	buffoonery
bubonic plague		bug, bugged, bugging	

bugbare	bugbear
bugbear	
bugel	bugle
bugerigar	budgerigar
buget	budget
buggy, -gies	
bugie	buggy
bugle, -gled, -gling	
bugler	
bugy	buggy
build, built, building	
builder	
build-up	
buisness	business
bukshee	

For **buk-** words, look under **buc-**.

bul	bull
bulb	
bulbar	bull-bar
bulbous	
bulbul	
buldog	bulldog
buldoze	bulldoze
bulet	bullet
buletin	bulletin
bulfight	bullfight
bulfrog	bullfrog
bul-headed	bull-headed
bulion	bullion
bulk	
bulkhead	
bulky, bulkier, bulkiest	
bull-bar	
bulldog	
bulldoze, -dozed, -dozing	
bulldozer	
bullet	
bulletin	
bullfight	
bullfrog	
bull-headed	
bullion	
bullock	
bullring	
bullroarer	

bullrush	
bullseye	
bull-terrier	
bullwark	bulwark
bully, -lies	
bully, -lied, -lying	
bulock	bullock
bulring	bullring
bulroarer	bullroarer
bulrush	
bulseye	bullseye
bulwalk	bulwark
bulwark	
buly	bully
bulyun	bullion
bum, bummed, bumming	
bumbel	bumble
bumble, bumbled, bumbling	
bumf	
bump, -ed, -ing	
bumper	
bumpey	bumpy
bumpiness	
bumpkin	
bumpshus	bumptious
bumptious, -ly	
bumptiousness	
bumpy, bumpier, bumpiest	
bumshus	bumptious
bunch, -ches	
bunch, -ed, -ing	
buncum	bunkum
bundel	bundle
bundle, -dled, -dling	
bundul	bundle
bundy	
buney	bunny
bung, -ed, -ing	
bungaloe	bungalow
bungalow	
bungel	bungle
bunger	
bunghole	
bungkum	bunkum
bungle, -gled, -gling	
bungler	
bungul	bungle

bunie	bunny	burial	
bunion		burke, burked, burking	
bunk, -ed, -ing		burl, -ed, -ing	
bunker, -ed, -ing		burlap	
bunkum		burlesk	burlesque
bunny, -nies		burlesque, -lesqued, -lesquing	
bunnyip	bunyip	burlie	burly (large)
Bunsen burner		burly, -lier, -liest (large)	
bunt		burly	berley (bait)
bunting		burn, burnt, burned, burning	
buny	bunny	burnable	
bunyip		burn-back	
bunyon	bunion	burner	
buoy, -ed, -ing (float)		burnish, -ed, -ing	
buoy	boy (child)	buro	bureau
buoyancy		buro	burro
buoyansy	buoyancy	burocrasy	bureaucracy
buoyant, -ly		burocrat	bureaucrat
burbel	burble	burow	bureau
burble, -bled, -bling		burow	burrow (hole)
burbul	burble	burr, burred, burring	
burch	birch	burra	borough (town)
burd	bird	burro, -ros (donkey)	
burden, -ed, -ing		burro	bureau
burdensome		burrocracy	bureaucracy
burdensum	burdensome	burrocrat	bureaucrat
burdie	birdie	burrow, -ed, -ing (hole)	
burdseye	bird's-eye	burrow	borough (town)
bureau, -eaus, -eaux		burrow	burro (donkey)
bureaucracy, -cies		bursar	
bureaucrasy	bureaucracy	bursary, -ries	
bureaucrat		burser	bursar
bureaucratic		bursery	bursary
buret	burette	burst, burst, bursting	
burette		burth	berth (ship)
burgandy	burgundy	burth	birth (born)
burgel	burgle	bury, buried, burying (cover)	
burgeon, -ed, -ing		bury	berry (fruit)
burger	burgher	bus, buses, busses	
burgess		bus, bused, busing or bussed, bussing	
burgher		busbie	busby
burglar		busby, -bies	
burglary, -ries		busel	bustle
burgle, -gled, -gling		bush, -ed, -ing	
burgler	burglar	bushcraft	
burgul	burgle	bushel	
burgundy		bushfire	

bushie (farmer)
    bushie   bushy
bush-lawyer
bushman, -men
bushranger
bushranging
bushwalk
bushy, bushier, bushiest
busier
busily
business
businesslike
businessman, -men
businesswoman, -women
busk, -ed, -ing
busker
bust, -ed, -ing
bustard
    busted   bustard
    bustel   bustle
buster
bustle, -tled, -tling
bust-up
    busul   bustle
busy, busied, busying
busy, busier, busiest
busybody, -bodies
but (contrary)
    but   butt (end)
butane
butcher, -ed, -ing
    buteek   boutique
    buten   button
    buter   butter
    buterfly   butterfly
    butey   beauty
    butician   beautician
    butify   beautify
    butique   boutique
    butishun   beautician
butler
    butock   buttock
    buton   button
    butress   buttress
butt, -ed, -ing (end)
    butt   but (contrary)
butter, -ed, -ing

butter-fingers
butterfly, -flies
butterscotch
buttock
button
buttonhole, -holed, -holing
buttress, buttresses
buxom, -ly
buy, bought, buying (purchase)
    buy   by (near to)
    buy   bye (sport)
buyer
    buz   buzz
    buzard   buzzard
    buzer   buzzer
    buz-saw   buzz-saw
buzz, -ed, -ing
buzz, -es
buzzard
buzzer
buzz-saw
by (near to)
    by   bye (sport)
    by   buy (purchase)
bye (sport)
    bye   by (near to)
    bye   buy (purchase)
bye-bye, bye-byes
by-election
    byennial   biennial
    byer   buyer
    byer   byre (shed)
    byfocal   bifocal
bygone
    bying   buying
    byke   bike
by-law
    byle   bile
    bylore   by-law
    bymetallic   bimetallic
    bymonthly   bimonthly
    bynominal   binominal
    byopsey   biopsy
    bypartisan   bipartisan
    bypartite   bipartite
bypass
    byped   biped

byplane	biplane
by-product	
byre (shed)	
bysecshun	bisection
bysect	bisect
byseksual	bisexual
bystander	
byte (computer)	
byte	bite (chew)
byway	
byword	
Byzantine	

Cc

cab
cabal, -balled, -balling
cabaray — cabaret
cabaret
cabbage
cabbidge — cabbage
cabby, cabbies
cabel — cable
cabey — cabby
cabie — cabby
cabige — cabbage
cabin
cabinet
cable, -bled, -bling
caboose
cabul — cable
cacao, -caos
cach — cache
cach — catch
cachay — cachet
cache, cached, caching (hide)
cache — cash (money)
cachet
cachou — cashew
cachword — catchword
cackel — cackle
cackle, -led, -ling
cacktus — cactus
cackul — cackle
cacofony — cacophony
cacophony, -nies
cactoblastis
cactus, -ti, -tuses
cacul — cackle
cad
cadaver
cadaverous, -ly
caddey — caddie (golf)

caddey — caddy (tea)
caddie, -died, -dying (golf)
caddie — caddy (tea)
caddy, -ies (tea)
caddie — caddie (golf)
cadence
cadense — cadence
cadenza
cadet
cadetship
cadge, cadged, cadging
cadjole — cajole
cadmium
Caesar
caesarean section
cafay — cafe
cafe
cafeen — caffeine
cafeteria
caffeine
caffeteria — cafeteria
cafiene — caffeine
cafiteria — cafeteria
caftan
cage, caged, caging
cagey, cagier, cagiest
cagy — cagey
cahoots
cain — cane
cairn
caisson
caje — cage
cajole, -joled, -joling
cake, caked, caking
calabash
calamari
calamine
calamitous, -ly
calamity, -ties
calarie — calorie
calcareous
calcarious — calcareous
calcification
calcify, -fied, -fying
calcium
calculable
calculabul — calculable

calculate, -lated, -lating		calm, -ly	
calculation		calmness	
calculative		calorie	
calculator		calorific	
		calorimeter	
calculaytor	calculator		
calculus, -luses		calory	calorie
Caledonian		calow	callow
calendar (time)		calsify	calcify
calender (roll)		calsium	calcium
calendula		calumniate, -ated, -ating	
calf, calves		calumniation	
calfskin		calumnious, -ly	
caliber	calibre		
calibrate, -brated, -brating		calumnius	calumnious
calibration		calumny, -nies	
calibrator		calus	callous (cruel)
calibre		calus	callus (skin)
calicks	calyx	Calvary	
calico, -coes, -cos		calve, calved, calving (give birth)	
calif	caliph	calve	carve (cut)
caligraphy	calligraphy	Calvinism	
caling	calling	Calvinist	
caliper		calypso, -sos	
caliph		calyx, calyces, calyxes	
calipso	calypso	cam	
calisthenics		camaflage	camouflage
calix	calyx	camaraderie	
calk	caulk	camber	
call, -ed, -ing (cry out)		cambric	
call	caul (membrane)	came	
		camel	
callamity	calamity	camelhair	
calldron	cauldron	camellia	
caller		camelya	camellia
callgirl		camember	camembert
calligrapher		camembert	
calligraphy		cameo, -os	
calliper		camera	
callistemon		cameraman	
callisthenics		camerardery	camaraderie
callosity, -ties		camfer	camphor
callous, -ly (cruel)		camio	cameo
callous	callus (skin)	camisole	
callousness		camle	camel
callow		camouflage, -flaged, -flaging	
callus, calluses (skin)		camp, -ed, -ing	
callus	callous (cruel)	campaign	
		campain	campaign

campanology
camper
campervan
  campher — camphor
camphor
campus, -es
camshaft
  camul — camel
can, could (able to)
can, canned, canning (tinned)
  canabis — cannabis
Canadian
canal
canape
canary, -ries
canasta
cancan
cancel, -celled, -celling
  cancelation — cancellation
cancellation
cancer
cancerous
  cancerus — cancerous
  candel — candle
candelabrum
  candellight — candlelight
  candelstick — candlestick
  cander — candour
  candey — candy
candid (open)
  candid — candied (sugar)
candidate
candied (sugar)
  candied — candid (open)
candle
candlelight
candlestick
candour
  candul — candle
  candulstick — candlestick
candy, -dies
candy, candied, candying (sugar)
cane, caned, caning (hit)
  caned — canned (tinned)
  canee — canny
  canery — cannery
cane-sugar

  canibal — cannibal
  canibalism — cannibalism
  canie — canny
canine
canister
cannabis
  cannary — canary
canned (tinned)
  canned — caned (hit)
cannelloni
cannery, -ries
cannibal
cannibalism
canniness
cannon (gun)
  cannon — canon (law)
cannot
canny, -nier, -niest

> For other **cann**- words,
> look under **can**-.

canoe, -es
canoe, -noed, -noeing
canoeist
canon (law)
  canon — cannon (gun)
canonical
canonisation
canonise, -nised, -nising
  canoo — canoe
canoodle, -dled, -dling
  canooist — canoeist
canopy, -pies
  cansel — cancel
  canser — cancer
  canserous — cancerous
cant (insincere)
can't (cannot)
cantaloup
cantaloupe
cantankerous, -ly
  cantankerus — cantankerous
cantata
canteen
canter, -ed, -ing
cantilever
canto, -tos

canton

cantor

  canue   canoe

canvas, -es (tent)

  canvas   canvass
                    (gather)

canvass, -ed, -ing (gather)

  canvass   canvas (tent)
  cany   canny

canyon

cap, capped, capping

capability, -ties

capable, -bly

  capabul   capable

capacious, -ly

capacitor

capacity, -ties

  capasitor   capacitor
  capasity   capacity
  capchure   capture

cape

caper, -ed, -ing

  capilary   capillary

capillary, -laries

capital

capitalisation

capitalise, -lised, -lising

capitalism

capitalist

capitalistic

capitulate, -lated, -lating

capitulation

capon

cappuccino

> For all other **capp**-words,
> look under **cap-**.

caprice

capricious, -ly

capriciousness

Capricorn

  caprise   caprice
  caprishus   capricious
  capshulate   capsulate
  capshun   caption
  capshus   captious

capsicum

capsize, -sized, -sizing

capstan

capsule

captain, -ed, -ing

captaincy

  capter   captor
  captin   captain

caption

captious, -ly

captiousness

  captius   captious

captivate, -vated, -vating

captivation

captive

captivity, -ties

captor

capture, -tured, -turing

  caracter   character
  caracteristic   characteristic

carafe

  caraffe   carafe

caramel

  caramul   caramel

carat (weight)

  carat   carrot (food)
  carate   karate

caravan, -vanned, -vanning

caraway

carbine

carbohydrate

carbon

carbonate, -nated, -nating

carbon dioxide

carbonise, -nised, -nising

carbon monoxide

carbuncle

  carbuncul   carbuncle

carburettor

carcase

carcass

carcinogen

carcinogenic

carcinoma, -mata, -mas

card, -ed, -ing

  cardagan   cardigan

cardboard

  cardbord   cardboard

cardiac
cardigan
cardinal, -ly
  cardiograf   cardiograph
cardiologist
cardiology
cardiovascular
cardsharp
care, cared, caring
careen
career, -ed, -ing
carefree
careful, -ly
careless, -ly
carelessness
caress, -ed, -ing
caressingly
caret (mark)
  caret   carat (weight)
caretaker
cargo, -goes
caribou, -bou
caricature, -tured, -turing
caricaturist
  caricter   character
  caricteristic   characteristic
  caridge   carriage
  carie   carry (bear)
  carier   carrier
caries (decay)
  caries   carries (bear)
  carillion   carillon
carillon
  carillyon   carillon
  carion   carrion
carisma   charisma
  carkey   khaki
  carki   khaki
  carm   calm
carmine
carnage
carnal, -ly
carnality
carnation
  carnidge   carnage
  carnije   carnage
carnival

carnivore
carnivorous, -ly
carol, -rolled, -rolling (song)
  carol   carrel (study)
  carol   corral (yard)
caroller
  carot   carat (weight)
carousal (feast)
  carousal   carousel (merry-go-round)
carouse, -roused, -rousing
carousel (merry-go-round)
  carousel   carousal (feast)
carp, -ed, -ing
carpenter
carpentry
carpet, -ed, -ing
carrel (study)
  carrel   carol (song)
  carrel   corral (yard)
carriage
carriageway
carrier
carries (bears)
  carries   caries (decay)
carrion
carrot (food)
  carrot   carat (weight)
carry, -ried, -rying
  carryon   carrion
  carsinoma   carcinoma
cart, -ed, -ing
carte blanche
cartel
cartilage
  cartilege   cartilage
  cartilidge   cartilage
  cartografy   cartography
cartographer
cartographic
cartography
carton
cartoon, -ed, -ing
cartoonist
cartridge
  cartrige   cartridge

cartrije	cartridge
cartwheel	
carve, carved, carving (cut)	
carve	calve (give birth)
cary	carry
casava	cassava
cascade, -caded, -cading	
case, cased, casing	
caseen	casein
casein	
casement	
caserole	casserole
casette	cassette
casock	cassock
casowary	cassowary
cash, -ed, -ing (money)	
cash	cache (hide)
cashay	cachet
casheer	cashier
cashew	
cashier	
cashmear	cashmere
cashmere	
cashoo	cashew
casia	cassia
casing	
casino, -nos	
cask	
caskade	cascade
casket	
caskit	casket
casock	cassock
cassava	
cassel	castle
casserole, -roled, -roling	
casset	cassette
cassette	
cassia	
cassock	
cassowary, -ries	
cast, cast, casting (fling)	
cast	caste (class)
castanet	
castaway	
caste (class)	
caster or castor (sugar)	

caster	castor (oil)
castigate, -gated, -gating	
castigation	
cast-iron	
castle, -tled, -tling	
castor (oil)	
castrait	castrate
castrate, -trated, -trating	
castration	
castrayte	castrate
casual, -ly	
casuality	casualty
casualty, -ties	
casuarina	
casuistic	
casuistry, -tries	
casulty	casualty
catachism	catechism
cataclysm	
cataclysmic	
catacomb	
catalise	catalyse
catalist	catalyst
catalitic	catalytic
catalog	catalogue
catalogue, -logued, -loguing	
cataloguer	
catalyse, -lysed, -lysing	
catalyst	
catalytic	
catamaran	
catapiler	caterpillar
catapult	
catar	catarrh
cataract	
catarh	catarrh
catarrh	
catarrhal	
catastrofic	catastrophic
catastrofy	catastrophe
catastrophe	
catastrophic, -ally	
catcall, -ed, -ing	
catch, caught, catching	
catcher	
catchment	
catchword	

catchy, catchier, catchiest
catechise, -chised, -chising
catechism
catechist
categorical, -ly
categorise, -rised, -rising
categorist
category, -ries
catel   cattle
cater, -ed, -ing
caterer
caterpillar
caterpiller   caterpillar
caterwall   caterwaul
caterwaul
catfish, -fishes, -fish
catgut
catharsis
cathartic
cathedral
catheter
cathode
catholic (universal)
Catholic (religion)
Catholicism
Catholicity
caticise   catechise
catigoric   categoric
catigorise   categorise
catigory   category
catikism   catechism
catish   cattish
catkin
catle   cattle
catnap, -ed, -ing
cat-o'-nine-tails
cattel   cattle
catterpillar   caterpillar
cattle
cattlegrid
cattle-run
cattish, -ly
catty, -ier, -iest
catul   cattle
catwalk
Caucasian
caucus, -ed, -ing

caught (did catch)
caught   court (law)
cauk   caulk
caul (membrane)
caul   call (cry)
cauldron
cauliflour   cauliflower
cauliflower
caulk, -ed, -ing
causal, -ly
causal   casual
causality, -ties
causation
causative, -ly
cause, caused, causing
causeway
caustic, -ally
cauterise, -rised, -rising
caution, -ed, -ing
cautionary
cautious, -ly
cavalcade, -caded, -cading
cavaleer   cavalier
cavalier
cavalry, -ries
cavalryman, -men
cave, caved, caving
caveman, -men
cavern
cavernous
caviar
cavil, -illed, -illing
cavity, -ties
caw   core (heart)
caw   corps (group)
cawcas   caucus
Cawcasian   Caucasian
cawcus   caucus
cay
cayenne
cease, ceased, ceasing
cease-fire
ceaseless, -ly
cedar
cede, ceded, ceding (yield)
cede   seed (plant)
ceder   cedar

ceeling	ceiling (roof)	censorious, -ly	
ceese	cease	censorship	
cefalic	cephalic	censurable	
ceiling (roof)		censurabul	censurable
ceiling	sealing (close)	censure, -sured, -suring	
celebrant		census	
celebrate, -brated, -brating		cent (coin)	
celebration		cent	scent (perfume)
celebrity, -ties		cent	sent (away)
celerity		centaur	
celery (food)		centenarian	
celery	salary (wage)	centenary, -ries	
celestial, -ly		centenery	centenary
celibacy, -cies		centennial, -ly	
celibasy	celibacy	center	centre
celibate		Centigrade	
celibrant	celebrant	centimeter	centimetre
celibrate	celebrate	centimetre	
cell (prison)		centipede	
cell	sell (goods)	centor	centaur
cellar (basement)		central, -ly	
cellar	seller (goods)	Centralia	
cellarman, -men		centralisation	
celler	seller (goods)	centralise, -lised, -lising	
cellist		centralism	
cello, -los		centralist	
cellofane	cellophane	centrality	
cellophane		centre, -tred, -tring	
cellular		centreboard	
celluler	cellular	centrefold	
celluloid		centrepiece	
cellulose		centrifugal, -ly	
celofane	cellophane	centrifuge	
Celsius		centripetal, -ly	
cement, -ed, -ing		centupel	centuple
cemetary	cemetery	centuple, -pled, -pling	
cemetery, -teries		centupul	centuple
cemical	chemical	centurion	
cemist	chemist	century, -ries	
cemistry	chemistry	cephalic	
cenotaf	cenotaph	ceramic	
censer (incense)		ceramicist	
censer	censor (books)	ceramics	
censership	censorship	ceramist	
censhure	censure		
censor (books)			
censor	censer (incense)		

> For any cerc- words,
> look under circ-.

cereal (grain)

cereal	serial (part)
cerebelum	cerebellum

cerebellum, -bella
cerebral
cerebrate, -brated, -brating
cerebration
cerebrum, -bra
ceremonial, -ly
ceremonious, -ly

ceremonius	ceremonious

ceremony, -monies

cerial	cereal (grain)
cerial	serial (part)
ceribellum	cerebellum
ceribrum	cerebrum

cerise

> For any cerk words,
> look under **circ-**.

certain, -ly
certainty, -ties

certanty	certainty
certen	certain
certenty	certainty

certifiable, -fiably

certifiabul	certifiable

certificate, -cated, -cating
certification
certifier
certify, -fied, -fying

certinty	certainty

certitude
cervical

cervicul	cervical
cerviks	cervix

cervix, cervixes, cervices

cesation	cessation
ceshun	session (time)
cesion	cession (yield)
cespit	cesspit
cespool	cesspool

cessation
cession(yield)

cession	session (time)

cesspit
cesspool

chablis
cha-cha

chacoal	charcoal

chafe, chafed, chafing (rub)

chafe	chaff (straw)

chaff (straw)
chaffinch, -es
chagrin, -ed, -ing
chain
chain-drive
chain-reaction
chainsaw
chain-smoke, -smoked, -smoking
chain-stitch, -ed, -ing
chain-store
chair, -ed, -ing
chairlift
chairman, -men
chairperson
chairwoman, -women

chaise	chase

chalet
chalice

chalinge	challenge
chalis	chalice

chalk, -ed, -ing
challenge, -lenged, -lenging
challenger

chamba	chamber

chamber
chamberlain

chamberlin	chamberlain
chambermade	chambermaid

chambermaid
chameleon

chamee	chamois

chamfer, -ed, -ing

chamie	chamois

chamois
champ, -ed, -ing
champagne

champaign	champagne

champers
champignon
champion, -ed, -ing
championship

champiun	champion

chance, chanced, chancing

chancel

chanceler	chancellor
chancelery	chancellery
chanceller	chancellor

chancellery, -ries

chancellor

chancellorship

chancery, -ceries

chancy, chancier, chanciest

chandeleer	chandelier

chandelier

chandler

chane	chain
chane-drive	chain-drive
chanel	channel
chane-reaction	chain-reaction
chanesaw	chainsaw

change, changed, changing

changeable, -bly

changeabul	changeable

changeling

changeover

channel, -nelled, -nelling

chanse	chance
chansel	chancel
chanseler	chancellor
chanselery	chancellery
chansey	chancy

chant, -ed, -ing

chaos

chaotic, -ally

chap, chapped, chapping

chapel

chaperone

chaple	chapel

chaplain

chaplaincy

chaplet

chaplin	chaplain

chapter

char, charred, charring

character

characterise, -rised, -rising

characteristic, -ally

charade

charaid	charade

charcoal

chare	chair
chareman	chairman
chareperson	chairperson
charewoman	chairwoman
charey	chary

charge, charged, charging

charger

chariot

charioteer

charisma

charismatic

charitable

charitableness

charitably

charitabul	charitable

charity, -ties

charlady, -ladies

charlatan

charleston

charm, -ed, -ing

charmer

chart, -ed, -ing

charter, -ed, -ing

chartreuse

chartroos	chartreuse

chary, charier, chariest

chase, chased, chasing

chased (follow)

chased	chaste (pure)
chasen	chasten

chaser

chasis	chassis

chasm

chassie	chassis

chassis, chassis

chaste (pure)

chaste	chased (follow)

chasten, -ed, -ing

chastener

chastise, -tised, -tising

chastisement

chastiser

chastity

chat, chatted, chatting

chateau, -teaus, -teaux

chatel	chattel

chater	chatter	cheerie	cheery
chatily	chattily	cheerily	
chatiness	chattiness	cheeriness	
chattel		cheerio, -os	
chatter, -ed, -ing		cheery, -rier, -riest	
chatterbox, -boxes		cheese	
chattily		cheesecake	
chattiness		cheesecloth	
chatty, -tier, -tiest		cheesed-off	
chaty	chatty	cheeseparing	
chauffer	chauffeur	cheesy, -sier, -siest	
chauffeur		cheet	cheat
chauvinism		cheeta	cheetah
chauvinist		cheetah	
chauvinistic, -ally		cheeter	cheetah
cheap (price)		chef	
cheap	cheep (sound)	chef-d'oeuvre, chefs-d'oeuvre	
cheapen, -ed, -ing		cheif	chief
cheapish, -ly		cheiftan	chieftain
cheapskate		chelist	cellist
chear	cheer	chelo	cello
chearful	cheerful	chemical, -ly	
chease	cheese	chemise	
cheat, -ed, -ing		chemist	
cheater		chemistrey	chemistry
check, -ed, -ing (stop)		chemistry, -tries	
check	cheque (money)	chemotherapist	
Check	Czech (person)	chemotherapy	
checkers		chenille	
checkmate, -mated, -mating		cheongsam	
checkout		cheque (money)	
checkpoint		cheque	check (stop)
checkup		Cheque	Czech (person)
chedar	cheddar	cheque-book	
cheddar		chequer	
cheder	cheddar	chequered	
cheef	chief	cherie	cherry
cheeftan	chieftain	cherio	cheerio
cheekily		cherish, -ed, -ing	
cheekiness		cheroot	
cheeky, cheekier, cheekiest		cherp	chirp
cheep, -ed, -ing (sound)		cherry, -ries	
cheep	cheap (price)	cherub, cherubim, cherubs	
cheer, cheered, cheering		cherubic, -ally	
cheerey	cheery	chery	cheery
cheerful, -ly		chery	cherry
cheerfulness		ches	chess

chesbord	chessboard	childproof	
chess		chili, -ies (fruit)	
chessboard		chili	chilly (cold)
chessnut	chestnut	chill, -ed, -ing	
chest		chilli, -ies (fruit)	
chesterfield		chilli	chilly (cold)
chestnut		chilliness	
chevalier		chilly, -ier, -iest (cold)	
chevon (goat meat)		chilly	chilli (fruit)
chevron (stripe)		chimbly	chimney
chew, -ed, -ing (eat)		chime, chimed, chiming	
chewie		chimera, -ras	
chewing gum		chimeric, -ally	
chews	choose (select)	chimnee	chimney
chewy		chimney, -neys	
chiack, -ed, -ing		chimpanzee	
chic (stylish)		chin	
chicanery, -ries		china	
chick (young bird)		chinchilla	
chickenfeed		Chinese	
chickenpox		chink, -ed, -ing	
chickpea		chintz, chintzes	
chickweed		chintzy	
chicle		chip, chipped, chipping	
chicory, -ries		chipboard	
chide, chided, chiding		chipmonk	chipmunk
chidingly		chipmunk	
chief, chiefs		chipolata	
chiefly		chiropodey	chiropody
chieftain		chiropodist	
chieftaincy		chiropody	
chiffon		chiropracter	chiropractor
chiffonier		chiropractic	
chifon	chiffon	chiropractor	
chignon		chirp, -ed, -ing	
chihuahua		chirpily	
chil	chill	chirpy, -pier, -piest	
chilblain		chisel, -elled, -elling	
chilblane	chilblain	chiseller	
child, children		chit	
childbaring	childbearing	chitchat	
childbearing		chivalrous, -ly	
childberth	childbirth	chivalrus	chivalrous
childbirth		chivalry	
childhood		chive	
childish, -ly		chivvy, -ied, -ying	
childlike		chloride	

chlorinate, -nated, -nating
chlorination
chlorine
  chlorofill   chlorophyll
chloroform, -ed, -ing
chlorophyll
chock, -ed, -ing
chock-a-block
chock-full
chocks
  choclat   chocolate
chocolate
choice, choicer, choicest
choir (singers)
  choir   quire (measure)
  choise   choice
choke, choked, choking
choker
choko
choler (anger)
  choler   collar (neck)
cholera
choleric
cholesterol
  choo   chew
chook
choose, chose, chosen, choosing (select)
  choose   chews (eats)
choosy
chop, chopped, chopping
chopper
choppy, -pier, -piest
  chopsooey   chop suey
chopstick
  chopy   choppy
choral, -ly (sing)
  choral   chorale (tune)
chorale (tune)
  chorale   choral (sing)
chord (music)
  chord   cord (string)
chore
  choreograf   choreograph
choreograph, -ed, -ing
choreographer
choreographic

choreography
chorister
chortle, -tled, -tling
  chortul   chortle
chorus, -ruses
chorus, -rused, -rusing
chose
chosen
chow
chowder
chow mein
  chrisalis   chrysalis
chrism
  Chrismas   Christmas
Christ
  Christain   Christian
christen, -ed, -ing
christendom
Christian
Christianity
Christmas
chromatic, -ally
chrome
chromium
chromosome
  chronalogical   chronological
chronic, -ally
  chronical   chronicle
chronicle, -cled, -cling
chronicler
chronologer
chronological, -ly
chronology, -gies
chronometer
chrysalis, chrysalises
chrysanthemum
chubbily
chubbiness
chubby, -bier, -biest
  chubier   chubbier
  chuby   chubby
chuck, -ed, -ing
  chuckel   chuckle
chuckle, chuckled, chuckling
chuckler
chuff, -ed, -ing
chug, chugged, chugging

chum, chummed, chumming
chummy, -mier, -miest
chump
chunk
chunkiness
chunky, -kier, -kiest
church, -es
churinga
churl
churlish, -ly
churn, -ed, -ing

churp	chirp
chute (drop)	
chute	shoot (gun)

chutney, -neys

chutny	chutney

chutzpah

cianide	cyanide
cibernetics	cybernetics

cicada, -dae, -das

cicatriss	cicatrix

cicatrix, cicatrices, cicatrixes

> For all other **cic**-words,
> look under **cyc**-.

cider

cifer	cipher

cigar

cigaret	cigarette

cigarette

cignet	cygnet (swan)
cignet	signet (ring)
cilestial	celestial

cilium, cilia

cilinder	cylinder
cilindrical	cylindrical
cimbal	cymbal(music)
cimbal	symbol (sign)
ciment	cement
cinamon	cinnamon

cinch, -ches
cincture
cinder
cinderella
cinema
cinemascope
cinematic, -ally

cinematograph
cineraria

cinic	cynic
cinical	cynical
cinicul	cynical
cinima	cinema
cinimatograf	cinematograph
cinimatograph	cinematograph
cinimon	cinnamon

cinnamon

cinosure	cynosure

cipher

cipress	cypress

circa

circel	circle
circit	circuit

circle, -cled, -cling
circlet
circuit, -ed, -ing
circuit-breaker
circuitous, -ly
circuitry

circul	circle

circular, -ly
circularise, -rised, -rising
circularity
circulate, -lated, -lating
circulation
circulator
circulatory
circumcise, -cised, -cising
circumcision
circumference

circumferense	circumference

circumnavigate, -gated, -gating
circumnavigation
circumnavigator
circumscribe, -ribed, -ribing
circumscription
circumspect
circumspection
circumstance

circumstanse	circumstance
circumstanshul	circumstantial

circumstantial, -ly
circumvent, -ed, -ing
circumvention

circus, circuses
cirrhosis
cirriculum — curriculum
cirrosis — cirrhosis
cirrus
cissy, cissies
cist — cyst
cistern
cistitis — cystitis
citadel
citation
cite, cited, citing (quote)
cite — sight (see)
cite — site (place)
citie — city
citizen
citric acid
citris — citrus
citron
citronella
citros — citrus
citrous
citrus
city, cities
civet
civic
civies — civvies
civik — civic
civil, -ly
civilian
civilisation
civilise, -lised, -lising
civility, -ties
civit — civet
civvies
clad
cladding
claim, -ed, -ing
claimable
claimabul — claimable
claimant
claimer
clairvoyance
clairvoyant
clam, clammed, clamming
clamber, -ed, -ing
clame — claim

clamer — clamour
clamerus — clamorous
clammily
clamminess
clammy, -mier, -miest
clamorous, -ly
clamour, -ed, -ing
clamp, -ed, -ing
clamy — clammy
clan
clandestine, -ly
clang, -ed, -ing
clanger (error)
clangour (loud sound)
clangourous, -ly
clank, -ed, -ing
clannish, -ly
clap, clapped, clapping
clapper
clapperboard
claptrap
claret
clarify, -fied, -fying
clarification
clarifier
clarinet
clarinettist
clarion
clarionet
clarity
clark — clerk
claryon — clarion
clash, -ed, -ing
clasify — classify
clasp, -ed, -ing
clasroom — classroom
class, classes
classable
classabul — classable
classer
classic
classical, -ly
classicism
classicist
classifiable
classifiabul — classifiable
classification

classify, -fied, -fying
classroom
classy, classier, classiest
clatter, -ed, -ing
clause (grammar)

clause	claws (animal)
claustrofobia	claustrophobia

claustrophobia
claves

clavicel	clavicle

clavichord

clavicord	clavichord

clavier
claw, -ed, -ing
claws (animal)

claws	clause (grammar)

clay
clayey

clayie	clayey

clayish

claym	claim

clean, -ed, -ing
cleanliness
cleanse, cleansed, cleansing
cleanskin
clear, -ed, -ing
clearance
clearly
clearness
clearway
cleat
cleavage
cleave, cleaved, cleaving
cleaver

cleavidge	cleavage
cleek	clique
cleeshay	cliché
cleet	cleat
cleeve	cleave
cleevage	cleavage
cleever	cleaver
cleevidge	cleavage

clef
cleft
clematis
clemency

clemensy	clemency

clement
clench, -ed, -ing

clenliness	cleanliness
clense	cleanse

cleptomania
clergy, -gies
clergyman, -men
cleric
clerical, -ly
clerk
clever, cleverer, cleverest
cleverly
cleverness
clew (ball)

clew	clue (hint)

clianthus

clichay	cliché

cliché, -chés
click, -ed, -ing (sound)

click	clique (group)

clicker

clidesdale	clydesdale

client
clientele

clientell	clientele

cliff
cliff-hanger
climacteric (crucial)
climactic (climax)

climaks	climax

climate (weather)
climatic, -ally
climatology
climax, -maxes
climb, -ed, -ing (upward)
clime (region)
clinch, -ed, -ing
clincher
cling, clung, clinging
clinger
clinic
clinical, -ly
clink, -ed, -ing
clinker, -ed, -ing
clip, clipped, clipping
clipper

clique (group)	
clique	click (sound)
clitoris	
clitris	clitoris
cloak	
cloak-and-dagger	
cloakroom	
clobber, -ed, -ing	
clock, -ed, -ing	
clockwise	
clockwork	
clod	
cloddish	
clodhopper	
clog, clogged, clogging	
cloggy	
cloister, -ed, -ing	
cloistral	
cloke	cloak
clone, cloned, cloning	
cloride	chloride
clorinate	chlorinate
clorine	chlorine
clorofil	chlorophyll
cloroform	chloroform
clorophyll	chlorophyll
close, closed, closing	
close, closer, closest	
closed-circuit	
closeness	
closet, -ed, -ing	
closure	
clot, clotted, clotting	
cloth, cloths (fabric)	
clothe, clothed, clothing	
clothes (garments)	
clothier	
cloud, -ed, -ing	
cloudbank	
cloudburst	
cloudless, -ly	
cloudy, cloudier, cloudiest	
clout, -ed, -ing	
clove	
cloven	
cloven-hoofed	
clover	

cloverleaf, -leaves	
clowd	cloud
clowdless	cloudless
clowdy	cloudy
clown, -ed, -ing	
clownery	
clownish, -ly	
clowt	clout
cloy, -ed, -ing	
cloyster	cloister
club, clubbed, clubbing	
clubhouse	
cluch	clutch
cluck, -ed, -ing	
clucky	
clue, clued, cluing (hint)	
clue	clew (ball)
clump, -ed, -ing	
clumpish	
clumpy	
clumsily	
clumsiness	
clumsy, -sier, -siest	
clung	
clurgy	clergy
cluster, -ed, -ing	
clutch, -ed, -ing	
clutch-start	
clutter, -ed, -ing	
Clydesdale	
coach, -ed, -ing	
coachman, -men	
coacksial	coaxial
coagulate, -lated, -lating	
coagulation	
coagulator	
coaks	coax
coal	
coaldust	
coalesce, -lesced, -lescing	
coalescence	
coalescent	
coaless	coalesce
coalessence	coalescence
coalessent	coalescent
coalface	
coalfield	

coalishun	coalition
coalition	
coalitionist	
coalmine	
coalminer	
coalmining	
coarse, coarser, coarsest (rough)	
coarse	course (path)
coarsen, -ed, -ing	
coast, -ed, -ing	
coastal	
coaster	
coastgard	coastguard
coastguard	
coastline	
coat, -ed, -ing	
coat-hanger	
coatless	
coax, -ed, -ing	
coaxial	
coaxingly	
coaxiul	coaxial
cobalt	
cobber	
cobble, -bled, -bling	
cobbler	
cobblestone	
cober	cobber
coble	cobble
cobler	cobbler
coblestone	cobblestone
cobulstone	cobblestone
cobra	
cobweb	
cocain	
cocaine	
cocane	cocaine
cocanut	coconut
cocatoo	cockatoo
coccix	coccyx
coccyx, -coccyges	
coch	coach
cochineal	
cochineel	cochineal
cock, -ed, -ing	
cockade	
cockatoo	

cockatrice	
cockatriss	cockatrice
cockcrow	
cockelshell	cockleshell
cockerel	
cocker spaniel	
cocket	coquette
cocketry	coquetry
cockeyed	
cockfight	
cockily	
cockiness	
cockle	
cockleshell	
cockney, -neys	
cockpit	
cockroach, -es	
cockroch	cockroach
cockscomb	
cockshure	cocksure
cocksure	
cocktail	
cocktale	cocktail
cockul	cockle
cocky, cockier, cockiest	
coco, -cos (palm tree)	
cocoa (drink)	
coconut	
cocoon	
coddle, -dled, -dling	
code, coded, coding	
codecks	codex
codeen	codeine
codeine	
codex, codices	
codger	
codicil	
codiene	codeine
codification	
codifier	
codify, -fied, -fying	
codisil	codicil
codle	coddle
codswallop	
codul	coddle
co-ed	
coeducashun	coeducation

coeducation		cohabit, -ed, -ing	
coeducational		cohabitation	
coefficient		coherent	coherent
coefishent	coefficient	cohere, -hered, -hering	
coegsist	coexist	coherence	
coequal, -ly		coherense	coherence
coequality		coherent, -ly	
coerce, -erced, -ercing		coheshun	cohesion
coercible		cohesion	
coercibul	coercible	cohesive, -ly	
coercion		cohort	
coercive, -ly		coiffure	
coerse	coerce	coifur	coiffure
coershun	coercion	coil, -ed, -ing	
coersible	coercible	coin, -ed, -ing	
coersive	coercive	coinage	
coeval, -ly		coincide, -cided, -ciding	
coevil	coeval	coincidence	
coevul	coeval	coincident, -ly	
coexist, -ed, -ing		coinidge	coinage
coexistence		coinsidence	coincidence
coexistense	coexistence	coinsident	coincident
coexistent		coir	
cofee	coffee	coishun	coition
cofer	coffer	coition	
cofey	coffee	coitus	
coff	cough	coke, coked, coking	
coffee		coket	coquette
coffer		cokoon	cocoon
coffin		col	
cofin	coffin	cola	
cog		colander	
cogency		colapse	collapse
cogenital	congenital	cold, -er, -est	
cogent, -ly		cole	coal
coger	codger	colender	colander
cogitate, -tated, -tating		coler	choler (anger)
cogitation		colera	cholera
cogitative		coleric	choleric
cognac		colesterol	cholesterol
cognate		coleus	
cognisance		colic	
cognisanse	cognisance	colicky	
cognisant		colitis	
cognishun	cognition	collaborate, -rated, -rating	
cognition		collaboration	
cognitive		collaborator	

collage
collapsable
collapse, -lapsed, -lapsing
collapsible
collar, -ed, -ing (neck)
   collar   choler (anger)
collarbone
collate, -lated, -lating
collateral
collation
collator
colleague
collect, -ed, -ing
collectable
collection
collective, -ly
collectivism
collector
college
collegian
collegiate
   coller   choler (anger)
   coller   collar (neck)
collide, -lided, -liding
collie
collier
colliery, -ries
collinear, -ly
collision
collocate, -cated, -cating
collocation
   colonial   colonial
colloquial, -ally
colloquialism
colloquy, -quies
collusion
collusive, -ly
cologne
colon
   colonade   colonnade

> For other **col-** words,
> look under **coll-**.

colonel
colonial, -ly
colonisation
colonise, -nised, -nising

coloniser
colonnade
colony, -nies
   color   colour
coloratura
   colorful   colourful
colossal, -ly
colossus, -lossuses
colour, -ed, -ing
colour-bar
colour-blindness
colourful, -fully
colt
coltish, -ly
   colum   column
columbine
column

> For other **col-** words,
> look under **coll-**.

columnist
coma (sleep)
   coma   comma (mark)
comatose, -ly
comb, -ed, -ing
combat, -bated, -bating
combatant
combative, -ly
comber
combination
combine, -bined, -bining
combustible
combustibility
   combustibul   combustible
combustion
come, came, come, coming
comeback
comedian
comedienne
comedy, -dies
comeliness
comely, -lier, -liest
   comend   commend
comestible
   comestibul   comestible
comet
comeuppance

comfert — comfort
comfertable — comfortable
comferter — comforter
comfort, -ed, -ing
comfortable, -bly
comforter
comfortless, -ly
comfy
comic
comical, -ly
comicality

> Look under **comm-** if the word is not under **com-**.

comma (mark)
comma — coma (sleep)
command, -ed, -ing
commandant
commander
commandment
commando, -dos, -does
commemorate, -rated, -rating
commemoration
commemorative, -ly
commence, -menced, -mencing
commencement
commend, -ed, -ing
commendable, -bly
commendabul — commendable
commendation
commendatory
commense — commence
commensurable, -bly
commensurabul — commensurable
commensurate
comment, -ed, -ing
commentary, -aries
commentater — commentator
commentator
commentry — commentary
commer — comma
commerce
commercial, -ly
commercialisation
commercialise, -lised, -lising
commercialism
commershal — commercial

commershalise — commercialise
commisar — commissar
commisariat — commissariat
commisary — commissary
commiserate, -rated, -rating
commiseration
commishun — commission
commision — commission
commisionaire — commissionaire
commisioner — commissioner
commissar
commissariat
commissary, -saries
commission
commissionaire
commissioner
commit, -mitted, -mitting
commitment
committal
committee
commitul — committal
commo
commodaty — commodity
commode
commodious, -ly
commodity, -ties
commodius — commodious
commodoor — commodore
commodore
common, -ly
commonality, -ties
commoner
commonplace
Commons
commonsense
commonsensical
Commonwealth
Commonwelth — Commonwealth
commoshun — commotion
commotion
communal, -ly
commune, -muned, -muning
communicable
communicabul — communicable
communicate, -cated, -cating
communication
communicative

communicator
  communikay   communique
communion
communique
communism
communist
communistic
community, -ties
commutation
commute, -muted, -muting
commuter

> Look under **comm-** if the word is not under **com-**.

compact
  compair   compare (liken)
  compair   compere (stage)
companion
companionable, -bly
companionship
company, -nies
  companyun   companion
comparable, -bly
  comparabul   comparable
comparative, -ly
compare, -pared, -paring (liken)
  compare   compere (stage)
comparison
compartment
compartmentalise, -ised, -ising
  compas   compass
  compashun   compassion
  compashunate   compassionate
compass, -es
compass, -ed, -ing
compassion
compassionate, -nated, -nating
compatibility
compatible, -bly
  compatibul   compatible
  compatition   competition
compatriot
compel, -pelled, -pelling
compendium, -diums, -dia
compensate, -sated, -sating
compensation
compensator

compensatory
  compensatry   compensatory
  compeny   company
compere, -pered, -pering (stage)
  compere   compare (liken)
  competant   competent
  competative   competitive
compete, -peted, -peting
competency
  competense   competence
competent, -ly
  competishun   competition
competition
competitive, -ly
competitor
compilation
compile, -piled, -piling
compiler
  compinsation   compensation
complacency, -cies
complacent, -ly (smug)
complain, -ed, -ing
complainant
complaint
complaisant (obliging)
  complanant   complainant
  complane   complain
  complant   complaint
  complasense   complacence
  complasent   complacent
complement, -ed, -ing (complete)
  complement   compliment (praise)
complementary (completing)
  complementary   complimentary (free)
complete, -pleted, -pleting
completion
complex, -ly
complexion
complexity, -ties
compliable
  compliabul   compliable
compliance
compliant, -ly
complicate, -cated, -cating
complication

complicity
  complient   compliant
compliment, -ed, -ing (praise)
  compliment   complement
                    (completely)
complimentary (free)
  complimentary   complementary
  complissity   complicity
comply, -plied, -plying
compo
component
comport
comportment
compose, -posed, -posing
composedly
  composhure   composure
  composishun   composition
composite, -ly
composition
compositor
compost
composure
  compot   compote
compote
compound, -ed, -ing
compoundable
  compoundabul   compoundable
comprehend, -ed, -ing
comprehendingly
  comprehenshun   comprehension
comprehensible, -bly
comprehension
comprehensive, -ly
comprehensiveness
compress, -ed, -ing
compressibility
compressible
  compressibul   compressible
compression
compressor
comprisal
comprise, -prised, -prising
compromise, -mised, -mising
comptroller
  compulsery   compulsory
  compulshun   compulsion
compulsion

compulsive, -ly
compulsorily
compulsory
  compulsrey   compulsory
compunction
computability
computation
compute, -puted, -puting
computer
computerisation
computer program
computer terminal
  comrad   comrade
comrade
comradeship

> Look under **comm-** if the
> word is not under **com-**.

con, conned, conning
  conbine   combine
concave, -ly
concavity, -ties
conceal, -ed, -ing
concealable
  concealabul   concealable
concealment
concede, -ceded, -ceding
conceit
conceited, -ly
conceivable
conceivably
  conceivabul   conceivable
conceive, -ceived, -ceiving
  concensus   consensus
concentrate, -trated, -trating
concentration
concentric
concentricity
  concepshun   conception
concept
conception
conceptual, -ly
conceptualise, -lised, -lising
concern, -ed, -ing
concert, -ed, -ing
concertina
concertmaster

concerto, -tos, -ti

concession

conch, conchs, conches

concherto	concerto
conciet	conceit
concieted	conceited
concievable	conceivable
concieve	conceive

conciliate, -ated, -ating

conciliation

conciliator

conciliatory

concise, -ly

> Look under **cons-** if the word is not under **conc-**.

conciseness

conclave

conclude, -cluded, -cluding

| conclushun | conclusion |

conclusion

conclusive, -ly

concoct, -ed, -ing

concoction

concomitance

concomitancy

concomitant, -ly

concord

concordance

| concordanse | concordance |

concordant

| concorse | concourse |

concourse

| concreet | concrete |

concrete, -creted, -creting

concretely

concreteness

concubinage

concubine

concupiscence

concupiscent

| concupissense | concupiscence |
| concupissent | concupiscent |

concur, -curred, -curring

| concurence | concurrence |
| concurent | concurrent |

concurrence

concurrent, -ly

| concus | concuss |
| concushun | concussion |

concuss, -ed, -ing

concussion

concussive

condament	condiment
condaminium	condominium
condansation	condensation
condem	condemn

condemn, -ed, -ing

condemnation

condemnatory

| condence | condense |
| condencer | condenser |

condensation

condense, -densed, -densing

condenser

| condensor | condenser |

condescend, -ed, -ing

condescension

condiment

condisend	condescend
condisension	condescension
condishun	condition
condishunal	conditional

condition, -ed, -ing

conditional, -ly

condolatory

condole, -doled, -doling

condolence

| condolense | condolence |

condolingly

condominium

condonation

condone, -doned, -doning

condor

conducive

| conducshun | conduction |

conduct, -ed, -ing

| conducter | conductor |

conductible

conductibility

| conductibul | conductible |

conduction

conductivity, -ties

conductor

conductress	confluent
conduit	conform, -ed, -ing
condusive — conducive	conformable, -bly
cone	conformabul — conformable
conecshun — connection	conformist
conect — connect	conformity, -ties
conective — connective	confound, -ed, -ing
confection	confownd — confound
confectionary, -aries (factory)	confrence — conference
confectionery, -eries (sweets)	confront, -ed, -ing
confedence — confidence	confrontation
confederacy, -cies	confurm — confirm
confederasy — confederacy	confuse, -fused, -fusing
confederate, -rated, -rating	confusion
confederation	confutation
confer, -ferred, -ferring	confute, -futed, -futing
conference	conga (dance)
conferm — confirm	conga — conger (eel)
confess, -ed, -ing	congeal, -ed, -ing
confesser	congeel — congeal
confession	congeneal — congenial
confessional	congenial, -ly
confessor	congeniality
confetti	congenital, -ly
confidant (trusted man)	conger (eel)
confidant — confident (sure)	conger — conga (dance)
confidante (trusted woman)	congest, -ed, -ing
confide, -fided, -fiding	congestion
confidence	congestive
confidenshul — confidential	conglomerate, -rated, -rating
confident (sure)	conglomeration
confident — confidant	congradulation — congratulation
(trusted man)	congragation — congregation
confidential, -ly	congratulate, -lated, -lating
confidentiality	congratulation
configeration — configuration	congratulatory
configuration	congregate, -gated, -gating
confine, -fined, -fining	congregation
confinement	congregational
confirm, -ed, -ing	congress
confirmable	congressional
confirmation	congrewent — congruent
confiscate, -cated, -cating	congrewus — congruous
confiscation	congruence
conflagration	congruent
conflict, -ed, -ing	congruity, -ties
confluence	congruous, -ly

conic
conical, -ly
conifer
coniferous
   conjeckture   conjecture
conjecturable, -bly
conjecture, -tured, -turing
   conjenial   congenial
   conjestion   congestion
conjoin, -ed, -ing
conjoint, -ly
   conjuce   conduce
conjugal, -ly
conjugality
conjugate, -gated, -gating
conjugation
   conjugel   conjugal
   conjuice   conduce
   conjuncshun   conjunction
conjunct, -ly
conjunction
conjunctional, -ly
conjunctive, -ly
conjunctivitis
conjuncture
conjuration
conjure, -jured, -juring
conjurer
conjuror
conk, -ed, -ing
conker (nut)
   conker   conquer (win)
   conkwest   conquest
con man, -men
connect, -ed, -ing
connectedly
connecter
connection
connective, -ly
connector
   connesser   connoisseur
   connewbial   connubial
conning tower
connivance
   connivanse   connivance
connive, -nived, -niving
connoisseur

connotation
connote, -noted, -noting
connubial, -ly
   connubiul   connubial
   conosseur   connoisseur
   conote   connote
conquer, -ed, -ing
conquerable
   conquerabul   conquerable
   conquerer   conqueror
conqueror
conquest
conquistador
consanguine
consanguineous, -ly
consanguinity
   consceintious   conscientious
conscience
   conscienshus   conscientious
conscientious, -ly
conscious, -ly
consciousness
   conscripshun   conscription
conscript, -ed, -ing
conscription
   conseal   conceal
   conseat   conceit
consecrate, -crated, -crating
consecration
consecutive
   consede   concede
   consekwence   consequence
consensus
consent, -ed, -ing
consequence
consequent
consequential, -ly
   conservatery   conservatory
conservation
conservational
conservationist
conservative, -ly
conservatism
conservatoire
conservatorium
conservatory, -tries
   conservatry   conservatory

conserve, -served, -serving
conserver
  consession   concession
  consicrate   consecrate
consider, -ed, -ing
considerable, -ably
  considerabul   considerable
considerate, -ly
consideration
consign, -ed, -ing
consignable
  consignabul   consignable
consignee
consigner
  consignible   consignable
consignment
consignor
  consiliate   conciliate
  consine   consign
  consinee   consignee
  consinement   consignment
  consinor   consignor
  consise   concise
consist, -ed, -ing
consistence
consistency, -cies
  consistense   consistence
  consistensy   consistency
consistent, -ly
consolable
  consolabul   consolable
consolation
console, -soled, -soling
consoler
consolingly
consolidate, -dated, -dating
consolidated revenue
consolidation
consolidator
consommé
consonance
consonant, -ly
consort, -ed, -ing
consortium, -tia
conspicuous, -ly
conspicuousness
conspiracy, -cies

  conspirasy   conspiracy
  conspirater   conspirator
conspirator
conspiratory
  conspiratry   conspiratory
conspire, -spired, -spiring
constable
  constabul   constable
constabulary, -ries
constancy
  constansy   constancy
constant, -ly
  constapation   constipation
constellation
consternation
constipate, -pated, -pating
constipation
constituency, -cies
  constituensy   constituency
constituent
constitute, -tuted, -tuting
constitution
constitutional, -ly
constrain, -ed, -ing
constraint
  constrickshun   constriction
constrict, -ed, -ing
constriction
construct, -ed, -ing
construction
constructive, -ly
constructor
construe, -strued, -struing
consul
consular
consulate
  consuler   consular
consult, -ed, -ing
consultant
consultation
consultative
  consultent   consultant
consulter
consumable
  consumabul   consumable
consume, -sumed, -suming
consumer

consumerism
consummate, -mated, -mating
consummation
consummative
 consummé   consommé
 consumpshun consumption
consumption
consumptive, -ly
contact, -ed, -ing
contact lenses
 contageous   contagious
contagion
contagious, -ly
 contagus   contagious
 contajus   contagious
contain, -ed, -ing
container
containment
contaminate, -nated, -nating
contamination
 contane   contain
 contanement   containment
 contaner   container
contemplate, -plated, -plating
contemplation
contemplative, -ly
contemporaneous, -ly
contemporary, -raries
contempt
 contemptable contemptible
contemptible, -bly
 contemptibul contemptible
contemptuous, -ly
contend, -ed, -ing
contender
 contenshun   contention
 contenshus   contentious
content
contented, -ly
contention
contentious, -ly
contentment
contest, -ed, -ing
contestant
 contestent   contestant
context
contextual, -ly

contiguity
contiguous, -ly
continence
 continense   continence
continent
continental
contingency, -cies
 contingensy   contingency
contingent, -ly
 continnuation continuation
continual, -ly
continuance
 continuanse   continuance
continuation
continue, -ued, -uing
continuity, -ties
continuous, -ly
continuum, -tinuums, -tinua
 contorshun   contortion
contort, -ed, -ing
contortion
contortionist
contour
contraband
contraception
contraceptive, -ly
 contrackshun contraction
contract, -ed, -ing
contraction
contractor
contractual
 contradickshun contradiction
contradict, -ed, -ing
contradiction
contradictory, -ries
contralto, -ti
 contrapshun   contraption
contraption
contrarily
contrariness
contrariwise
contrary, -ries
 contrasepshun contraception
 contraseptive contraceptive
contrast, -ed, -ing
contravene, -vened, -vening
 contravenshun contravention

contribushun   contribution
contribute, -buted, -buting
contribution
contributor
contributory
   contributry   contributory
   contrishun   contrition
contrite, -ly
contrition
contrivance
   contrivanse   contrivance
contrive, -trived, -triving
control, -trolled, -trolling
controllable
   controllabul   controllable
controller
   controvershal   controversial
controversial, -ly
controversy, -sies
contumely, -lies
contuse, -tused, -tusing
   contushun   contusion
contusion
contusive
conurbation
convalesce, -lesced, -lescing
convalescence
   convalescense   convalescent
convalescent
   convaless   convalesce
   convalessence   convalescence
convection
convective, -ly
convector
convene, -vened, -vening
convenience
   conveniense   convenience
convenient, -ly
convenor
   convenshun   convention
   convenshunal   conventional
convent
convention
conventional, -ly
conventionalism
converge, -verged, -verging
conversant, -ly

conversation
conversational, -ly
conversationalist
converse, -versed, -versing
conversely
   conversent   conversant
   convershun   conversion
conversion
convert, -ed, -ing
   convertabul   convertible
converter
convertible, -ly
   convertibul   convertible
convex, -ly
convexity, -ties
convey, -ed, -ing
conveyance
conveyancer
conveyancing
   conveyanse   conveyance
conveyor belt
   convickshun   conviction
convict, -ed, -ing
conviction
   convienence   convenience
convince, -vinced, -vincing
convincible
   convincibul   convincible
convincingly
convivial, -ly
convivialty
convocation
convoke, -voked, -voking
   convolushun   convolution
convolute, -luted, -luting
convolution
convoy, -ed, -ing
convulse, -vulsed, -vulsing
   convulshun   convulsion
convulsion
convulsive, -ly
   conyac   cognac
coo, cooed, cooing
cooee, cooeed, cooeeing
   cooger   cougar
cook, -ed, -ing
cookery, -eries

cookhouse
cookie, cookies
  cookoo — cuckoo
cool, -ed, -ing
coolabah
  coolabar — coolabah
coolamon
coolant
coolie (labourer)
coolly (calmly)
coop, -ed, -ing
co-op
cooper
cooperage
cooperate, -rated, -rating
cooperation
cooperative, -ly
  coopon — coupon
co-opt, -ed, -ing
coordinate, -nated, -nating
coordination
coordinator
cop, copped, copping (accept)
  coparison — comparison
cope, coped, coping (put up with)
  coper — copper
copha
copier
co-pilot
copious, -ly
cop-out
copper
copperhead
copperplate
  coppy — copy
copra
  cops — copse
copse
cop shop
copula, -lae
copulate, -lated, -lating
copulation
copulative, -ly
copy, copies
copy, copied, copying
copybook
copycat, -catted, -catting

  copyer — copier
copyist
copyright, -ed, -ing (licence)
  copyrite — copyright
copywriter
coquet, -quetted, -quetting
coquetry
coquette
coquettish, -ly
coral (reef)
  coral — choral (sing)
  coral — corral (yard)
coralfish
  corcus — caucus
cord (rope)
  cord — chord (music)
cordage
corded
cordial, -ly
cordiality
  cordige — cordage
cordon, -ed, -ing
cordon bleu
cords (trousers)
corduroy
core, cored, coring (centre)
  core — caw (cry)
  core — corps (group)
  corecshun — correction
  corect — correct
  corection — correction
  corective — corrective
  corelate — correlate
corella
  coreografy — choreography
  corespond — correspond
  corespondence — correspondence
  corespondense — correspondence
co-respondent (divorce)
  corespondent — correspondent
coriander
  coridoor — corridor
  coridor — corridor
Corinthian
  coriografy — choreography
  corispond — correspond
  corispondence — correspondence

corispondent	correspondent	corpse (body)	
corister	chorister	corpse	corps (group)
cork, -ed, -ing		corpulence	
corkage		corpulense	corpulence
corker		corpulent, -ly	
corkscrew, -ed, -ing		corpus, -pora	
corm		corpuscle	
cormorant		corpuscular	
corn		corpusle	corpuscle
corncob		corpussel	corpuscle
cornea, -neas, -neae		corral, -ralled, -ralling (yard)	
corneal		corral	choral (sing)
corned beef		correckshun	correction
corneel	corneal	correct, -ed, -ing	
corner, -ed, -ing		correction	
cornerstone		correctional	
cornet		corrective, -ly	
cornflour		correlate, -lated, -lating	
cornia	cornea	correlation	
cornice, -niced, -nicing		correlative, -ly	
cornstalk		correlativity	
cornucopia		correspond, -ed, -ing	
corny, -nier, -niest		correspondence	
coroborate	corroborate	correspondent	
coroborator	corroborator	corridor	
coroboree	corroboree	Corriedale	
corode	corrode	corroborate, -rated, -rating	
corola	corolla	corroboration	
corolary	corollary	corroborative, -ly	
corolla		corroborator	
corollary, -ries		corroboree	
corona, -nas, -nae		corrode, -roded, -roding	
coronary		corrodible	
coronary thrombosis		corrodibul	corrodible
coronation		corrollary	corollary
coroner		corroshun	corrosion
coronet		corrosion	
coroshun	corrosion	corrosive, -ly	
corosive	corrosive	corrugate, -gated, -gating	
corparation	corporation	corrugated iron	
corperal	corporal	corrugation	
corporal, -ly		corrupshun	corruption
corporate, -ly		corrupt, -ed, -ing	
corporation		corruptabul	corruptible
corporeal, -ly		corruptible, -bly	
corps (group)		corruptibility	
corps	corpse (body)	corruptibul	corruptible

corruption		cost, cost, costed, costing	
corsage		cost	coast
corsair		co-star, -starred, -starring	
corsashun	causation	coster	
corse	coarse (rough)	costguard	coastguard
corse	course (path)	costliness	
corsen	coarsen	costly, -lier, -liest	
corset		costume, -tumed, -tuming	
corsetry		costume jewellery	
corshun	caution	cosy, -sies	
corshus	cautious	cosy, -sier, -siest	
corsit	corset	cot	
cort	caught (held)	cotage	cottage
cort	court (law)	cotchineal	cochineal
cort marshal	court martial	cote (shelter)	
cortage	cortege	cote	coat (garment)
cortege		coterie	
corterise	cauterise	cotige	cottage
cortex, -tices		coton	cotton
cortier	courtier	cotoneaster	
cortion	caution	cotonwool	cottonwool
cortious	cautious	cottage	
cortisan	courtesan	cotter pin	
cortisone		cotton	
cortly	courtly	cottonbush	
cortroom	courtroom	cottonwood	
cortship	courtship	cottonwool	
cortyard	courtyard	cottony	
corugate	corrugate	cou daytar	coup d'état
corupt	corrupt	couch	
coruptible	corruptible	cougar	
coruption	corruption	cough, -ed, -ing	
corus	chorus	could	
corvet	corvette	couldn't (could not)	
corvette		couldnt	couldn't
cos		coulter	
cosh		councel	council (meeting)
cosmetic		councel	counsel (advice)
cosmetically			
cosmografy	cosmography	council (meeting)	
cosmography, -phies		council	counsel (advice)
cosmology			
cosmonaut		counciller	councillor
cosmonort	cosmonaut	councillor (member)	
cosmopolitan		councillor	counsellor (adviser)
cosmos			
Cossack			

counsel, -selled, -selling (advice)

counsel   council (meeting)

counseller   counsellor
counsellor (adviser)

counsellor   councillor (member)

count, -ed, -ing
countdown
countenance, -nanced, -nancing

countenanse   countenance

counter
counteract, -ed, -ing
counteraction
counteractive, -ly
counterattack, -ed, -ing
counterbalance, -anced, -ancing
counter culture
counterespionage

counterfeet   counterfeit

counterfeit, -ed, -ing
counterfeiter
counterintelligence
countermand, -ed, -ing
counterpane
counterpart
counterpoint
counterproductive
counter-revolution
counter-revolutionary, -aries
countersign, -ed, -ing
countersignature

countersine   countersign
counterwait   counterweight

counterweight
countess

countie   county

countless
country, -tries
countryman, -men
countryside
county, -ties
coup, -coups

coupay   coupé

coup de grace
coup d'état
coupé

couple, -led, -ling
couplet
coupon
courage
courageous, -ly
courier
course (path)

course   coarse (rough)
coursen   coarsen

court, -ed, -ing (law)

court   caught (held)

courtesan
courtesy, -sies
courthouse
courtier
courtly, -lier, -liest

court marshal   court martial

court martial
courtroom
courtyard
cousin
couture
couturier
covenant
cover, -ed, -ing
coverage
covert, -ly
cover-up
covet, -ed, -ing
covetous, -ly
covey, -eys
coward (scared)

coward   cowered (cringed)

cowardice

cowardiss   cowardice

cowardly
cowboy
cower, -ed, -ing (cringe)

cowerd   coward
cowered   coward (scared)

cowl, -ed, -ing
cowlick
cowling

> For cown-words,
> look under **coun-**.

cowslip
cox
coxcomb
  coxe   coax
coxswain
coy, -ly
  coyn   coin
coyote
crab, crabbed, crabbing
crab-apple
crabby, -bier, -biest
crablouse
crack, -ed, -ing
crackdown
cracker
crackle, -led, -ling
crackpot
  crackul   crackle
cradle, -dled, -dling
cradle-snatcher
  cradul   cradle
craft
craftily
craftiness
craftsman, -men
craftsmanship
crafty, -tier, -tiest
crag
cragged
craggy, -gier, -giest
  crain   crane
crake
cram, crammed, cramming
cramp, -ed, -ing
cranberry, -ries
crane, craned, craning
cranial, -ly
cranium, -nia
crank, -ed, -ing
crankcase
crankiness
crankshaft
cranky, -kier, -kiest
cranny, -nies
craps
crapulous
crash, -ed, -ing

crasher
crass
crate, crated, crating
crater
cravat
crave, craved, craving
craven, -ly
craw
crawl, -ed, -ing
crawler
crayfish, -fishes, -fish
crayon, -ed, -ing
  craype   crepe
craypot
  craysh   crèche
craze, crazed, crazing
crazily
craziness
crazy, -zier, -ziest
  creacher   creature
creak, -ed, -ing (squeak)
  creak   creek (stream)
cream, -ed, -ing
creaminess
creamy, -mier, -miest
  creap   creep
crease, creased, creasing
create, -ated, -ating
  creater   creator
creation
creative, -ly
creativeness
creativity
creator
creature
crèche
  creecher   creature
credence
  credense   credence
  credenshul   credential
credential
credibility
credible
credibly
  credibul   credible
credit, -ed, -ing
creditable, -bly

creditabul	creditable	crewel	cruel (harsh)
credit card		crewl	cruel
crediter	creditor	crew neck	
creditor		crews (sailors)	
credo, -dos		crews	cruise (ship)
credulity		crib, cribbed, cribbing	
credulous, -ly		cribage	cribbage
credulousness		cribbage	
creed		cribbidge	cribbage
creek (stream)		crick	
creek	creak (squeak)	cricket	
creel		cricketer	
creem	cream	crier	
creep, crept, creeping		crime	
creeper		criminal, -ly	
creepiness		criminality, -ties	
creeps		criminologist	
creepy, -pier, -piest		criminology	
cremate, -mated, -mating		crimp, -ed, -ing	
cremation		crimpy, -pier, -piest	
crematorium		crimson	
creme		cringe, cringed, cringing	
crenellate, -lated, -lating		crinkle, -kled, -kling	
creole		crinkul	crinkle
creosote, -soted, -soting		crinkly	
crepe, creped, creping		crinoline	
crept		cripple, -pled, -pling	
crepuscular		cript	crypt
crescendo, -dos		criptic	cryptic
crescent		criptograf	cryptograph
cresh	crèche	criptogram	cryptogram
creshendo	crescendo	criptograph	cryptograph
cress		cripul	cripple
cressent	crescent	crisalis	chrysalis
crest, -ed, -ing		crisalus	chrysalis
crestfallen, -ly		criscros	crisscross
cretin		crisen	christen
cretinism		Crisendom	Christendom
cretinous		crisis, -ses	
creture	creature	crisp, -ed, -ing	
crevase	crevasse	crispness	
crevase	crevice	crispy	
crevasse, -vassed, -vassing		crisscross	
crevice		Crist	Christ
creviss	crevice	cristal	crystal
crew, -ed, -ing		cristaline	crystalline
crewel (yarn)		cristalise	crystallise

Cristian — Christian
Cristianity — Christianity
criteek — critique
criterion, -teria
critic
critical, -ly
criticise, -cised, -cising
criticism
critique
critisise — criticise
croak, -ed, -ing
croaky
crochet, -ed, -ing
crock
crockadile — crocodile
crockery
crocodile
crocus, crocuses
croft
crofter
croissant
crokay — croquet
cromatic — chromatic
crome — chrome
cromosome — chromosome
crone
crony, -nies
crood — crude
crook
crooked, -ly
crookedness
croon, -ed, -ing
crooner
crop, cropped, cropping
crop-dust, -ed, -ing
crop-duster
cropper
croquet (sport)
croquette (food)
crosier
cross, -ed, -ing
crossbar
crossbench
crossbencher
crossbones
crossbow
crossbreed, -bred, -breeding

crosscheck
cross-country
crosscut, -cut, -cutting
cross-examination
cross-examine, -ined, -ining
cross-examiner
cross-eyed
cross-fertilisation
cross-fertilise, -lised, -lising
crossover
cross-pollinate, -nated, -nating
cross-purpose
cross-reference, -renced, -rencing
crossroad
cross-section
cross-stitch, -ed, -ing
crosswise
crossword puzzle
crotch
crotchet
crotchetiness
crotchety
crouch, -ed, -ing
croup
croupier
crouton
crow, crowed, crowing
crowbar
crowd, -ed, -ing
croweater
crown, -ed, -ing
crown-of-thorns
crow's-foot, -feet
crow's-nest
crucial, -ly
crucibel — crucible
crucible
crucibul — crucible
crucifix
crucifixion
cruciform, -ly
crucify, -fied, -fying
crude, cruder, crudest
crudeness
crudity, -ties
cruel, cruelled, cruelling
cruelty, -ties

cruet
cruise, cruised, cruising (ship)
  cruise   crews (sailors)
cruiser
  crum   crumb
crumb, -ed, -ing
crumble, -bled, -bling
crumbly, -blier, -bliest
  crumbul   crumble
crummy, -mier, -miest
crumpet
crumple, -pled, -pling
  crumpul   crumple
  crumy   crummy
crunch, -ed, -ing
crunchy, -chier, -chiest
crusade, -saded, -sading
crusader
crush, -ed, -ing
  crushal   crucial
crusher
  crusibul   crucible
crust
crustacean
  crustashun   crustacean
crustiness
crusty, crustier, crustiest
crutch, -ed, -ing
crux, cruxes, cruces
  cruze   cruise
cry, cries
cry, cried, crying
crypt
cryptic, -ally
cryptogram
cryptograph
cryptographer
cryptographic
cryptography
  crysalis   chrysalis
crystal
crystalline
crystallisation
crystallise, -lised, -lising
cub
cubby, -bies
cubbyhole

cubbyhouse
cube, cubed, cubing
cubic
cubical, -ly (cube-shaped)
cubicle (room)
cubism
cubist
cubmaster
  cuboard   cupboard
  cuby   cubby
  cubyhole   cubbyhole
  cubyhouse   cubbyhouse
cuckold, -ed, -ing
cuckoldry
cuckoo
cucumber
cud
  cuddel   cuddle
cuddle, -dled, -dling
cuddlesome
cuddly
cuddy, -dies
cudgel, -elled, -elling
cudgerie
  cudly   cuddly
  cudos   kudos
cue, cued, cuing (billiards)
  cue   queue (line)
cuff, -ed, -ing
cuisine
  culcher   culture
cul-de-sac
  culer   colour
culinary
cull, -ed, -ing
culminate, -nated, -nating
culmination
  culots   culottes
culottes
culpability
culpable, -bly
  culpabul   culpable
culprit
cult
cultism
cultist
cultivate, -vated, -vating

cultivater → cultivator
cultivation
cultivator
cultural, -ly
culture, -tured, -turing
cultured pearl
culture shock
culvert
cumbasome → cumbersome
cumbersome, -ly
cumbersum → cumbersome
cumfurt → comfort
cumin
cummerbund
cumpass → compass
cumquat
cumulative, -ly
cumulus
cuning → cunning
cunning, -ly
cuntry → country
cup, cupped, cupping
cupboard
cupbord → cupboard
cupful, cupfuls
cupid
cupidity
cupola
cuppa
cur
curable, -bly
curacao
curacy, -cies
curage → courage
curant → currant (fruit)
curare
curate
curater → curator
curative, -ly
curator
curatorial
curb, -ed, -ing (control)
curb → kerb (gutter)
curcuit → circuit
curd
curdle, -dled, -dling
curdul → curdle

cure, cured, curing
curency → currency
curent → current (flow)
curette, -retted, -retting
curfew
curiculum → curriculum
curio, curios
curiosity, -ties
curious, -ly
curiousness
curius → curious
curl, -ed, -ing
curler
curlew
curly, -lier, -liest
curnel → colonel
currage → courage
curragus → courageous
currajong
currant (fruit)
currant → current (flow)
currawong
currency, -cies
currensy → currency
current (flow)
current → currant (fruit)
current account
currently
curriculum, -lums, -la
curriculum vitae
curry, -ries
curry, -ried, -rying
curse, cursed, cursing
cursive, -ly
cursor
curt, -ly
curtail, -ed, -ing
curtailment
curtain, -ed, -ing
curtale → curtail
curtsy, -sies
curtsy, -sied, -sying
curvaceous
curvachure → curvature
curvashus → curvaceous
curvature
curve, curved, curving

curvilinear
cushion, -ed, -ing
cushon — cushion
cushy, cushier, cushiest
cusp
cuspid
cuss
cussed, -ly
custard
custard-apple
custodial
custodian
custodiul — custodial
custodiun — custodian
custom
customarily
customary, -aries
custom-built
customer
custom-made
cut, cut, cutting
cutback
cute, cuter, cutest
cuteness
cutical — cuticle
cuticle
cuticul — cuticle
cutlass
cutlery
cutlet
cut-off
cut-out
cut-price
cutter
cutthroat
cuttlebone
cuttlefish, -fishes, -fish
cuttulbone — cuttlebone
cutworm
cuvenant — covenant
cuver — cover
cuvet — covet
cuvey — covey
cyanide
cybernetics
cyclamate
cyclamen

cycle, cycled, cycling
cyclic
cyclist
cycloid
cyclone
cyclonic
cyclostyle, -led, -ling
cyder
cygnet (swan)
cygnet — signet (ring)
cylinder
cymbal (instrument)
cymbal — symbol (sign)
cymbalist
cymbidium
cynic
cynical, -ly
cynicism
cynoshure — cynosure
cynosure
cypher
cypress
cyst
cystitis
cytology
czar
czarina
czarist
Czech
Czechoslovak
Czechoslovakia

Dd

dab, dabbed, dabbing
dabble, -bled, -bling
dabed — dabbed
dabing — dabbing
dable — dabble
dabul — dabble
dachshund
dacks — daks
dacor — decor
dad
daddy-long-legs
daemon
daffodil
daffodill — daffodil
daffy, daffier, daffiest
dafny — daphne
dafodil — daffodil
daft
dager — dagger
dagger
dahlia
dail — dale
daily
daim — dame
daintie — dainty
daintily
dainty, -tier, -tiest
dair — dare
dairy, -ries (milk)
dairy — diary (book)
dais
daisie — daisy
daisy
daks
dalee — dally
dalia — dahlia
dally, -lied, -lying
Dalmatian

daly — daily
dam, dammed, damming (water)
dam — damn (swear)
damage, -aged, -aging
damageable
damask
dame
damedge — damage
damestic — domestic
damn, -ed, -ing (swear)
damn — dam (water)
damnable, -bly
damnabul — damnable
damnation
damp
dampcourse
dampen, -ed, -ing
damper
damsel
damsil — damsel
damsul — damsel
dance, danced, dancing
dancer
dandelion
dandilion — dandelion
dandle, -dled, -dling
dandruff
dane — deign
dangel — dangle
danger
dangerous, -ly
dangerus — dangerous
dangle, -gled, -gling
dangul — dangle
danjer — danger
danjerus — dangerous
daper — dapper
dappel — dapple
dapper, -ly
dapple, -pled, -pling
darby — derby
dare, dared, daring
daredevil
darey — dairy
dark, -ly
darken, -ed, -ing
darkin — darken

darkness
darkroom
darlin — darling
darling
darn, -ed, -ing
dart, -ed, -ing
darta — data
dartabase — database
darter
dash, -ed, -ing
dashboard
dashbord — dashboard
dashound — dachshund
dastard, -ly
dastid — dastard
dastud — dastard
data
database
date, dated, dating
dater — data
datim — datum
datum
daub
daufin — dauphin
daughter
daunt, -ed, -ing
dauphin
dauter — daughter
dawb — daub
dawdle, -dled, -dling
dawdul — dawdle
dawn, -ed, -ing
dawnt — daunt
dawter — daughter
day
daybrake — daybreak
daybreak
daydream
daycor — decor
dayify — deify
dayis — dais
dayity — deity
daylia — dahlia
daylight
daylite — daylight
dayly — daily
dayn — deign

daysy — daisy
daze, dazed, dazing (stun)
daze — days (time)
dazzle, -zled, -zling
dazzler
deacon
deactivate, -ated, -ating
dead, -ly
dead centre
deaden, -ed, -ing
dead heart
dead heat
deadline
deadlock
deadly, -lier, -liest
deadpan
dead reckoning
dead weight
deadwood
deaf
deafen, -ed, -ing
deaft — deft
deal, dealt, dealing
dealer
deam — deem
dean
deanery
dear, -ly (loved)
dear — deer (animal)
dearth
death
death adder
deathly
death-wish

> Look under **di-** if the
> word is not under **de-**.

debacle
debacul — debacle
debar, -barred, -barring
debase, -based, -basing
debasement
debatable, -bly
debatabul — debatable
debate, -bated, -bating
debatible — debatable
debauch, -ed, -ing

debauchery, -ries

debbit — debit

debensher — debenture

debenshure — debenture

debenture

debilitate, -tated, -tating

debilitation

debility, -ties

debit, -ed, -ing

debonair

deboo — debut

debree — debris

debrief, -ed, -ing

debris

debt

debter — debtor

debtor

debug, -bugged, -bugging

debunk, -ed, -ing

debut

debutante

decade

decadence

decadense — decadence

decadent, -ly

decamp, -ed, -ing

decant, -ed, -ing

decanter

decapitate, -tated, -tating

decapitation

decathalon — decathlon

decathlon

decay, -ed, -ing

decease, -ceased, -ceasing

deceit

deceitful, -ly

deceive, deceived, deceiving

decelerate, -rated, -rating

December

decency, -cies

decent, -ly

decentralisation

decentralise, -lised, -lising

decepshun — deception

deception

deceptive, -ly

decibel

decibell — decibel

decide, -cided, -ciding

decidedly

deciduous

decieve — deceive

decifer — decipher

decimal

decimate, -mated, -mating

decipher, -ed, -ing

decishun — decision

decision

decisive, -ly

deck, -ed, -ing

deckade — decade

deckchair

deckchare — deckchair

deckerate — decorate

deckhand

deckle

deckul — deckle

declaim, -ed, -ing

declamation

declarable

declarabul — declarable

declaratory

declaratry — declaratory

declare, -clared, -claring

declassify, -fied, -fying

decline, -clined, -clining

decode, -coded, -coding

decompose, -posed, -posing

decomposishun — decomposition

decomposition

decompreshun — decompression

decompress, -ed, -ing

decompression

decongestant

decor

decorate, -rated, -rating

decoration

decorative, -ly

decorous, -ly

decorum

decorus — decorous

decoy, -ed, -ing

decrease, -creased, -creasing

decree, -creed, -creeing

decreese → decrease
decrepit
decrepitude
decrese → decrease
decry, -cried, -crying
ded → dead
deden → deaden

> Look under **di-** if the word
> is not under **de-**.

dedicate, -cated, -cating
dedication
dedly → deadly
deduce, -duced, -ducing
deduct, -ed, -ing
deductible
deductibul → deductible
deduction
deed
deel → deal
deem, -ed, -ing
deen → dean
deep, -ly
deepen, -ed, -ing
deep freeze, -frozen, -freezing
deepwater
deer (animal)
deer → dear (loved)
de-escalate, -lated, -lating
def → deaf
deface, -faced, -facing
defacit → deficit
de facto
defamation
defamatory
defamatry → defamatory
defame, -famed, -faming
default, -ed, -ing
defaulter
defeat, -ed, -ing
defeatism
defeatist
defecate, -cated, -cating
defeckshun → defection
defect, -ed, -ing
defection
defective, -ly

defector
defeet → defeat
defen → deafen
defence
defend, -ed, -ing
defendant
defendent → defendant
defensable → defensible
defensible
defensibul → defensible
defensive, -ly
defer, -ferred, -ferring
deferance → deference
deference
deferense → deference
deferenshul → deferential
deferential, -ly

> For **deff-**words,
> look under **def-**.

defiance
defianse → defiance
defiant, -ly
deficiency, -cies
deficit
defience → defiance
defile, -filed, -filing
definate → definite
define, -fined, -fining
definishun → definition
definit → definite
definite, -ly
definition
definitive, -ly
defishency → deficiency
defishent → deficient
defisit → deficit
deflate, -flated, -flating
deflation
deflationary
defleckshun → deflection
deflect, -ed, -ing
deflection
defnite → definite
defoliant
defoliate, -ated, -ating
defoliation

deform, -ed, -ing
deformity, -ies
defraud, -ed, -ing
defrauder
defray, -ed, -ing
defreeze, -frozen, -freezing
   defrord — defraud
defrost, -ed, -ing
deft, -ly
deftness
defunct
defuse, -fused, -fusing
defy, -fied, -fying
   defyance — defiance
   defyant — defiant

> Look under **di-** if the word is
> not under **de-**.

degeneracy
   degenerasy — degeneracy
degenerate, -rated, -rating
degeneration
degradation
degrade, -graded, -grading
degree
   degridation — degradation
   dehidrate — dehydrate
dehydrate, -drated, -drating
dehydration
   deifie — deify
deify, -fied, -fying
   deisel — diesel
   deitee — deity
deity, -ties
   dejeckshun — dejection
dejection
   dekay — decay
delay, -ed, -ing
   delecate — delicate
delectable, -bly
   delectabul — delectable
delegate, -gated, -gating
delegation
   delerious — delirious
   deleshun — deletion
delete, -leted, -leting

deleterious, -ly
deletion
   delfinium — delphinium
deli
deliberate, -rated, -rating
deliberately
deliberation
deliberative, -ly
delicacy, -cies
delicate, -ly
delicatessen
delicious, -ly
   delicous — delicious
   deligate — delegate
delight, -ed, -ing
delightful, -ly
delineate, -ed, -ing
delineation
   deliniate — delineate
   delinkwency — delinquency
   delinkwent — delinquent
   delinquancy — delinquency
delinquency
delinquent
delirious, -ly
delirium
   delirius — delirious
   delishus — delicious
   delite — delight
   deliteful — delightful
deliver, -ed, -ing
deliverance
   deliverence — deliverance
delivery, -eries
dell
dellie

> For other **dell-** words, look
> under **del-**.

   delood — delude
delphinium
   delt — dealt
delta
delude, -luded, -luding
deluge, -uged, -uging
   deluks — de luxe
   delushun — delusion

delusion
delusive, -ly
delusory
delve, delved, delving
demagogue
demagogy
demand, -ed, -ing
demarcate, -cated, -cating
demarcation
demean, -ed, -ing
  demeaner   demeanour
demeanour
  demensha   dementia
demented, -ly
dementia
demerara
demerit
demigod
demilitarised zone
demise
demister
demo
demob
demobilisation
demobilise, -lised, -lising
democracy, -cies
  democrasy   democracy
democrat
democratic, -ally
democratisation
  demografy   demography
demographic, -ally
demography
demolish, -ed, -ing
  demolishun   demolition
demolition
demolitionist
demon
demonic
demonology
demonstrable, -bly
  demonstrabul   demonstrable
demonstrate, -strated, -strating
  demonstrater   demonstrator
demonstration
demonstrator
demoralise, -lised, -lising

demote, -moted, -moting
demur, -murred, -murring (object)
  demur   demure (coy)
demure, -murer, -murest (coy)
  demure   demur (object)
den
  dence   dense
  dencher   denture
  dencity   density
  denem   denim
dengue
  deni   deny
denial
denigrate, -grated, -grating
denigration
denim
denizen

For denn- words, look under
den-.

denominate, -nated, -nating
denomination
denominational, -ly
denominator
denotable
  denotabul   denotable
denote, -noted, -noting
denounce, -nounced, -nouncing
denouncement
  denownse   denounce
dense, denser, densest
densely
  densitee   density
density
dent, -ed, -ing
dental
dentist
dentistry
denture
denude, -nuded, -nuding
denunciate, -ated, -ating
deny, denied, denying
  deoderant   deodorant
  deoderise   deodorise
deodorant
deodorise, -rised, -rising
  deparcher   departure

depart, -ed, -ing
department
departmental, -ly
departure
depen   deepen
depend, -ed, -ing
dependable, -bly
dependabul   dependable
dependant (noun)
dependence
dependency, -cies
dependensy   dependency
dependent, -ly (adjective)
dependible   dependable
depickshun   depiction
depict, -ed, -ing
depiction
depilatery   depilatory
depilatory, -ries
depilatry   depilatory
depleshun   depletion
deplete, -pleted, -pleting
depletion
deploi   deploy
deplorable, -bly
deplorabul   deplorable
deplore, -plored, -ploring
deploy, -ed, -ing
deployment
depo   depot
deport, -ed, -ing
deportation
deportee
depose, -posed, -posing
deposit, -ed, -ing
deposishun   deposition
depositer   depositor
deposition
depositor
depository, -ries
depositry   depository
depot

> For depp- words, look under
> **dep-**.

depraved
depravity, -ties

deprecate, -cated, -cating
deprecation
depreciate, -ated, -ating
depreciation
depredation
depresherise   depressurise
depreshiate   depreciate
depreshun   depression
depresive   depressive
depresor   depressor
depress, -ed, -ing
depressant
depressent   depressant
depresshun   depression
depression
depressive, -ly
depressor
depressurise, -ised, -ising
depricate   deprecate
deprive, -prived, -priving
depth
deputation
depute, -puted, -puting
deputey   deputy
deputise, -tised, -tising
deputy, -ties

> Look under **di-** if the word is
> not under **de-**.

derail, -ed, -ing
derailment
derale   derail
derange, -ranged, -ranging
derby, -bies
deregister, -ed, -ing
derelickshun   dereliction
derelict
dereliction
derick   derrick
deride, -rided, -riding
derigible   dirigible
derishun   derision
derision
derisive, -ly
derivation
derivative
derive, -rived, -riving

dermatitis
dermatologist
dermatology
derogatery / derogatory
derogatory
derogatry / derogatory
derrick

> For other derr- words, look
> under der-.

dert / dirt
derth / dearth
derty / dirty
dervish
desalination
desastrous / disastrous
descant
descend, -ed, -ing
descendant (noun)
descendent (adjective)
descent (down)
descent / dissent (differ)
desciple / disciple
describe, -scribed, -scribing
descripshun / description
description
descriptive, -ly
descry, -cried, -crying
desease / disease
deseat / deceit
deseave / deceive
desecrate, -crated, -crating
desecration
desegregate, -gated, -gating
desegregation
desel / diesel
deselerate / decelerate
Desember / December
desency / decency
desend / descend
desensitise, -tised, -tising
desent / decent
desent / descent
desentralise / decentralise
desershun / desertion
desert, deserts
desert, -ed, -ing (leave)

desert / dessert (food)
deserter
desertion
deserve, -served, -serving
desese / disease
desibel / decibel
de-sex, -sexed, -sexing
desicate / desiccate
desication / desiccation
desiccate, -cated, -cating
desiccation
deside / decide
desiduous / deciduous
design, -ed, -ing
designate, -nated, -nating
designation
desimal / decimal
desimate / decimate
desimul / decimal
desine / design
desipher / decipher
desirability
desirable, -bly
desirabul / desirable
desire, -sired, -siring
desirous
desirus / desirous
desist, -ed, -ing
desk
deskant / descant

> Look under di- if the word is
> not under de-.

desolate, -lated, -lating
desolation
despach / despatch
despair, -ed, -ing
despare / despair
despatch, -ed, -ing
despensable / dispensable
desperado, -does, -dos
desperate, -ly
desperation
despicable, -bly
despicabul / despicable
despise, -spised, -spising
despite

despoil, -ed, -ing
despoliation
despondency
  despondensy — despondency
despondent, -ly
despot
despotic
despotism
  desprate — desperate
dessert (food)
  dessert — desert (leave)
dessertspoon
destination
destine, -tined, -tining
destiny, -nies
  destitushen — destitution
destitute
destitution
destroy, -ed, -ing
destroyer
  destruckshun — destruction
destruct, -ed, -ing
destructible
  destructibul — destructible
destruction
destructive, -ly
desultory
  det — debt
detach, -ed, -ing
detachable
  detachabul — detachable
detail, -ed, -ing
detain, -ed, -ing
detainee
detainment
  detale — detail
  detane — detain
  deteckshun — detection
detect, -ed, -ing
detectable
  detectabul — detectable
detection
detective
detector
  detektive — detective
  detenshun — detention
detention

deter, -terred, -terring
  deter — debtor
  deterent — deterrent
detergent
  deterjent — detergent
deteriorate, -rated, -rating
deterioration
determinant
determination
determine, -mined, -mining
determinism
deterrence
deterrent
detest, -ed, -ing
detestable, -bly
  detestabul — detestable
detestation
  deth — death
detonate, -nated, -nating
detonation
detonator
detour, -ed, -ing
  detrackshun — detraction
detract, -ed, -ing
detraction
detractor
  detramental — detrimental
detriment
detrimental, -ly
  detterent — deterrent
  dettor — debtor
deuce
deutschmark
devaluation
devalue, -valued, -valuing
devastate, -tated, -tating
devastation
  devel — devil
develop, -ed, -ing
  develope — develop
  developement — development
developer
development
developmental, -ly
deviance
deviancy
  devianse — deviance

deviansy — deviancy
deviant, -ly
deviate, -ated, -ating
deviation
device (thing)
device — devise (plan)
devide — divide
devil
devilish, -ly
devilment
devilry
devil's advocate
devious, -ly
devise, -vised, -vising (plan)
devise — device (thing)
devius — devious
devoid
devolushun — devolution
devolution
devolutionary
devolve, -volved, -volving
Devonshire tea
devoshun — devotion
devote, -voted, -voting
devotee
devotion
devour, -ed, -ing
devout, -ly
dew (water)
dew — due (payable)
dewdrop
dewey — dewy
dewy, dewier, dewiest
dexterity
dexterous, -ly
dexterus — dexterous

> Look under **de-** if the word is
> not under **di-**.

diabeetes — diabetes
diabetes
diabetic
diabolic
diabolical, -ly
diadem
diafanus — diaphanous
diafram — diaphragm

diagnose, -nosed, -nosing
diagnosis, -ses
diagnostic
diagnostician
diagnostishun — diagnostician
diagonal, -ly
diagram
diagrammatic, -ally
dial, dialled, dialling
dialect
dialectic
dialectician
dialectishun — dialectician
dialise — dialyse
dialisis — dialysis
dialog — dialogue
dialogue
dialyse, -lysed, -lysing
dialysis, -ses
diamante
diameter
diametrical, -ly
diamond
diaper
diaphanous, -ly
diaphanus — diaphanous
diaphragm
diarea — diarrhoea
diarist
diarrhoea
diary, -ries (book)
diary — dairy (milk)
diatonic, -ally
diatribe
dibase — debase
dibate — debate
dibs
dice, diced, dicing
dicey
dichotomy, -mies
dicipul — disciple
dick
dickens
dicky
dicotomy — dichotomy
dicshun — diction
dicshunry — dictionary

dictate, -tated, -tating
dictation
dictator
dictatorial, -ly
  dictatoriul — dictatorial
  dictayshun — dictation
diction
dictionary, -aries
dictum, -ta, -tums
did
didactic, -ally
  diddel — diddle
diddle, -dled, -dling
diddler
  didel — diddle
didgeridoo
  didgit — digit
  didgitalis — digitalis
didn't (did not)
  didnt — didn't
  didul — diddle
die (singular of dice)
die, dies (tool)
die, died, dying (death)
  die — dye (colour)
dieback
die-casting
diehard
  dieing — dying (death)
  dieing — dyeing (colour)
  diernal — diurnal
diesel
diet, dieted, dieting
dietary
dietician
  dietishen — dietician

> For dif- words, look under
> **diff-**.

differ, -ed, -ing
difference
  differense — difference
  differenshul — differential
different, -ly
differential, -ly
differentiate, -ated, -ating
differentiation

difficult
difficulty, -ties
diffidence
diffident, -ly
diffuse, -fused, -fusing
  diffushun — diffusion
diffusion
  diflect — deflect
dig, dug, digging
  diger — digger
digest, -ed, -ing
digestible
  digestibul — digestible
digestion
digger
diggings
digit
digital
digital computer
digitalis
dignify, -fied, -fying
dignitary, -taries
  dignitry — dignitary
dignity, -ties
digress, -ed, -ing
  digresshun — digression
digression
digs
dike
  dil — dill
dilapidated
dilapidation
dilate, -lated, -lating
dilation
dilatory
  dilatry — dilatory
  dilema — dilemma
dilemma
  dilatent — dilettante
dilettante, -ti
  dilibag — dillybag
  dilidali — dilly dally
diligence
  diligense — diligence
diligent, -ly
dill
dillybag

dilly dally
dilushen — dilution
dilution
diluvial
diluvian

> Look under **de-** if the word is not under **di-**.

dim, dimmed, dimming
dim, dimmer, dimmest
dime
dimenshun — dimension
dimension
dimensional,-ly
dimer — dimmer
diminish, -ed, -ing
diminishing returns
diminushen — diminution
diminution
diminutive, -ly
dimmer
dimple, -pled, -pling
dimpul — dimple
dim sim
dimwit
dimwitted, -ly
dinamic — dynamic
dinamite — dynamite
dinamo — dynamo
dinasty — dynasty
dine, dined, dining (eat)
dine — dyne (unit)
diner (eating)
diner — dinner (food)
ding
dingbats
ding-dong
dinghy, -ghies (boat)
dingie — dinghy
dingo, -goes, -gos
dingy, -gier, -giest (dull)
dingy — dinghy (boat)
dink, -ed, -ing
dinkum
dinky, dinkier, dinkiest
dinky-di
dinner (food)

dinner — diner (eating)
dinosaur
dinosoar — dinosaur
dinosore — dinosaur
dint, -ed, -ing
diocese
diode
diokside — dioxide
dioxide
dip, dipped, dipping
diper — diaper
diper — dipper
diphtheria
diphthong
diploma
diplomacy, -cies
diplomasy — diplomacy
diplomat
diplomatic, -ally
dipper
dipsomania
dipsomaniac
diptych
dire, direr, direst
direckshun — direction
direct, -ed, -ing
direct current
directer — director
direct evidence
direction
directional
direction-finder
directive
directly
director
directory, -ries
directry — directory
direct tax
dirge
dirigible
dirigibul — dirigible
dirk
dirt
dirtily
dirty, dirtied, dirtying
dirty, dirtier, dirtiest
disable, -bled, -bling

disabul — disable
disabuse, -bused, -busing
disadvantage, -taged, -taging
disadvantageous, -ly
disadvantige — disadvantage
disadvantij — disadvantage
disafect — disaffect
disaffect, -ed, -ing
disaffection
disagree, -greed, -greeing
disagreeable, -bly
disagreeableness
disagreeabul — disagreeable
disagreement
disallow, -ed, -ing
disalow — disallow
disapear — disappear
disapoint — disappoint
disappear, -ed, -ing
disappearance
disappearanse — disappearance
disappoint, -ed, -ing
disappointment
disapproval
disapprove, -proved, -proving
disaprove — disapprove
disaray — disarray
disarray
disasociate — disassociate
disassociate, -ated, -ating
disassociation
disaster
disastrous, -ly
disastrus — disastrous
disatisfy — dissatisfy
disavow, -ed, -ing
disavowal
disband, -ed, -ing
disbandment
disbeleif — disbelief
disbeleive — disbelieve
disbelief
disbelieve, -lieved, -lieving
disc
discard, -ed, -ing
disc brake
discern, -ed, -ing

discernible, -bly
discernibul — discernible
discernment
discharge, -charged, -charging
disciple
disciplinarian
disciplinary
discipline, -plined, -plining
discipul — disciple
disc jockey
disclaim, -ed, -ing
disclaimer
disclaym — disclaim
disclose, -closed, -closing
disclosure
disco
discolor — discolour
discolour, -ed, -ing
discolouration
discomfert — discomfort
discomfit, -ed, -ing (thwart)
discomfit — discomfort
discomfort, -ed, -ing (pain)

> Look under **de-** if the word is not under **di-**.

discompose, -posed, -posing
discomposhur — discomposure
discomposure
disconcert, -ed, -ing
disconneckshun — disconnection
disconnection
disconsert — disconcert
disconsolate, -ly
discontent
discontinue, -tinued, -tinuing
discontinuity
discontinuous, -ly
discord
discordance
discordanse — discordance
discordant, -ly
discotheque
discount, -ed, -ing
discourage, -raged, -raging
discouragement
discourse, -coursed, -coursing

discourteous, -ly
discourtesy
discourtius — discourteous
discover, -ed, -ing
discoverer
discovery, -eries
discownt — discount
discredit, -ed, -ing
discreditable, -bly
discreditabul — discreditable
discreet (prudent)
discreet — discrete (apart)
discrepancy
discrepansy — discrepancy
discreshun — discretion
discreshunry — discretionary
discrete (apart)
discretion
discretionary
discribe — describe
discriminate, -nated, -nating
discrimination
discriminator
discriminatory
discriminatry — discriminatory
discripshun — description
discriptive — descriptive
discuridge — discourage
discursive, -ly
discurtius — discourteous
discus (sport)
discushun — discussion
discuss, -ed, -ing (talk)
discussion
disdain, -ed, -ing
disdainful, -ly
dise — dice
disease
diseased
diseave — deceive
diseckshun — dissection
disect — dissect
disembark, -ed, -ing
disembarkation
disemble — disembowel
disembodied
disembowel, -elled, -elling

diseminate — disseminate
disenchant, -ed, -ing
disenchantment
disenshun — dissension
disentangle, -gled, -gling
disentanglement
disentry — dysentery
disern — discern
disernibul — discernible
disertation — dissertation
diservise — disservice
disesed — diseased
disfaver — disfavour
disfavour, -ed, -ing
disfiger — disfigure
disfigure, -ed, -ing
disfranchise, -chised, -chising
disfranchisement
disgise — disguise
disgorge, -gorged, -gorging
disgrace, -graced, -gracing
disgraceful, -ly
disgracefull — disgraceful
disgruntled
disguise, -guised, -guising
disgust, -ed, -ing
disgustedly
dish, -ed, -ing
disharmoney — disharmony
disharmony
disharten — dishearten
dishcloth
dishearten, -ed, -ing
dishevelled
dishonest, -ly
dishonesty
dishonor — dishonour
dishonour, -ed, -ing
dishonourabel — dishonourable
dishonourable, -bly
dishonourabul — dishonourable
disidence — dissidence
disident — dissident
disign — design
disillusion, -ed, -ing
disillusionment
disilushun — disillusion

disimilar	dissimilar
disimulate	dissimulate
disinclination	
disincline, -clined, -clining	
disinfect, -ed, -ing	
disinfectant	
disinfectent	disinfectant
disinherit, -ed, -ing	
disinheritance	
disintegrate, -grated, -grating	
disintegration	
disinter, -terred, -terring	
disinterment	
disinterested, -ly	
disintigrate	disintegrate
disipate	dissipate
disipation	dissipation
disiple	disciple
disiplinary	disciplinary
disipline	discipline
disjoint, -ed, -ing	
disk	
diskwalify	disqualify
diskwiet	disquiet
diskwolify	disqualify
dislexia	dyslexia
dislike, -liked, -liking	
dislocate, -cated, -cating	
dislocation	
dislodge, -lodged, -lodging	
disloge	dislodge
disloyal, -ly	
disloyalty, -ties	
dismal, -ly	
dismantel	dismantle
dismantle, -tled, -tling	
dismantul	dismantle
dismay, -ed, -ing	
dismember, -ed, -ing	
dismemberment	
dismisal	dismissal
dismiss, -ed, -ing	
dismissal	
dismount, -ed, -ing	
dismownt	dismount
disobay	disobey
disobedience	

disobediense	disobedience
disobedient, -ly	
disobey, -ed, -ing	
disoblige, -bliged, -bliging	
disoloot	dissolute
disoluble	dissoluble
disolute	dissolute
disolution	dissolution
disolve	dissolve
disonance	dissonance
disonanse	dissonance
disonant	dissonant
disone	disown
disoner	dishonour
disonerable	dishonourable
disonest	dishonest

> Look under **de-** if the word is
> not under **di-**.

disorder	
disorderliness	
disorderly	
disorganisation	
disorganise, -nised, -nising	
disorientate, -tated, -tating	
disown, -ed, -ing	
dispair	despair
disparage, -raged, -raging	
disparagement	
disparagingly	
disparate, -ly	
disparidge	disparage
disparige	disparage
disparity, -ties	
dispashonate	dispassionate
dispashunate	dispassionate
dispassionate, -ly	
dispatch, -ed, -ing	
dispel, -pelled, -pelling	
dispencable	dispensable
dispencary	dispensary
dispence	dispense
dispensable	
dispensabul	dispensable
dispensary, -saries	
dispensry	dispensary
dispensation	

dispenser
   dispepsia   dyspepsia
dispersal
disperse, -persed, -persing
   dispershun   dispersion
dispersion
   dispicable   despicable
dispirit, -ed, -ing
   dispite   despite
displace, -placed, -placing
displaceable
   displaceabul   displaceable
displacement
   displacment   displacement
   displase   displace
display, -ed, -ing
displease, -pleased, -pleasing
displeasure
   displese   displease
   displeshur   displeasure
   displesure   displeasure
disport, -ed, -ing
disposable
disposable income
   disposabul   disposable
dispose, -posed, -posing
   disposeshun   dispossession
   disposess   dispossess
   disposishun   disposition
disposition
dispossess, -ed, -ing
dispossession
disprin
   disproporshun   disproportion
disproportion
disproportionate, -ly
disprove, -proved, -proving
   dispursal   dispersal
   dispurse   disperse
   dispurshun   dispersion
disputable, -bly
   disputabul   disputable
disputation
disputatious
dispute, -puted, -puting
disqualification
disqualify, -fied, -fying

disquiet, -ed, -ing
disquietude
   disquite   disquiet
disregard, -ed, -ing
   disreguard   disregard
disrepair
   disrepare   disrepair
disreputable, -bly
   disreputible   disreputable
disrespect
disrespectful, -ly
   disrespectfull   disrespectful
   disrigard   disregard
   disrispect   disrespect
disrobe, -robed, -robing
   disrupshun   disruption
disrupt, -ed, -ing
disruption
disruptive, -ly
   dissapate   dissipate
   dissapear   disappear
   dissapoint   disappoint
   dissaprove   disapprove
dissatisfaction
dissatisfy, -fied, -fying
   disscord   discord
dissect, -ed, -ing
dissemble, -bled, -bling
disseminate, -nated, -nating
dissemination
   dissenshun   dissension
dissension
dissent, -ed, -ing
dissenter
dissertation
   disservicabul   disserviceable
disservice
disserviceable
dissidence
   dissidense   dissidence
dissident, -ly
dissimilar, -ly
dissimilarity
dissimulate, -lated, -lating
dissimulation
dissipate, -pated, -pating
dissipation

dissociate, -ated, -ating
dissociation
   disoloot — dissolute
dissoluble
   dissolubul — dissoluble
   dissolushun — dissolution
dissolute, -ly
dissolution
dissolvable
   dissolvabul — dissolvable
dissolve, -solved, -solving
dissonance
   dissonanse — dissonance
dissonant, -ly
   disstil — distil
dissuade, -suaded, -suading
distaff
distance, distanced, distancing
   distanse — distance
distant, -ly
distaste
distasteful, -ly
   distastefull — distasteful
distemper, -ed, -ing
distend, -ed, -ing
   distenshun — distention
   distent — distant
distention
   disterb — disturb
   disterbance — disturbance
distil, -tilled, -tilling
distillate
distillation
distillery, -eries
   distillry — distillery
   distincshun — distinction
distinct, -ly
distinction
distinctive, -ly
distinguish, -ed, -ing
distinguishable, -bly
   distingwish — distinguish
   distink — distinct
   distorshun — distortion
distort, -ed, -ing
distortion
   distrackshun — distraction

distract, -ed, -ing
distraction
distraught, -ly
   distrawt — distraught
distress, -ed, -ing
distressful, -ly
   distressfull — distressful
distressingly
distress signal
   distribushun — distribution
distribution
distributive, -ly
distributor
district
distrust, -ed, -ing
disturb, -ed, -ing
disturbance
   disturbanse — disturbance
disunion
disunite, -nited, -niting
disunity, -ties
   disurn — discern
   disurnible — discernible
disuse, -used, -using
   diswade — dissuade
   diswashun — dissuasion
   diswasive — dissuasive
ditch, -ed, -ing
ditch, -ditches
dither
dithering
dithery
   dito — ditto
ditto
ditty, -ties
   dity — ditty
divan
dive, dived, diving
dive-bomb
diver
diverge, -verged, -verging
divergence
   divergense — divergence
divergent, -ly
diverse, -ly
   divershun — diversion
diversification

diversify, -fied, -fying

> Look under **de-** if the word is
> not under **di-**.

diversion

diversionary

diversionry   diversionary

diversity, -ties

divert, -ed, -ing

divest, -ed, -ing

divestible

divide, -vided, -viding

dividend

divider

divination

divinatory

divine, -vined, -vining

divinely

diviner

divinitey   divinity

divinity, -ties

diviser   divisor

divishun   division

divisible, -bly

divisibul   divisible

divisif   divisive

division

divisional, -ly

divisive, -ly

divisor

divorce, -vorced, -vorcing

divorcee

divorse   divorce

divorsee   divorcee

divulge, -vulged, -vulging

divulgence

divulgense   divulgence

divvy, -vies

divvy, -vied, -vying

dixie

dizier   dizzier

diziest   dizziest

dizmal   dismal

dizolve   dissolve

dizy   dizzy

dizzily

dizziness

dizzy, dizzied, dizzying

dizzy, dizzier, dizziest

do, did, done, doing

do   doe (animal)

dob, dobbed, dobbing

dobbin

docile, -ly

docility

dock, -ed, -ing

docker

docket

dockit   docket

dockyard

docter   doctor

doctor, -ed, -ing

doctoral

doctorate

doctrin   doctrine

doctrinair   doctrinaire

doctrinaire

doctrinal, -ly

doctrine

doctrinul   doctrinal

doctrut   doctorate

document, -ed, -ing

documentary, -ries

documentation

documentry   documentary

dodder, -ed, -ing

doddery

doddle

doder   dodder

dodge, dodged, dodging

dodgem

dodger

dodgy, dodgier, dodgiest

dodje   dodge

dodjy   dodgy

dodo, -does, -dos

doe (animal)

doe   dough (bread)

doer

does

doesn't (does not)

doesnt   doesn't

dof   doff

doff, -ed, -ing

doffin   dauphin
dog, dogged, dogging
dogbox
    dogerul   doggerel
dogfight
dogfish
    dogfite   dogfight
doggerel
doggo
doghouse
dogleg
doglegged
dogma, -mas, -mata
dogmatic
dogmatical, -ly
dogmatism
dogmatist
dog paddle
    dog paddul   dog paddle
dog watch
    doilie   doily
doily, -lies
doings
    dol   dole (pay)
    dol   doll (toy)
    dolar   dollar
Dolby system
doldrums
dole, doled, doling (pay)
    dole   doll (toy)
    doler   dollar
    dolerus   dolorous
    dolfin   dolphin
doll, -ed, -ing (toy)
    doll   dole (pay)
dollar
    doller   dollar
dollop
dolly, dollies
dolomite
dolorous, -ly
    dolorus   dolorous
dolour
dolphin
dolt
doltish, -ly
domain

    domane   domain
dome
domed
domestic, -ally
domesticate, -cated, -cating
domestication
domesticity
    domestisity   domesticity
domicile, -ciled, -ciling
domiciliary
dominance
    dominanse   dominance
dominant, -ly
dominate, -nated, -nating
    dominater   dominator
domination
dominative
dominator
    dominear   domineer
domineer, -ed, -ing
    dominent   dominant
dominion
domino, -noes
domino theory
    dominyun   dominion
    domisile   domicile
    dommimate   dominate
don, donned, donning
donate, -nated, -nating
    donater   donator
donation
donator
done
    doner   donor
dong, -ed, -ing
donkey, -keys
donkey vote
donkey's years
    donky   donkey
donnybrook
donor
don't (do not)
    dont   don't
donut
    dooch   douche
doodad
doodah

doodle, -dled, -dling
   doodul — doodle
doom, -ed, -ing
doomsday
door
   door — dour
doorjamb
doorknock, -ed, -ing
   doornock — doorknock
   doosh — douche
dope, doped, doping
dopey, dopier, dopiest
   dophin — dauphin
   dore — door
dormancy
   dormansy — dormancy
dormant
   dormitery — dormitory
   dormitry — dormitory
   dorn — dawn
dorsal
   dorsul — dorsal
   dorter — daughter
dory, -ries
dosage
dose, dosed, dosing
   dosier — dossier
   dosige — dosage
   dosije — dosage
   dosile — docile
   dosility — docility
doss, -ed, -ing
dossier
dot, dotted, dotting
dotage
dote, doted, doting
   dotidge — dotage
   dotije — dotage
dotterel
dottle
dotty, dottier, dottiest
   doubel — double
double, -led, -ling
double agent
double-barrelled
double bass
double-breasted

doublecross, -ed, -ing
double-dealing
double dissolution
double-dutch
double exposure
double-jointed
double standard
doublet
doublethink
double time
doubloon
doubt, -ed, -ing
doubtful, -ly
   doubtfull — doubtful
doubtingly
doubtless, -ly
douche, douched, douching
   douel — dowel
dough
doughnut
doughty, -tier, -tiest
dour, -ly
dourness
douse, doused, dousing
   dout — doubt
   doutful — doubtful
   doutless — doubtless
   douty — doughty
dove
dover
dovetail
   dovetale — dovetail
   dow — dhow (boat)
   dow — doe (animal)
   dow — dough (bread)
dowager
   dowdie — dowdy
dowdily
dowdiness
dowdy, -dier, -diest
   dowery — dowry
   dowey — doughy
down, -ed, -ing
down-and-out
downcast
   downey — downy
downfall

downfallen
downgrade, -graded, -grading
downhearted, -ly
downhill
down payment
downpipe
downpore   downpour
downpour
downright, -ly
downrite   downright
downstairs
downstream
down-to-earth
downtown
downtrodden
down-under
downward, -ly
downwards
downwerds   downwards
downwind
downy, downier, downiest
dowrie   dowry
dowry, -ries
dowse, dowsed, dowsing
dowt   doubt
dowtey   doughty
dowtful   doubtful
dowtless   doubtless
doxology, -gies
doyen
doze, dozed, dozing (sleep)
doze   does
dozen, dozen, dozens
dozily
doziness
drab, drabber, drabbest
draconean   draconian
draconian
draft, -ed, -ing (plan)
draft   draught (air)
draft dodger
draftey   draughty
draftiness   draughtiness
drafts   draughts
draftsman, -men
drafty   draughty
drag, dragged, dragging

dragnet
dragonfly, -flies
dragoon, -ed, -ing
drag race
dragster
drain, -ed, -ing
drainage
drainige   drainage
drainpipe
drake
dram
drama
dramatic, -ally
dramatics
dramatisation
dramatise, -tised, -tising
dramatist
drank
drape, draped, draping
draper
drapery, -eries
drastic, -ally
draught (air)
draught   draft (plan)
draughtboard
draughthorse
draughts
draughtsman, -men
draughty, -tier, -tiest
draw, drew, drawn, drawing
drawback
drawbridge
drawbrije   drawbridge
drawcard
drawer
drawing-pin
drawl, -ed, -ing
drawn
dray
dread, -ed, -ing
dreadful, -ly
dreadfull   dreadful
dreadnort   dreadnought
dreadnought
dream, dreamed, dreamt, dreaming
dreamer
dreamily

dreamless, -ly		drink-driving	
dreamy, dreamier, dreamiest		drive-in	
drearily		drivel, -elled, -elling	
dreariness		driver	
dreary, drearier, dreariest		driveway	
dred	dread	drizzle, -zled, -zling	
dredful	dreadful	drizzly	
dredger		drizzul	drizzle
drednort	dreadnought	droll	
dreem	dream	drollery, -eries	
drege	dredge	drolly	
dregs		dromedary, -daries	
dreje	dredge	drone, droned, droning	
dremt	dreamt	drongo, -gos	
drench, -ed, -ing		drool, -ed, -ing	
drerie	dreary	droop, -ed, -ing	
drery	dreary	droopy, -ier, -iest	
dres	dress	drop, dropped, dropping	
dresie	dressy	droplet	
desige	dressage	drop-out	
dresmaker	dressmaker	dropper	
dress, -ed, -ing		dropsey	dropsy
dressage		dropsy	
dress circle		dross	
dress down		drought	
dresser		drousy	drowsy
dressmaker		drout	drought
dressmaking		drove, droved, droving	
dressy		drover	
drew		drown, -ed, -ing	
dri	dry	drowse, drowsed, drowsing	
dribble, -bled, -bling		drowsey	drowsy
dribbler		drowsily	
dribbul	dribble	drowsy, drowsier, drowsiest	
dribs and drabs		drowt	drought
dribul	dribble	drub, drubbed, drubbing	
dried		drudge, drudged, drudging	
drier		drudgery, -eries	
driest		drug, drugged, drugging	
drift, -ed, -ing		druge	drudge
drifter		drugery	drudgery
driftwood		drugstore	
drill, -ed, -ing		drum, drummed, drumming	
drily		drummer	
drink, drunk, drinking		drumstick	
drinkable		drunk	
drinkabul	drinkable	drunkard	

drunken, -ly
drunkenness
dry, dried, drying
dry, drier, driest
dry cell
dry-clean
dryer
dryly
dryness
dual, -ly (two)
   dual   duel (fight)
dualism
duality
dub, dubbed, dubbing
   dubel   double
dubious, -ly
   dubius   dubious
   duble   double
   dubly   doubly
ducal, -ly
   duce   deuce
duck, -ed, -ing
duckbill
duckling
   ducktile   ductile
duco
duct
ductile
dud
dudgeon
due (owing)
   due   dew (water)
   duedrop   dewdrop
duel, -ed, -ing (fight)
   duel   dual (two)
   duelist   duellist
duellist
duet
duettist
   dufel   duffle
duffer
duffle
   dufful   duffle
dugong
dugout
duke
   dul   dull

dulcet
   duler   duller
   dulie   duly
dull
dullard
dullness
dully
   dulset   dulcet
duly
   dum   dumb
dumb, -ly
dumbbell
   dumbell   dumbbell
dumbfound, -ed, -ing
dumbness
   dumfound   dumbfound
dummy, -mies
dummy, -mied, -mying
   dumness   dumbness
dump, -ed, -ing
dumper
dumpling
   dumy   dummy
dun, dunned, dunning (demand)
   dun   done
dunce
dunderhead
dune
dung
dungaree
   dungen   dungeon
dungeon
   dunjun   dungeon
dunk, -ed, -ing
dunny
   dunse   dunce
duodenal
duodenum
dupe, duped, duping
   duplacate   duplicate
   duplecks   duplex
duplex
duplicate, -cated, -cating
duplication
duplicity, -ties
   duplisity   duplicity
durable, -bly

durability
durabul	durable

duration

duress
durge	dirge
durible	durable

during
durt	dirt
durtie	dirty
durty	dirty

dusk

duskiness

dusky, duskier, duskiest

dust, -ed, -ing

dustbin

duster

dustman, -men

dustpan

dust-up

dusty, dustier, dustiest

Dutch courage
Dutch curije	Dutch courage

duteous, -ly

dutiable
dutiabul	dutiable
dutifree	duty-free

dutiful, -ly

duty, -ties

duty-free
duv	dove

duvet
duvtail	dovetail
duvtale	dovetail

dux
duzen	dozen

dwarf, dwarfs, dwarves

dwarfish, -ly

dwell, dwelt, dwelled, dwelling

dwindle, -dled, -dling
dworf	dwarf
dworves	dwarfs

dye, dyed, dyeing (colour)
dye	die (dead)
dyed	died (dead)
dyehard	diehard
dyeing	dying (death)

dyer

dyke, dyked, dyking

dynamic, -ally

dynamics

dynamism

dynamite, -mited, -miting

dynamo, -mos

dynasty, -ties

dyne (unit)
dyne	dine (eat)

dysentery
dysentry	dysentery

dysfunction

dyslectic

dyslexia

dyslexic

dyspepsia

dyspeptic

dystrophy

Ee

each
eagel — eagle
eager
eagle
eaglehawk
eaglet
eal — eel
ear
earache
eardrum
earfone — earphone
earie — eerie (weird)
earie — eyrie (nest)
earing — earring
early, -lier, -liest
earmark, -ed, -ing
earmuf — earmuff
earmuff
earn, -ed, -ing
earner
earnest, -ly
earnestness
earnings
earphone
earring
earshot
earth, -ed, -ing
earthbound
earthen
earthenware
earthiness
earthling
earthly, -lier, -liest
earthquake
earthworm
earthy, earthier, earthiest
earwig
ease, eased, easing

easel
easement
easily
east
easten — eastern
East End
Easter
easterly
eastern
eastward, -ly
eastwards
easiness
easy, easier, easiest
eat, ate, eaten, eating
eatable
eatabul — eatable
eater
eau-de-Cologne
eaves
eavesdrop, -dropped, -dropping
eavesdropper
ebb, -ed, -ing
ebbony — ebony
ebonie — ebony
ebony, -onies
ebuliense — ebullience
ebulient — ebullient
ebullience
ebullient, -ly
eccentric, -ally
eccentricity, -ties
ecclesiastic
ecclesiastical, -ly
ecentric — eccentric
ech — each
echelon
echidna
echo, echoes
echo, echoed, echoing
eclair
eclare — eclair
eclectic, -ally
eclesiastic — ecclesiastic
eclipse, eclipsed, eclipsing
ecliptical, -ly
ecologey — ecology
ecological, -ly

ecologist
ecology
economic
economical, -ly
economics
economise, -mised, -mising
economist
economy, -mies
ecosphere
ecosystem

   ecsema   eczema
   ecsentric   eccentric

ecstasy, -sies
ecstatic, -ally
ecumenical, -ly
ecumenism
eczema
edam

   edem   edam

eddy, eddies
eddy, eddied, eddying
edelweiss
edge, edged, edging
edger
edgeways

   edgey   edgy

edginess
edgy, -ier, -iest
edible
edibility

   edibul   edible

edict

   edie   eddy

edify, -fied, -fying
edit, -ed, -ing

   editer   editor

edition (book)

   edition   addition (add)

editor
editorial, -ly
educable

   educabul   educable

educate, -cated, -cating
education
educational, -ly
educationalist
educative

educator
Edwardian

   edy   eddy
   eeger   eager
   eegle   eagle

eel

   eenin   oenin
   eer   ear

eerie, eerier, eeriest (weird)

   eerie   eyrie (nest)

eerily
eeriness

   eermark   earmark

> For ef- words,
> look under **eff-**.

efface, -faced, -facing
effect, -ed, -ing
effective, -ly
effectual, -ly
effeminacy

   effeminasy   effeminacy

effeminate, -ly
effervesce, -vesced, -vescing
effervescence
effervescent, -ly

   effervesent   effervescent
   effervess   effervesce
   effervessence   effervescence

efficacious, -ly
efficacy, -cies

   efficayshus   efficacious

efficiency, -cies

   efficiensy   efficiency

efficient, -ly
effigy, -gies
effloresce, -resced, -rescing
efflorescence
efflorescent
effluent
effluvium, -via, -viums
effort
effortless, -ly
effrontery, -teries

   effrontrey   effrontery
   effushun   effusion

effusion

effusive, -ly

effigy   effigy
eg   egg
egalitarian
egalitarianism
egg, -ed, -ing
eggcup
egghead
eggplant
eggshell
eggwhite

eggwite   eggwhite
Egipshun   Egyptian
Egipt   Egypt
egis   aegis
ego, egos
egocentric
egocentricity
egoism
egoist
egoistical, -ly

egosentric   egocentric
egotism
egotist
egotistical, -ly
egress
egret

For egs- words,
look under ex-.

Egypt
Egyptian
eiderdown
eight
eighteen
eighth
eightieth
eighty, eighties
eisteddfod
either
ejaculate, -lated, -lating
ejaculation

ejeckshun   ejection
eject, -ed, -ing
ejection
ejector
eke, eked, eking

eklipse   eclipse
eko   echo

For eks- words,
look under ex-.

ekumenical   ecumenical

For ekw- words,
look under eq-.

elaborate, -rated, -rating
elaborately
elaboration
elan
eland
elapse, elapsed, elapsing
elastic, -ally
elasticity

elastisitey   elasticity
elate, elated, elating
elbow, -ed, -ing
elbowroom
elder, -ly
elderberry, -ries
eldest

elecshun   election
elect, -ed, -ing
election
electioneer, -ed, -ing
elective
elector
electoral, -ly
electorate
electric
electrical, -ly
electrician
electricity
electrification

electrishun   electrician
electrisity   electricity
electrocardiogram
electrocardiograph

electrocushun   electrocution
electrocute, -cuted, -cuting
electrode
electrolysis
electromagnet
electromagnetic

electromotive
electron
electronic
electronic data processing
electronics
electroplate, -plated, -plating
electrostatic
elegance
eleganse → elegance
elegant, -ly
elegey → elegy
elegy, -gies
element
elemental, -ly
elementary
elementery → elementary
elementul → elemental
elephant
elephantine
elevan → eleven
elevate, -vated, -vating
elevater → elevator
elevation
elevator
eleven
eleventh
elf, elves
elfin
elfish
elfs → elves
elicit, -ed, -ing (draw)
elicit → illicit (wrong)
elifant → elephant
eliganse → elegance
eligant → elegant
eligible, -bly
eligibility
eligibul → eligible
elikser → elixir
eliment → element
elimentry → elementary
eliminate, -nated, -nating
eliminator
elipse → ellipse
elipsis → ellipsis
elishun → elision
elision

elite
elitism
elitist
elivate → elevate
elixir
Elizabethan
elk
ellipse
ellipsis, -ses
elliptical, -ly
ellite → elite
elm
elocushun → elocution
elocution
elocutionist
elokwence → eloquence
elongate, -gated, -gating
elongation
elope, eloped, eloping
elopement
eloper
eloquant → eloquent
eloquence
eloquense → eloquence
eloquent, -ly
else
elsewere → elsewhere
elsewhere
elswhere → elsewhere
elucidate, -dated, -dating
elucidation
elucidatory
elude, eluded, eluding (evade)
elude → allude (say)
elusidate → elucidate
elusive, -ly
elves
emaciate, -ated, -ating
emaciation
emanate, -nated, -nating
emanation
emancipate, -pated, -pating
emancipation
emancipator
emancipist
emanent → eminent
emansipate → emancipate

emasculate, -lated, -lating
emasculation
  emasiate — emaciate
embalm, -ed, -ing
embankment
  embarass — embarrass
embargo, -goes
embargo, -goed, -going
embark, -ed, -ing
embarkation
embarrass, -ed, -ing
embarrassment
embassy, -sies
embed, -bedded, -bedding
embellish, -ed, -ing
embellishment
ember
  embezel — embezzle
embezzle, -zled, -zling
embezzlement
embitter, -ed, -ing
emblazon, -ed, -ing
emblem
emblematic, -ally
  embodie — embody
embodiment
embody, -bodied, -bodying
embolism
  embos — emboss
emboss, -ed, -ing
embrace, -braced, -bracing
embraceable
  embrase — embrace
  embrio — embryo
embroider, -ed, -ing
embroidery, -deries
embroil, -ed, -ing
embryo, -os
embryonic
emend, -ed, -ing
emerald
  emerey — emery
emerge, emerged, emerging
emergence
emergency
  emergense — emergence
  emergensy — emergency

emergent
  emerie — emery
emeritus
emery
emetic
  emfasema — emphysema
  emfasise — emphasise
  emfatic — emphatic
emigrant
emigrate, -grated, -grating
eminence (high)
  eminense — eminence
eminent, -ly (known)
  eminent — imminent (near)
  emisary — emissary
  emishun — emission
emissary, -saries
emission
emit, emitted, emitting
emitter
emollient
emolument
  emoshun — emotion
emotion
emotional, -ly
emotionalism
emotionless, -ly
emotive, -ly
empanel, -elled, -elling
empathy
  emperer — emperor
emperor
emphasis, -ses
emphasise, -sised, -sising
emphatic, -ally
emphysema
empire
empirical, -ly
empiricism
empiricist
  empirisism — empiricism
employ, -ed, -ing
employable
  employabul — employable
employee
employer

employment
emporium, -poriums, -poria
empower, -ed, -ing
empress
emptie → empty
emptiness
empty, -tied, -tying
empty, -tier, -tiest
emrald → emerald
emu
emulate, -lated, -lating
emulation
emulshun → emulsion
emulsion
enable, -bled, -bling
enabul → enable
enact, -ed, -ing
enactment
enamel, -elled, -elling
enameller
enamer → enamour
enamour, -ed, -ing
encapsulate, -lated, -lating
encephalitis
encephalogram
enchant, -ed, -ing
enchantment
enciclical → encyclical
enciclopedia → encyclopaedia
encircle, -cled, -cling
encirclement
encircul → encircle
enclave
enclose, -closed, -closing
encloshur → enclosure
enclosure
encode, -coded, -coding
encompass, -ed, -ing
encore, -cored, -coring
encounter
encownter → encounter
encourage, -raged, -raging
encouragement
encroach, -ed, -ing
encumber, -ed, -ing
encumbrance
encumbranse → encumbrance

encyclical
encyclopaedia
encyclopaedic
end, -ed, -ing
endanger, -ed, -ing
endear, -ed, -ing
endearment
endeavour, -ed, -ing
endeer → endear
endemic, -ally
endever → endeavour
endive
endless, -ly
endorse, -dorsed, -dorsing
endorsement
endow, -ed, -ing
endowment
endurable, -bly
endurance
enduranse → endurance
endure, -dured, -during
endurible → endurable
endways
enema
enemy, -mies
energetic, -ally
energy, -gies
enervate, -vated, -vating
enervative
enfeeble, -bled, -bling
enfeebul → enfeeble
enfold, -ed, -ing
enforce, -forced, -forcing
enforceable
enforceabul → enforceable
enforcement
enforcer
enforse → enforce
enforsibul → enforceable
enfranchise, -chised, -chising
engage, -gaged, -gaging
engagement
engajment → engagement
engender, -ed, -ing
engine
enginear → engineer
engineer, -ed, -ing

English
engrave, -graved, -graving
engraver
engross, -ed, -ing
engulf, -ed, -ing
enhance, -hanced, -hancing
enhancement
  enhanse — enhance
enigma
enigmatic, -ally
  enima — enema
  enimy — enemy
  enithing — anything
  eniwhere — anywhere
  enjender — engender
  enjin — engine
  enjineer — engineer
  enjoi — enjoy
  enjoiabul — enjoyable
  enjoiment — enjoyment
enjoin, -ed, -ing
enjoy, -ed, -ing
enjoyable, -bly
  enjoyabul — enjoyable
enjoyment
enlarge, -larged, -larging
enlargement
enlarger
enlighten, -ed, -ing
enlightenment
enlist, -ed, -ing
enlistment
  enliten — enlighten
enliven, -ed, -ing
en masse
enmity, -ties
ennoble, -bled, -bling
enoblement
ennui
  enobul — ennoble
enormity, -ties
enormous, -ly
  enormus — enormous
enough
enquire, -quired, -quiring
enquirer
enquiry, -ries

enrage, -raged, -raging
  enrap — enwrap
  enrapcher — enrapture
enrich, -ed, -ing
enrichment
enrol, -rolled, -rolling
enrolment
en route
ensconce, -ed, -ing
  ensconse — ensconce
ensemble
  ensembul — ensemble
  ensercul — encircle
  enshure — ensure
ensign
  ensine — ensign
ensue, -sued, -suing
en suite
ensure, -sured, -suring
  ensweet — en suite
entail, -ed, -ing
  entale — entail
entangle, -gled, -gling
entanglement
  entangul — entangle
entente
enter, -ed, -ing
enteritis
enterprise
enterprising, -ly
entertain, -ed, -ing
entertainer
entertainment
  entertane — entertain
enthral, -led, -ling
enthuse, -thused, -thusing
enthusiasm
enthusiast
enthusiastic, -ally
entice, -ticed, -ticing
entire, -ly
entirety
  entise — entice
  entitel — entitle
  entitey — entity
entitle, -tled, -tling
entitlement

entity, -ties		enzyme	
entourage		epaulet	
entouraje	entourage	epawlet	epaulet
entrails		ephemeral, -ly	
entrance		epic	
entranse	entrance	epical, -ly	
entrant		epicenter	epicentre
entre	entree	epicentre	
entreat, -ed, -ing		epicure	
entreaty, -treaties		epicurean	
entree		epidemic	
entreet	entreat	epidemical, -ly	
entreprener	entrepreneur	epidermal	
entrepreneur		epidermis	
entrepreneurial		epigraf	epigraph
entrust, -ed, -ing		epigram	
entry, -tries		epigrammatic, -ally	
enuff	enough	epigraph	
enumerable		epilepsy	
enumerabul	enumerable	epileptic	
enumerate, -rated, -rating		epilog	epilogue
enumeration		epilogue	
enunciate, -ated, -ating		episcopacy, -cies	
enunciation		episcopal	
enunsiate	enunciate	Episcopalian	
enuresis		episode	
envelop, -ed, -ing (wrap up)		episodic, -ally	
envelope (letter)		epissel	epistle
enviable, -bly		epitaph	
enviabul	enviable	epitarf	epitaph
envie	envy	epithet	
envious, -ly		epitome	
envirament	environment	epitomise, -mised, -mising	
environment		epoch	
environmental, -ly		epochal	
environmentalism		epok	epoch
environmentalist		eppigram	epigram
environs		equable, -bly	
envisage, -aged, -aging		equal, equalled, equalling	
envisidge	envisage	equalise, -lised, -lising	
envius	envious	equality, -ties	
envoi	envoy	equanimity, -ties	
envoy		equate, equated, equating	
envy, -vies		equater	equator
envy, envied, envying		equation	
enwrap, enwrapped, enwrapping		equator	
enzime	enzyme	equatorial	

equestrian		erl	earl
equidistant, -ly		erly	early
equilateral		ermine	
equilibrium		ern	earn (money)
equine		ern	urn (vessel)
equinocks	equinox	ernest	earnest
equinoctial		erode, eroded, eroding	
equinox		erogenous	
equip, equipped, equipping		eroneous	erroneous
equipment		eror	error
equitable, -bly		Eros	
equitabul	equitable	eroshun	erosion
equity, -ties		erosion	
equivalence		erotic, -ally	
equivalense	equivalence	erotica	
equivocal, -ly		eroticism	
equivocate, -cated, -cating		erotisism	eroticism
equivocation		err, -ed, -ing	
era		errand	
eradicable, -bly		erratic, -ally	
eradicate, -cated, -cating		erratum, -ta	
eradication		erroneous, -ly	
erand	errand	erronius	erroneous
erant	errant	error	
erase, erased, erasing		errupt	erupt
eraser		ersatz	
erasion		erstwhile	
erata	errata	erth	earth
eratic	erratic	erthen	earthen
erayshure	erasure	erthly	earthly
erban	urban	erudishun	erudition
erbane	urbane	erudition	
erbanise	urbanise	erupt, -ed, -ing	
erbanity	urbanity	eruption	
erchun	urchin	erwig	earwig
erecshun	erection	esay	essay
erect, -ed, -ing		escalate, -lated, -lating	
erection		escalater	escalator
erer	error	escalation	
erge	urge	escalator	
ergent	urgent	escapade	
ergonomics		escape, -caped, -caping	
erie	eerie (weird)	escapee	
erie	eyrie (nest)	escaper	
erk (rank)		escapement	
erk	irk (bore)	escapism	
erksome	irksome	escapist	

escarpment	et cetera
eschew, -ed, -ing	etch, -ed, -ing
eschue → eschew	etcher
escort, -ed, -ing	eternal, -ly
escutcheon	eternity, -ties
escutshun → escutcheon	ether
esel → easel	ether → either
esence → essence	ethereal, -ly
esenshul → essential	ethic
Eskimo, -mos	ethical, -ly
eskwire → esquire	ethics
esky	ethnic, -ally
esophagus → oesophagus	ethnology
esoteric, -ally	ethos
especial, -ly	etiket → etiquette
espeshul → especial	etimology → etymology
espionage	etiquet → etiquette
esplanade	etymology, -gies
esplanaid → esplanade	eucalyptus, -tuses, -ti
espousal	euchre, -chred, -chring
espouse, -poused, -pousing	Euclid
espowse → espouse	
espresso	For **euf**-words, look under **euph**-.
esprit	
espy, -pied, -pying	eugenics
esquire	Euklid → Euclid
essay, -ed, -ing (try)	eulogise, -gised, -gising
essay → assay (analyse)	eulogy, -gies
essayist	eunuch
essence	euphemism
essense → essence	euphemistic, -ally
essenshul → essential	euphony, -nies
essential, -ly	euphoria
establish, -ed, -ing	euphoric
establishment	Eurapean → European
estate	Eurashun → Eurasian
esteem, -ed, -ing	Eurasian
Ester → Easter	eureka flag
estern → eastern	eurhythmics
estimable, -bly	eurithmics → eurhythmics
estimabul → estimable	European
estimate, -mated, -mating	euthanasia
estimation	evacuate, -uated, -uating
estimator	evacuation
estrange, estranged, estranging	evacuee
estrogen → oestrogen	evade, evaded, evading
estuary, -aries	evaluate, -ated, -ating

evaluation		ewe (sheep)		
evangalist	evangelist	ewe	yew (tree)	
evangelical, -ly		exacerbate, -bated, -bating		
envangelicul	evangelical	exacerbation		
evangelism		exackly	exactly	
evangelist		exact, -ed, -ing		
evaperate	evaporate	exactitude		
evaporate, -rated, -rating		exactly		
evaporation		exactness		
evasion		exagerate	exaggerate	
evasive, -ly		exaggerate, -rated, -rating		
eve		exaggeration		
evedence	evidence	exalt, -ed, -ing		
even, -ed, -ing		exaltation		
evenly		examination		
evenness		examine, -ined, -ining		
event		examiner		
eventual, -ly		example		
eventuality, -ties		exampul	example	
eventuate, -ated, -ating		exaserbate	exacerbate	
ever		exasperate, -rated, -rating		
evergreen		exasperation		
everlasting, -ly		excavate, -vated, -vating		
every		excavation		
everybody		excavator		
everyday		exceed, -ed, -ing (surpass)		
everyone		exceed	accede (agree)	
everything		exceedingly		
everywhere		excel, -celled, -celling		
eves	eaves	excell	excel	
evict, -ed, -ing		excellence		
eviction		excellency, -cies		
evictor		excellense	excellence	
evictshun	eviction	excellent, -ly		
evidence, -denced, -dencing		excepshun	exception	
evident, -ly		except, -ed, -ing		
evil, -ly		exception		
evince, evinced, evincing		exceptional, -ly		
evinse	evince	excerpt		
eviscerate, -rated, -rating		excess		
evocative		excessive, -ly		
evoke, evoked, evoking		exchange, -changed, -changing		
evolushun	evolution	exchangeable		
evolution		exchequer		
evolve, evolved, evolving		excise, -cised, -cising		
evolvement		excishun	excision	
evry	every	excision		

excitable, -bly
   excitabul   excitable
excite, -cited, -citing
excitement
exclaim, -ed, -ing
exclamation
exclamatory
   exclamatry   exclamatory
exclude, -luded, -luding
   exclushun   exclusion
exclusion
exclusive, -ly
excommunicate, -cated, -cating
excommunication
excrement
excrescence
   excreshun   excretion
   excressense   excrescence
excreta
excrete, -creted, -creting
excretion
excretory
excruciating, -ly
excursion
excusable, -bly
excuse, -cused, -cusing
execrable, -bly
execrate, -crated, -crating
   execushun   execution
execute, -cuted, -cuting
execution
executioner
executive
executor
exemplary
exemplify, -fied, -fying
   exempshun   exemption
exempt
exemptible
   exemptibul   exemptible
exemption
exercise, -cised, -cising
   exershun   exertion
exert, -ed, -ing
exertion
ex gratia
exhalation

exhale, -haled, -haling
exhaust, -ed, -ing
exhaustion
exhaustive, -ly
   exhibishun   exhibition
exhibit, -ed, -ing
exhibition
exhibitionism
exhibitionist
exhibitor
exhilarate, -rated, -rating
exhilaration
exhort, -ed, -ing
exhortation
exhume, -humed, -huming
exhumation
   exibit   exhibit
exigency, -cies
   exigensy   exigency
exile, -iled, -iling
exist, -ed, -ing
existence
   existense   existence
   existenshul   existential
existent
existential, -ly
existentialism
existentialist
exit
exodus
exonerate, -rated, -rating
exorbitant, -ly
exorcise, -cised, -cising
exorcism
exorcist
   exorsism   exorcism
   exorst   exhaust
   exort   exhort
   exortashun   exhortation
exoteric, -ally
exotic, -ally
expand, -ed, -ing
expanse
   expanshun   expansion
expansion
expansive, -ly
expansiveness

expatiate, -ated, -ating
expatriate, -ated, -ating
expatriation
expect, -ed, -ing
expectancy, -cies
expectant, -ly
expectation
expectorant
expectorate, -rated, -rating
expediency
   expediensy   expediency
expedient, -ly
   expedishun   expedition
expedite, -dited, -diting
expedition
expeditionary
expeditious, -ly
expeditiousness
expel, -pelled, -pelling
expend, -ed, -ing
expendable
   expendicher   expenditure
expenditure
expense
expensive, -ly
experience, -enced, -encing
experiment, -ed, -ing
experimental, -ly
experimentation
expert, -ly
expertise
expiate, -ated, -ating
expiation
expiration
expire, -pired, -piring
expiry, -ries
explain, -ed, -ing
explanation
explanatory
   explane   explain
   explanetry   explanatory
expletive
explicable, -bly
   explicabul   explicable
explicate, -cated, -cating
explicit, -ly
   explisit   explicit

explode, -ploded, -ploding
exploit, -ed, -ing
exploitation
exploration
exploratory
explore, -plored, -ploring
explorer
explosion
explosive, -ly
exponent
exponential, -ly
export, -ed, -ing
exporter
   exposay   exposé
expose, -posed, -posing
exposé
   exposhur   exposure
expostulate, -lated, -lating
exposure
expound, -ed, -ing
   expreshun   expression
   expresive   expressive
express, -ly
express, -ed, -ing
expression
expressionism
expressionist
expressive, -ly
   expresso   espresso
expressway
expropriate, -ated, -ating
expropriation
expulsion
expunction
expunge, -punged, -punging
expurgate, -gated, -gating
expurgation
exquisite, -ly
exquisiteness
   exseed   exceed
   exsel   excel
   exselence   excellence
   exserpt   excerpt
ex-serviceman, -men
extant
   extasy   ecstasy
   extatic   ecstatic

extemporaneous, -ly
extempore
extend, -ed, -ing
extendible
  extendibul — extendible
  extenshun — extension
extension
extensive, -ly
extent
extenuate, -ated, -ating
extenuation
  exterier — exterior
exterior
exterminate, -nated, -nating
extermination
exterminator
external, -ly
extinct
extinction
  extingshun — extinction
extinguish, -ed, -ing
extinguisher
extol, -tolled, -tolling
  extorshun — extortion
extort, -ed, -ing
extortion
extortionate, -ly
extortioner
extortionist
extra
  extracshun — extraction
extract, -ed, -ing
extractable
extraction
extracurricular
  extradishun — extradition
extradite, -dited, -diting
extradition
extramarital
extraneous, -ly
extraordinary
extrapolate, -ated, -ating
extrapolation
extrasensory
extraterrestrial
extravagance
extravagancy

extravagant, -ly
extravaganza
  extravert — extrovert
  extremast — extremist
extreme, -tremer, -tremest
extremely
extremism
extremist
extremity, -ties
extricate, -cated, -cating
extrication
extrovert
extrude, -truded, -truding
extrusion
exuberance
  exuberanse — exuberance
exuberant, -ly
exude, -uded, -uding
exult, -ed, -ing
exultant, -ly
exultation
  exume — exhume
eye, eyed, eyeing
eyeball
eyebrow
eyelash
eyelet
eyelid
eyesight
eyesore
eyetooth, -teeth
eyewash
eyewitness, -nesses
eyrie (nest)
  eyrie — eerie (weird)
  eze — ease
  ezel — easel
  ezy — easy

Ff

fable, -bled, -bling
fabric
fabricate, -cated -cating
fabrication
fabulous, -ly
  fabulus   fabulous
facade
face, faced, facing
faceless
facelift
  faceshus   facetious
facet, -eted, -eting
facetious, -ly
facia (panel)
  facia   fascia (band)
facial, -ly
facile, -ly
facilitate, -tated, -tating
facility, -ties
  facist   fascist
facsimile, -led, -leing
fact
faction
factionalism
factor
factory, -ries
factotum
factual, -ly
faculty, -ties
fad
faddish, -ly
fade, faded, fading
faeces
fag, fagged, fagging
faggot
  fagot   faggot
Fahrenheit
fail, -ed, -ing

fail-safe
failure
  failyer   failure
  faim   fame
  faimus   famous
fain (gladly)
  fain   feign (pretend)
faint, -ed, -ing (weak)
  faint   feint (pretend)
fair, -ly (honest)
  fair   fare (price)
fair game
fairway
fair-weather
  fairwell   farewell
fairy, -ries
fairytale
  fait   fate
  faitful   fateful
fait accompli
faith
faithful, -ly
faith-healing
fake, faked, faking
faker (fraud)
fakir (holy)
  falacy   fallacy
  falanx   phalanx
  falasius   fallacious
  falasy   fallacy
falcon
falconry
  fale   fail
  falesy   fallacy
  falible   fallible
  falic   phallic
fall, fell, fallen, falling
fallacious, -ly
fallacy, -cies
fallible, -bly
  fallibul   fallible
fallout
fallow
  fallus   phallus
  falow   fallow
false, falser, falsest
falsehood

falsetto, -tos	
falsification	
falsify, -fied, -fying	
falt	fault
falter, -ed, -ing	
falteringly	
falure	failure
falus	phallus
fame, famed, faming	
familial	
familiar, -ly	
familiarisation	
familiarise, -rised, -rising	
familiarity, -ties	
familier	familiar
family, -lies	
famine	
famished	
famous, -ly	
famus	famous
fan, fanned, fanning	
fanatic	
fanatical, -ly	
fanaticism	
fancier	
fanciful, -ly	
fancy, -cies	
fancy, -cied, -cying	
fancy, -cier, -ciest	
fane	fain (glad)
fane	feign (pretend)
fanfair	fanfare
fanfare	
fang	
fanlight	
fansie	fancy
fansiful	fanciful
fansy	fancy
fantam	phantom
fantasey	fantasy
fantasia	
fantasise, -sised, -sising	
fantastic, -ally	
fantasy, -ies	
fantom	phantom
far, farther, farthest	
far, further, furthest	

faranyx	pharynx
faraway	
farce	
fare, fared, faring (get on)	
fare	fair (honest)
farenhite	Fahrenheit
farewell	
far-fetched	
farm, -ed, -ing	
farmacist	pharmacist
farmacy	pharmacy
farmasist	pharmacist
farmer	
farmstead	
farrago, -goes	
farrier	
farrow, -ed, -ing	
far-sighted	
farther (away)	
farther	father (parent)
farthing	
faryngitis	pharyngitis
farytale	fairytale
fascia, fasciae (band)	
fascia	facia (panel)
fascinate, -nated, -nating	
fascination	
fascism	
fascist	
fase	face
fase	phase
fasen	fasten
faset	facet
fasetious	facetious
fasha	facia (panel)
fasha	fascia (band)
fashal	facial
fashion, -ed, -ing	
fashionable, -bly	
fashism	fascism
fashist	fascist
fashon	fashion
fashonabul	fashionable
fasilitate	facilitate
fasility	facility
fasinate	fascinate
fasination	fascination

fast, -ed, -ing
fasten, -ed, -ing
fastener
fastidious, -ly
fastidiousness
   fastidius   fastidious
fat, fatted, fatting
fat, fatter, fattest
fatal, -ly
fatalism
fatalist
fatalistic, -ally
fatality, -ties
fate (destiny)
   fate   fete (fair)
fated
fateful, -ly
   faten   fatten
father, -ed, -ing (parent)
   father   farther (away)
Father Christmas
fatherhood
father-in-law, fathers-in-law
fatherland
fatherly
fathom, -ed, -ing
fathomable
fatigue, -tigued, -tiguing
fatten, -ed, -ing
fattener
fatty, -tier, -tiest
fatuous, -ly
faucet
fault, -ed, -ing
faultless, -ly
faulty, faultier, faultiest
faun (god)
   faun   fawn (deer)
fauna
faux pas
   faver   favour
   faverite   favourite
   faveritism   favouritism
   favorite   favourite
favour, -ed, -ing
favourable, -bly
favourite

favouritism
fawn, -ed, -ing (deer)
   fawn   faun (god)
   fawna   fauna
   faysha   facia (panel)
   faysha   fascia (band)
   fayshal   facial
faze, fazed, fazing
   feacher   feature
fealty, -ties
fear, -ed, -ing
fearful, -ly
   fearfull   fearful
fearless, -ly
fearsome, -ly
feasible, -bly
feasibility
   feasibul   feasible
feast, -ed, -ing
feat (act)
   feat   feet (body)
feather, -ed, -ing
featherbed, -bedded, -bedding
featherweight
feathery
feature, -tured, -turing
febrile
February
   Febuary   February
   feces   faeces
   fech   fetch
feckless, -ly
fecund
fecundity
   fedaration   federation
federal, -ly
federalism
federalist
federate, -rated, -rating
federation
fee
feeble, -bler, -blest
   feebul   feeble
feebleness
feebly
feed, fed, feeding
feedback

feeder		fer	fir (tree)
feel, felt, feeling		fer	fur (pelt)
feeld	field	feral	
feeler		feret	ferret
feend	fiend	ferie	ferry
feest	feast	ferl	furl
feet (body)		ferlong	furlong
feet	feat (act)	ferment, -ed, -ing	
feetul	foetal	fermentation	
feetus	foetus	fern	
feign, -ed, -ing (pretend)		fernery, -ries	
feign	fain (glad)	ferny	
feild	field	fernice	furnace
feind	fiend	fernish	furnish
feint, -ed, -ing (pretend)		ferniture	furniture
feint	faint (weak)	ferocious, -ly	
fekund	fecund	ferocity	
fekundity	fecundity	feroshus	ferocious
felicitate, -tated, -tating		ferret, -ed, -ing	
felicitation		ferrous	
felicitous, -ly		ferrule , -ruled, -ruling (tip)	
felicity, -ties		ferrule	ferule (rod)
feline, -ly		ferry, -ries	
felisitous	felicitous	ferry, -ried, -rying	
felisity	felicity	ferryboat	
fell		ferther	further
fellow		ferthest	furthest
fellowship		fertile, -ly	
felon		fertilisation	
felonious, -ly		fertilise, -lised, -lising	
felony, -nies		fertiliser	
felow	fellow	fertility	
felt		ferule, -ruled, -ruling (rod)	
female		ferule	ferrule (tip)
feminine, -ly		fervency	
femininity		fervent, -ly	
feminism		ferver	fervour
femme fatale		fervid, -ly	
femur		fervour	
fence, fenced, fencing		fery	ferry
fend, -ed, -ing		fesant	pheasant
fender		fesible	feasible
fenix	phoenix	festal, -ly	
fennel		fester, -ed, -ing	
fenomenon	phenomenon	festival	
fenominal	phenomenal	festive, -ly	
fense	fence	festivity, -ties	

festoon, -ed, -ing
feta   fetta (cheese)
fetch, -ed, -ing
fete, feted, feting (fair)
fete   fate (destiny)
feter   fetter (chain)
fether   feather
fetid, -ly
fetish
fetishism
fetlock
fetta (cheese)
fetter, -ed, -ing (chain)
fettle
fettler
feud, -ed, -ing
feudal, -ly
feudalism
fever
fevered
feverish, -ly
fewd   feud
fewdal   feudal
fey, -ly
fez, fezzes
fezant   pheasant
fial   file (papers)
fial   phial (tube)
fiance (man)
fiancee (woman)
fiansey   fiancee
fiasco, -cos
fib, fibbed, fibbing
fibber
fiber   fibber
fiber   fibre
fibre
fibreglass
fibro
fibrositis
fibrous, -ly
fibrus   fibrous
fibula
fickle, -kly
fickleness
ficshun   fiction

fiction
fictional, -ly
fictishus   fictitious
fictitious, -ly
fiddle, -dled, -dling
fiddler
fiddlesticks
fiddly
fidelity, -ties
fidget, -ed, -ing
fidgety
fidle   fiddle
field, -ed, -ing
fielder
fieldsman, -men
fiend
fiendish, -ly
fierce, fiercer, fiercest
fiercely
fierceness
fierey   fiery
fierse   fierce
fiery, fierier, fieriest
fiesta
fife
fifteen
fifteenth
fifth
fiftieth
fifty
fifty-fifty
fig
figer   figure
figerative   figurative
figet   fidget
fight, fought, fighting
fighter
figment
figuration
figurative, -ly
figure, -ured, -uring
figurehead
figurine
Fiji
Fijian
fiksation   fixation
fiksative   fixative

fikscher — fixture

For other fila- words,
look under **phila-**.

filch, -ed, -ing
filcher
file, filed, filing (paper)
file — phial (tube)
filet — fillet
filial, -ly
filibuster
filie — filly
filigree
filip — fillip
Filipino
Filippines — Philippines
filistine — philistine
fill, -ed, -ing
filler
fillet
fillip
filly, -lies
film, -ed, -ing
filmy, filmier, filmiest

For filo- words,
look under **philo-**.

filter, -ed, -ing
filth
filthily
filthiness
filthy, filthier, filthiest
filtrate, -trated, -trating
filtration
fily — filly
fin, finned, finning
final, -ly (end)
finale (last part)
finalisation
finalise, -lised, -lising
finalist
finality, -ties
finance, -nanced, -nancing
financial, -ly
financier
finanse — finance
finch, -ches

find, found, finding
finder
fine, fined, fining
fine, finer, finest
finely
fineness
finery, -ries
finesse, -nessed, -nessing
finetuner
finger
fingernail
fingerprint
fingertip
finical, -ly
finicky
finis (conclusion)
finish, -ed, -ing
finisher
finite, -ly
fiord
fir (tree)
fir — fur (pelt)
fire, fired, firing
firearm
firebreak
fire-escape
fire-extinguisher
firefly, -flies
fireman, -men
fireplace
fireproof
firescreen
fireworks
firm, -ed, -ing
firmament
first, -ly
first-hand
first-past-the-post
fiscal, -ly
fish, fishes, fish
fisherman, -men
fishery, -ries
fish-eye lens
fishmonger
fish-net
fishplate
fishun — fission

fishy, fishier, fishiest
  fisile   fissile
  fision   fission

> For other fisi- words,
> look under **physi-**.

  fiskle   fiscal
fissile
fission
fissure, -sured, -suring
fist
fisticuff
fistula, -las, -lae
fit, fitted, fitting
fit, fitter, fittest
  fite   fight
fitful, -ly
  fitfull   fitful
fitness
fitter
five
fiver
fix, fixed, fixing
fixated
fixation
fixative
  fixcher   fixture
fixity, -ties
fixture
fizz, -ed, -ing
fizzer
fizzle, -zled, -zling
  fizzul   fizzle
fizzy, -zier, -ziest
fjord
flabbergast, -ed, -ing
flabbily
flabbiness
flabby, -bier, -biest
  flabergast   flabbergast
  flaby   flabby
flaccid, -ly
flaccidity
flag, flagged, flagging
flagellate, -lated, -lating
flagon
flagrant, -ly

flagship
flagstone
flail, -ed, -ing
flair (talent)
  flair   flare (blaze)
flak
flake, flaked, flaking
flakily
flaky, flakier, flakiest
flamboyance
flamboyancy
flamboyant, -ly
flame, flamed, flaming
flamenco, -cos
flamethrower
flame-tree
flamingo, -gos, -goes
flammable
  flammabul   flammable
flan
  flanel   flannel
flange, flanged, flanging
  flanje   flange
flank, -ed, -ing
flannel, -elled, -elling
flannelette
  flanul   flannel
flap, flapped, flapping
flapjack
flapper
flare, flared, flaring (blaze)
  flare   flair (talent)
flash, -ed, -ing
flashback
flashbulb
flashgun
flashlight
flashpoint
flashy, flashier, flashiest
flask
flat, flatted, flatting
flat, flatter, flattest
  flaten   flatten
  flater   flatter
flatette
flatfoot, -feet
flat-footed, -ly

flathead
flatten, -ed, -ing
flatter, -ed, -ing
flatterer
flattery, -teries
flatulence
flatulense → flatulence
flatulent, -ly
flaunt, -ed, -ing
flautist
flaver → flavour
flavour, -ed, -ing
flaw, -ed, -ing (fault)
flaw → floor (room)
flax
flaxen
flay, -ed, -ing
flea (insect)
flea → flee (escape)
flea-bitten
fleat → fleet
fleck, -ed, -ing
flecks (spots)
flecks → flex (bend)
fledge, fledged, fledging
flee, fled, fleeing (escape)
flee → flea (insect)
fleece, fleeced, fleecing
fleeciness
fleecy, fleecier, fleeciest
fleese → fleece
fleet, -ly
fleeting, -ly
fleetness
flegling → fledgling
flegmatic → phlegmatic
fleks → flecks (spots)
fleksible → flexible
flem → phlegm
flert → flirt
flesh
fleshy, fleshier, fleshiest
fleur-de-lis, fleurs-de-lis
flew (fly)
flew → flu (ill)
flew → flue (passage)
flex, -ed, -ing (bend)

flex
flecks (spots)
flexible, -bly
flexitime
fli → fly
flibbertigibbet
flick, -ed, -ing
flicker, -ed, -ing
flick-knife, flick-knives
flier
flight
flightiness
flighty, -tier, -tiest
flimsily
flimsiness
flimsy, -sies
flimsy, -sier, -siest
flinch, -ed, -ing
flinchingly
fling, flung, flinging
flint
flinty, flintier, flintiest
flip, flipped, flipping
flipansy → flippancy
flipant → flippant
fliper → flipper
flippancy
flippant, -ly
flipper
flirt, -ed, -ing
flirtation
flirtatious, -ly
flit, flitted, flitting
flite → flight
flo → floe (ice)
flo → flow (pour)
float, -ed, -ing
floatation
floater
flock, -ed, -ing
flocks (groups)
flocks → phlox (plant)
floe (ice)
floe → flow (pour)
flog, flogged, flogging
flood, -ed, -ing
floodgate
floodlight, -lit, -lighting

floor, -ed, -ing (room)
floor   flaw (fault)
floorboard
flooride   fluoride
floot   flute
flop, flopped, flopping
floppily
floppy, -pier, -piest
floppy disc
flora, floras, florae
floral, -ly
florescence (flowering)
florescence   fluorescence (giving light)
florescent
florescent   fluorescent
florid, -ly
floridate   fluoridate
florin
florish   flourish
florist
floss
flossy, flossier, flossiest
flotation
flote   float
flotilla
flotsam and jetsam
flounce, flounced, flouncing
flounder, -ed, -ing
flounse   flounce
flour (grain)
flour   flower (plant)
flourish, -ed, -ing
floury
flout, -ed, -ing
flow, -ed, -ing
flower, -ed, -ing (plant)
flower   flour (grain)
flowerbed
flowery, -rier, -riest
flown
flownder   flounder
flownse   flounce
flow-on
flowt   flout
flox   phlox
flu (ill)

flu   flew (fly)
flu   flue (passage)
fluctuate, -ated, -ating
fluctuation
flue (passage)
flue   flew (fly)
flue   flu (ill)
fluency
fluensy   fluency
fluent, -ly
fluff, -ed, -ing
fluffily
fluffiness
fluffy, fluffier, fluffiest
fluid, -ly
fluidity
fluke, fluked, fluking
fluks   flux
fluky, flukier, flukiest
flunk, -ed, -ing
fluoresce, -resced, -rescing
fluorescence (giving light)
fluoridate, -dated, -dating
fluoridation
flurish   flourish
flurry, -ries
flurry, -ried, -rying
flurt   flirt
flurtation   flirtation
flury   flurry
flush, -ed, -ing
fluster, -ed, -ing
flute, fluted, fluting
flutter, -ed, -ing
fluvial
flux
fly, flies
fly, flew, flown, flying
flyblown
flycatcher
flyleaf, -leaves
flyover
flytrap
flyweight
flywheel
foal, -ed, -ing
foam, -ed, -ing

fob, fobbed, fobbing
    fobia   phobia
focal, -ly
focus, -ci or -cuses
focus, -cused, -cusing or -cussed,
  -cussing
focuser
fodder
foe
    foe pas   faux pas
foetal
foetus
fog, fogged, fogging
fogey, fogeys
fogginess
foggy, -gier, -giest
foghorn
fogy, -gies
foible
    foier   foyer
foil, -ed, -ing
foist, -ed, -ing
    foks   fox
fold, -ed, -ing
folder
    fole   foal
foliage
foliaged
    foliaje   foliage
foliation
    folie   folly
folio, -lios
folk
folk dance
    folklaw   folklore
folklore
follicle
    follicul   follicle
follow, -ed, -ing
follower
folly, -lies
    folow   follow
    foly   folly
    fome   foam
foment, -ed, -ing
fond, -ly
fondant

fondle, -dled, -dling
fondness
fondue
    fondul   fondle
    fone   phone
    fonetic   phonetic
    fonograf   phonograph
font
    fony   phony
food
foodstuff
fool, -ed, -ing
foolery, -eries
foolhardiness
foolhardy, -dier, -diest
foolish, -ly
foolishness
foolproof
foolscap
foot, feet
football
footballer
foothill
foothold
footie
footing
footlights
footloose
footman, -men
footnote
footpath
footprint
footsore
footstep
footwork
fop
foppish, -ly
for (with the purpose of)
    for   fore (front)
    for   four (number)
forage, -raged, -raging
foray
    forbarance   forbearance
forbear, -bore, -borne, -bearing
forbearance
forbid, -bad, -bidden, -bidding
    forbode   forebode

forcasle / forecastle
forcast / forecast
forcastle / forecastle
force, forced, forcing
forceful, -ly
forceps, -ceps, -cipes
forcible, -bly
forcibul / forcible
forclose / foreclose
ford, -ed, -ing
fordable
fore (front)
fore / four (number)
forearm
forebear
forebode, -boded, -boding
forecast, -ed, -ing
forecaster
forecastle
foreclose, -closed, -closing
forefather
forefinger
forego, -gone, -going (go before)
forego / forgo (give up)
foreground
forehand
forehead
foreign
foreigner
foreknow, -knew, -knowing
foreknowledge
foreman, -men
foren / foreign
forener / foreigner
forerunner
foresee, -saw, -seeing
foreshadow, -ed, -ing
foreshore
foresight
foreskin
forest, -ed, -ing
forestall, -ed, -ing
forester
forestry
foretaste, -tasted, -tasting
foretell, -told, -telling
forethought

forever
forewarn, -ed, -ing
foreword (book)
foreword / forward (ahead)
forfeit, -ed, -ing
forfeiture
forfit / forfeit
forfiture / forfeiture
forgary / forgery
forge, forged, forging
forgery, -eries
forget, -got, -gotten -getting
forgetful, -ly
forget-me-not
forgettable
forgive, -gave, -given, -giving
forgiveness
forgo, -went, -gone, -going (give up)
forgo / forego (go before)

For for-words, also
look under fore-.

---

forige / forage
forin / foreign
fork, -ed, -ing
fork-lift
forlorn, -ly
form, -ed, -ing
formal, -ly
formalise, -lised, -lising
formality, -ties
format
formation
formative, -ly
former, -ly
formica
formidable, -bly
formidabul / formidable
formula, -las, -lae
formulate, -lated, -lating
formulation
formulator
forn / faun (god)
forn / fawn (deer)
fornicate, -cated, -cating

fornication	
forsable	forcible
forsake, -sook, -saken, -saking	
forse	force
forseps	forceps
forsful	forceful
forsible	forcible
forsight	foresight
fort (soldiers)	
fort	fought (fight)
forte (strong)	
forth (away)	
forth	fourth (number)
forthcoming	
forthright	
forthwith	
fortieth	
fortification	
fortify, -fied, -fying	
fortitude	
fortnight	
fortnightly	
fortnite	fortnight
fortress	
fortuitous, -ly	
fortuitus	fortuitous
fortunate, -ly	
fortune	
fortune-teller	
forty, -ties	
forum, forums, fora	
forward (ahead)	
foreward	foreword (book)
forwards	
fosfate	phosphate
fosforesent	phosphorescent
fosforus	phosphorus
fosil	fossil
fossick, -ed, -ing	
fossil	
foster, -ed, -ing	

> For *foto-* words,
> look under **photo-**.

foul, -ed, -ing (dirt)

foul	fowl (bird)
found, -ed, -ing	
foundation	
founder, -ed, -ing	
foundling	
foundry, -dries	
fount	
fountain	
four (number)	
four	fore (ahead)
four-stroke	
fourt	fort (soldiers)
fourt	fought (fight)
fourteen	
fourteenth	
fourth, -ly	
fourty	forty
fowl (bird)	
fowl	foul (dirt)
fownd	found
fowndation	foundation
fowndry	foundry
fownt	fount
fowntain	fountain
fox, foxes	
foxhole	
fox-hunting	
foxtrot	
foxy, foxier, foxiest	
foyble	foible
foyer	
fracas	
fracshun	fraction
fracshus	fractious
fraction	
fractional, -ly	
fractious, -ly	
fracture, -tured, -turing	
fragile, -ly	
fragility, -ties	
fragment, -ed, -ing	
fragmentary	
fragmentation	
fragmented	
fragmentry	fragmentary
fragrance	
fragranse	fragrance

fragrant, -ly
frail, -ly
frailty, -ties
frame, framed, framing
frame-up
framework
franc (money)
franc   frank (mark)
franchise
frangipanni, -nies
frank, -ed, -ing (mark)
frank   franc (money)
frankfurt
frankincense
frantic, -ally
frase   phrase
frate   freight
fraternal, -ly
fraternisation
fraternise, -nised, -nising
fraternity, -ties
fraud
fraudulence
fraudulense   fraudulence
fraudulent, -ly
fraught
fraut   fraught
frawd   fraud
frawdulence   fraudulence
frawdulent   fraudulent
frawt   fraught
fray, -ed, -ing
frazzle, -zled, -zling
frazzul   frazzle
freak
freakish, -ly
freckle, -led, -ling
free, freed, freeing
free, freer, freest
freeborn
freedom
freehand
freehold
freelance, -lanced, -lancing
freelancer
freeload, -ed, -ing
freeloader

freely
freeman, -men
Freemason
Freemasonry
free-range
freesia
freestanding
freestyle
freeway
freewheel, -ed, -ing
freeze, froze, frozen, freezing (cold)
freeze   frieze (band)
freezer
freight, -ed, -ing
freighter
freind   friend
frekwency   frequency
frekwent   frequent
French
frend   friend
frendly   friendly
frendship   friendship
frenetic, -ally
frenzie   frenzy
frenzied
frenzy, -zies
frenzy, -zied, -zying
frequency, -cies
frequensy   frequency
frequent, -ly
fresco, -coes
fresco, -coed, -coing
fresh, -ly
freshen, -ed, -ing
freshener
fresher
freshness
freshwater
fresko   fresco
fret, fretted, fretting
fretful, -ly
fretwork
Freudian
fri   fry
friable
friabul   friable
friar

fricassee, -seed, -seeing
fricshun → friction
friction
frictional, -ly
Friday
fridge
friend
friendliness
friendly, -lier, -liest
friendship
frier → friar
Friesian
frieze (band)
frieze → freeze (cold)
frigate
fright
frighten, -ed, -ing
frightener
frightful, -ly
frightfull → frightful
frigid, -ly
frigidity, -ties
frigidness
frill, -ed, -ing
frill-necked lizard
fringe, fringed, fringing
frippery, -ries
frisk, -ed, -ing
friskily
frisky, friskier, friskiest
frite → fright
friteful → frightful
friten → frighten
friter → fritter
fritter, -ed, -ing
frivolity, -ties
frivolous, -ly
frivolus → frivolous
frizz, frizzes
frizz, frizzed, frizzing
frizzle, -zled, -zling
frizzy
frizzul → frizzle
fro
frock, -ed, -ing
frog
frogman, -men

frogmarch, -ed, -ing
frogmouth
Froidian → Freudian
frolic, -icked, -icking
frolicsome, -ly
frond
front, -ed, -ing
frontage
frontal, -ly
frontbencher
frontier
frontige → frontage
froogal → frugal
frooishun → fruition
froot → fruit
frootful → fruitful
frost, -ed, -ing
frostbite, -bit, -bitten, -biting
frostily
frosty, -tier, -tiest
froth, -ed, -ing
frothiness
frothy, frothier, frothiest
frown, -ed, -ing
frowzy, -zier, -ziest
froze
frozen, -ly
fructose
frugal, -ly
frugality, -ties
fruishun → fruition
fruit, -ed, -ing
fruiterer
fruit-fly
fruitful, -ly
fruition
fruitless, -ly
fruity, -tier, -tiest
frump
frumpish, -ly
frunt → front
fruntal → frontal
fruntier → frontier
frustrate, -trated, -trating
frustration
frut → fruit
fruterer → fruiterer

frutful	fruitful
frutie	fruity

fry, fried, frying
fry, fries

fucher	future
fucheristic	futuristic

fuchsia

fudal	feudal
fudalism	feudalism

fuddle, -dled, -dling

fuddul	fuddle
fude	feud

fudge, fudged, fudging
fuel, fuelled, fuelling
fuel-injection
fuel-injector
fugitive
fugue

ful	full

fulcrum, -crums, -cra
fulfil, -filled, -filling
fulfilment
full
full-back
full-blooded

fullfil	fulfil

fully
fully-fledged
fulminate, -ated, -ating

fulscap	foolscap

fulsome, -ly
fulsomeness
fumble, -bled, -bling
fumbler

fumbul	fumble

fume, fumed, fuming
fumigant
fumigate, -gated, -gating
fumigation
fumigator
fun

funcshun	function

function
functional, -ly
functionalism
functionary, -ries
fund, -ed, -ing

fundamental, -ly

funel	funnel

funeral
funereal, -ly
funfair
fungicide
fungus, fungi
funicular

funily	funnily

funk, -ed, -ing
funnel, -nelled, -nelling
funnel-web
funnily
funny, -nier, -niest
fur, furred, furring (pelt)

fur	fir (tree)

furbish, -ed, -ing

furie	furry (fur)
furie	fury (anger)
furier	furrier

furious, -ly

furius	furious

furl, -ed, -ing
furlong
furlough

furm	firm
furmament	firmament
furment	ferment
furmentation	fermentation
furn	fern

furnace
furnish, -ed, -ing
furnisher
furnishings
furniture
furore
furphy, -phies
furrier
furrow, -ed, -ing
furry, -rier, -riest (fur)

furst	first

further
furtherance
furthest
furtive, -ly
fury, -ries (anger)

fus	fuss

fuse, fused, fusing
fuselage

fusha	fuchsia
fusier	fussier
fusiest	fussiest
fusilade	fusillade
fusilage	fuselage

fusilier
fusillade
fusion
fuss, -ed, -ing
fusspot
fussy, -sier, -siest
futile, -ly
futility, -ties
future
futurism
futuristic
futurology
fuzz
fuzzily
fuzziness
fuzzy, -zier, -ziest

fyord	fiord
fyord	fjord

For fysi- words, look under **physi-**.

Gg

gab, gabbed, gabbing
gabardine
gabble, -bled, -bling (talk)
gable (roof)

gabul	gabble (talk)
gabul	gable (roof)

gadget
Gaelic

gaf	gaff (hook)
gaf	gaffe (mistake)

gaff (hook)
gaffe (mistake)
gag, gagged, gagging
gaga

gage	gauge
gaget	gadget

gaggle

gagit	gadget
gagul	gaggle

gaiety, -ties

gail	gale

gaily
gain, -ed, -ing
gainful, -ly
gainsay, -said, -saying
gait (walk)

gait	gate (opening)

gaiter

gaitey	gaiety

gala (festival)

gala	galah (bird)

galah (bird)

galaksey	galaxy
galant	gallant
galantry	gallantry
galaw	galore

galaxy, -axies
gale

galery	gallery
galey	galley
galivant	gallivant

gall, -ed, -ing
gallant, -ly
gallantry, -tries
galleon
gallery, -leries
galley, -leys
gallivant, -vanted, -vanting
gallon
gallop, galloped, galloping (pace)
gallows
gallstone
gallup poll (survey)

galon	gallon
galop	gallop (pace)

galore
galoshes

galows	gallows
galup poll	gallup poll

galvanise, -nised, -nising
galvanised iron

galy	galley

gambit
gamble, -bled, -bling (chance)
gambol, -bolled, -bolling (frolic)
game, gamed, gaming
gamesmanship
gamin (urchin)
gamma
gammon (bacon)
gammy, -mier, -miest
gamut
gander
gang
gangling
ganglion, -glia, -glions
gangplank

gangreen	gangrene

gangrene
gangrenous

gangrenus	gangrenous

gangster
gangway
gannet
gantry, -tries

gaol (prison)
   gaol   goal (aim)
gaolbird
gaoler
gap
gape, -ed, -ing
garage, -raged, -raging
   garantee   guarantee
   garantee   guaranty
   garantor   guarantor
garb, -ed, -ing
garbage
   garbige   garbage
garble, -bled, -bling
   garbul   garble
   gard   guard
garden, -ed, -ing
gardener
gardenia
   gardian   guardian
garfish, -fish, -fishes
gargle, -gled, -gling
   gargoil   gargoyle
gargoyle
   gargul   gargle
garish, -ly
   garison   garrison
garland, -landed, -landing
garlic
garment
garner, -ed, -ing
garnet
garnish, -ed, -ing
garnishee, -sheed, -sheeing
   garnit   garnet
garrison, -ed, -ing
   garrot   garrotte
garrotte, -rotted, -rotting
garrulity
garrulous, -ly
garter
   garulus   garrulous
gas, gases
gas, gassed, gassing
gasbag, -bagged, -bagging
   gasebo   gazebo
   gaselene   gasoline

gaseous
gash, gashed, gashing
   gasious   gaseous
gasket
gasmask
gasolene
gasoline
gasometer
gasp, -ed, -ing
   gassey   gassy
gassy, -sier, -siest
   gastley   ghastly
gastric
gastritis
gastroenteritis
gastronome
gastronomy
gate (opening)
   gate   gait (walk)
gateau, -teaux
gatecrash, -crashed, -crashing
   gater   gaiter
gateway
gather, -ed, -ing
gauche
   gaudie   gaudy
gauge, gauged, gauging
gaunt, -ly
gauntlet
gauze
gave
gavel
   gavot   gavotte
gavotte
   gawdie   gaudy
gawk, -ed, -ing
gawky, -kier, -kiest
   gawl   gall
   gawnt   gaunt
   gawntlet   gauntlet
   gawse   gauze
gay, gayer, gayest
   Gaylic   Gaelic
   gayn   gain
   gaysha   geisha
gaze, -ed, -ing
gazebo, -bos, -boes

gazel   gazelle
gazelle
gazette, -etted, -etting
gazump, -ed, -ing
gear, -ed, -ing
gearbox, -boxes
gear-ratio
gearstick
gearwheel
gecko, -os, -oes
geebung
geek
gees   geese
geese
geezer
Geiger counter
geisha, -shas
gel, gelled, gelling
gelatin   gelatine
gelatine
gelatinous, -ly
gelatinus   gelatinous
gelato
geld, gelded, gelding
gelignite
gem, gemmed, gemming
gemfish, -fish, -fishes
Gemini
gen, genned, genning
gendarme, -darmes
gender
gene
genealogist
genealogy, -gies
genee   genie
general, -ly
generalise, -ised, -ising
generality, -ties
generate, -ed, -ing
generation
generation-gap
generator
generic
generical, -ly
generosity, -ties
generous, -ly
generus   generous

genesis, -ses
genetic
genetical, -ly
genetics
geney   genie
genial, -ly
genie
geniology   genealogy
genital
genius, geniuses
genocide
genoside   genocide
genre
gent
genteel, -ly (proper)
genteel   gentle
gentile (Christian)
gentility, -ties
gentle, -tler, -tlest
gentleman, -men
gentlewoman, -women
gentrey   gentry
gentrification
gentry
gentul   gentle
gentulman   gentleman
genuflect, -ed, -ing
genuin   genuine
genuine, -ly
genuineness
genus, genera
geny   genie
geofysics   geophysics
geografey   geography
geography, -phies
geologist
geology, -gies
geometrey   geometry
geometric
geometrical, -ly
geometry, -tries
geophysicist
geophysics
georgette
geranium
gerd   gird
gerder   girder

gerdle	girdle	giddy, -dier, -diest	
gerdul	girdle	gide	guide
geriatric		gidgee	
gerilla	gorilla	gidgie	gidgee
gerilla	guerilla	gidie	giddy
gerkin	gherkin	gidy	giddy
gerl	girl	gift	
germ		gig, gigged, gigging	
German		gigantic, -ally	
germane		giggle, -gled, -gling	
germinal		gigolo, -los	
germinate, -nated, -nating		gigul	giggle
gerontology		gil	gill
gerth	girth	gild, gilded, gilding (gold)	
gerund		gild	guild (union)
gerymander	gerrymander	gile	guile
gescha	gesture	gilgai	
geser	geyser	gilgy	gilgai
gess	guess	gill	
gest	guest	giloteen	guillotine
gestate, -tated, -tating		gilotine	guillotine
gestation		gilt (gold)	
gesticulate, -lated, -lating		gilt	guilt
gesture, -tured, -turing		giltey	guilty
get, got, getting		gilty	guilty
getaway		gim	gym
getto	ghetto	gimick	gimmick
geyser		gimkana	gymkhana
ghastly, -lier, -liest		gimlet	
gherkin		gimmick	
ghetto, ghettos, ghettoes		gimnasium	gymnasium
ghost, -ly		gimnastics	gymnastics
ghoul		gin, ginned, ginning	
ghoulish, -ly		ginecology	gynaecology
ghoulishness		giney	guinea
giant		gineypig	guineapig
gibber		gingam	gingham
gibberish		ginger	
gibbet, -beted, -beting		gingerley	gingerly
gibe, gibed, gibing (mock)		gingerly	
gibe	jibe (sail)	gingham	
giber	gibber	gingivitis	
giberish	gibberish	ginie	guinea
gibet	gibbet	giniepig	guineapig
giblet		ginjer	ginger
gidance	guidance	ginjivitis	gingivitis
gidanse	guidance	ginseng	

gip	gyp		glaze, glazed, glazing	
gipsey	gipsy		glazier	
gipsie	gipsy		glea	glee
gipsum	gypsum		gleam, -ed, -ing	
gipsy, -sies			glean, -ed, -ing	
giraf	giraffe		glee	
gird, -ed, -ing			gleem	gleam
girder			gleen	glean
girdle, -dled, -dling			glib, glibber, glibbest	
girdul	girdle		glicerine	glycerine
girl			glide, glided, gliding	
girocompass	gyrocompass		glider	
giroscope	gyroscope		glimmer, -ered, -ering	
girth			glimpse, glimpsed, glimpsing	
gise	guise		glimse	glimpse
gismo			glint, -ed, -ing	
gist			glisen	glisten
gitar	guitar		gliserin	glycerine
give, gave, given, giving			glisten, -ed, -ing	
giy	guy		glitter, -ed, -ing	
gizerd	gizzard		glo	glow
gizzard			gloat, -ed, -ing	
glacial, -ly			glob	
glacier			global, -ly	
glad, gladded, gladding			globe, globed, globing	
glad, gladder, gladdest			globule	
glade			gloo	glue
gladen	gladden		gloocose	glucose
gladiater	gladiator		gloom	
gladiator			gloomily	
glamer	glamour		gloomy, -mier, -miest	
glamorous, -ly			glooten	gluten
glamour			glorie	glory
glance, -ed, -ing			glorify, -fied, -fying	
gland			glorious, -ly	
glandular			glorius	glorious
glanduler	glandular		glory, glories	
glanse	glance		glory, gloried, glorying	
glare, glared, glaring			glos	gloss
glas	glass		glosary	glossary
glashal	glacial		gloss, glossed, glossing	
glasier	glacier		glossary, -ries	
glass, glasses			glossie	glossy
glasshouse			glossy, glossier, glossiest	
glassy, -sier, -siest			glote	gloat
glaucoma			glove	
glawcoma	glaucoma		glow, -ed, -ing	

glower, -ered, -ering
glucose
glue, glued, gluing
glum, -ly
glut, glutted, glutting
gluten (glue)

  glutten   glutton

glutton (eat)

  gluv   glove

glycerine
gnarled
gnash, -ed, -ing
gnat
gnaw, gnawed, gnawing
gnome
gnu, gnus
go, gone, going
goad, -ed, -ing
goal (aim)

  goal   gaol (prison)

goalkeeper
goanna
goat
goatee
gob

  gobbel   gobble

gobble, -bled, -bling
gobbledegook
gobbler
go-between
goblet
goblin

  gobul   gobble

go-cart
God
godchild, -children
goddess
godforsaken
godly, -lier, -liest
godparent
godsend, -sent, -sending
godspeed
goer
goes
goggle, -gled, -gling

  gogul   goggle
  goiter   goitre

goitre
go-kart
gold
golden, -ly
goldfield
goldfish
goldmine

  gole   goal (aim)

golf (game)

  golf   gulf (bay)

golliwog
gollywog

  gon   gone

gondola
gondolier
gone
goner
gong
goo
good, better, best

  gooda   gouda

goodbye, -byes
goodnight
goodwill
gooey, gooier, gooiest
goof, goofed, goofing
googly

  gool   ghoul
  goolash   goulash
  goormand   gourmand
  goormay   gourmet

goose, geese

  gooseberie   gooseberry

gooseberry, -ries
goosestep, -stepped, -stepping
gopher
gore, gored, goring
gorge, gorged, gorging
gorgeous, -ly

  gorgus   gorgeous

gorilla (ape)

  gorilla   guerilla (soldier)

gormandise, -dised, -dising
gorse
gory, gorier, goriest

  gosamer   gossamer

goshawk
gosip	gossip

gosling
go-slow
gospel
gospeller
gossamer
gossip, -ed, -ing
gost	ghost
gote	goat

Gothic
gouda
gouge, gouged, gouging
goul	ghoul

goulash
gourd
gourmand
gourmet
gout
goven	govern

govern, -ed, -ing
governer	governor

governess
government
governmental, -ly
governor
governor-general, governors-general
govner	governor
gowge	gouge
gawt	gout

grab, grabbed, grabbing
grace, graced, gracing
graceful, -ly
gracious, -ly
gradation
grade, graded, grading
grader
gradient
gradual, -ly
graduate, -ated, -ating
graduation
graf	graph

graffiti
grafic	graphic
grafics	graphics
grafite	graphite
grafiti	graffiti

graft, grafted, grafting
grail
grain
graling	grayling

gram
gramar	grammar
gramarian	grammarian
gramatical	grammatical
gramer	grammar
gramerfone	gramophone

grammar
grammarian
grammatical, -ly
gramophone
grampus
gran
granary, -ries
grand
grandeur
grandiloquent, -ly
grandiose, -ly
grandiosity
grandparent
grandstand
grane	grain

grange
granie	granny
granit	granite

granite
granny, grannies
grant, -ed, -ing
granular
granulate, -lated, -lating
granule
grany	granny

grape
grapefruit, grapefruit
grapevine
graph, -ed, -ing
graphic
graphical, -ly
graphics
graphite
graple	grapple

grapnel
grapple, -pled, -pling
grappul	grapple

gras	grass	greed	
grase	grace	greedily	
grashoper	grasshopper	greedy, greedier, greediest	
grashus	gracious	greef	grief
grasp, -ed, -ing		green	
grass		greenery, -eries	
grasshopper		greengrocer	
glassland		greenhorn	
grassroots		greenhouse	
grassy, -sier, -siest		greese	grease
grate (fireplace)		greet, -ed, -ing	
grate, grated, grating (rub)		gregarious, -ly	
grate	great (large)	gregarius	gregarious
grateful, -ly		greif	grief
gratification		greive	grieve
gratify, -fied, -fying		greivus	grievous
gratingly		gremlin	
gratis		grenade	
gratitude		grenadier	
gratuitey	gratuity	grene	green
gratuitous, -ly		grenery	greenery
gratuitousness		grengroser	greengrocer
gratuitus	gratuitous	grenhorn	greenhorn
gratuity		grenhous	greenhouse
grave		grese	grease
gravel, gravelled, gravelling		grete	greet
gravelly		grevance	grievance
gravie	gravy	grevanse	grievance
gravitashun	gravitation	greve	grieve
gravitate, -tated, -tating		grevillea	
gravitation		grevus	grievous
gravity, -ties		grew	
gravure		grey	
gravvity	gravity	greyhound	
gravy, -vies		greyness	
grayhownd	greyhound	grid	
grayl	grail	griddle, -dled, -dling	
grayling		griddul	griddle
grayn	grain	gridiron	
graze, grazed, grazing		grief	
grazier		grief-stricken	
grease, greased, greasing		grievance	
greasepaint		grievanse	grievance
great (large)		grieve, -ed, -ing	
great	grate (rub)	griever	
greatful	grateful	grievous, -ly	
grede	greed	griffin	

grill, -ed, -ing (cook)
grille (screen)
griller (barbeque)
grooyere — gruyere
grope, groped, groping
groper
gros — gross
groser — grocer
gross, grosses
grotesk — grotesque
grotesque, -ly
groto — grotto
grotto, -toes, -tos
grotty, -tier, -tiest
groty — grotty
grouch, -ed, -ing
groun — grown
ground, -ed, -ing
groundsheat — groundsheet
groundsheet
groundsman, -men
group, -ed, -ing
grouse, groused, grousing
grout, -ed, -ing
grove
grovel, -elled, -elling
grovle — grovel
grow, grew, grown, growing
grower
growl, -ed, -ing
grown (mature)
grown — groan (moan)
grownd — ground
growse — grouse
growth
groyne (jetty)
groyne — groin (body)
grub, grubbed, grubbing
grubber
grubby, -bier, -biest
grudge, -ed, -ing
gruel, gruelled, gruelling
gruesome, -ly
gruesomeness
gruf — gruff
gruff, -ly
gruge — grudge
grumble, -led, -ling
grumbul — grumble
grummet

griller — gorilla
griller — guerilla
grim, grimmer, grimmest
grimace, -maced, -macing
grimase — grimace
grime, grimed, griming
grimy, grimier, grimiest
grin, grinned, grinning
grind, ground, grinding
grinder
grindstone
grined — grind
grip, gripped, gripping (hold)
gripe, griped, griping (pain)
grippe (flu)
grisel — gristle (fibre)
grisel — grizzle (whine)
grisly, -lier, -liest
grissle — gristle (fibre)
grissle — grizzle (whine)
grist
gristle (fibre)
grit, gritted, gritting
grizzle, -zled, -zling (whine)
grizzle — gristle (fibre)
grizzleguts
gro — grow
groan, groaned, groaning (moan)
groan — grown (mature)
grocer
grocery, -ceries
grog
groggy, -gier, -giest
groin (body)
groin — groyne (jetty)
grone — groan
grone — grown
groo — grew
grool — gruel
groop — group
groosum — gruesome
groove, grooved, grooving
groovey — groovy
groovy, -vier, -viest

grumpie   grumpy
grumpy, -pier, -piest
grunt, -ed, -ing
grunter
grusome   gruesome
grusum   gruesome
gruyaire   gruyère
gruyare   gruyère
gruyère
G-string
guano, -nos
guarantee, -teed, -teeing
guarantor
guaranty, -tied, -tying
guaranty, -ties
guard, -ed, -ing
guardian
guava
gudgeon
guerilla (soldier)
guerilla   gorilla (ape)
guernsey, -seys
guess, -ed, -ing
guest
guesthouse, -houses
gufaw   guffaw
guffaw, -awed, -awing
guidance
guide, guided, guiding
guideline
guild (union)
guild   gild (gold)
guile
guileless, -ly
guillotine, -tined, -tining
guiloteen   guillotine
guilotine   guillotine
guilt
guiltily
guilty, -tier, -tiest
guinea
guineapig
guise, guised, guising
guitar
gul   gull
gulash   goulash
gulch

gulet   gullet
guley   gully
gulf (bay)
gulf   golf (game)
gulible   gullible
gulie   gully
gull, -ed, -ing
gullet
gullible, -bly
gullibility
gullibul   gullible
gully, gullies
gulp, -ed, -ing
guly   gully
gum, gummed, gumming
gumboil
gumboot
gummy, -mier, -miest
gumnut
gumption
gumshun   gumption
gun, gunned, gunning
gung ho
gunk
gunl   gunwale
gunman, -men
gunmetal
gunnel   gunwale
gunner
gunnery, -eries
gunny, -nies
gunnysack
gunpowder
gunsmith
gunwale
guppy, -pies
gurdle   girdle
gurgle, -gled, -gling
gurgul   gurgle
gurnard, -nards
gurnerd   gurnard
gurth   girth
guru, gurus
gush, gushed, gushing
gusset
gussit   gusset
gust, -ed, -ing

gusto
gut, gutted, gutting
   guter   gutter
   guteral   guttural
   gutersnipe   guttersnipe
gutless, -ly
   gutsa   gutser
gutser
   gutsie   gutsy
gutsy
gutter
guttersnipe
guttural, -ly
   guvern   govern
   guverness   governess
   guvernment   government
   guvner   governor
guy
   guzul   guzzle
guzzle, guzzled, guzzling
   gwano   guano
   gwava   guava
   gybe   gibe
gym
   gymkana   gymkhana
gymkhana
gymnasium, -nasiums, -nasia
gymnastics
gynaecological
gynaecologist
gynaecology
gyp, gypped, gypping
gypsum
gypsy, -sies
gyrate, -ed, -ing
gyrocompass
gyroscope

Hh

habeas corpus
haberdasher
haberdashery, -ries

habet	habit
habias corpus	habeas corpus
habichual	habitual
habichuate	habituate

habit
habitable, -bly

| habitabul | habitable |

habitat
habitation
habitual, -ly
habituate, -ated, -ating

hach	hatch
hachery	hatchery
hachett	hatchet

hacienda
hack, -ed, -ing
hackle, -led, -ling
hackney, -neyed, -neying
hacksaw

| hackul | hackle |

hackwork
haddock
hades
hadn't (had not)

| hadnt | hadn't |

haematology

| haemefilia | haemophilia |

haemoglobin
haemophilia

| haemorage | haemorrhage |

haemorrhage, -haged, -haging
haemorrhoid

| haemorroid | haemorrhoid |

haft, -ed, -ing
hag

| hagard | haggard |
| hagerd | haggard |

haggard, -ly
haggis
haggle, -gled, -gling
hagiography, -phies

| hagis | haggis |
| hagul | haggle |

haiku
hail (ice)

| hail | hale (robust) |

hailstone
hailstorm
hair (head)

| hair | hare (animal) |
| hair | heir (inherit) |

hairdo, -dos
hairdresser
hairline
hairpiece
hairpin
hairspring
hair-trigger
hairy, -rier, -riest
haka
hake, hake, hakes
hakea

| halcion | halcyon |

halcyon
hale, haler, halest (robust)

hale	hail (ice)
haleluya	hallelujah
halestone	hailstone
halestorm	hailstorm

half
half-back
half-baked
half-blood
half-breed
half-brother
half-caste
half-cock
half-forward
half-hearted, -ly
half-life
half-mast
half-measure

half-mesure	half-measure
half-moon	
half-sister	
half-time	
half-truth	
halfway	
halfway house	
halfwit	
halibut, -buts	
halilooya	hallelujah
halitosis	
hall (room)	
hall	haul (carry)
hallelujah	
halleluyah	hallelujah
hallmark	
hallo (greet)	
hallow, -ed, -ing (holy)	
Halloween	
hallucinate, -nated, -nating	
hallucination	
hallucinogen	
halmark	hallmark
halo, -loes, -los (light)	
halo	hallo (greet)
halo	hallow (holy)
halogen	
Haloween	Halloween
halsiun	halcyon
halt, -ed, -ing	
halter	
halusinate	hallucinate
halusinogen	hallucinogen
halve, -ed, -ing	
halyard	
halyerd	halyard
ham, hammed, hamming	
hamburger	
hamer	hammer
ham-fisted	
hamlet	
hammer, -ed, -ing	
hammerhead	
hammock	
hamper, -ered, -ering	
hamster	
hamstring, -strung, -stringing	

hand, handed, handing	
handbag	
handball	
handbill	
handbook	
handbrake	
handclap, -clapped, -clapping	
handcuff, -cuffed, -cuffing	
handey	handy
handeywork	handiwork
handicap, -capped, -capping	
handicraft	
handie	handy
handiwork	
handkerchief, -chiefs, -chieves	
handle, -dled, -dling	
handlebar	
handler	
handmade (article)	
handmaid (servant)	
hand-me-down	
handout	
hand-pick, -picked, -picking	
handpiece	
handrail	
handriting	handwriting
handset	
handshake	
handsome, -somer, -somest (fine)	
handspring	
handstand	
hand-to-mouth	
handul	handle
handwriting	
handy, -dier, -diest	
handyman	
hang, hung or hanged, hanging	
hangar (shed)	
hangar	hanger (clothes)
hangdog	
hanger (clothes)	
hanger	hangar (shed)
hanger-on, hangers-on	
hang-glider	
hangi	
hangkerchief	handkerchief

hangman	hardnose
hangover	hard-pressed
hang-up	hardship
hank	hardtop
hanker, -ed, -ing	hardware
hankerchief — handkerchief	hardwear — hardware
hankie	hardwood
hankuff — handcuff	hardy, hardier, hardiest
hanky, hankies	hare (animal)
hanky-panky	hare — hair (head)
Hansard	hare — heir (inherit)
hansom (cab)	harebrained
hansom — handsome (fine)	harelip
	harem
hansum — handsome	harico — haricot
hapen — happen	haricot
haphazard, -ly	hark, -ed, -ing
hapie — happy	harlot
hapless, -ly	harm, -ed, -ing
happen, -ened, -ening	harmonic
happily	harmonica
happy, happier, happiest	harmonious, -ly
happy-go-lucky	harmonise, -nised, -nising
hapy — happy	harmonium
harang — harangue	harmonius — harmonious
harangue, -rangued, -ranguing	harmony, -nies
haras — harass	harness, -ed, -ing
harass, -ed, -ing	harow — harrow
harassment	harp, -ed, -ing
harber — harbour	harpoon
harbinger	harpsichord
harbour, -ed, -ing	harpsicord — harpsichord
hard, -ly	harpy
hardback	harrier
hard-bitten	harrow, -ed, -ing
hardboard	harry, -ried, -rying
hard-core	harsh, -ly
hard-court	hart (deer)
harden, -ed, -ing	hart — heart (body)
hard-hearted, -ly	
hardie — hardy	For all other **hart**- words, look under **heart**-.
hard-hit	
hardihood	harum-scarum
hardiness	harve — halve
hardlie — hardly	harvest, -ed, -ing
hardline	harvester
hardness	harvist — harvest

hary	hairy
has-been	
hasen	hasten
hash, -ed, -ing	
hashish	
hasnt	hasn't
hasock	hassock
hasp	
hassel	hassle
hassle, -led, -ling	
hassock	
haste, -tily	
hasten, -ed, -ing	
hasty, hastier, hastiest	
hatch, -ed, -ing	
hatchback	
hatcherey	hatchery
hatchery, -eries	
hatchet	
hatchway	
hate, -ed, -ing	
hateful, -ly	
hatred	
hatrid	hatred
hatstand	
hatter	
hat-trick	
haughty, -tier, -tiest	
haul, -ed, -ing (carry)	
haul	hall (room)
haulage	
haulier	
haulige	haulage
haunch	
haunt, -ed, -ing	
haute cuisine	
hav	have
have	
haven	
haven't (have not)	
havent	haven't
haversack	
havoc, -ocked, -ocking	
hawk, -ed, -ing	
hawker	
hawl	haul

hawlidge	haulage
hawlige	haulage
hawlier	haulier
hawnch	haunch
hawnet	hornet
hawnt	haunt
hawse (ship)	
hawse	horse (animal)
hawser	
hawthorn	
hawticulcher	horticulture
hawticulture	horticulture
hawtie	haughty
hawty	haughty
hay (grass)	
hay	hey (cry)
hayday	heyday
hayfever	
haystack	
haywire	
hazard	
hazardous, -ly	
haze, hazed, hazing	
hazel	
hazerd	hazard
head, -ed, -ing	
headache	
headcount, -ed, -ing	
headdress	
header	
headfirst	
headfone	headphone
head-hunting	
headlamp	
headland	
headlight	
headline, -lined, -lining	
headlite	headlight
headlong	
headman	
headmaster	
headmistress	
head-on	
headphone	
headquarters	
headset	
headshrinker	

headspring
headstand
head start
headstone
headstream
headstrong
headwaters
headway
headwind
headword
heady, -dier, -diest
heal (health)

| heal | heel (shoe) |

health
healthy, -thier, -thiest
heap, -ed, -ing
hear, heard, hearing (listen)

| hear | here (place) |

heard (listen)

| heard | herd (animals) |

hearer
hearing aid
hearsay
hearse
heart (body)
heartache
heart attack
heartbeat
heartbreak
heartbroken, -ly
heartburn
hearten, -ed, -ing
heartfelt
hearth
heartless, -ly
heart-rending, -ly
heartstring
heart-throb
hearty, -tily
heat, -ed, -ing
heater
heath
heathen, -then, -thens
heather
heatwave
heave, -ed, -ing
heave-ho

heaven, -ly
heavy, -ily
heavy-duty
heavy-handed, -ly
heavy-hearted, -ly
heavy-laden
heavyweight
Hebrew

| Hebroo | Hebrew |

heck
heckle, -led, -ling
hectare
hectic, -ally
hector, -ed, -ing
he'd (he would)

| hed | head (body) |
| hed | he'd (he would) |

hedge, hedged, hedging
hedgehog
hedonism
heed, -ed, -ing
heedless, -ly
heehaw
heel (shoe)

| heel | heal (health) |

heeler

heematology	haematology
heemoglobin	haemoglobin
heemophilia	haemophilia
heep	heap
heer	hear (listen)
heer	here (place)
heet	heat
heeth	heath
hefer	heifer
heftie	hefty

heft, -ed, -ing
hefty, -tier, -tiest

| hege | hedge |

hegemony, -nies
heifer
height
heighten, -ed, -ing

| heighth | height |

heinous, -ly

| heinus | heinous |

heir (inherit)

heir	hair (head)	hena	henna
heir	here (place)	hence	
heir apparent, heirs apparent		henchman, -men	
heiress		henge	
heirloom		henna	
heist, -ed, -ing		henpeck, -pecked, -pecking	
heith	height	hens	hence
hel	hell	henus	heinous
held		hepatic	
helicopter		hepatitis	
heliograf	heliograph	heptagon	
heliograph		herald, -ed, -ing	
heliotrope		heraldic, -ally	
helipad		heraldrey	heraldry
heliport		heraldry, -dries	
helium		herb	
hell		herbaceous	
he'll (he will)		herbage	
hell	he'll	herbalist	
hell-bent		herbashus	herbaceous
hellcat		herbicide	
Hellenic		herbiside	herbicide
hellfire		herbivore	
hello, -los		herbivorous	
hello, -loed, -loing		herbivorus	herbivorous
hell's angel		herculean	
helm		herd (animals)	
helmet		herd	heard (listen)
helmsman, -men		herdsman, -men	
helo	hello	here (place)	
helot		here	hear (listen)
help, -ed, -ing		hereafter	
helpless, -ly		hereby	
helpmate		hereditary	
helter-skelter		hereditey	heredity
helth	health	hereditrey	hereditary
helthy	healthy	heredity, -ties	
hemerige	haemorrhage	Hereford	
hemeroid	haemorrhoid	herein	
hem, hemmed, hemming		hereof	
hemisfare	hemisphere	heresay	hearsay
hemisfear	hemisphere	heresie	heresy
hemisphere		heresy, -sies	
hemlock		heretic	
hemp		hereto	
hemstitch, -stitched, -stitching		hereunder	
hen		hereupon	

herewith
   hering — herring
heritable, -ly
heritage
   heritige — heritage
   herl — hurl
   hermafrodite — hermaphrodite
hermaphrodite
hermaphroditism
   hermatage — hermitage
hermetic
hermetical, -ly
hermit
hermitage
   hermitige — hermitage
hernia, -nias
hero, -roes
heroic
heroical, -ly
   heroicle — heroical
heroin (drug)
heroine (female hero)
heroism
heron
hero-worship, -shipped, -shipping
   herpeas — herpes
herpes
herring, -rings, -ring
herringbone
hers
   herse — hearse
herself
   hert — hurt
   hertle — hurtle
   hertul — hurtle
hertz
he's (he is, or he has)
   hes — he's
   hesian — hessian
hesitancy
   hesitansey — hesitancy
hesitant, -ly
hesitate, -tated, -tating
hesitation
hessian
heterogeneity
heterogeneous, -ly

   heterogenius — heterogeneous
heterosexual, -ly
   hethen — heathen
   hether — heather
het-up
heuristic, -ally
   heve — heave
   heven — heaven
   hevenly — heavenly
   hevie — heavy
   hevily — heavily
   heviwait — heavyweight
   hevy — heavy
hew, hewed, hewn, hewing (cut)
   hew — hue (colour)
hex
hexagon
hexagonal, -ly
hexameter
hey (cry)
   hey — hay (grass)
heyday

For other **hi**-words, look
under **hy**-.

---

hi (cry)
   hi — high (up)
   hiasinth — hyacinth
hiatus, -tuses
hiatus hernia
hibernate, -nated, -nating
hibiscus
   hibrid — hybrid
hiccup, -ed, -ing
   hich — hitch
   hichhike — hitchhike
hick
hickory, -ries
   hicup — hiccup
hidden
hide, hid, hiding
hideaway
hidebound
hideous, -ly
hide-out
   hidius — hideous
hidy-hole

hier	hire	hind	
hierarchy, -chies		hinder, -ed, -ing	
hierarkey	hierarchy	hinderanse	hindrance
hieroglific	hieroglyphic	Hindoo, -doos	
hieroglyphic, -ally		Hindooism	
hi-fi		hindquarter	
high, -ly		hindrance	
highborn		hindranse	hindrance
highbrow		hindsight	
high-class		hindsite	hindsight
higher (up)		Hindu	
higher	hire (rent)	Hinduism	
highfalutin		hiness	highness
high-fidelity		hinge, -ed, -ing	
high-grade		hint, -ed, -ing	
high-handed, -ly		hinterland	
highland		hip, hipped, hipping	
highlight		hipbath	
highly-wrought		hipie	hippie
high-minded, -ly		hipopotamus	hippopotamus
highness		hippie, -ies	
high-pitched		Hippocratic oath	
high-powered		hippopotamus, -muses, -mi	
high-pressure		hipster	
high-rise		hipy	hippie
high-speed		hire, hired, hiring (rent)	
high-spirited		hire	higher (up)
hight	height	hireling	
high-tension		hire-purchase	
highway		hiroglific	hieroglyphic
highwayman, -men		hiss, -ed, -ing	
hijack, -ed, -ing		histerey	history
hike, -ed, -ing		histeria	hysteria
hil	hill	histogram	
hiland	highland	historian	
hilarious, -ly		historic	
hilarius	hilarious	historiography	
hilight	highlight	history, -ries	
hilite	highlight	histrey	history
hill		histrionic, -ally	
hillbilly, -lies		hit, hit, hitting	
hillock		hitch, -ed, -ing	
hilly, hillier, hilliest		hitchhike, -hiked, -hiking	
hilt		hite	height
him (he)		hither	
him	hymn (song)	hitherto	
himself		hive, -ed, -ing	

hiway	highway

> For other **hi-** words,
> look under **hy-**.

ho	hoe
hoaks	hoax

hoard, -ed, -ing (gather)

hoard	horde (mob)

hoarding

hoare	whore

hoarse, hoarser, hoarsest (voice)

hoarse	hawse (ship)
hoarse	horse (animal)

hoary, hoarier, hoariest (old)
hoax, -ed, -ing
hob

hobbel	hobble

hobble, -bled, -bling
hobby, -bies
hobbyhorse

hobie	hobby

hobnail
hobnob, -nobbed, -nobbing
hobo, -bos, -boes

hochpoch	hotchpotch

hock, -ed, -ing
hockey

hockie	hockey

hocus-pocus, -cussed, -cussing
hod
hoe, hoed, hoeing (tool)

hoes	hose (water)

hog, hogged, hogging
hogget
hogshead

hogshed	hogshead

hogwash
hoi polloi
hoist, -ed, -ing

hokem	hokum

hokey pokey
hokum
hold, held, holding
holdfast
hold-up
hole, holed, holing (opening)

hole	whole (all)

holey	wholly

holiday

holie	holly (plant)
holie	holy (saint)
holie	wholly (all)
holihock	hollyhock

holiness
holland
holler, -ed, -ing (shout)
hollow, -ly (hole)
holly, -lies (plant)

holly	holy (saint)
holly	wholly (all)

hollyhock
holocaust

holocost	holocaust
holow	hollow

holster
holus-bolus
holy, -lier, -liest (saint)

holy	holly (plant)
holy	wholly (all)

homage
homburg
home, -ed, -ing
home-brew
homeland
homely, -lier, -liest
homeopathy
homesick
homespun
homestead
homeward
homework
homicide

homige	homage
homiley	homily

homily, -lies

homiopathy	homeopathy
homiside	homicide

homogeneous, -ly
homogenise, -nised, -nising

homogenius	homogeneous
homonim	homonym

homonym
homophone
Homo sapiens

homoseksual	homosexual	hope, hoped, hoping	
homoseksuality	homosexuality	hopeful	
homosexual		hopefull	hopeful
homosexuality		hopeless, -ly	
hone, honed, honing		hopper	
honest, -ly		hopping-mouse	
honesty		hopsack	
honey, honeys		hopscotch	
honeybee		horde, horded, hording (animals)	
honeycomb		horde	hoard (gather)
honeydew		hore	whore
honeyeater		horendus	horrendous
honeymoon		horer	horror
honeysuckle		horible	horrible
hongi		horid	horrid
honie	honey	horific	horrific
honk,-ed, -ing		horify	horrify
honorarium, -rariums, -raria		horizon	
honorary		horizontal, -ly	
honorific, -ally		hormone	
honour, -ed, -ing		horn, -ed, -ing	
honourable, -bly		hornbill	
hony	honey	hornpipe	
hood, -ed, -ing		horn-rimmed	
hoodlum		horny, -nier, -niest	
hoodwink, -ed, -ing		horology	
hoof, hoofs, hooves		horor	horror
hook, -ed, -ing		horoscope	
hookah		horrendous, -ly	
hooker		horrible, -bly	
hookie	hooky	horribul	horrible
hook-up		horrid, -ly	
hookworm		horrific	
hooky		horrify, -fied, -fying	
hoola-hoola	hula-hula	horror	
hooligan		hors d'oeuvre	
hoop		horse, horses (animal)	
hooping coff	whooping cough	horse, horsed, horsing	
		horse	hawse (ship)
hoopla		horse	hoarse (voice)
hooray		horseflesh	
hooroo		horseplay	
hoot, -ed, -ing		horsepower	
hooter		horserace	
hoover		horseradish	
hop, hopped, hopping		horseshoe, -shoed, -shoeing	
		horsy, -sier, -siest	

hortative, -ly
hortatory
  horthorn   hawthorn
  horticulcher   horticulture
horticulture
  hortie   haughty
hose, hosed, hosing (water)
  hose   hoes (tools)
hosiery
hospice
hospitable, -bly
  hospitabul   hospitable
hospital
hospitality, -ties
host, -ed, -ing
hostage
  hostaple   hospital
hostel
hostess
  hostige   hostage
hostile, -ly
hostility, -ties
hot, hotted, hotting
hot, hotter, hottest
hot-blooded
hotchpotch
hotel
hotelier
  hoter   hotter
  hotest   hottest
hotfoot
hothead
hot-headed, -ly
  hothed   hothead
  hotheded   hotheaded
hothouse
hotplate
hotpot
hot rod
hot seat
hot-shot
hot-water bottle
hound, -ed, -ing
hound's-tooth
hour (time)
  hour   our
hourglass

houri, -ris
hourly
house, houses
house, housed, housing
houseboat
housebreaker
housebroken
housecoat
housefly, -flies
household
housekeeper
housemaid
House of Commons
houseproud
house-train
house-warming
housewife, -wives
housey-housey
housie-housie
housing
hovel, -elled, -elling
hover, -ed, -ing
hovercraft
how
however
howl, -ed, -ing
howler
  hownd   hound
  howse   house
howsoever
hoy
hoyden
  hu   hew (cut)
  hu   hue (colour)
hubbub
  huch   hutch
huckster
huddle, -dled, -dling
hue (colour)
  hue   hew (cut)
  huf   huff
huff, -ed, -ing
hug, hugged, hugging
huge, huger, hugest
  hul   hull
hula-hula
  hulabaloo   hullabaloo

hulk
hull,-ed, -ing
hullabaloo
hullo
hum, hummed, humming
human
humane, -ly
humanism
humanist
humanitarian
humanity, -ties
humanly
humanoid
humble, -bled, -bling
humble, -bler, -blest
humble pie
humbug, -bugged, -bugging
humbul   humble
humdinger
humdrum
humer   humour
humerist   humorist
humerus, -meri (bone)
humerus   humorous (funny)
humid, -ly
humidifier
humidity
humiliate, -ated, -ating
humiliation
humility, -ties
hummingbird
hummock
humock   hummock
humorist
humorous, -ly (funny)
humorous   humerus (bone)
humour, -ed, -ing
hump, -ed, -ing
humpback
humpy, -pier, -piest
humus
hunch, -ed, -ing
hunchback
hundred, -dreds
hundredfold
hundredth

huney   honey
hunger
hungrie   hungry
hungry, -grier, -griest
hunie   honey
hunk
hunt, -ed, -ing
hunter
huntress
huntsman, -men
Huon pine
huray   hurray
hurd   heard (listen)
hurd   herd (animals)
hurdiegurdie   hurdy-gurdy
hurdle, -dled, -dling
hurdul   hurdle
hurdy-gurdy, -dies
huricane   hurricane
hurie   hurry
hurl, -ed, -ing
hurlie-burlie   hurly-burly
hurly-burly, -burlies
hurmit   hermit
hurnia   hernia
hurray
hurricane
hurry, -ried, -rying
hurse   hearse
hurt, hurt, hurting
hurtel   hurtle
hurtle, -tled, -tling
hurtul   hurtle
hurtz   hertz
hury   hurry
husband
husbandry
hush, -ed, -ing
husie   hussy
husk
huskie   husky
husky, -kier, -kiest (hoarse)
husky, -kies (dog)
hussar
hussel   hustle
hussey   hussy
hussul   hustle

hussy, -sies
hustings
hustle, -tled, -tling
hut, hutted, hutting
hutch
hutkeeper
hyacinth
hybrid
hydatids
hydra, -dras, -drae
hydrangea
   hydranja   hydrangea
hydrant
hydrate, -drated, -drating
hydration
hydraulic, -ally
hydrocarbon
hydrochloric acid
hydro-electric
   hydrofobia   hydrophobia
hydrofoil
hydrogen
hydrologist
hydrology
   hydrolic   hydraulic
hydrolysis, -ses
hydrometer
hydroplane, -planed, -planing
hydroponics
hydrous
hydroxide
hyena
   hygene   hygiene
hygiene
hygienic, -ally
hygroscopic
   hym   hymn
hymen
hymn (song)
hymnal
hype, hyped, hyping
hyperactive
hyperbola, -las (curve)
hyperbole (overstatement)
hypersensitive
hypertension
hyphen

hyphenate, -nated, -nating
hypnosis, -ses
hypnotherapy
hypnotise, -tised, -tising
hypnotism
hypo
hypochondria
hypocrisy, -sies
hypocrite
hypodermic
hypodermic syringe
hypotenuse
hypothesis, -ses
hypothesise, -sised, -sising
hypothetical, -ly
hysterectomy, -mies
hysteria
hysteric
hysterical, -ly

Ii

ibis
ice, iced, icing
iceberg
icebound
icebox
icebreaker
ice-cream
icepack
icepick
ich — itch
icicle
iclesiastic — ecclesiastic
iclipse — eclipse
icon, icons
iconoclast
iconomey — economy
iconomist — economist
icy, icier, iciest
idea
ideal, -ly
idealise, -ised, -ising
idealism
idem
identical, -ly
identicul — identical
identification
identify, -fied, -fying
identikit
identity, -ties
ideology, -gies
iderdown — eiderdown
ides
idilic — idyllic
idill — idyll
idiocy, -cies
idiologey — ideology
idiom
idiomatic, -ally

idiosincrasy — idiosyncrasy
idiosyncrasy, -sies
idiot
idium — idiom
idle, idled, idling (not busy)
idle — idol (statue)
idler
idol (statue)
idol — idle (not busy)
idolatry, -tries
idolise, -lised, -lising
idyl — idyll
idyll
idyllic, -ally
iface — efface
ifect — effect
ifel — Eiffel
ifeminite — effeminate
ificiency — efficiency
igalitarian — egalitarian
igloo, -loos
igneous
ignishun — ignition
ignite, -nited, -niting
ignition
ignition coil
ignius — igneous
ignoble, -bly
ignominy, -minies
ignor — ignore
ignoramus, -muses
ignorant, -ly
ignore, -nored, -noring
iguana
iguarna — iguana
ijaculation — ejaculation
ijection — ejection
ikon, ikons
ikuip — equip
ikwivocal — equivocal
ikwivocate — equivocate
il — I'll (I will)
il — ill (sick)
ilaberate — elaborate
iland — island
ilapse — elapse
ilation — elation

ilastic	elastic
ilate	elate
ile	aisle (passage)
Ile	I'll (I will)
ile	isle (island)
ilect	elect
ilection	election
ilectorate	electorate
ilectrocute	electrocute
ilectronic	electronic
ilegal	illegal
ilegibul	illegible
ilegitimate	illegitimate
ileven	eleven
ilicit	elicit
ilicit	illicit
ilikser	elixir
iliminate	eliminate
ilimination	elimination
ilipse	ellipse
iliptic	elliptic
ilisit	elicit
ilisit	illicit
iliteracy	illiteracy
iliterate	illiterate
ilixir	elixir

ilk

I'll (I will)

ill, worse, worst (sick)

ill-advised, -ly

ill-assorted

ill-bred

ill-defined

illegal, -ly

illegible, -bly

illegibul	illegible

illegitimate, -ly

ill-fated

ill-gotten

ill health

illiberal, -ly

illicit, -ly (unlawful)

illicit	elicit (evoke)

illiteracy

illiterate

ill-mannered, -ly

ill-natured, -ly

illness

illogical, -ly

ill-treat, -ed, -ing

illuminate, -nated, -nating

illumination

illumine, -mined, -mining

ill-use, -used, -using

illusion (deception)

illusion	allusion (brief reference)
illusion	elusion (evade)

illusive (deceptive)

illusive	allusive
illusive	elusive

illusory

illustrate, -strated, -strating

illustration

illustrative, -ly

illustrator

illustrious, -ly

ill will

ilogical	illogical
ilope	elope
ilucidate	elucidate
ilude	elude
iluminate	illuminate
ilumination	illumination
ilusidate	elucidate
ilusion	allusion
ilusion	elusion
ilusion	illusion
ilusive	allusive
ilusive	elusive
ilusive	illusive
ilustrate	illustrate
ilustration	illustration
ilustrator	illustrator
ilustrius	illustrious

I'm (I am)

Im	I'm
imaciate	emaciate
imaculate	immaculate

image, -aged, -aging

imagery, -ries

imagin	imagine

imaginary, -ries

imagination

imaginative
imagine, -ined, -ining
  imancipate — emancipate
  imansipation — emancipation
  imashiate — emaciate
  imaterial — immaterial
  imature — immature
  imaturity — immaturity
imbalance
  imbalanse — imbalance
  imbarrass — embarrass
imbecile, -ly
  imbeseal — imbecile
imbibe, -bibed, -bibing
imbroglio, -os
imbue, -bued, -buing
  imerge — emerge
  imergence — emergence
  imergency — emergency
  imergent — emergent
  imetic — emetic
  imission — emission
  imit — emit

> For other im- words, look
> under imm-.

imitate, -tated, -tating
imitation
immaculate, -ly
immanent (inherent)
  immanent — eminent (known)
  immanent — imminent (near)
immaterial, -ly
immature
immeasurable, -bly
immediate, -ly
immemorial, -ly
immense, -ly
immerse, -mersed, -mersing
  immershun — immersion
immersion
  immesurable — immeasurable
immigrant
immigrate, -grated, -grating
imminent (near)

imminent — eminent (known)
imminent — immanent (inherent)
immobile
immobility
immoderate, -ly
immodest, -ly
immolate, -lated, -lating
immoral, -ly
immortal, -ly
immortalise, -lised, -lising
immortality, -ties
immovable, -bly
immune, -ly
immunise, -nised, -nising
immunology
immure, -mured, -muring
immutable, -bly
  imolient — emollient
  imolument — emolument
  imoshen — emotion
  imoshun — emotion
  imoshunal — emotional
  imotion — emotion
  imotive — emotive
imp
impact, -ed, -ing
impair, -ed, -ing
impale, -paled, -paling
impalpable, -bly
  impare — impair
  imparshal — impartial
impart, -ed, -ing
impartial, -ly
  impasable — impassable
  impashent — impatient
  impasioned — impassioned
  impasive — impassive
impassable, -bly
impasse
impassioned, -ly
impassive, -ly
impatient, -ly
impeach, -ed, -ing
  impecabul — impeccable
impeccable, -bly

impecunious, -ly
impecunius   impecunious
impede, -peded, -peding
impediment, -ary
impeech   impeach
impel, -pelled, -pelling
impenetrable, -bly
impenge   impinge
imperative, -ly
imperceptibel   imperceptible
imperceptible, -bly
imperfect, -ly
imperial, -ly
imperialism
imperil, -rilled, -rilling
imperious, -ly
imperius   imperious
impermeable, -bly
impermeabul   impermeable
imperseptibul   imperceptible
impersonal, -ly
impersonate, -nated, -nating
impertinence
impertinense   impertinence
imperturbable, -bly
impervious, -ly
impervius   impervious
impetuous, -ly
impetus, -tuses
impiety, -ties
impinge, -pinged, -pinging
impious, -ly
impish, -ly
impius   impious
implacable, -bly
implacabul   implacable
implant, -ed, -ing
implausible, -bly
implausibul   implausible
implement, -ed, -ing
implicate, -cated, -cating
implication
implicit, -ly
implie   imply
implied
implisit   implicit
implode, -ploded, -ploding

implore, -plored, -ploring
imply, -plied, -plying
impolite, -ly
impolitic, -ly
import, -ed, -ing
importance
importanse   importance
important, -ly
importunate, -ly
importune, -tuned, -tuning
imposcher   imposture
impose, -posed, -posing
imposibul   impossible
imposishun   imposition
imposition
impossible, -bly
imposter   impostor
impostor
imposture
impotence
impotent, -ly
impound, -ed, -ing
impoverish, -ed, -ing
impracticability
impracticable, -bly
impracticabul   impracticable
impractical, -ly
imprecate, -cated, -cating
imprecise, -ly
impregnable, -bly
impregnabul   impregnable
impregnate, -nated, -nating
impres   impress
impresario, -os
impreshun   impression
impreshunable   impressionable
impreshunism   impressionism
impresise   imprecise
impresive   impressive
impress, -pressed, -pressing
impression
impressionable, -bly
impressionism
impressive, -ly
imprimatur
imprint, -ed, -ing
imprison, -ed, -ing

improbable, -bly
impromptu
improper, -ly
impropriety, -ties
improve, -proved, -proving
improvement
improvident, -ly
improvise, -vised, -vising
imprudent, -ly
   impruve   improve
impudent, -ly
impugn, -ed, -ing
impulse
   impune   impugn
impunity
impure, impurer, impurist
impute, -puted, -puting
   imulshun   emulsion
   imune   immune
   imunologey   immunology
   imurge   emerge
in
   in   inn (hotel)
inability
   in absenshia   in absentia
in absentia
   inaccessabul   inaccessible
inaccessible, -bly
inaccuracy, -cies
inactive, -ly
   inacuracy   inaccuracy
   inacurasey   inaccuracy
   inadekwat   inadequate
inadequate, -ly
inadvertent, -ly
inalienable, -bly
   inalienabul   inalienable
inane, -ly
inanimate, -ly
inappreciable, -bly
   inappreciabul   inappreciable
inappropriate, -ly
   inapropriate   inappropriate
inapt, -ly
inaptitude
inarticulate, -ly
inasmuch as

   inate   innate
   inatentive   inattentive
inattentive, -ly
inaugural
inaugurate, -rated, -rating
inauspicious, -ly
   inawmus   enormous
   inawspishus   inauspicious
inborn
inbreed, -bred, -breeding
incalculable, -bly
in camera
incandescence
incandescent, -ly
   incandesence   incandescence
incantation
incapable, -bly
   incapabul   incapable
incapacitate, -tated, -tating
incapacity, -ties
   incapasitate   incapacitate
   incapasitey   incapacity
incarcerate, -rated, -rating
incarnate, -nated, -nating
   incarserate   incarcerate
incendiary, -aries
incense (perfume)
incense, -censed, -censing (angry)
incentive
inception
incessant, -ly
   incessent   incessant
incest
incestuous, -ly
inch, -ed, -ing
incidence
incident
incidental, -ly
incinerate, -rated, -rating
incinerator
incipient, -ly
incise, -cised, -cising
incision
incisive, -ly
incisor
incite, -cited, -citing (urge)
   incite   insight (see)

incivility, -ties
inclement, -ly
inclination
incline, -clined, -clining
inclose   enclose
include, -cluded, -cluding
inclusion
inclusive, -ly
incognito, -tos
incoherent, -ly
income
incommensurable, -bly
incommensurate, -ly
incommode, -moded, -moding
incommodity, -ties
incommunicability
incommunicable, -bly
incommunicado
incommunicative, -ly
incomparable, -bly
incompatible, -bly
incompatibul   incompatible
incompetent, -ly
incomplete, -ly
incomprehensible, -bly
incomprehension
incomunicado   incommunicado
inconceivable, -bly
inconcievable   inconceivable
inconclusive, -ly
incongruous, -ly
incongruus   incongruous
inconseavable   inconceivable
inconsequent, -ly
inconsequential, -ly
inconsiderate, -ly
inconsistant   inconsistent
inconsistent, -ly
inconsolable, -bly
inconsolabul   inconsolable
inconspicuous, -ly
inconstant, -ly
incontestable, -bly
incontestabul   incontestable
incontinent, -ly
incontrovertible, -bly
inconvenience, -ienced, -iencing

inconvenient, -ly
incorect   incorrect
incorigibul   incorrigible
incorporate, -rated, -rating
incorporation
incorrect, -ly
incorrigible, -bly
incorrupt, -ly
incorruptible, -bly
increase, -creased, -creasing
incredible, -bly
incredibul   incredible
incredulity
incredulous, -ly
incredulus   incredulous
increment
incremental
increse   increase
incriminate, -nated, -nating
incubate, -bated, -bating
incubator
inculcate, -cated, -cating
incum   income
incumbent, -ly
incumbrance
incur, -curred, -curring
incurable, -bly
incurabul   incurable
incurshun   incursion
incursion
indebted
indecent, -ly
indecipherable
indecishun   indecision
indecision
indecisive, -ly
indeclinable
indeclinabul   indeclinable
indecorous, -ly
indecorus   indecorous
indeed
indefatigable, -bly
indefatigabul   indefatigable
indefeasible, -bly
indefeasibul   indefeasible
indefensible, -bly
indefensibul   indefensible

indefinable, -bly
   indefinabul — indefinable
indefinite, -ly
   indeks — index
indelible, -bly
   indelibul — indelible
indelicate, -ly
   indemnifie — indemnify
indemnify, -fied, -fying
indemnity, -ties
   indencher — indenture
indent, -ed, -ing
indenture, -tured, -turing
independent, -ly
in-depth
indescribable, -bly
   indescribabul — indescribable
   indesent — indecent
   indesiferable — indecipherable
   indespensable — indispensable
indestructible, -bly
   indestructibul — indestructible
   indeted — indebted
indeterminate, -ly
index, -dexes, -dices
indexation
Indian
indiarubber
indicate, -cated, -cating
indicative, -ly
indicator
indices
indict, -ed, -ing
indictment
   indiferent — indifferent
indifferent, -ly
indigenous, -ly
indigent, -ly
indigestible, -bly
   indigestibul — indigestible
indigestion
indignant, -ly
indignation
indignity, -ties
indigo, -gos
   indipendent — independent
indirect, -ly

indiscreet, -ly
   indiscreshun — indiscretion
   indiscrete — indiscreet
indiscretion
indiscriminate, -ly
   indisishun — indecision
   indisisive — indecisive
   indisoluble — indissoluble
indispensable, -bly
   indispensabul — indispensable
indisposed
indisposition
indisputable, -bly
   indisputabul — indisputable
indissoluble, -bly
indistinct, -ly
indistinguishable, -bly
indite, -dited, -diting (write)
   indite — indict (accuse)
individual, -ly
individualism
individualist
individuality, -ties
indivisible, -bly
   indivisibul — indivisible
indoctrinate, -nated, -nating
indolent, -ly
indomitable, -bly
   indomitabul — indomitable
indoor
indubitable, -bly
   indubitabul — indubitable
induce, -duced, -ducing
   inducshion — induction
   inducshun — induction
induct, -ed, -ing
induction
inductive, -ly
inductor
indulge, -dulged, -dulging
indulgence
   indulgense — indulgence
indulgent, -ly
   industrey — industry
industrial, -ly
industrialise, -lised, -lising
industrialism

industrialist
industrious, -ly
  industrius — industrious
industry, -tries
inebriate, -ated, -ating
inebriation
inedible
  inedibul — inedible
  inefable — ineffable
  inefective — ineffective
  inefectual — ineffectual
ineffable, -bly
ineffective, -ly
ineffectual, -ly
inefficient, -ly

> For ineks- words, look
> under inex-.

inelegant, -ly
ineligible, -bly
  ineligibul — ineligible
inept, -ly
inequality, -ties
inequitable, -bly
  inequitabul — inequitable
inequity, -ties
ineradicable, -bly
  ineradicabul — ineradicable
  inersha — inertia
inert, -ly
inertia
inescapable, -bly
  inescapabul — inescapable
  inesenshul — inessential
inessential, -ly
inestimable, -bly
  inestimabul — inestimable
inevitable, -bly
  inevitabul — inevitable
inexact, -ly
inexcusable, -bly
inexhaustible, -bly
inexorable, -bly
  inexorabul — inexorable
inexpedient, -ly
inexpensive, -ly
inexperienced

  inexperiense — inexperience
inexpert, -ly
inexplicable, -bly
inexplicit, -ly
inexpressible, -bly
in extremis
inextricable, -bly
  infalible — infallible
  infalibul — infallible
infallible, -bly
  infamey — infamy
infamous, -ly
  infamus — infamous
infamy, -mies
infancy, -cies
  infansey — infancy
infant
infanticide
  infantiside — infanticide
infantile
  infantrey — infantry
infantry
infatuate, -ated, -ating
infatuation
  infecshun — infection
infect, -ed, -ing
infection
infectious, -ly
infelicity, -ties
infer, -ferred, -ferring
inference
  inferense — inference
  inferier — inferior
inferior
inferiority complex
  inferm — infirm
  infermarey — infirmary
infernal, -ly
inferno, -nos
infertile
infest, -ed, -ing
infidel
infidelity, -ties
infighting
infiltrate, -trated, -trating
infinite, -ly
infinitesimal, -ly

infinitey | infinity
infinitive, -ly
infinity, -ties
infirior | inferior
infirm, -ly
infirmary, -ries
inflamabul | inflammable
inflamatry | inflammatory
inflame, -flamed, -flaming
inflammable, -bly
inflammation
inflammatory
inflatable
inflate, -flated, -flating
inflation
inflect, -ed, -ing
inflection
inflexible, -bly
inflict, -ed, -ing
infliction
inflow
influence, -enced, -encing
influense | influence
influenshul | influential
influential, -ly
influenza
influks | influx
inform, -ed, -ing
informal, -ly
informant
information
informer
infracshun | infraction
infraction
infra-red
infrastructure
infrekwency | infrequency
infrekwent | infrequent
infrequency
infrequent, -ly
infringe, -fringed, -fringing
infuriate, -ated, -ating
infurnal | infernal
infuse, -fused, -fusing
infusion
infusun | infusion
ingenious, -ly (clever)

ingenius | ingenious
ingenue
ingenuity, -ties
ingenuous, -ly (innocent)
ingenuus | ingenuous
ingest, -ed, -ing
ingestion
English | English
ingot
ingrain, -ed, -ing
ingrashiate | ingratiate
ingrate
ingratiate, -ated, -ating
ingratitude
ingrave | engrave
ingredient
ingress
in-groop | in-group
in-group
ingrown
inhabit, -ed, -ing
inhalant
inhalation
inhale, -haled, -haling
inhear | inhere
inhere, -hered, -hering
inherent, -ly
inherit, -ed, -ing
inheritance
inheritanse | inheritance
inhibishun | inhibition
inhibit, -ed, -ing
inhospitable, -bly
inhospitabul | inhospitable
inhospitality
inhuman, -ly
inhumane, -ly
inhumanity, -ties
inikwality | inequality
inikwity | iniquity
inikwitus | iniquitous
inimical, -ly
inimitable, -bly
inimitability
inimitabul | inimitable
inings | innings
iniquitey | iniquity

iniquitous, -ly		innards	
iniquitus	iniquitous	innate, -ly	
iniquity, -ties (sin)		inner	
iniquity	inequity	innerject	interject
	(unfair)	innermost	
inishal	initial	innings	
inishative	initiative	innkeeper	
inishiate	initiate	innocence	
initial, -ialled, -ialling		innocent, -ly	
initiate, -ated, -ating		innocuous, -ly	
initiation		innovate, -vated, -vating	
initiative		innovation	
inject, -ed, -ing		innovative, -ly	
injection		innovatory	
injenue	ingenue	innuendo, -dos	
injere	injure	innumerable, -bly	
in-joke		innumerate	
injudicious, -ly		inocent	innocent
injudishus	injudicious	inoculate, -lated, -lating	
injunction		inoculation	
injunkshun	injunction	inocuus	innocuous
injure, -jured, -juring		inofensive	inoffensive
injurey	injury	inoffensive, -ly	
injurius	injurious	inoperable, -bly	
injury, -ries		inoperative, -ly	
injustice		inoportune	inopportune
injustise	injustice	inopportune, -ly	
ink		inordible	inaudible
inkeeper	innkeeper	inordibul	inaudible
inkling		inordinate, -ly	
inkwest	inquest	inorganic, -ally	
inkwire	enquire	inorgural	inaugural
inkwisitive	inquisitive	inorgurate	inaugurate
inkwisitor	inquisitor	inormity	enormity
		inormous	enormous

For other ink- words,
look under **inc-**.

		inorspishus	inauspicious
inlade	inlaid	inosence	innocence
inland		inosent	innocent
in-law		inough	enough
inlay, -laid, -laying		inovate	innovate
inlet		in-patient	
in loco parentis		in-payshent	in-patient
inmate		input	
in memoriam		inquest	
inmost		inquietude	
inn (hotel)		inquire, -quired, -quiring	
		inquiry, -ries	

inquisitive, -ly	
inrage	enrage
inroad	
inrode	inroad
insalubrious, -ly	
insalubrius	insalubrious
insaine	insane
insane, -ly	
insanitary	
insanitey	insanity
insanirty	insanitary
insanity, -ties	
insatiable, -bly	
insayshabul	insatiable
inscribe, -scribed, -scribing	
inscription	
inscrutable, -bly	
inscrutability	
insect	
insecticide	
insectiside	insecticide
insecure, -ly	
insecurity, -ties	
inseminate, -nated, -nating	
insemination	
insendiary	incendiary
insensate, -ly	
insense	incense
insensible, -bly	
insensibility, -ties	
insensibul	insensible
insensitive, -ly	
insensitivity	
insentive	incentive
inseparable, -bly	
inseperabul	inseparable
inseprabul	inseparable
insepshun	inception
insert, -ed, -ing	
insertion	
insertitude	incertitude
in-service	
insesent	incessant
insest	incest
insestuous	incestuous
inset, -set, -setting	
inshoranse	insurance

inshore	ensure (certain)
inshore	insure (protect)
inshorense	insurance
inside	
insidense	incidence
insident	incident
insidentul	incidental
insidious, -ly	
insidius	insidious
insight, (see)	
insight	incite (urge)
insignia	
insignificance	
insignificant, -ly	
insincere, -ly	
insincerity, -ties	
insinerate	incinerate
insinerater	incinerator
insinsere	insincere
insinserity	insincerity
insinuate, -ated, -ating	
insipid, -ly	
insipient	incipient
insiser	inciser
insision	incision
insisive	incisive
insist, -ed, -ing	
insistence	
insistent, -ly	
insite	incite (urge)
insite	insight (see)
insivility	incivility
insobriety	
insofar	
insolence	
insolense	insolence
insolent, -ly	
insolubility	
insoluble, -bly	
insolubul	insoluble
insolvency	
insolvensy	insolvency
insolvent	
insomnia	
inspechun	inspection
inspect, -ed, -ing	
inspecter	inspector

inspection
inspector
inspiration
inspire, -spired, -spiring
instability
  instagate — instigate
  instal — install
install, -ed, -ing
  installment — instalment
instalment
instance, -stanced, -stancing
  instanse — instance
instant, -ly
instantaneous, -ly
  instantanius — instantaneous
  instatution — institution
instead
  insted — instead
instep
instigate, -gated, -gating
  instigater — instigator
instigation
instigator
  instil — instill
  instilashun — instillation
instill, -stilled, -stilling
instillation
instinct
instinctive, -ly
  institushen — institution
institute, -tuted, -tuting
institution
institutional, -ly
institutionalise, -lised, -lising
  instremunt — instrument
instruct, -ed, -ing
instruction
instructive, -ly
instrument
instrumental, -ly
instrumentalist
instrumentation
instrument panel
insubordinate, -ly
insubordination
  insubstanshul — insubstantial
insubstantial, -ly

  insue — ensue
insufferable, -bly
insufficiency
insufficient, -ly
  insuffishency — insufficiency
  insufrabul — insufferable
insular, -ly
insularity
insulate, -lated, -lating
insulation
insulin
insult, -ed, -ing
insuperable, -bly
  insuperabul — insuperable
insurance
  insuranse — insurance
insure, -sured, -suring
  insurecshun — insurrection
insurgence
insurgency
  insurgense — insurgence
insurgent
insurmountable, -bly
insurrection
  insurshun — insertion
  insurt — insert
intact
intaglio, intaglios, intagli
  intail — entail
intake
intangible, -bly
  intangibul — intangible
integer
integral, -ly
integrate, -grated, -grating
integrated circuit
integration
integrity
  intelect — intellect
  intelectual — intellectual
  inteligense — intelligence
  inteligensia — intelligentsia
  inteligent — intelligent
  inteligibul — intelligible
intellect
intellectual, -ly
intelligence

intelligent, -ly
intelligentsia
intemperance
   intemperanse   intemperance
intemperate, -ly
intend, -ed, -ing
intense, -ly
   intenshun   intention
intensify, -fied, -fying
intensive, -ly
intent, -ly
intention
intentional, -ly
inter, -terred, -terring
interact, -ed, -ing
interaction
inter alia
intercede, -ceded, -ceding
intercept, -ed, -ing
interception
interceptor
   interceshun   intercession
intercession
intercessor
interchange, -changed, -changing
interchangeable, -bly
intercom
intercontinental
   intercorse   intercourse
intercourse
interdependence
interdependency
interdependent, -ly
interdict
interdisciplinary
   interelate   interrelate
interest, -ed, -ing
interface, -faced, -facing
   interfear   interfere
interfere, -fered, -fering
interference
interfuse, -fused, -fusing
intergalactic
   interier   interior
interim
interior
interject, -ed, -ing

interjection
injector
interlace, -laced, -lacing
interline, -lined, -lining
interlock, -ed, -ing
   interloap   interlope
   interlood   interlude
interlope, -loped, -loping
interloper
interlude
   intermarie   intermarry
intermarry, -ried, -rying
intermediary, -aries
intermediate, -ly
interment
intermesh, -ed, -ing
intermezzo, -zos, -zi
interminable, -bly
   interminabul   interminable
   intermishun   intermission
intermission
intermittent, -ly
intern
internal, -ly
internal-combustion engine
internalise, -lised, -lising
   internashunal   international
international, -ly
internationale
internationalism
internecine
internee
   internisine   internecine
   interogate   interrogate
interpersonal, -ly
interplay, -ed, -ing
interpolate, -lated, -lating
interpose, -posed, -posing
interpret, -ed, -ing
interpretation
interpreter
interracial, -ly
interregnum, -nums
interrelate, -lated, -lating
interrogate, -gated, -gating
interrogation
interrogative, -ly

interrogator	
interrupt, -ed, -ing	
interruption	
intersect, -ed, -ing	
intersection	
intersede	intercede
intersepshun	interception
intersept	intercept
interseshun	intercession
intersperse, -spersed, -spersing	
interspurse	intersperse
interstate	
interstice, -tices	
intertwine, -twined, -twining	
interupshun	interruption
interurban	
interval	
interveiw	interview
intervene, -vened, -vening	
intervener	
intervenor	intervener
intervenshun	intervention
intervention	
interview, -ed, -ing	
interviewer	
intervue	interview
interweave, -woven, -weaving	
interweaver	
intestate	
intestine	
intice	entice
intiger	integer
intigral	integral
intigrate	integrate
intimacy, -cies	
intimasy	intimacy
intimate, -ly	
intimate, -mated, -mating	
intimation	
intimidate, -dated, -dating	
intimidation	
intimidator	
intoksicate	intoxicate
intolerable, -bly	
intolerabul	intolerable
intolerance	
intoleranse	intolerance

intolerant, -ly	
intonation	
intone, -toned, -toning	
in toto	
intoxicant	
intoxicate, -cated, -cating	
intoxication	
intractable, -bly	
intractabul	intractable
intransigence	
intransigency	
intransigense	intransigence
intransigensy	intransigency
intransigent, -ly	
intransitive, -ly	
intrastate	
intra-uterine device	
intravenous, -ly	
intravenus	intravenous
in-tray	
intreege	intrigue
intrepid, -ly	
intricacy, -cies	
intricasey	intricacy
intricate, -ly	
intrigue, -trigued, -triguing	
intriguer	
intrinsic, -ally	
introduce, -duced, -ducing	
introducshun	introduction
introduction	
introductory	
introduse	introduce
introode	intrude
introosive	intrusive
introspection	
introvert, -ly	
intrude, -truded, -truding	
intruder	
intrushun	intrusion
intrusion	
intrusive, -ly	
intrust	entrust
intuishun	intuition
intuition	
intuitive, -ly	
inturn	intern

inturnal	internal
inuendo	innuendo
inumerabul	innumerable
inumerate	enumerate
inumeration	enumeration
inunciate	enunciate

inundate, -dated, -dating
inundation

inunsiate	enunciate

inure, inured, inuring

inursha	inertia
inurt	inert

invade, -vaded, -vading
invalid, -ly
invalidate, -dated, -dating
invalidation
invaluable, -bly

invaluabul	invaluable
invaluble	invaluable

invariability
invariable, -bly

invariabul	invariable

invasion

invatation	invitation
invay	inveigh
invaygul	inveigle

invective, -ly
inveigh, -ed, -ing
inveigle, -gled, -gling

inveigul	inveigle
invenshun	invention

invent, -ed, -ing
invention
inventive, -ly
inventor
inventory, -tories

inventry	inventory

inverse, -ly

invershun	inversion

inversion
invert, -ed, -ing
invertebrate
invest, -ed, -ing

investagation	investigation
investichure	investiture

investigate, -gated, -gating
investigation

investigator
investiture
investment
inveterate

invidios	invidious

invidious, -ly
invidiousness

inviegh	inveigh
inviegle	inveigle

invigorate, -rated, -rating
invincible, -bly

invinsibul	invincible

inviolable, -bly

inviolabul	inviolable

inviolate, -ly
invisibility
invisible, -bly

invisibul	invisible

invitation
invite, -vited, -viting
in vitro
invocation
invoice, -voiced, -voicing

invoise	invoice

invoke, -voked, -voking
involuntary, -tarily

involuntrey	involuntary
involushun	involution

involution
involve, -volved, -volving
involvement
invulnerable, -bly

invulnerabul	invulnerable
inverce	inverse
invirt	invert

inward, -ly
inwardness
inwards

inwood	inward
inyure	inure
iodene	iodine

iodine
ion (atom)

ion	iron (metal)
ionesfere	ionosphere

ionise, -nised, -nising
ionosphere

iony	irony
iota	
IOU	
iradiate	irradiate
iradicate	eradicate
irascibility	
irascible, -bly	
irascibleness	
irascibul	irascible
irase	erase
irate, -ly	
irational	irrational
ire	

For other ir- words,
look under irr-.

iridesense	iridescence
iridesent	iridescent
iridescence	
iris, irises	
Irish	
irk (bore)	
irk	erk (rank)
irksome, -ly	
irksum	irksome
iron, -ed, -ing (metal)	
iron	ion (atom)
ironbark	
ironeus	erroneous
ironic, -ally	
ironmonger	
ironmongery	
ironware	
irony, -nies	
iroshun	erosion
irosion	erosion
irotic	erotic
irradiashun	irradiation
irradiate, -ated, -ating	
irradiation	
irrashionul	irrational
irrational, -ly	
irreconcilable, -bly	
irrecoverable, -bly	
irrecoverabul	irrecoverable
irredeemable, -bly	
irredeemabul	irredeemable

irreducibility	
irreducible, -bly	
irreducibul	irreducible
irrefutable, -bly	
irrefutabul	irrefutable
irregardless	
irregular, -ly	
irregularity, -ties	
irrelevance	
irrelevancy	
irrelevansey	irrelevancy
irrelevant, -ly	
irreligious, -ly	
irreligus	irreligious
irreparable, -bly	
irreparabul	irreparable
irreplacabul	irreplaceable
irreplaceable, -bly	
irrepresibul	irrepressible
irrepressible, -bly	
irreproachable, -bly	
irreprochabul	irreproachable
irresistabul	irresistible
irresistible, -bly	
irresolute, -ly	
irrespective, -ly	
irresponsibility	
irresponsible, -bly	
irresponsibul	irresponsible
irretraceable, -bly	
irretraseabul	irretraceable
irretrievable, -bly	
irretrievabul	irretrievable
irreverant	irreverent
irreverence	
irreverent, -ly	
irreverint	irreverent
irreversibility	
irreversible, -bly	
irreversibul	irreversible
irrevocable, -bly	
irrevocabul	irrevocable
irridescent	iridescent
irrigate, -gated, -gating	
irrigation	
irrisistabel	irresistible
irrisistabul	irresistible

irritability
irritable, -bly
  irritabul — irritable
irritancy
  irritansey — irritancy
irritant
irritate, -tated, -tating
irritation
  irrupshun — irruption
irrupt, -ed, -ing
irruption
irruptive, -ly
  isalate — isolate
  isatope — isotope
  ise — ice
  ishue — issue
  isicul — icicle
  isight — eyesight
Islam
Islamic
island
islander
isle (island)
  isle — aisle (passage)
isn't (is not)
  isnt — isn't
isobar
isolate, -lated, -lating
isolation
isolationism
isolationist
isosceles
  isosilese — isosceles
isotope
Israeli
  Isralie — Israeli
issue, issued, issuing
isthmus, -muses
  istmus — isthmus
italic
itch, -ed, -ing
item
itemise, -mised, -mising
iterate, -rated, -rating
iteration
  iternal — eternal
  iternally — eternally
  iternity — eternity
itinerant, -ly
itinerary, -ries
it'll (it will)
  itll — it'll
it's (it is)
its (possessive)
  its — it's (it is)
itself
  ivacuate — evacuate
  ivacuation — evacuation
  ivade — evade
  ivaluate — evaluate
  ivaluation — evaluation
  ivaporate — evaporate
  ivaporation — evaporation
  ivasion — evasion
  ivasive — evasive
I've (I have)
  Ive — I've
  ivent — event
  iventual — eventual
  ivery — ivory
  ivey — ivy
  ivict — evict
  iviction — eviction
  ivoke — evoke
  ivolve — evolve
ivory, -ries
ivory tower
  ivry — ivory
ivy, ivies
Ivy League

Jj

jab, jabbed, jabbing
jabber
jabiru
jacana
jacaranda
jack
jackal
jackass
jackdaw
jackdoor — jackdaw
jackeroo
jacket
jackhammer
jack-in-the-box
jackknife, -knives
jack-of-all-trades
jackpot, -potted, -potting
Jacobean
jade, jaded, jading
jaffle
jafful — jaffle
jag, jagged, jagging
jaguar
jail
jake
jalopy, -lopies
jam, jammed, jamming
jam (food)
jam — jamb (door)
jamb (door)
jamboree
jamborie — jamboree
jangle, -gled, -gling
jangul — jangle
janiter — janitor
janitor
January
Janurey — January

Japanese, -nese
japonica
jar, jarred, jarring
jargon
jarrah
jarrar — jarrah
jasmin — jasmine
jasper
jaundice, -diced, -dicing
jaundise — jaundice
jaunt, -ed, -ing
jauntie — jaunty
jaunty, -tier, -tiest
javelin
javlin — javelin
jaw
jawndise — jaundice
jawnt — jaunt
jay
jaywalk, -ed, -ing
jaywalker
jaz — jazz
jazz
jazzy, -zier, -ziest
jealous, -ly
jealousy, -ousies
jealus — jealous
jeans
jeep
jeer, -ed, -ing
Jehovah
Jehovah's Witness
jejune
jelie — jelly
jelly, -lies
jelly, -lied, -lying
jellyfish, -fish, -fishes
jelous — jealous
jelus — jealous
jely — jelly
jemey — jemmy
jemie — jemmy
jemmy, -mies
jemmy, -mied, -mying
jemy — jemmy
jeopardise, -dised, -dising
jeopardy

jepardise	jeopardise	jigsaw	
jepardy	jeopardy	jillaroo	
jerboa		jilt, -ed, -ing	
jeribilt	jerry-built	jim	gym
jerk, -ed, -ing		jimkana	gymkhana
jerkin		jin	gin
jerky, -kily		jingel	jingle
jerry, -ries		jingle, -gled, -gling	
jerry-build, -built, -building		jingoism	
jerry can		jingul	jingle
jersey		jinks	jinx
jersie	jersey	jinx, -es	
jest, -ed, -ing		jirashun	gyration
jester		jiration	gyration
Jesuit		jiro	gyro
Jesus		jiroscope	gyroscope
jet, jetted, jetting		jist	gist
jetie	jetty	jiter	jitter
jetison	jettison	jitter, -ed, -ing	
jet lag		jittery	
jettison, -ed, -ing		jive, jived, jiving	
jetty, -ties		job, jobbed, jobbing	
jety	jetty	jobber	
Jew		jockey, -eys	
Jewish		jockey, -eyed, -eying	
jewel, -elled, -elling (cut gem)		jockie	jockey
jewel	dual (two)	jockstrap	
jewel	duel (fight)	jocky	jockey
jewel	joule (unit)	jocose, -ly	
jeweler	jeweller	jocosity, -ties	
jeweller		jocular, -ly	
jewellery		jocularity, -ties	
jewelrey	jewellery	jocund, -ly	
jewfish		jocundity, -ties	
Jewry (Jewish people)		jodhpurs	
jewry	jury (court)	jodpurs	jodhpurs
jew's harp		joey, -eys	
jib, jibbed, jibbing		jog, jogged, jogging	
jibe, jibed, jibing (sail)		jogger	
jibe	gibe (scoff)	jogtrot, -trotted, -trotting	
jiffy, -fies		johnnycake	
jifie	jiffy	joi	joy
jify	jiffy	join, joined, joining	
jig, jigged, jigging		joiner	
jigger		joinery	
jiggle, -gled, -gling		joint, -ly	
jiggul	jiggle	joist	

joke, joked, joking		jubilate, -lated, -lating	
joker		jubilation	
jollitey	jollity	jubilee	
jollity, -ties		jubilie	jubilee
jolly, -lier, -liest		juce	deuce (two)
jolt, -ed, -ing		juce	juice (liquid)
joly	jolly	Judaism	
jonah		judas	
jonathan		judge, judged, judging	
jonquil		judgement	
Joo	Jew	judgment	
Jooish	Jewish	judicacher	judicature
jool	joule (unit)	judicachur	judicature
Joone	June	judicature	
joopiter	Jupiter	judicial, -ly	
joose	deuce (two)	judiciary, -aries	
joose	juice (liquid)	judicious, -ly	
joote	jute	judishul	judicial
jostle, -tled, -tling		judisharey	judiciary
josul	jostle	judishous	judicious
jot, jotted, jotting		judishus	judicious
jotter		judo	
joule (unit)		juel	dual (two)
joule	dual (two)	juel	duel (fight)
joule	duel (fight)	juel	jewel (gem)
joule	jewel (gem)	juel	joule (unit)
journal		jug, jugged, jugging	
journalese		juge	judge
journalism		juggement	judgement
journalist		juggernaut	
journel	journal	juggle, -gled, -gling	
journey, -neys		juggler	
journey, -neyed, -neying		jugul	juggle
joust, -ed, -ing		jugular	
Jove		juice (liquid)	
jovial, -ly		juice	deuce (two)
joviality		juiciness	
jowl		juicy, -cier, -ciest	
joy		Juish	Jewish
joyful, -ly		jujitsu	
joyous, -ly		jukebox	
joy-ride, -rode, -riding		jukstapose	juxtapose
joystick		julep	
joyus	joyous	Juli	July
ju	Jew	July	
jube		jumble, -bled, -bling	
jubilant, -ly		jumbo, -bos	

jumbuck		justify, -fied, -fying
jumbul	jumble	justise	justice
jump, -ed, -ing		jut, jutted, jutting
jumper		jute
jump-start		juvenile, -ly
jump suit		juwel	dual (two)
jumpy, jumpier, jumpiest		juwel	duel (fight)
junction		juwel	jewel (gem)
juncture		juwel	joule (unit)
June		juxapose	juxtapose
jungle		juxaposition	juxtaposition
jungul	jungle	juxtapose, -posed, -posing
junier	junior	juxtaposition
junior		jym	gym
juniper		jyroscope	gyroscope
junk			
junkcher	juncture		
junket			
junkie			
junkshere	juncture		
junkshun	junction		
junkshure	juncture		
junta			
Jupiter			
jurer	juror		
juri	jury		
juridical, -ly			
jurisdickshion	jurisdiction		
jurisdickshun	jurisdiction		
jurisdiction			
jurisprudence			
jurisprudense	jurisprudence		
jurisprudunse	jurisprudence		
jurist			
jurnal	journal		
jurney	journey		
juror			
jury, -ries			
juse	juice		
jusie	juicy		
jussive			
just, -ly			
justice			
justice of the peace			
justifiabel	justifiable		
justifiable, -bly			
justification			

Kk

Look under **c** if the word is not under **k**

kadaicha man
kaleidoscope

| kalidascope | kaleidoscope |
| kalidescope | kaleidoscope |

kalsomine, -mined, -mining
kamikaze
kampong
kanaka
kangaroo
kaolin
ka pai
kapok
kaput
karate

| karkey | khaki |
| karki | khaki |

karma
karri, -ris (tree)

| karri | carry (bring) |

kauri, -ris
kayak
kebab
kedgeree
keel, -ed, -ing
keen, -ly
keenness
keep, kept, keeping
keeper
keg
kelp

| kelpey | kelpie |

kelpie

| kelt | Celt |
| keltic | Celtic |

ken, kenned, kenning

| kenel | kennel |

kennel, -nelled, -nelling
kept
keratin
kerb (gutter)

| kerb | curb (check) |

kerchief
kerfuffle
kernel (core)

| kernel | colonel (army) |

kero

| keropody | chiropody |
| keroseen | kerosene |

kerosene

kerosine
kestrel
ketch
ketchup

| ketle | kettle |

kettle
kettledrum

kettul	kettle
kew	cue
kew	queue (line)

kewpie
key, keys (lock)
key, keyed, keying

| key | quay (wharf) |

keyboard
keystone
khaki, -kis
kibble, -bled, -bling

| kibbul | kibble |
| kiak | kayak |

kibbutz
kick, kicked, kicking
kick-off
kid, kidded, kidding
kidnap, -napped, -napping
kidney, -neys
kikuyu
kill, killed, killing
killer
killjoy
kiln
kilo
kilogram

kilojoule
kilometer   kilometre
kilometre
kilowatt
kilowatt-hour
kilt
kilter
kimono, -nos
kin
kina
kind, -ly
kindness
kindergarten
kindle, -dled, -dling
kindly, -lier, -liest
kindred
kindrid   kindred
kindrud   kindred
kindul   kindle
kinetics
king
kingdom
kingly
kingfish
kingfisher
kingpin
kink, kinked, kinking
kinkiness
kinky, -kier, -kiest
kinsfolk
kinship
kinsman, -men
kiosk
kip, kipped, kipping
kipper
kirk
kiropody   chiropody
kismet
kiss, kissed, kissing
kissable
kit, kitted, kitting
kitbag
kitchen
kite
kiten   kitten
kith
kitie   kitty

kitsch
kitten
kittenish, -ly
kitty, -ties
kity   kitty
kiwi
kiyak   kayak
klaxon
kleptomania
knack
knacker
knapsack
knave (rogue)
knave   nave (church)
knead, -ed, -ing, (dough)
knead   need (want)
knee, kneed, kneeing
kneecap
kneel, knelt, kneeling
knell, -ed, -ing
knew
knew   gnu (animal)
knew   new
knickerbockers
knick-knack
knife, knives
knife, knifed, knifing
knight (lord)
knight   night (time)
knighthood
knit, knitted, knitting
knitwear
knob, knobbed, knobbing (handle)
knobbly
knobby, -bier, -biest
knock, -ed, -ing
knockabout
knock-back
knockdown
knocker
knock-knee
knockout
knoll
knot, knotted, knotting (tie)
knot   not (denial)
knothole
knotty, -tier, -tiest

know, knew, known, knowing
know-all
know how
knowledge
knowledgeable, -bly
knuckle, -led, -ling
knuckle-duster
koala
  kola   koala
kookaburra
koori
korodji
Koran
korowai
  koroway   korowai
kosher
kowtow, -ed, -ing
Kremlin
kris
Krishna
kudos
kumquat
kung-fu
kurrajong

> For kw- words, look under
> **qu-**.

kylie

Ll

label, -belled, -belling
  laber — labour
labial, -ly
labiate
  labirinth — labyrinth
labium, -bia
  lable — label
  labor — labour
laboratory, -ries
  laboratrey — laboratory
laborious, -ly
  laborius — laborious
labour, -ed, -ing
labourer
labour-intensive
Labrador
  labratory — laboratory
  labrinth — labyrinth
  laburnem — laburnum
laburnum
labyrinth
labyrinthine
lace, laced, lacing
lacebark
lacerate, -rated, -rating
laceration
  lach — latch
lack, -ed, -ing
lackadaisical, -ly
  lacker — lacquer
lackey, -eys
lackey, -eyed, -eying
  lacky — lackey
laconic, -ally
lacquer, -ed, -ing
  lacross — lacrosse
lacrosse
lactate, -tated, -tating

lactation
lacteal, -ly
lactic
lactose
lad
ladder
lade, laded, laden, lading (load)
  lade — laid (placed)
  ladel — ladle
  lader — ladder
  ladie — lady
ladle, -dled, -dling
  ladul — ladle
lady, -dies
ladybird
lag, lagged, lagging
  lagard — laggard
lager
laggard, -ly
  laghable — laughable
lagoon
laid (placed)
  laid — lade (load)
laid-back
  laim — lame
lain (did lie)
  lain — lane (passage)
lair (den)
  lair — layer
  laissay fair — laissez faire
laissez faire
  laitie — laity
laity
lake
  lakross — lacrosse
  laks — lax
  laksative — laxative
lam, lammed, lamming (spike)
  lam — lamb (sheep)
lama
lamb (sheep)
  lamb — lam (spike)
lambaste, -basted, -basting
lame, lamed, laming
lame, lamer, lamest
lament, -ed, -ing
lamentable, -bly

lamentation
laminate, -nated, -nating
lamington
lamp
lampoon, -ed, -ing
lampoonist
lamp-post
  lampray   lamprey
lamprey, -reys
lance, lanced, lancing
lancet
land, -ed, -ing
landfall
landform
landlady, -dies
landlocked
landlord
landlubber
landmark
landmass
landmine
land rights
landscape, -scaped, -scaping
landslide
lane (passage)
  lane   lain (did lie)
language
languid, -ly
languish, -ed, -ing
  languer   languor
languorous, -ly
  langwid   languid
  langwidge   language
  langwish   languish
lank, -ly
  landladie   landlady
  lanladie   landlady
  lanlady   landlady
  lanlord   landlord
lanolin
lanoline
  lanse   lance
  lanser   lancer
  lanset   lancet
lantana
lantern
lanyard

lap, lapped, lapping
lapel
lapelled
lapidary, -ries
lapis lazuli
lap-lap
lapse, lapsed, lapsing
larceny, -nies
larcenous, -ly
  larconic   laconic
lard
larder
large, -ly
largess
lariat
  laringitis   laryngitis
  larinx   larynx
lark
larrikin
  larseny   larceny
larva, -vae (insect)
  larva   lava (rock)
laryngitis
larynx, larynxes
lascivious, -ly
  lase   lace
laser
  laserate   lacerate
lash, -ed, -ing
  lasitude   lassitude
  lasivious   lascivious
  lasivius   lascivious
  lasoo   lasso
  lasor   laser
lass
lassitude
lasso, -sos, -soes
lasso, -soed, -soing
last, lasted, lasting
last-ditch
lastly
latch, -ed, -ing
latchkey
late, later, latest
lately
latency
  latensey   latency

latent, -ly
lateral, -ly
latex, latexes
lath (strip)
lathe (machine)
lather, -ed, -ing
lathery
Latin
  latise   lattice
latitude
latrine
latter
lattice
laud, lauded, lauding (praise)
  laud   lord (ruler)
laudable, -bly
laudanum
laudation
laudatory
laugh, laughed, laughing
laughable, -bly
laughter
  laun   lawn
launch, launched, launching
launder, -ed, -ing
  laundrey   laundry
laundromat
laundry, -dries
laureate
laurel, -relled, -relling
  lauyer   lawyer
lava (rock)
  lava   larva (insect)
lavatory, -ries
  lavatree   lavatory
  lavatrey   lavatory
lave, laved, laving
lavender
lavish, lavished, lavishing
law (rule)
  law   lore (learn)
  lawd   laud (praise)
  lawd   lord (ruler)
  lawdabul   laudable
lawful, -ly
lawless, -ly
lawn

  lawnch   launch
  lawnder   launder
  lawndrey   laundry
  lawndromat laundromat
  lawndry   laundry
lawsuit
  lawsute   lawsuit
lawyer
lax, -ly
  lax   lacks
  laxadasical lackadaisical
laxative
laxity
lay, laid, laying (rest)
  lay   lei (flowers)
  laybie   lay-by
lay-by
layer
layette
layman, -men
layout
laze, lazed, lazing
lazily
lazy, -zier, -ziest
lea (meadow)
  lea   lee (shelter)
leach, -ed, -ing (filter)
  leach   leech (worm)
lead, led, leading (show)
lead (metal)
  lead   led (shown)
leaden, -ly
leader
leadership
leaf, leaves
leaflet
league
leak (hole)
  leak   leek (food)
leakage
lean, leant or leaned, leaning (bend)
  leant   Lent (season)
  leant   lent (did lend)
lean-to
leap, leapt or leaped, leaping
leapfrog, -frogged, -frogging
learn, learnt or learned, learning

learner
lease, leased, leasing
leasehold
leash, -ed, -ing
  leashur   leisure
  leason   liaison
least
  leasure   leisure
  leasurely   leisurely
leather
leatherjacket
leave, left, leaving
leaven, -ed, -ing
  leaver   lever
lecher (man)
  lecher   lecture (talk)
lecherous, -ly
  lecherus   lecherous
lechery
lectern
lector
lecture, -tured, -turing
lecturer
led (shown)
  led   lead (metal)
ledge
ledger (book)
  ledger   leger (stand)
lee (shelter)
  lee   lea (meadow)
  leeason   liaison
leech (worm)
  leech   leach (filter)
  leed   lead
  leef   leaf
  leeflet   leaflet
  leege   liege
  leegue   league
leek (food)
  leek   leak (hole)
  leen   lean
  leep   leap
leer, -ed, -ing
lees
  leese   lease
  leesh   leash
  leesion   lesion

  leesiun   lesion
leeward
leeway
  leewood   leeward
left
  leftenant   lieutenant
  leftenent   lieutenant
left-footer
left-handed
leftist
leftward
left-winger
leg, legged, legging
legacy, -cies
legal, -ly
legalese (language)
legalisation
legalise, -lised, -lising (authorise)
legalism
legality, -ties
  legand   legend
  legasey   legacy
  legashen   legation
legate
legation
legend
legendary, -ries
  legendrey   legendary
leger (stand)
  leger   ledger (book)
leghorn
  legibel   legible
legibility
legible, -bly
legion
legionary, -ries
legionnaire
  legislachur   legislature
legislate, -lated, -lating
legislation
legislative, -ly
legislator
legislature
legitimacy
  legitimasey   legitimacy
legitimate, -mated, -mating
legume

lei, leis (flowers)
   lei   lay (rest)
leisure
leisurely
   lejun   legion
   lejunry   legionary
   leksicografer   lexicographer
   leksicografey   lexicography
   leksicographer   lexicographer
   leksicon   lexicon
   leming   lemming
lemming
lemon
lemonade
lemur
lend, lent, lending
lender
length
lengthen, -ed, -ing
lengthily
lengthways
lengthwise
lengthy, -thier, -thiest
lenience
leniency
   leniense   lenience
   leniensy   leniency
lenient, -ly
lenity, -ties
lens, lenses
   lense   lens
Lent (season)
   lent   leant (bent)
   lenth   length
lentil (pea)
   lentil   lintel (beam)
Leo
leonine
leopard
leotard
   lepard   leopard
leper
   leperd   leopard
leprechaun
   leprechorn   leprechaun
leprosy
   lept   leapt

   lerch   lurch
   lerk   lurk
   lern   learn
   lesen   lessen (reduce)
   lesen   lesson (study)
lesbian
lesbianism
   leishur   leisure
lesion
   leson   lessen (reduce)
   leson   lesson (study)
less
lessee
lessen (reduce)
lesson (study)
lessor
lest
   lesure   leisure
let, let, letting
letdown
   leter   letter
   leter   litre
lethal, -ly
   lethargey   lethargy
lethargic, -ally
lethargy, -gies
   lether   leather
   letice   lettuce
   letise   lettuce
   letre   litre
letter
lettered
letterhead
letterpress
lettuce
let-up
   letuse   lettuce
leucosis
leukaemia
   leve   leave
levee (bank)
   levee   levy (tax)
level, -elled, -elling
leveller
level-headed
   levelheded   level-headed
   leven   leaven

lever, -ed, -ing
leverage
leviathan
levie   levee (bank)
levie   levy (tax)
levitate, -tated, -tating
levitation
levity, -ties
levrage   leverage
levy, levies (tax)
levy, levied, levying (tax)
levy   levee (bank)
lewd, -ly
lexicografer   lexicographer
lexicografey   lexicography
lexicographer
lexicography
lexicon
lezbian   lesbian
li   lie
liability, -ties
liable (legal)
liabul   libel (crime)
liabul   liable (legal)
liaise, -aised, -aising
liaison
liana
liar (tell lies)
liar   lyre (music)
liason   liaison
libarian   librarian
libary   library
libel, -belled, -belling (crime)
libel   liable (legal)
libelus   libellous
libul   liable
libellous, -ly
liberal, -ly
liberalism
liberate, -rated, -rating
liberation
liberator
libertey   liberty
libertine
liberty, -ties
libidinal
libidinous, -ly

libido
Libra
libralism   liberalism
librarian
library, -ries
libretto, -tos, -ti
librian   librarian
lice
licee   lychee
licence (noun)
license, -censed, -censing
licensee
licenshiate   licentiate
licenshius   licentious
licenshus   licentious
licentiate
licentious, -ly
lichee   lychee
lichen
lichenis   lichenous
lichenous
lichenus   lichenous
lick, -ed, -ing
licker   liqueur
licker   liquor
licorice
licorish   licorice
licoriss   licorice
lickrish   licorice
lid
lie, lied, lying (untruth)
lie, lay, lain, lying (recline)
lie   lye (solution)
liege
lien
liesure   leisure
lieu (instead)
lieu   loo (toilet)
lieutenant
life, lives
lifebelt
lifeboat
lifeboy   lifebuoy
lifebuoy
lifeguard
lifeless, -ly
lifelike

lifelong
lifesaver
lifestyle
lifetime
lift, -ed, -ing
lift-off
ligacher — ligature
ligachur — ligature
ligament
light, lighted, lighting
lighten, -ed, -ing
light-fingered
light-headed
light-hearted, -ly
lighthouse
lightly
lightning
lightweight
ligneous
lignite
like, liked, liking
likeable
likelihood
likely, -lier, -liest
likelyhood — likelihood
liken, likened, likening
likeness
likewise
likorish — licorice
likoriss — licorice
likrish — licorice

For likw- words, look under **liqu-**.

lilac
lilak — lilac
lile — lisle
lilie — lily
Lilliputian
lilly pilly
lilt, -ed, -ing
lily, -ies
lily-livered
limb
limber, limbered, limbering
limbo, -bos
lime, limed, liming

limelight
limelite — limelight
limerick
limersene — limousine
limestone
limey, -meys
limf — lymph
limfatic — lymphatic
limit, -ed, -ing
limitation
limousine
limp, -ed, -ing
limpet
limph — lymph
limphatic — lymphatic
limpid, -ly
linchpin
linch — lynch
linctus
line, lined, lining (mark)
line — lion (cat)
lineage
lineal, -ly
lineament (detail)
linear, -ly
lineige — lineage
linen
liner
linesman, -men
line-up
ling, lings
linger, -ed, -ing
lingerie
lingo, -goes
lingual, -ly
linguist
linguistic, -ally
lingwal — lingual
lingwist — linguist
linier — linear
liniment (oil)
liniment — lineament (detail)
link, linked, linking
linkage
linnet
linocut

linoleum
linolium   linoleum
linotype, -typed, -typing
linseed
lint
lintel (beam)
lintel   lentil (pea)
linx   lynx
lion (cat)
lion   line (mark)
lioness
lion-hearted, -ly
lionisation
lionise, -nised, -nising
liotard   leotard
lip
lip-read, -read, -reading
lip-salve
lip-service
lipstick
liquefier
liquefy, -fied, -fying
liquer   liqueur
liquer   liquor
liqueur (drink)
liqueur   liquor (spirits)
liquid
liquidambar
liquidate, -dated, -dating
liquidation
liquidator
liquidity
liquor (spirits)
liquor   liqueur (drink)
liquorice
liquoris   liquorice
liquorish   liquorice
lire   lyre
lirebird   lyrebird
liric   lyric
lirical   lyrical
lise   lice
lisen   listen
lisence   licence (noun)
lisence   license (verb)
lisen   listen
lisensee   licensee

lisentiate   licentiate
lisentius   licentious
lisle
lisp, -ed, -ing
lissom
lissum   lissom
list, -ed, -ing
listen, -ed, -ing
listless, -ly
lit
litany, -nies
lite   light
litel   little
liter   litre
liter   litter
literacher   literature
literachur   literature
literacy
literal, -ly
literary, -ily
literasy   literacy
literat   literate
literate
literati
literature
litergy   liturgy
litewait   light-weight
lithe, -ly
lithesome
lithium
lithograf   lithograph
lithograph
lithographic, -ally
lithography
litigant
litigation
litigator
litle   little
litmus
litening   lightning
litracher   literature
litrachur   literature
litre
litter, -ed, -ing
litterbug
little, less, least
litul   little

liturgey — liturgy
liturgical, -ly
liturgy, -gies
liv — live
livary — livery
live, lived, living
livelihood
lively, -lier, -liest
livelyhood — livelihood
liven, -ed, -ing
liver
liverish
liverwurst
livery, -ries
livestock
livewire
livid, -ly
livlie — lively
livrey — livery
liying — lying
lizard
lizerd — lizard
llama
lo — low
load, -ed, -ing (burden)
load — lode (ore)
loaf, loaves
loam, -ed, -ing
loan (lend)
loan — lone (alone)
loath (unwilling)
loathe, loathed, loathing (hate)
loathsome, -ly
lob, lobbed, lobbing
lobby, -bies
lobby, -bied, -bying
lobe
lobie — lobby
lobotomy
lobster
loby — lobby
local, -ly
locale
localise, -lised, -lising
locality, -ties
locate, -cated, -cating
location

loch (lake)
lock (door)
locker
locket
lockjaw
locksmith
lockup
locomoshun — locomotion
locomotion
locomotive
locum
locust
lode (ore)
lode — load (burden)
lodestar
lodestone
lodge, lodged, lodging
lodger
lofe — loaf
loft, lofted, lofting
loftily
lofty, -tier, -tiest
log, logged, logging
loganberie — loganberry
loganberry, -ries
logarithm
logbook
loge — lodge
loger — logger
logerithm — logarithm
loggerhead
logic
logical, -ly
logicality
logistics
loier — lawyer
loin
loincloth
loiter, -ed, -ing
loiterer
lol — loll
lolipop — lollipop
loll, -ed, -ing
lollipop
lolly, -lies
lome — loam
lone (alone)

lone	loan (lend)	loot	lute (music)
loneliness		lop, lopped, lopping (cut)	
lonely, -lier, -liest		lope, loped, loping (run)	
loner		lopsided, -ly	
lonesome, -ly		loquacious, -ly	
lonesum	lonesome	loquacity	
long, -ed, -ing		loquashius	loquacious
longevity		loquashus	loquacious
longhand		loquat	
longing, -ly		lord (ruler)	
longitude		lord	laud (praise)
longitudinal, -ly		lordly, -lier, -liest	
long-playing		lord mayor	
long-sighted		lore (learn)	
longstanding		lore	law (rule)
long-suffering		lorel	laurel
long-term		lorgnette	
longwinded, -ly		loriat	laureate
loo (toilet)		lorie	lorry
loo	lieu (instead)	lorikeet	
loobricant	lubricant	lornch	launch
loobricate	lubricate	lornyet	lorgnette
loocid	lucid	lorry, lorries (truck)	
loocrative	lucrative	lory, lories (bird)	
loodicrous	ludicrous	los	loss
loodicrus	ludicrous	lose, lost, losing (fail)	
loofah		lose	loose (free)
look, -ed, -ing		loser	
lookemia	leukaemia	loshion	lotion
looker	lucre	loshun	lotion
lookout		loss	
lookwarm	lukewarm	lot, lotted, lotting	
loom, -ed, -ing		lotery	lottery
loominus	luminous	lothe	loathe
loon		lothsum	loathsome
loona	luna	lotion	
loonatic	lunatic	lotry	lottery
loony, loonier, looniest		lots	
loop, -ed, -ing		lottery, -teries	
loophole		lotto	
loose, loosed, loosing (free)		lotus	
loose, looser, loosest		loud, -ly	
loose	lose (fail)	loudhailer	
loose-leaf		loudspeaker	
loosen, -ed, -ing		lounge, lounged, lounging	
loosing	losing	louse, lice	
loot (booty)		louse, loused, lousing	

lousy, lousier, lousiest
lout
   louver → louvre
louvre
love, loved, loving
loveliness
lovelorn
lovely, -lier, -liest
lover
   loves → loaves
low, lower, lowest
lowboy
lowbrow
   lowd → loud
low-down (mean)
lowdown (truth)
lower, -ed, -ing
low-key
lowland
lowly, -lier, -liest
   lownge → lounge
low-pressure
   lowse → louse
   lowt → lout
low-voltage
loyal, -ly
loyalty, -ties
   loyle → loyal
lozenge
   lozinge → lozenge
   lu → lieu (instead)
   lu → loo (toilet)
lubber, -ly
   luber → lubber
lubricant
lubricate, -cated, -cating
lubrication
   lucer → lucre
lucerne
lucid, -ly
Lucifer
luck, -ily
lucky, -ier, -iest
lucky dip
lucrative, -ly
lucre
   lude → lewd

ludicrous, -ly
ludo
luff, -ed, -ing
lug, lugged, lugging
   lugage → luggage
luggage
lugger
   lugige → luggage
   lugsuriant → luxuriant
lugubrious, -ly
   lukemia → leukaemia
lukewarm
   luksuriant → luxuriant
   luksuriate → luxuriate
   luksurius → luxurious
   luksury → luxury
   lul → lull
   lulabie → lullaby
lull, -ed, -ing
lullaby, -bies
lullaby, -bied, -bying
lumbago
lumbar (back)
lumber (timber)
lumberjack
luminance
luminary, -naries
luminescence
luminescent
   luminessence → luminescence
   luminessent → luminescent
luminosity, -ties
luminous, -ly
   luminus → luminous
lump, -ed, -ing
lunacy, -cies
lunar
   lunasey → lunacy
lunatic
lunch, -ed, -ing
luncheon
lung
lunge, lunged, lunging
lungfish
lupin
lupus
lurch, lurched, lurching

lure, lured, luring
lurex
lurid, -ly
lurk, lurked, lurking
  lurn — learn
luscious, -ly
lush, -ly
  lushes — luscious
  lushious — luscious
  lushus — luscious
  lused — lucid
  lusid — lucid
lust, lusted, lusting
  luster — lustre
lustful, -ly
  lustie — lusty
lustre
lustrous, -ly
lusty, -tier, -tiest
lute, luted, luting (music)
  lute — loot (booty)
Lutheran
  luv — love
  luve — love
  luver — lover
  luvley — lovely
  luvlier — lovelier
lux
  luxery — luxury
luxuriance
luxuriant, -ly
luxuriate, -ated, -ating
luxurious, -ly
luxury, -ries
lyceum
lychee
lye (solution)
  lye — lie (untruth)
  lye — lie (recline)
lying-in
lymph
lymphatic
lynch, -ed, -ing
lynx, lynxes (wildcat)
  lynx — links
lyre (musical instrument)
  lyre — liar (tell lies)

lyrebird
lyric
lyrical, -ly
lyricist

Mm

macabre
macadam
macadamia nut
macaroni, -nis, -nies
macaw
mace
  mach   match
machete
machinate, -nated, -nating
machination
machine, -chined, -chining
machinery, -ries
mackerel
mackintosh, mackintoshes
macramé
mad, madder, maddest
mad, madded, madding
madam
madcap
made (produced)
  made   maid (girl)
madeira
mademoiselle
  maden   madden
  madera   madeira
madness
madonna
madrigal
maelstrom
maestro
mafia
magazine
maggot
magic
magical, -ly
magician
  magishion   magician
  magishun   magician

magisterial, -ly
magistrate
  magizine   magazine
  magnanimis   magnanimous
magnanimity
magnanimous, -ly
  magnanimus magnanimous
  magnat   magnate
  magnat   magnet
magnate (wealth)
magnesium
magnet (attract)
magnetic, -ally
magnetisation
magnetise, -tised, -tising
magnetism
magnetite
magneto, -tos
magnification
magnificence
magnificent, -ly
magnifier
  magnifisense magnificence
  magnifisent   magnificent
  magnifisunt   magnificent
magnify, -fied, -fying
magnitude
magnolia
magnum, -nums
  magot   maggot
magpie
  mahem   mayhem
mah-jong
mahogany, -nies
maid (girl)
  maid   made
maiden
mail (letters)
  mail   male (man)
mailbox, mailboxes
maim, -ed, -ing
main (chief)
  main   mane (hair)
mainland
mainline, -lined, -lining
mainliner
mainstay

mainstream	
maintain, -ed, -ing	
maintenance	
maintananse	maintenance
maisonette	
maize (corn)	
maize	maze (puzzle)
majer	major
majestey	majesty
majestic, -ally	
majesty, -ties	
majong	mah-jong
major	
majority, -ties	
makaber	macabre
makadam	macadam
make, made, making	
makeshift	
make-up	
mako	
maladey	malady
maladjusted	
maladjustment	
malady, -dies	
malaise	
malapropism	
malard	mallard
malaria	
malase	malaise
male (man)	
male	mail (letters)
maleable	malleable
malefacshun	malefaction
malefaction	
malefactor	
malet	mallet
malevolence	
malevolense	malevolence
malevolent, -ly	
malformation	
malformed	
malfuncshion	malfunction
malfuncshun	malfunction
malfunction, -ed, -ing	
maliable	malleable
malice	
malicious, -ly	

malign, -ed, -ing	
malignance	
malignancy	
malignansey	malignancy
malignant, -ly	
maline	malign
malinger, -ed, -ing	
malingerer	
malise	malice
malishus	malicious
mall	
mallard, -lards, -lard	
malleability	
malleable	
malleabul	malleable
mallee	
mallet	
mallow	mellow
malnutrishun	malnutrition
malnutrition	
malpractice	
malpractise	malpractice
malstrom	maelstrom
malt (liquor)	
malt	moult (lose)
Malthusian	
maltreat, -ed, -ing	
maltreet	maltreat
maluka	
mamal	mammal
mamarey	mammary
mame	maim
mamilla, -millae	
mamma, mammae	
mammal	
mammary	
mammon	
mammoth	
mamon	mammon
mamoth	mammoth
man, men	
man, manned, manning	
manacle, -cled, -cling	
manacul	manacle
manage, -aged, -aging	
manageability	
manageable, -bly	

management
manager
manageress
managerial, -ly
manana
manchester
mandarin (bureaucrat)
mandarine (fruit)
mandate, -dated, -dating
mandatory, -ries
   mandatry — mandatory
mandolin
mandrax
mane (hair)
   mane — main (chief)
   maner — manner (way)
   maner — manor (house)
mange
   mangel — mangle
manger
mangle, -gled, -gling
mango, -goes, -gos
mangrove
   mangul — mangle
mangy, -gier, -giest
   manhandel — manhandle
manhandle, -dled, -dling
   manhandul — manhandle
manhole
manhood
mania
maniacal, -ly
manic
manic-depression
manic-depressive
manicure, -cured, -curing
   manidge — manage
manifest, -ed, -ing
manifestation
manifesto, -tos
manifold
   manige — manage
manikin (dwarf)
   manikin — mannequin (model)
manila
   manipulashun — manipulation

manipulate, -lated, -lating
manipulation
manipulative
manipulator
manipulatory
   manje — mange
   manjer — manger
   manjy — mangy
mankind
manly, -lier, -liest
manna (food)
   manna — manner (way)
   manna — manor (house)
mannequin
manner (way)
   manner — manna (food)
   manner — manor (house)
mannered
mannerism
manoeuvrability
manoeuvrable
manoeuvre, -vred, -vring
   manoover — manoeuvre
   manoovrabul — manoeuvrable
manor (house)
   manor — manna (food)
   manor — manner (way)
manpower
manse
   manshun — mansion
mansion
manslaughter
   manslorter — manslaughter
mantel (shelf)
   mantel — mantle (cloak)
mantelpiece
mantilla
mantis, -tises
mantissa
mantle (cloak)
   mantle — mantel (shelf)
   mantul — mantel (shelf)
   mantul — mantle (cloak)
manual, -ly
   manufacsher — manufacture
manufacture, -tured, -turing
manure, -nured, -nuring

manuscript		markuis	marquis
many, more, most		marlin	
maonaise	mayonnaise	marlock	
Maori, -ris		marmalade	
map, mapped, mapping		marone	maroon
mapel	maple	maroon	
maple		marow	marrow
mar, marred, marring		marquee (tent)	
marathon		marquis (nobleman)	
maraud, -ed, -ing		marri (tree)	
marawed	maraud	marri	marry (unite)
marble, -bled, -bling		marriage	
marbul	marble	marrow	
marcasite		marry, -ried, -rying (unite)	
March		marry	marri (tree)
march, -ed, -ing		Mars	
marcher		marsh	
marchioness		marshal, -shalled, -shalling (officer)	
mare (horse)		marshal	martial (brave)
mare	mayor (chief)	marshland	
mareene	marine	marshmallow	
margarine		marshul	marshal
margin		marshul	martial
marginal, -ly		marshy, -shier, -shiest	
mariage	marriage	marsupial	
marie	marry	mart	
marijuana		marter	martyr
marina		martial (brave)	
marinade, -naded, -nading		martial	marshal
marinate, -nated, -nating			(officer)
marine		martinet	
mariner		martini	
marionet	marionette	martyr	
marionette		martyrdom	
marital, -ly		marvel, -velled, -velling	
maritime		marvellous, -ly	
maritul	marital	Marxism	
mariwana	marijuana	Marxist	
marjoram		mary	marry
mark, marked, marking		marzipan	
marker		mas	mass
market, -ed, -ing		masacer	massacre
marketeer		masacre	massacre
markey	marquee	masage	massage
markey	marquis	mascara	
marksman, -men		mascot	
marksmanship		masculine, -ly	

masculinity
   mase   mace
mash, -ed, -ing
   mashene   machine
   mashine   machine
   mashinry   machinery
   masive   massive
mask, -ed, -ing
   maskerade   masquerade
masochism
masochist
   masocism   masochism
mason
masonic
masonite
masonry, -ries
masquerade, -raded, -rading
mass, -ed, -ing
   massacer   massacre
massacre, -cred, -cring
massage, -saged, -saging
masseur
massif (mountain)
massive, -ly (large)
mass media
mass-produce, -duced, -ducing
   massur   masseur
mast
mastectomy, -mies
master
   masterbate   masturbate
masterful, -ly
mastermind
   masterpeace   masterpiece
masterpiece
masthead
mastiff
masturbate, -bated, -bating
masturbation
mat, matted, matting (rug)
   mat   matt (dull)
matador
match, -ed, -ing
matchmaker
mate, mated, mating
   mater   matter
material, -ly

materialisation
materialise, -lised, -lising
materialism
materialist
maternal, -ly
maternity
mateship
matey
mathematical, -ly
mathematician
mathematics
   mathematisian   mathematician
maths
matilda
   matinay   matinee
matinee
   mating   matting
   matress   mattress
matriarch
matriarchal
matriarchic
matriarchy, -chies
matriculant
matriculate, -lated, -lating
matriculation
matrimony, -nies
matrix, matrices
matron, -ly
matt (dull)
matter
matting
mattock
mattress
maturation
mature, -tured, -turing
maturity
maudlin, -ly
maul, -ed, -ing
mausoleum, -leums, -lea
mauve
maverick
   mawgage   mortgage
mawkish, -ly
   mawl   maul
   mawsoleum   mausoleum
maxi
maxim

maximisation		media	
maximise, -mised, -mising		mediaeval	
maximum, -ma, -mums		median	
maybe		mediashun	mediation
May Day		mediate, -ated, -ating	
mayhem		mediation	
mayonnaise		meditator	
mayor (chief)		medic	
mayor	mare (horse)	medical, -ly	
mayoralty, -ties		medicate, -cated, -cating	
mayoress		medication	
maypole		medicinal, -ly	
maze (puzzle)		medicine	
maze	maize (corn)	medieval, -ly	
mazurka		mediocer	mediocre
mead		mediocre	
meadow		mediocrity, -ties	
meager	meagre	medisinal	medicinal
meagre, -ly		medisine	medicine
meak	meek	meditate, -tated, -tating	
meal		meditation	
mean, meant, meaning (intend)		meditator	
mean	mien (show)	medium, -dia, -diums	
meander, -ed, -ing		medle	meddle
meantime		medler	meddler
meanwhile		medley, -leys	
measels	measles	medly	medley
measles		medow	meadow
measure, -ured, -uring		medsine	medicine
measurement		medul	meddle
meat (flesh)		meed	mead
meat	meet (contact)	meek, -ly	
meat	mete (measure)	meel	meal
mecanic	mechanic	meen	mean (intend)
mecanise	mechanise	meen	mien (show)
mecanism	mechanism	meening	meaning
mechanic		meerschaum	
mechanical, -ly		meershum	meerschaum
mechanisation		meesels	measles
mechanise, -nised, -nising		meet, met, meeting (contact)	
mechanism		meet	meat (flesh)
medal, -alled, -alling (award)		meet	mete (measure)
medallion		megafone	megaphone
medcine	medicine	megalomania	
meddle, -dled, -dling (interfere)		megalomaniac	
meddler		megaphone	
medeval	mediaeval	meger	meagre

mekanic   mechanic
mekanical   mechanical
mekanise   mechanise
mekanism   mechanism
melaleuca
melancholia
melancholic, -ally
melancholy, -cholies
Melanesian
melee
meliflous   mellifluous
meliorate, -rated, -rating
melioration
meliorator
mellifluous, -ly
mellow, -ly
melodey   melody
melodic, -ally
melodious, -ly
melodius   melodious
melodrama
melodramatic, -ally
melody, -dies
melon
melow   mellow
melt, melted, melting
member
membership
membrain   membrane
memento, -tos
memo, memos
memoir
memorabel   memorable
memorabilia
memorable,-bly
memorabul   memorable
memorandum, -dums
memorey   memory
memorial, -ly
memorise, -rised, -rising
memory, -ries
memrable   memorable
menace, -aced, -acing
menagerie
menajery   menagerie
menase   menace
mend, -ed, -ing

mendacious, -ly
mendacity, -ties
mendashus   mendacious
mendasity   mendacity
mendicant
menial, -ly
meningitis
meninjitis   meningitis
meniscus, -nisci
menopause
menopaws   menopause
menshion   mention
menshun   mention
menstruate, -ated, -ating
menstruation
mensuration
ment   meant
mental, -ly
mentalitey   mentality
mentality, -ties
menthol
mentholated
mention, -ed, -ing
mentor
menu
merang   meringue
mercantile
mercenary, -naries
mercenrey   mercenary
mercer
mercerise, -rised, -rising
mercery, -ries
merchandise, -dised, -dising
merchant
merchantman, -men
merciful, -ly
merciless, -ly
mercurial, -ly
mercury, -ries
mercy, -cies
mere, -ly
meretricious, -ly
meretrishious   meretricious
meretrishus   meretricious
merge, merged, merging
merger
meridian

merie	merry	metalurgey	metallurgy
meringue		metamorfic	metamorphic
merino, -nos		metamorfosus	metamorphosis
merit, -ed, -ing		metamorphic	
meritories	meritorious	metamorphosis, -ses	
meritorious, -ly		metaphor	
meritorius	meritorious	metaphoric	
mermade	mermaid	metamorphical, -ly	
mermaid		metaphrase, -phrased, -phrasing	
merriment		metaphysical, -ly	
merry, -rier, -riest		metaphysics	
merry-go-round		metastasise, -sised, -sising	
merrymaker		mete, meted, meting (measure)	
mersenry	mercenary	mete	meat (flesh)
mersy	mercy	mete	meet (contact)
mery	merry	meteor (streak)	
mesa		meteor	metier (trade)
mescalin		meteoric, -ally	
mesenger	messenger	meteorite	
mesh, -ed, -ing		meteorological, -ly	
mesige	message	meteorology	
mesmerise, -rised, -rising		meter (measure)	
mesmerism		meter	metre (distance)
mess, -ed, -ing			
message		methadone	
messenger		methane	
Messiah		methed	method
Messianic		methedrine	
messmate		methilate	methylate
Messrs		metho	
mesure	measure	method	
metabolic		methodical, -ly	
metabolise, -lised, -lising		Methodist	
metabolism		methodology, -gies	
metafisicul	metaphysical	methylate, -lated, -lating	
metafisics	metaphysics	meticulous, -ly	
metafor	metaphor	meticulus	meticulous
metaforic	metaphoric	metier (trade)	
metaforicul	metaphorical	metier	meteor (streak)
metal, -alled, -alling (element)		metiorology	meteorology
metal	mettle (energy)	metre (distance)	
metalic	metallic	metre	meter (measure)
metallic			
metallurgic		metric	
metallurgical, -ly		metricate, -cated, -cating	
metallurgist		metrication	
metallurgy		metric system	

metronome		middul	middle
metropolis, -lises		middy, -dies (beer)	
metropolitan		middy	midi (skirt)
mettle (energy)		midel	middle
mettle	metal (element)	midge	
metul	mettle (energy)	midget	
mew, -ed, -ing		midi (skirt)	
mews (stables)		midi	middy (beer)
mews	muse (think)	midil	middle
mezanine	mezzanine	midling	middling
mezzanine		midnight	
mi	my	midnite	midnight
mia-mia		mid-off	
miander	meander	mid-on	
miaow, -ed, -ing		midriff	
miasma, -mas, -mata		midshipman, -men	
miasmatical		midst	
miasmic		midul	middle
mica		mid wicket	
mice		midwife, -wives	
microbe		mien (show)	
microbial		mien	mean (intend)
microbic		miff	
microbiological		mige	midge
microbiologist		might (power)	
microbiology		might	mite (small)
micro-economics		mighty, -tier, -tiest	
microfiche		migit	midget
microfilm		migraine	
microfone	microphone	migrane	migraine
micrometer		migrant	
micron		migrate, -grated, -grating	
microphone		migration	
microprocessor		migratory	
microprosessor	microprocessor	migreat	migrate
microscope		mika	mica
microscopic, -ally		mikado, -dos	
microwave		miksamotosis	myxomatosis
midair		mikscher	mixture
midday		mikschur	mixture
middel	middle	mikser	mixer
middle, -led, -ling		miksture	mixture
middleman, -men		mil (millilitre)	
middle-of-the-road		mil	mill (grind)
middlewait	middleweight	mild, -ly	
middleweight		mildew, -ed, -ing	
middling		mildu	mildew

mile		mime, mimed, miming	
mileage		mimic, -icked, -icking	
milestone		mimicry, -ries	
mileniem	millennium	mimosa	
milenium	millennium	minaret	
milet	millet	mince, minced, mincing	
milibar	millibar	mincemeat	
milieu		mincer	
mililiter	millilitre	mind, minded, minding	
milimeter	millimetre	mindful, -ly	
miliner	milliner	mine, mined, mining	
miling	milling	minefield	
milinry	millinery	miner (worker)	
milion	million	miner	minor (less)
milionair	millionaire	miner	myna (bird)
milipeed	millipede	mineral	
milisha	militia	mineralogical, -ly	
militancy		mineralogist	
militansy	militancy	mineralogy	
militant, -ly		minestrone	
militarism		minestroney	minestrone
militarist		minestrony	minestrone
militaristic, -ally		minesweeper	
military		mingel	mingle
militia		mingle, -led, -ling	
milk, -ed, -ing		mingul	mingle
milksop		mingy, -gier, -giest	
milky, -kier, -kiest		mini	
Milky Way		miniature	
mill, milled, milling (grind)		minibus	
millennial, -ly		minicher	miniature
millennium, -niums, -nia		minichur	miniature
miller		minim	
millet		minimal, -ly	
millibar		minimise, -mised, -mising	
milligram		minimiser	
millilitre		minimum, -mums, -ma	
millimetre		minion	
milliner		miniscule	minuscule
millinery		miniskirt	
million		minister	
millionaire		ministerial, -ly	
millipede		ministration	
millpond		ministrative, -ly	
millstone		ministrey	ministry
millwheel		ministry, -tries	
milyou	milieu	minit	minute

mink, minks (animal)

   minks   minx (girl)

minnow, -nows

minor (lesser)

   minor   miner (worker)
   minor   myna (bird)

minority, -ties

   minow   minnow
   minse   mince

minstrel

mint, -ed, -ing

minuet

minus

minuscule

minute, -uted, -uting

minx (girl)

   minx   minks (animals)

   minyouet   minuet
   miopia   myopia
   miow   miaow
   miracel   miracle

miracle

   miracul   miracle

miraculous, -ly

   miraculus   miraculous

mirage

mire, mired, miring

   mirer   mirror
   miriad   myriad

mirrnyong

mirror, -ed, -ing

mirth

mirthful, -ly

   mis   miss
   misadvencher   misadventure
   misadvenchur   misadventure

misadventure

   misal   missal

misanthrope

misanthropic, -ally

misanthropist

misanthropy

misapprehension

misappropriate, -ated, -ating

misappropriation

   misapropriate   misappropriate

misbehave, -haved, -having

miscarriage

miscarry, -ried, -rying

   miscariage   miscarriage
   miscarie   miscarry
   miscarige   miscarriage

miscast, -cast, -casting

miscellaneous, -ly

miscellany, -nies

mischance

   mischanse   mischance

mischief

   mischievious   mischievous

mischievous, -ly

   mischif   mischief
   mischivus   mischievous

misconceive, -ceived, -ceiving

misconceiver

   misconcepshun   misconception

misconception

   misconcieve   misconceive

misconduct

   misconsepshun   misconception

misconstrue, -strued, -struing

miscreant

misdeed

misdemeanour

   misdemener   misdemeanour

misdo, -did, -done, -doing

   mise   mice
   miselanius   miscellaneous
   miselany   miscellany
   miself   myself
   miseltoe   mistletoe

miser

miserable, -ly

   miserabul   miserable

misere

miserly

misery, -ries

misfit, -fitted, -fitting

misfortune

misgiving

mishap

   mishapen   misshapen
   mishion   mission

mishmash

misile	missile
misiltoe	mistletoe
misis	misses
misive	missive
misus	missus
mislay, -laid, -laying	
misle	missal (book)
misle	missile (weapon)
mislead, -led, -leading	
misleader	
misleed	mislead
misnoma	misnomer
misnomer	
misogynist	
misogynous	
misogyny	
misojonist	misogynist
misojonous	misogynous
misojony	misogyny
mispell	misspell
misplace, -placed, -placing	
misplacement	
misplase	misplace
misprint, -ed, -ing	
misrabul	miserable
misrepresent, -ed, -ing	
miss, misses	
miss, missed, missing	
missal (book)	
missal	missile (weapon)
misselaney	miscellany
misselanius	miscellaneous
misselany	miscellany
misses (fail)	
misses	missus (wife)
misshape, -shaped, -shaping	
missile (weapon)	
missile	missal (book)
mission	
missionary, -ries	
missive	
misspell, misspelt, misspelling	
missus (wife)	
mist (cloud)	
mist	missed

mistake, -took, -taking	
mistaken	
misteltoe	mistletoe
mister	
misterey	mystery
misterius	mysterious
mistery	mystery
mistic	mystic
mistic	mystique
mistify	mystify
mistletoe	
mistreat, -ed, -ing	
mistress	
mistrial	
mistrust, -ed, -ing	
misty, -tier, -tiest	
misul	missal
misul	missile
misultoe	mistletoe
misunderstand, -stood, -standing	
misuse, -used, -using	
mite (small)	
mite	might (power)
miten	mitten
miter	mitre
mith	myth
mithical	mythical
mithology	mythology
mitie	mighty
mitigate, -gated, -gating	
mitre, -tred, -tring	
mitt	
mitten	
mix, mixed, mixing	
mixamotosis	myxomatosis
mixcher	mixture
mixchur	mixture
mixer	
mixture	
mix-up	
mizzenmast	
mnemonics	
mo	mow
moa (bird)	
moa	mower (lawn)
moan, moaned, moaning	
moaner	

moat		mogul	
mob, mobbed, mobbing		mohair	
mobile, -ly		Mohammedan	
mobiliety	mobility	mohare	mohair
mobilisation		moiety, -ties	
mobilise, -lised, -lising		moischer	moisture
mobility		moischur	moisture
moccasin		moisen	moisten
mock, mocked, mocking		moisun	moisten
mocker		moist, -ly	
mockery, -ries		moisten, -ed, -ing	
mockingbird		moisture	
mockry	mockery	mokasin	moccasin
mock-up		moke	
modal (manner)		molar	
modal	model (example)	molases	molasses
		molasses	
moddul	modal	molasus	molasses
moddul	model	mold	mould
mode		mole	
model, -elled, -elling (example)		molecular, -ly	
modeller		molecule	
moden	modern	molest, -ed, -ing	
moderate, -rated, -rating		molestation	
moderation		molicodle	mollycoddle
moderator		molicodul	mollycoddle
modern, -ly		moll	
modernity, -ties		mollify, -fied, -fying	
modest, -ly		mollusc	
modesty, -ties		mollycoddle, -dled, -dling	
modicum		moloch	
modifi	modify	Molotov cocktail	
modifiable		molt	malt (liquor)
modifiabul	modifiable	molt	moult (lose)
modification		molten	
modifier		molusk	mollusc
modify, -fied, -fying		molybdenum	
modlin	maudlin	moment	
modul	model	momentarily	
modular		momentary	
modulate, -lated, -lating		momentous, -ly	
modulation		momentum, -ta	
modulator		monakey	monarchy
module		monarch	
moduler	modular	monarchal, -ly	
modulur	modular	monarchic, -ally	
mogo		monarchist	

monarchy, -chies
monastery, -teries
monastic, -ally
monasticism
  monastry — monastery
Monday
  mone — moan
monetary, -rily
money, monies
moneychanger
money-grubber
money-grubbing
moneylender
money market
money order
  monga — monger
mong
monger
Mongol
Mongolian
Mongolism
Mongoloid
mongoose, -gooses
mongrel
  mongrul — mongrel
  moniter — monitor
monitor, -ed, -ing
monk
monkey, -keys
monkey, -keyed, -keying
monkey-wrench
monochromatic, -ally
monochrome
monochromic
monocle
monocled
  monocul — monocle
monogamist
monogamous
  monogamus — monogamous
monogamy
  monograf — monograph
monogram
monograph
  monokrome — monochrome
  monokside — monoxide
monolith

monolithic
  monolog — monologue
monologue
  monoplain — monoplane
monoplane
  monopoley — monopoly
monopolisation
monopolise, -lised, -lising
monopoly, -lies
monorail
  monosilabic — monosyllabic
  monosilabul — monosyllable
monosyllabic, -ally
monosyllable
monotone
monotonous, -ly
  monotonus — monotonous
monotony
monoxide
monsoon
monsoonal
monster
monstera deliciosa
monstrosity, -ties
monstrous, -ly
  monstrus — monstrous
montage
month
monument
monumental, -ly
mooch, -ed, -ing
mood
moody, -dier, -diest
moon
moonlight
moonshine
moonstone
moony, -nier, -niest
moor, -ed, -ing (land)
  moor — more (further)
Moor (Muslim)
moorhen
moose, moose (animal)
  moose — mouse (rodent)
  moose — mousse (food)
  moosli — muesli
moot

moovabul	moveable	morrow	
moove	move	morse code	
mop, mopped, mopping		morsel	
mope, moped, moping		· *mortafy*	mortify
moped		mortal, -ly	
mopoke		mortality, -ties	
moral, -ly		mortar	
moralise, -lised, -lising		mortarboard	
moralist		mortgage, -gaged, -gaging	
moralistic		mortgagee	
moralitey	morality	mortgagor	
morality, -ties		mortice, -ticed, -ticing	
morass		*mortifi*	mortify
moratorium, -toria, -toriums		mortification	
moray, -rays (eel)		mortify, -fied, -fying	
morays	mores (custom)	*mortiss*	mortice
morbid, -ly		mortuary, -ries	
morbidity		*mos*	moss
mordant, -ly		mosaic	
mordern	modern	moselle	
more, most (further)		*moshun*	motion
more	moor (tie up)	*mosk*	mosque
moreover		*moskito*	mosquito
mores (custom)		mosque	
morfine	morphine	mosquito, -toes	
morg	morgue	moss	
morgage	mortgage	most, -ly	
morganatic, -ally		mot	
morgige	mortgage	mote (dust)	
morgue		*mote*	moat (ditch)
moribund, -ly		motel	
moribundity		*moter*	motor
Mormon		*motervate*	motivate
Mormonism		motet	
morn (morning)		moth, moths	
morn	mourn (sorrow)	mothballs	
mornay		mother	
mornful	mournful	motherland	
morning (day)		mother-of-pearl	
morning	mourning (sorrowing)	motif (figure)	
		motif	motive (reason)
moron		motion, -ed, -ing	
moronic		motivate, -vated, -vating	
morose, -ly		motivation	
morover	moreover	motivational	
morow	morrow	motive (reason)	
morphine			

motive	motif (figure)	moveable, -ly	
motle	mottle	movement	
motley, -leys		movie	
motly	motley	mow, mowed, mowing	
moto	motto	mower	
motor, -ed, -ing		mownd	mound
motorbike		mownt	mount
motorcycle		mowntain	mountain
motorcyclist		mowntenus	mountainous
motorist		mowntun	mountain
mottle, -tled, -tling		mowse	mouse
motto, -tos		mowth	mouth
mould, moulded, moulding		mozzarella	
moulder, -ed, -ing		Mr., Messrs.	
mouldy, -dier, -diest		Mrs.	
moult, -ed, -ing (lose)		Ms.	
moult	malt (liquor)	much, more, most	
mound		muchooal	mutual
mount, mounted, mounting		mucilage	
mountain		mucilaginous	
mountaineer		muck, mucked, mucking	
mountainous, -ly		muckrake, -raked, -raking	
mountenus	mountainous	muck-up	
mountun	mountain	mucky, -ier, -iest	
mourn, -ed, -ing (sorrow)		mucous (of mucus)	
mourn	morn (morning)	mucus	
mourner		mud, mudded, mudding	
mournful, -ly		muddie (crab)	
mourning (sorrowing)		muddie	muddy (dirty)
mourning	morning (day)	muddle, -dled, -dling	
mouse, mice (rodent)		muddler	
mouse, moused, mousing		muddy, -died, -dying (dirty)	
mouse	moose (animal)	muddy, -dier, -diest (dirty)	
mouse	mousse (food)	muddy	muddie (crab)
moussaka		mudel	muddle
mousse (food)		mudflat	
moustache		mudflow	
mousy, -sier, -siest		mudguard	
mouth, mouths		mudhopper	
mouthful, -fuls		mudlark	
mouthpeace	mouthpiece	mudle	muddle
mouthpiece		mudrunner	
mouth-to-mouth		mudskipper	
movabel	moveable	mudslinger	
movabul	moveable	muesli	
move, moved, moving		muezzin	
		muff, -ed, -ing	

muffin
muffle, -fled, -fling
muffler
  mufful   muffle
  mufin   muffin
mufti, -tis
mug, mugged, mugging
mugga
mugger
muggins
muggy, -gier, -giest
  mukus   mucous
  mukus   mucus
mulatto, -tos, -toes
  mulberie   mulberry
mulberry, -ries
mulch, -ed, -ing
mule
muleteer
mulga
mulgara
mulish, -ly
mull, -ed, -ing
mullet, -lets, -let
mulligatawny
mullion
mullock
mulloway
  multaple   multiple
  multch   mulch
multicultural
multifaceted
multifarious, -ly
  multifarius   multifarious
  multifaseted   multifaceted
multigrade
multilateral, -ly
multimillionaire
  multinashionul   multinational
multinational
multipartite
multiple
multiple sclerosis
  multipli   multiply
multiplication
multiplicative, -ly
multiplicity, -ties

multiplier
  multiplisity   multiplicity
multiply, -plied, -plying
  multipul   multiple
multitude
multitudinous, -ly
  multitudinus   multitudinous
  mulyun   mullion
mum
mumble, -bled, -bling
mumbo jumbo
  mumbul   mumble
  mumie   mummy
  mumifi   mummify
mummer
mummification
mummify, -fied, -fying
mummy, -mies
mummy, -mied -mying
mumps
  mumy   mummy
munch, munched, munching
munchies
  mundain   mundane
mundane, -ly
  Munday   Monday
  munetry   monetary
  mungrel   mongrel
municipal, -ly
municipality, -ties
  munie   money
  munishun   munition
  munisipality   municipality
  munk   monk
  munky   monkey
  munth   month
  muny   money
  mur   myrrh
mural
murder, -ed, -ing
murderer
murderess
murderous, -ly
murk, -ily
murky, -kier, -kiest
  murmer   murmur
murmur, -ed, -ing

murrain
murth   mirth
murtle   myrtle
mus   mews (stables)
mus   muse(think)
muscat
muscatel
muscle, -cled, -cling (body)
muscle   mussel (fish)
muscle-bound
Muscovy duck
muscular, -ly
muscularity
muse, mused, musing (think)
muse   mews (stables)
musel   muscle (body)
musel   mussel (fish)
museum
mush, -ed, -ing
mushroom, -ed, -ing
mushy, -ier, -iest
music
musical, -ly
musician
musishun   musician
musk
muskatel   muscatel
musket
musketeer
musketry
muskrat, -rats
Muslim, -lims
muslin
mussel (fish)
mussel   muscle (body)
must
mustache   moustache
mustash   moustache
mustang
mustard
muster, -ed, -ing
musterd   mustard
mustie   musty
mutant, -ly
mutate, -tated, -tating
mutation
mute, muted, muting

muter   mutter
mutilate, -lated, -lating
mutilation
mutilator
mutinear   mutineer
mutineer
mutinous, -ly
mutinus   mutinous
mutiny, -nies
mutiny, -nied, -nying
muton   mutton
mutt
mutter, -ed, -ing
mutton
mutton-bird
mutton-chops
mutual, -ly
mutuality
muu-muu
muzak
muzul   muzzle
muzzle, -zled, -zling
myall
myna (bird)
myna   miner (worker)
myna   minor (less)
myopia
myopic
myriad
myrrh
myrtle
myself
mysterious, -ly
mysterius   mysterious
mystery, -ries
mystic (symbol)
mystical, -ly
mysticism
mystification
mystify, -fied, -fying
mystique (secret)
mystisism   mysticism
mystry   mystery
myth
mythical, -ly
mythology, -gies
myxomatosis

Nn

nab, nabbed, nabbing
nabor	neighbour
nachur	nature
nachurul	natural
nack	knack
nacker	knacker
nacker	nacre

nacre (pearl)
nacreous
nadir
nag, nagged, nagging
nagger
nail, nailed, nailing
naive, -ly
naivety
naked, -ly
nakedness
nakid	naked
nale	nail

namby-pamby, -bies
name, named, naming
namely
namesake
nanie	nanny

nankeen kestrel
nanny, -ies
nannygai
nanny-goat
nany	nanny

nap, napped, napping
napalm
naparm	napalm

nape
napery
naphtha
naphthalene
napie	nappy

napkin

nappe (rock)
nappy, -pies (cloth)
napsack	knapsack
naptha	naphtha
narate	narrate
narative	narrative

narcissism
narcissistic
narcissus, -cissuses, -cissi
narcosis
narcotic
nark, -ed, -ing
narl	gnarl
narow	narrow

narrate, -rated, -rating
narration
narrative, -ly
narrator
narrow, -ly
narsissism	narcissism
narsissistic	narcissistic
narsisus	narcissus

nasal, -ly
nasalisation
nasalise, -lised, -lising
nasality
nascence
nascency
nascent, -ly
nasel	nasal
nash	gnash
nashun	nation
nashunal	national
nastie	nasty

nasty, -tier, -tiest
nat	gnat

natal
natch
natel	natal
nater	natter
nateral	natural
naty	natty

nation
national, -ly
nationalism
nationalist
nationalistic, -ally

nationality, -ties		nayl	nail
nation-state		Nazi, -zis	
native		Nazism	
Nativity		nead	knead
Natsi	Nazi	nead	need
natter, -ed, -ing		neadel	needle
natty, -tier, -tiest		neadil	needle
natul	natal	neadle	needle
natur	nature	neadless	needless
natural, -ly		neap	
naturalisation		near, -ed, -ing	
naturalise, -lised, -lising		nearby	
naturalism		nearly	
naturalist		nearside	
naturalistic		neat, -ly	
nature		nebula, -lae, -las	
naturopathy		nebulous, -ly	
naty	natty	nebulus	nebulous
naught		necesarey	necessary
naughty, -tier, -tiest		necesitate	necessitate
nausea		necesitey	necessity
nauseate, -ated, -ating		necessarily	
nauseation		necessary, -saries	
nauseous, -ly		necessitate, -tated, -tating	
nautical, -ly		necessity, -ties	
nautilus, -luses		neck	
naval (ship)		neckerchief	
naval	navel (body)	neckliss	necklace
nave (church)		necklace	
nave	knave (rogue)	necksus	nexus
navel (body)		necktie	
navel orange		necromancer	
navie	navvy	necromancy	
navie	navy	necromanser	necromancer
navigabel	navigable	necromansey	necromancy
navigable, -bly		necrofilia	necrophilia
navigate, -gated, -gating		necrofiliac	necrophiliac
navigation		necrofilism	necrophilism
navigator		necrophilia	
navul	naval (ship)	necrophiliac	
navul	navel (body)	necrophilism	
navvy, -vies (worker)		necropolis, -lises	
navy, -vies (warships)		nectar	
naw	gnaw	nectarine	
nay (no)		nee (name)	
nay	neigh (horse)	nee	knee (limb)
naybour	neighbour	need, -ed, -ing (necessary)	

need	knead (dough)	neither (nor)	
need	kneed (use	neither	nether (below)
	knee)	nek	neck
needful, -ly		neklace	necklace
needle, -dled, -dling		neklis	necklace
needless, -ly		nekrofilia	necrophilia
needlework		nekropolis	necropolis
needul	needle	nell	knell
neel	kneel	nemesis, -ses	
neer	near	nemisis	nemesis
ne'er-do-well		nemonics	mnemonics
neet	neat	neofite	neophyte
nefarious, -ly		Neolithic	
nefarius	nefarious	neologise, -gised, -gising	
nefew	nephew	neon	
negate, -gated, -gating		neophyte	
negation		nephew	
negative, -tived, -tiving		nephrism	
negativity		nephritic	
negatory		nephritis	
neglect, -ed, -ing		nepotism	
neglectful, -ly		Neptune	
negligee		nerd	
negligence		nerve, nerved, nerving	
negligense	negligence	nerve centre	
negligent, -ly		nerve-racking	
negligibility		nerveous	nervous
negligible, -bly		nerveus	nervous
negligibul	negligible	nervous, -ly	
neglijay	negligee	nervy, -vier, -viest	
negoshabul	negotiable	nesessary	necessary
negoshiate	negotiate	nesessitate	necessitate
negotiability		nesessitey	necessity
negotiable, -bly		nesessity	necessity
negotiant		nesle	nestle
negotiate, -ated, -ating		nest, -ed, -ing	
negotiation		nestle, -tled, -tling	
Negro, -groes		nesul	nestle
Negroid		net, netted, netting	
neice	niece	netball	
neigh (horse)		netha	neither (nor)
neigh	nay (no)	netha	nether (below)
neighbor	neighbour	nether (below)	
neighbour		nether	neither (nor)
neighbourhood		nettle, -tled, -tling	
neighbouring		nettul	nettle
neighbourly		network	

neumatic	pneumatic
neural, -ly	
neuralgia	
neuralgic	
neuritic	
neuritis	
neurological, -ly	
neurologist	
neurology	
neurone	
neurosis, -ses	
neurotic, -ally	
neuter	
neutral, -ly	
neutralisation	
neutralise, -lised, -lising	
neutrality	
neutron	
neva	never
never-never	
nevertheless	
new (novel)	
new	gnu (animal)
new	knew
newclear	nuclear
newcleus	nucleus
newcomer	
newfangled	
Newfoundland	
newmatic	pneumatic
newmonia	pneumonia
newral	neural
newrologist	neurologist
newrone	neurone
newrosis	neurosis
newrotic	neurotic
news	
newsagency	
newsagent	
newscast, -cast, -casting	
newscaster	
newsletter	
newsman, -men	
newspaper	
newspeak	
newsprint	
news reader	

newsreel	
newt	
newter	neuter
newtralise	neutralise
newtron	neutron
New Zealander	
next	
next of kin	
nexus, nexus	
ni	nigh
nib	
nibbel	nibble
nibble, -bled, -bling	
nibbler	
nibul	nibble
nice, nicer, nicest	
nicety, -ties	
niche	
nick, -ed, -ing	
nickel, -elled, -elling	
nickerbockers	knickerbockers
nickers	knickers
nickle	nickel
nicknack	knick-knack
nickname, -named, -naming	
nicks	nix
nicotine	
niece	
niether	neither
nifarius	nefarious
nife	knife
niftie	nifty
nifty, -tier, -tiest	
nigel	niggle
nigerd	niggard
niggard	
niggle, -gled, -gling	
nigh	
night, -ly (time)	
night	knight (lord)
nightcap	
nightclub	
nightdress	
nightingale	
nightjar	
nightmare	
nightmarish	

nightsoil
nightwatchman
  nigle   niggle
  niglect   neglect
  nigul   niggle
nihilism
nil
  nilon   nylon
nimble, -bler, -blest
  nimbul   nimble
nimbus, -bi, -buses
  nimf   nymph
  nimph   nymph
nine
ninepins
nineteen
nineteenth
ninety, -ties
  ninie   ninny
ninny, -nies
ninth, -ly
  nion   neon
nip, nipped, nipping
  nipie   nippy
  niple   nipple
nipper
nipple
nippy, -pier, -piest
  nipul   nipple
  nipy   nippy
nirvana
  nise   nice
  nisitey   nicety
nit (insect)
  nit   knit (stitch)
  nite   knight (lord)
  nite   night (time)
  niter   nitre
  nither   neither
nitpick, -ed, -ing
nitpicker
nitrate, -trated, -trating
nitration
nitre
nitric
  nitrifi   nitrify
nitrification

nitrify, -fied, -fying
nitrite
nitrogen
nitrogenous
  nitrogliserine   nitroglycerine
nitroglycerine
  nitrojen   nitrogen
  nitting   knitting
nitty-gritty
nitwit
  nives   knives
nix
no (denial)
  no   know
nob (person)
  nob   knob (handle)
no-ball
nobble, -bled, -bling
  nobie   knobby
nobility, -ties
noble, nobler, noblest
nobleman, -men
nobody, -bodies
  nobul   noble
  nock   knock
  nocker   knocker
  nockneed   knock-kneed
nocturnal, -ly
nocturne
nod, nodded, nodding
nodal
noddy, -dies
node
nodular
nodule
Noel
noes (denials)
  noes   knows
  noes   nose (on face)
noggin (cup, head)
nogging (timber)
no-go
no-hoper
noise, noised, noising
noisily
noisiness
noisome, -ly

noisy, noisier, noisiest
noisy miner
  noledge   knowledge
  noll   knoll
nomad
nomadic, -ally
nomadism
no-man's-land
nom de plume
  nome   gnome
nomenclature
nominal, -ly
nominate, -nated, -nating
nomination
nominative
nominator
nominee
  non   none
nonaggression
  nonagressiun   nonaggression
nonagon
nonce
nonchalance
non-combatant
non-commissioned
non-committal, -ly
non compos
  non compus   non compos
non-conducting
non-conformance
non-conformity
nondescript
none
nonentity, -ties
nonetheless
non-fiction
non-fictional
nonflammable
nong
  no-nonsence   no-nonsense
no-nonsense
nonpareil
nonplus, -plussed, -plussing
non-productive, -ly
non-proliferation
non-representational
non-sectarian

  nonsence   nonsense
nonsense
nonsensical, -ly
non-U
non-violence
non-violent, -ly
noodle
  noogar   nougat
nook
noon
noose, noosed, noosing
nope
nor
  nor   gnaw
Nordic
norm
normal, -ly
normalcy
normalisation
normalise, -lised, -lising
Norman
normative, -ly
  norsia   nausea
  norsiate   nauseate
  nort   naught (ruin)
  nort   nought (nil)
  nortey   naughty
north
northerly
northern
northerner
northward, -ly
  nortickel   nautical
  nortie   naughty
nose, nosed, nosing (on face)
  nose   knows
  nose   noes (denial)
nosebag
nosedive, -dived, -diving
nosegay
nosey, -sier, -siest
nosily
nosiness
nostalgia
nostalgic, -ally
  nostrem   nostrum
nostril

nostrim	nostrum
nostrum	
nosy, -sier, -siest	
not (denial)	
not	knot (tie)
nota bene	
notability	
notable, -bly	
notarial, -ly	
notary, -ries	
notation	
notch, -ed, -ing	
note, noted, noting	
notefy	notify
nothing	
notice, -ticed, -ticing	
noticeable, -bly	
noticeabul	noticeable
notifiable	
notification	
notifier	
notify, -fied, -fying	
notion	
notional, -ly	
not negotiable	
notories	notorious
notoriety, -ties	
notorious, -ly	
notorius	notorious
notwithstanding	
nougar	nougat
nougat	
nought	
noughts-and-crosses	
noun	
nourish, -ed, -ing	
nourishingly	
nourishment	
nous	
nouveau riche, nouveaux riches	
novel	
novelette	
novelist	
novella, novellas, novelle	
novelty, -ties	
November	
novice	

novitiate	
now	
nowadays	
nowhere	
nowing	knowing
nowledge	knowledge
noxious, -ly	
noxius	noxious
nozzle	
nozzul	nozzle
nu	gnu (animal)
nu	knew
nu	new (novel)
nuance	
nuanse	nuance
nub	
nubile	
nuckle	knuckle
nuclear	
nuclear bomb	
nuclear energy	
nuclear family	
nuclear fishun	nuclear fission
nuclear fission	
nuclear fusion	
nuclear power	
nuclear reaction	
nuclear reactor	
nucleus, -clei, -cleuses	
nude, -ly	
nudge, nudged, nudging	
nudism	
nudist	
nudity	
nuge	nudge
nugget	
nuisance	
nulifi	nullify
null	
nulla-nulla	
nullification	
nullify, -fied, -fying	
num	numb
numatic	pneumatic
numb, numbed, numbing	
number, -ed, -ing	
numberless	

numberplate	
numbness	
numbskull	
numeracy	
numeral	
numerasy	numeracy
numerate, -rated, -rating	
numeration	
numerator	
numerical, -ly	
numericul	numerical
numerological	
numerology	
numerous, -ly	
numerus	numerous
numismatics	
numismatist	
numonia	pneumonia
nun (woman)	
nun	none (no one)
nunnery, -neries	
nupshal	nuptial
nuptial	
nural	neural
nuralgia	neuralgia
nurcher	nurture
nuritis	neuritis
nurologist	neurologist
nurone	neurone
nurosis	neurosis
nurotic	neurotic
nurse, nursed, nursing	
nursery, -eries	
nursrey	nursery
nurture, -tured, -turing	
nurve	nerve
nusance	nuisance
nuse	news
nuspaper	newspaper
nut, nutted, nutting	
nuter	neuter
nutcracker	
nutmeg	
nutral	neutral
nutrient	
nutriment	
nutrishun	nutrition

nutrishus	nutritious
nutrition	
nutritional, -ly	
nutritionist	
nutritious, -ly	
nutron	neutron
nuts	
nutshell	
nutty, -tier, -tiest	
nuty	nutty
nuzul	nuzzle
nuzzle, -zled, -zling	
nylon	
nymf	nymph
nymph	
nymphomania	
nymphomaniac	

Oo

oaf
oak
oar (boat)

oar	awe (dread)
oar	or
oar	ore (rock)

oasis, oases
oat
oath, oaths
oatmeal

| obay | obey |
| obbese | obese |

obduracy

| obdurasey | obduracy |

obdurate, -ly
obedience

| obediense | obedience |

obedient, -ly
obeisance

| obeisanse | obeisance |

obelisk
obese, -ly
obesity

| obessence | obeisance |

obey, -ed, -ing
obituary, -aries

| objecshun | objection |
| objay dart | objet d'art |

object, -ed, -ing
objection
objectionable, -bly

| objectionabul | objectionable |

objective, -ly
objectivity
objector
objet d'art, objets d'art
oblation

| obleek | oblique |

obligate, -gated, -gating
obligation
obligatory
oblige, obliged, obliging

| oblik | oblique |

oblique, obliqued, obliquing
obliquity, -ties
obliterate, -rated, -rating
oblivion
oblivious, -ly

| oblivius | oblivious |

oblong
obloquy, -quies

| obnokshus | obnoxious |

obnoxious, -ly

| obo | oboe |

oboe
oboist
obscene, -ly
obscenity, -ties
obscure, -scured, -scuring
obscure, -scurer, -scurest
obscurity, -ties
obsecrate, -crated, -crating

obseen	obscene
obsekwies	obsequious
obsekwius	obsequious

obsequious, -ly
observance
observant, -ly
observation
observatory, -tories

| observatry | observatory |

observe, -served, -serving

| obseshun | obsession |

obsess, -ed, -ing
obsession
obsessive, -ly
obsolescence
obsolescent, -ly

| obsolesense | obsolescence |
| obsolesent | obsolescent |

obsolete, -ly
obstacle

| obstacul | obstacle |
| obstatrician | obstetrician |

obstetric, -ally

obstetrician
obstetrics
  obstetrishen — obstetrician
  obstetrishun — obstetrician
obstinacy, -cies
  obstinasey — obstinacy
obstinate, -ly
obstreperous, -ly
  obstreperus — obstreperous
  obstrucshun — obstruction
obstruct, -ed, -ing
obstruction
obstructive, -ly
obtain, -ed, -ing
  obtane — obtain
  obtroode — obtrude
  obtroosive — obtrusive
obtrude, -truded, -truding
obtrusive, -ly
obtuse, -ly
obverse, -ly
obviate, -ated, -ating
obviation
obvious, -ly
  obvius — obvious
  ocasion — occasion
  occashun — occasion
occasion, -ed, -ing
occasional, -ly
Occident
occidental
occlude, -cluded, -cluding
  occlushun — occlusion
occlusion
  occular — ocular
occult
occultism
occupancy
occupant
occupation
occupational
  occupent — occupant
  occupi — occupy
occupy, -pied, -pying
occur, -curred, -curring
  occurense — occurrence
occurrence

ocean
Oceania
oceanic
  oceanografey — oceanography
oceanographer
oceanography
ocelot
  ocher — ochre
ochre, ochred, ochring
ochrous
ocker
  Ocktober — October
o'clock
  oclood — occlude
  ocloosion — occlusion
  ocsident — Occident
octagon
octagonal, -ly
octane
octave
octavo
octet
October
octogenarian
octopus, -puses -pi
ocular, -ly
  ocult — occult
  ocupancy — occupancy
  ocupant — occupant
  ocupi — occupy
  ocur — occur
  ocurence — occurrence
  ocurents — occurrence
  od — odd
odd, -ly
oddball
oddbod
oddity, -ties
oddment
odds
odds-on
  odeclone — eau-de-Cologne
  oderus — odorous
  odiferus — odoriferous
odious, -ly
  odissey — odyssey
odium

odius	odious	offishul	official
odontology		offishus	officious
odor	odour	off-limits	
odoriferous, -ly		off-load, -loaded, -loading	
odorous, -ly		off-peak	
odour		off-putting	
odyssey		off-season	
Oedipus complex		offset, -set, -setting	
oenin		offshoot	
oesofagus	oesophagus	offshore	
oesophagus, -gi		off side (cricket)	
oestrogen		offside (rugby)	
of		offsider	
of	off (away)	offspring	
ofal	offal	oficial	official
ofence	offence	oficiate	officiate
ofend	offend	oficious	officious
ofen	often	ofis	office
ofense	offence	ofiser	officer
ofensive	offensive	ofishal	official
ofer	offer	ofishiate	officiate
off (away)		ofishus	officious
off	of	ofset	offset
offal		ofshoot	offshoot
off-beat		ofside	offside
off-colour		ofspring	offspring
offcourse		oft	
off-cut		often	
offence		ogel	ogle
offend, -ed, -ing		oger	ogre
offender		ogle, ogled, ogling	
offense	offence	ogre	
offensive, -ly		oh	
offer, -ed, -ing		ohm	
offering		oil, oiled, oiling	
offertory, -ries		oilcloth	
offhand		oilfield	
offhanded, -ly		oilly	oily
office		oil rig	
officer		oilskin	
official, -ly		oily, oilier, oiliest	
officialdom		ointment	
officiate, -ated, -ating		oister	oyster
officiation		ok	oak
officious, -ly		okay	
offing		oks	ox
offise	office	oksalic acid	oxalic acid

oksidate	oxidate	on	own
okside	oxide	once	
oksident	Occident	oncore	encore
oksidise	oxidise	oncourse	
oksyacetylene	oxyacetylene	one (number)	
oksygen	oxygen	one	won (win)
oksymoron	oxymoron	one-eyed	
old, older, oldest		one-off	
olden		oner	owner
oldish		oneres	onerous
old-timer		onerous, -ly	
oleaginous		onership	ownership
oleaginus	oleaginous	oneself	
oleander		one-sided, -ly	
olearia		onest	honest
olfachun	olfaction	one-upmanship	
olfaction		oniks	onyx
olfactory, -ries		onion	
olfactry	olfactory	onist	honest
oligarch		onor	honour
oligarchic		onistey	honesty
oligarchy, -chies		onley	only
oligarkey	oligarchy	only	
Olimpic	Olympic	onorarey	honorary
oliv	olive	onorarium	honorarium
olive		onrabul	honourable
omelette		onrush	
omen		onset	
ominous, -ly		on side (cricket)	
ominus	ominous	onside (rugby)	
omishun	omission	onslaught	
omission		onslawt	onslaught
omit, omitted, omitting		onslort	onslaught
omlet	omelette	onto	
omnibus, -buses		ontological	
omnipotence		ontology	
omnipotense	omnipotence	ontray	entree
omnipotent, -ly		ontreprener	entrepreneur
omnipresence		onus	
omnipresent		onward	
omniscience		onwards	
omniscient, -ly		onyx	
omnisiense	omniscience	oomph	
omnisient	omniscient	ooze, oozed, oozing	
omnivorous, -ly		opacity, -ties	
omnivorus	omnivorous	opake	opaque
on		opal	

opaline
opaque, opaqued, opaquing
  opasity   opacity
  opeate   opiate
open, -ed, -ing
openly
open-minded
open-range
open-verdict
opera
operable, -bly
  operabul   operable
operate, -rated, -rating
  operater   operator
operatic, -ally
operation
operational, -ly
operative, -ly
operator
operetta
ophthalmic
ophthalmologist
ophthalmology
opiate, -ated, -ating
opine, opined, opining
opinion
opinionated
  opinyun   opinion
opium
  oponent   opponent
  oportune   opportune
  oportunitey   opportunity
  opose   oppose
  oposishun   opposition
  oposite   opposite
  oposition   opposition
opossum
  oposum   opossum
opponency
opponent
opportune, -ly
opportunism
opportunist
opportunity, -ties
oppose, -posed, -posing
opposite
opposition

oppress, -ed, -ing
oppression
oppressive, -ly
oppressor
opprobrious, -ly
opprobrium
  oprabul   operable
  oprate   operate
  opreshun   oppression
  opresive   oppressive
  opress   oppress
  opshun   option
  opshunul   optional
opt, -ed, -ing
  opthalmic   ophthalmic
  opthalmology   ophthalmology
optic
optical, -ly
optician
optics
optimism
optimist
optimistic, -ally
optimum, -ma, -mums
option
optional, -ly
  optishun   optician
optometrist
optometry
opulence
  opulense   opulence
opulent, -ly
opus, opuses, opera
or
  or   awe (dread)
  or   oar (boat)
  or   ore (rock)
  ora   aura
oracle
  oracul   oracle
oracular, -ly
oral, -ly (spoken)
  oral   aural (hear)
  orangatang   orang-outang
orange
orang-outang
  orashun   oration

orater	orator	orfanaje	orphanage
oration		orful	awful
orator		orfun	orphan
oratorical, -ly		organ	
oratorio, -rios		organdie, -dies	
oratory, -ries		organic, -ally	
oratrey	oratory	organisation	
orb		organise, -nised, -nising	
orbit, -ed, -ing		organism	
orbital		organist	
orcestra	orchestra	organza	
orcestral	orchestral	orgasm	
orcestrate	orchestrate	orgenism	organism
orchard		orger	auger (tool)
orchardist		orger	augur (omen)
orchestra		orgey	orgy
orchestral, -ly		orgiastic	
orchestrate, -trated, -trating		orgy, -gies	
orchestration		orical	auricle (ear)
orchid		orical	oracle (seer)
orcid	orchid	oriel	
ordain, -ed, -ing		orient	
ordanal	ordinal	oriental	
ordane	ordain	orientate, -tated, -tating	
ordeal		orientation	
ordenrey	ordinary	orienteering	
order, -ed, -ing		orifice	
orderly, -lies		orifise	orifice
orderliness		origami	
ordinal		origin	
ordinance (law)		original, -ly	
ordinariness		originality, -ties	
ordinary, -ries		originate, -nated, -nating	
ordination		oringe	orange
ordinry	ordinary	oriole	
orditer	auditor	orjy	orgy
orditrey	auditory	orkestra	orchestra
ordnance (weapons)		orkestral	orchestral
ordnance	ordinance (law)	orkestrate	orchestrate
ordure		orkestration	orchestration
ore (rock)		orkid	orchid
ore	oar (boat)	ornament	
ore	or (either)	ornamental, -ly	
ore	awe (dread)	ornamentation	
oregano		ornate, -ly	
orfan	orphan	ornimant	ornament
orfanage	orphanage	orning	awning

ornithologist
ornithology
orotund
orphan
orphanage
Orphism
orris
  orspishus — auspicious
  orstruck — awestruck
  orsum — awesome
  ort — aught
  ort — ought
  orthedoks — orthodox
orthodontic
orthodontics
orthodontist
orthodox
orthodoxy, -doxies
  orthografey — orthography
orthography, -phies
orthopaedic
orthopaedics
orthopaedist
orthopaedy
  orthopeadic — orthopaedic
  orthority — authority
  oscilation — oscillation
oscillate, -lated, -lating (move)
  oscillate — osculate (kiss)
oscillation
oscillator
oscilloscope
osculate, -lated, -lating (kiss)
  osculate — oscillate (move)
  oseanic — oceanic
  oselot — ocelot
  oshun — ocean
osier
  osifi — ossify
  osler — ostler
osmosis
  ospray — osprey
osprey, -preys
  ossifi — ossify
ossification
ossify, -fied, -fying
  ossilate — oscillate

  ossilation — oscillation
  ossiloscope — oscilloscope
  osteapath — osteopath
ostensible, -bly
  ostensibul — ostensible
ostentation
ostentatious, -ly
osteoarthritis
osteomyelitis
osteopath
osteopathic
osteopathy
ostler
ostracise, -cised, -cising
ostracism
  ostrasise — ostracise
  ostrasism — ostracism
ostrich
  ote — oat
  oter — otter
  oth — oath
other
otherwise
otherworldly
otic
otiose, -ly
otiosity
  otoman — ottoman
otter
ottoman, -mans
ouch
ought (should)
  ought — aught (any part)
ouija
  oul — owl
ounce
  ounse — ounce
our (us)
  our — hour
  ourly — hourly
ours
ourself, -selves
oust, ousted, ousting
ouster
out, -ed, -ing
outback

outbilding	outbuilding
outboard	
outbrake	outbreak
outbreak	
outbuilding	
outburst	
outcast	
outcome	
outcri	outcry
outcrop, -cropped, -cropping	
outcry, -cries	
outdate, -dated, -dating	
outdo, -done, -doing	
outdoor	
outdoors	
outer	
outfall	
outfield	
outfit, -fitted, -fitting	
outflank, -ed, -ing	
outfox, -ed, -ing	
outgoing	
outgrow, -grew, -grown, -growing	
outgrowth	
outhouse	
outhowse	outhouse
outlandish, -ly	
outlast, -ed, -ing	
outlaw	
outlawry	
outlay, -laid, -laying	
outlet	
outline, -lined, -lining	
outlive, -lived, -living	
outlook	
outlying	
outmode, -moded, -moding	
out-of-date	
out-of-doors	
out-of-pocket	
out-of-the-way	
outpatient	
outpayshent	outpatient
outperform, -ed, -ing	
outplay, -ed, -ing	
outpoint, -ed, -ing	
outpooring	outpouring

outpost	
outpouring	
output	
outrage, -raged, -raging	
outrageous, -ly	
outraygus	outrageous
outrider	
outrigger	
outright	
outrite	outright
outset	
outside	
outsider	
outsize	
outskirts	
outspoken, -ly	
outstanding, -ly	
outstretch, -ed, -ing	
outstrip, -stripped, -stripping	
outward, -ly	
outwards	
outweigh	
outwit, -witted, -witting	
ouze	ooze
ov	of
oval, -ly	
ovarey	ovary
ovary, -ries	
ovate	
ovation	
oven	
ovenproof	
ovenware	
ovenwear	ovenware
over, -ly	
overall	
overarm	
overawe, -awed, -awing	
overawl	overall
overbalance, -anced, -ancing	
overbalanse	overbalance
overbare	overbear
overbear, -bore, -borne, -bearing	
overbid, -bid, -bidding	
overboard	
overbord	overboard
overbridge	

overcast, -cast, -casting
overcharge, -charged, -charging
overcoat
overcome, -came, -come, -coming
   overdew   overdue
overdo, -did, -done, -doing
overdose, -dosed, -dosing
overdraft
overdraw, -drew, -drawn, -drawing
overdress, -ed, -ing
overdrive, -drove, -driven, -driving
   overdu   overdue
overdue
overestimate, -mated, -mating
overestimation
overflow, -flowed, -flowing
overgrown
overhang, -hung, -hanging
overhaul, -ed, -ing
   overhawl   overhaul
overhead
overhear, -heard, -hearing
overhearer
   overhed   overhead
   overherd   overheard
   overhere   overhear
   overjoid   overjoyed
overjoyed
overkill
overland
overlander
overlap, -lapped, -lapping
overlay, -laid, -laying
overleaf
   overleef   overleaf
overlie, -lay, -lain, -lying (lie over)
   overlie   overly
overlook
overly (excessively)
   overly   overlie
overnight
   overnite   overnight
   overore   overawe
   overought   overwrought
overpass
overpower, -ed, -ing
   overeach   overreach

   overeech   overreach
   overiding   overriding
overreach, -ed, -ing
override, -rode, -ridden, -riding
   overrool   overrule
overrule, -ruled, -ruling
overrun, -ran, -run, -running
   overule   overrule
   overun   overrun
overseas (abroad)
oversee, -saw, -seen, -seeing
overseer
overshadow, -ed, -ing
overshoot, -shot, -shooting
oversight
   oversite   oversight
overstate, -stated, -stating
overstatement
overstay, -ed, -ing
overstep, -stepped, -stepping
overstock, -ed, -ing
oversubscribed
overt, -ly
overtake, -taken, -taking
   overtaks   overtax
overtax
overthrow, -thrown, -throwing
overtime, -timed, -timing
overtone
overture, -tured, -turing
overturn, -ed, -ing
overview
   overwait   overweight
   overwate   overweight
overweight
   overwelm   overwhelm
   overwerk   overwork
overwhelm, -ed, -ing
overwork, -worked, -working
overwrought
ovine
   ovipares   oviparous
   oviparis   oviparous
oviparous, -ly
   oviparus   oviparous
ovoid (egg)
   ovoid   avoid (evade)

ovulate, -lated, -lating
ovulation
ovule
ovum, ova
   owa   hour
   owa   our
owe, owed, owing (debt)
   owe   oh (cry)
owl
own, -ed, -ing
   ownce   ounce
owner
ownership
   ownly   only
   owst   oust
   owt   out
ox, oxen
oxalis
oxidate, -dated, -dating
oxidation
oxide
oxidisable
   oxidisabul   oxidisable
oxidisation
oxidise, -dised, -dising
oxidiser
   oxigenate   oxygenate
oxyacetylene
oxygen
oxygenate, -nated, -nating
oxygenation
oxygenise, -nised, -nising
oxymoron, -mora
oyster
Oz
ozone
ozonize, -ized, -izing
ozonosphere

Pp

pace, paced, pacing
pacemaker
pacer
  pach   patch
  pachwork   patchwork
pacific, -ally
pacification
pacifier
pacifism
pacifist
pacify, -fied, -fying
pack, -ed, -ing
package
packer
packet
packhorse
  packije   package
pact
pad, padded, padding
paddle, -dled, -dling
paddler
paddle-steamer
paddock
  paddul   paddle
paddy, -dies
paddy-wagon
  pade   paddy
  padie   paddy
padlock, -ed, -ing
padre
  padrey   padre
  pady   paddy
paediatrician
paediatrics
pagan
paganism
page, paged, paging
pageant

pageantry, -ries
  pagentry   pageantry
pageboy
pager
pagoda
pail (bucket)
  pail   pale (white)
pain (ache)
  pain   pane (glass)
painful, -ly
pain-killer
painstaking, -ly
paint, -ed, -ing
painter
pair, -ed, -ing (two)
  pair   pare (trim)
  pair   pear (fruit)
pakeha
pal, palled, palling (friend)
palace
  palase   palace
palatable, -bly
palatal, -ly (taste)
palate (mouth)
  palate   palette (board)
  palate   pallet (bed)
  palate   pellet (ball)
palatial, -ly (palace)
pale, paled, paling (white)
pale, paler, palest
  pale   pail (bucket)
palette (board)
  palette   pallet (bed)
  paliate   palliate
  palid   pallid
palindrome
paling
palisade, -saded, -sading
pall, palled, palling (satiate)
pallbearer
pallet (bed)
  pallet   palette (paint)
  pallet   pellet (ball)
palliate, -ated, -ating
palliation
palliative, -ly
pallid, -ly

pall-mall (game)
pall-mall — pell-mell
— (haste)
pallor
palm, -ed, -ing
palmist
palmistry
palmy, -mier, -miest
palomino, -nos
palor — pallor
palpable, -bly
palpabul — palpable
palpitate, -tated, -tating
palpitation
palsie — palsy
palsied
palsy, -sies
paltrie — paltry
paltriness
paltry, -trier, -triest
pamplet — pamphlet
pampas
pamper, -ed, -ing
pamphlet
pamphleteer
pan, panned, panning
panacea
panache
Panama hat
panash — panache
pancake, -caked, -caking
pancreas
pancreatic
panda (animal)
pandemonium
pander, -ed, -ing (indulge)
pane (glass)
pane — pain (ache)
paneful — painful
panegyric, -ally
panel, -elled, -elling
panellist
panestaking — painstaking
pang
panic, -icked, -icking
paniced — panicked
panicky

panic-stricken
panigiric — panegyric
panik — panic
pannier
pannikin
panorama
panoramic, -ally
pansie — pansy
pansy, -sies
pant, -ed, -ing
pantaloon
pantechnicon
pantheism
pantheist
pantheistic, -ally
pantheon
panther
panthion — pantheon
panties
pantihose
pantingly
pantograf — pantograph
pantograph
pantomime
pantomine — pantomime
pantrey — pantry
pantry, -ries
pants
panza — panzer
panzer
pap
papa
papacy, -cies
papal
papasy — papacy
paper
paperback
paperbark
paperboy
paperclip
paper-mache — papier-mâché
paperwait — paperweight
paperweight
papier-mâché
papirus — papyrus
papism
papoose

papouse	papoose	parameter	
pappa	papa	paramiter	parameter
pappoose	papoose	paramoor	paramour
papprika	paprika	paramount	
pappyrus	papyrus	paramour	
paprica	paprika	paramownt	paramount
paprika		paranoia	
papul	papal	paranoiac	
papyrus, -ri		paranoid	
parable		parapet	
parabola		paraphernalia	
parabul	parable	paraphrase, -phrased, -phrasing	
parachute		paraplegic	
paracide	parricide	paraplijic	paraplegic
paracleet	paraclete	parashoot	parachute
paraclete		parashute	parachute
parade, -raded, -rading		parasite	
paradice	paradise	parasitic, -ally	
paradigm		parasitism	
paradime	paradigm	parasol	
paradise		parasoll	parasol
paradoks	paradox	paratrooper	
paradox		parboil, -ed, -ing	
parady	parody	parboyle	parboil
parafernalia	paraphernalia	parcel, -celled, -celling	
paraffin		parch, -ed, -ing	
parafin	paraffin	parchment	
parafrase	paraphrase	pardon, -ed, -ing	
paragon		pardonable	
paragraf	paragraph	pardonabul	pardonable
paragraph		pardoner	
parakeet		pare (trim)	
parakete	parakeet	pare	pair (two)
paralax	parallax	pare	pear (fruit)
paralel	parallel	parent	
paralelagram	parallelogram	parentage	
paralise	paralyse	parental, -ly	
paralisis	paralysis	parenthesis, -ses	
paralitic	paralytic	parentige	parentage
parallax		**parfait**	
parallel, -leled, -leling or -lelled,		parfay	parfait
-lelling		**pariah**	
parallelogram		parie	parry
paralyse, -lysed, -lysing		**parish, parishes**	
paralysis		**parishioner**	
paralytic		parishoner	parishioner
paramedical		pariside	parricide

parisidul	parricidal
parity	
park, -ed, -ing	
parka	
parket	parquet
parking-meter	
Parkinson's disease	
parlament	parliament
parlance	
parlans	parlance
parlay	parley
parlement	parliament
parlementarey	parliamentary
parlementry	parliamentary
parler	parlour
parlermade	parlour-maid
parley, -leyed, -leying	
parliament	
parliamentarian	
parliamentary	
parlour	
parlour-maid	
parm	palm
parmist	palmist
parochial, -ly	
parochialism	
parody, -dies	
parody, -died, -dying	
parograf	paragraph
paragraph	paragraph
parokial	parochial
paroksism	paroxysm
parole, -roled, -roling	
paroll	parole
parot	parrot
paroxysm	
parquet, -queted, -queting	
parranoia	paranoia
parricide	
parrot	
parry, parried, parrying	
parse, parsed, parsing	
parsel	parcel
parshal	partial
parshialitey	partiality
parsimonious, -ly	
parsimonius	parsimonious

parsimony	
parsley	
parslie	parsley
parsly	parsley
parsnip	
parson	
parsonage	
parsonige	parsonage
parsul	parcel
part, -ed, -ing	
partake, -took, -taken, -taking	
partial, -ly	
partiality, -ties	
participant	
participate, -pated, -pating	
participle	
participul	participle
particle	
particul	particle
particular, -ly	
partie	party
partime	part-time
partisan	
partishun	partition
partisipant	participant
partisipate	participate
partisipul	participle
partition, -ed, -ing	
partly	
partner, -ed, -ing	
partridge	
partrige	partridge
part-time	
party, -ties	
pars	pass
pary	parry
pasabul	passable
pascal	paschal
paschal	
pascher	pasture
pase	pace
pasemaker	pacemaker
paserby	passer-by
pashonate	passionate
pashun	passion
pasific	pacific
pasify	pacify

pasige	passage		patchy, patchier, patchiest	
pasinger	passenger		pâté	
pasive	passive		patella, -tellae	
pasivitey	passivity		paten	pattern
Pasover	Passover		patent, -ed, -ing	
paspalum			patent-leather	
pasport	passport		pater	patter
pass, passed, passing			patern	pattern
passable, -bly			paternal, -ly	
passabul	passable		paternalism	
passage, -saged, -saging			paternity	
passbook			path	
passé			pathetic, -ally	
passenger			pathological, -ly	
passer-by, passers-by			pathology, -gies	
passige	passage		pathos	
passion			patie	patty
passionate, -ly			patience (calm)	
passionfruit			patient, patients (ill)	
passive, -ly			patient, -ly	
passivity			patina	
Passover			patio, patios	
passport			patiserey	patisserie
password			patisserie	
past			patois, patois	
pasta (dough)			patriarch	
pasta	pastor (priest)		patriarchal, -ly	
paste, pasted, pasting			patriarchy, -archies	
pasteboard			patriark	patriarch
pastel			patrician	
pasterise	pasteurise		patricide	
pasteurise, -ed, -ing			patrimony, -monies	
pastiche			patriot	
pastie	pasty		patriotic, -ally	
pastime			patriotism	
pastor (priest)			patrishun	patrician
pastoral, -ly			patriside	patricide
pastoralist			patrol, patrolled, patrolling	
pastrami			patron	
pastry, -tries			patronage	
pasture, -ed, -ing			patroness	
pasty, -ties			patronige	patronage
pasword	password		patronise, -ed, -ing	
pat, patter, patting			patter, -ed, -ing	
patay	pâté		pattern, -ed, -ing	
patch, -ed, -ing			patty, -ies	
patchwork			paturnal	paternal

paturnitey	paternity	paysnent	patient
patwa	patois	paytent	patent
paucity		pea	
paun	pawn	peace (calm)	
paunch, paunches		peace	piece (part)
paunchy		peaceable, -bly	
pauper		peaceabul	peaceable
pause, paused, pausing (stop)		peaceful, -ly	
pause	paws (feet)	peach, peaches	
pave, paved, paving		peacock	
pavement		peak, -ed, -ing (top)	
pavilion		peak	peek (look)
pavlova		peak	pique (anger)
paw (foot)		peal, -ed, -ing (ring)	
paw	poor (needy)	peal	peel (skin)
paw	pore (skin)	peanut	
paw	pour (flow)	peap	peep
pawcelain	porcelain	pear (fruit)	
pawch	porch	pear	pair (two)
pawk	pork	pear	pare (trim)
pawkupine	porcupine	pearage	peerage
pawl	pall	pearce	pierce
pawlbarer	pall-bearer	pearl (gem)	
pawlsied	palsied	pearl	purl (knit)
pawlsy	palsy	pearly, -lies	
pawltrey	paltry	peasant	
pawn, -ed, -ing		peasantry	
pawnbroker		peashooter	
pawnbroking		peashuter	peashooter
pawnch	paunch	peat	
pawnografey	pornography	pebble	
pawpaw		pecadillo, -loes, -los	
pawper	pauper	pecan	
pawpus	porpoise	peck, -ed, -ing	
pawse	pause (stop)	peckish, -ly	
pawselin	porcelain	pecock	peacock
pawshun	portion	pectin	
pawsitey	paucity	pectoral	
pay, paid, paying		peculiar, -ly	
payable		peculiarity, -ties	
payabul	payable	pecuniary	
payload		pedagog	pedagogue
payment		pedagogic, -ally	
paynt	paint	pedagogue	
payola		pedagogy	
payroll		pedal, -alled, -alling (bike)	
payshence	patience	pedant	

pedantic, -ally
pedantry, -ries
peddle, -dled, -dling (sell)
   peddle   pedal (bike)
pederast
pederastic, -ally
pederasty
pedestal, -stalled, -stalling
pedestrian
pedicure
pedigree
pedlar
peek, -ed, -ing (look)
   peek   peak (top)
   peek   pique (anger)
peel, -ed, -ing (skin)
   peel   peal (ring)
peep, -ed, -ing
peepshow
peer, -ed, -ing (look)
   peer   pier (wharf)
peerage
peeress
   peerige   peerage
peerless, -ly
peevish
peewee
peewit
peg, pegged, pegging
   peice   piece
pejorative, -ly
   pek   peck
   pekant   piquant
Pekinese
Pekingese
   pekish   peckish
pelargonium
pelican
pellet (ball)
   pellet   palate (mouth)
   pellet   palette (board)
   pellet   pallet (bed)
pell-mell (haste)
   pell-mell   pall-mall (game)
pellucid, -ly
pelmet

pelt, -ed, -ing
   pelusid   pellucid
pelvis, -ves
pen, penned, penning
penal
penalisation
penalise, -lised, -lising
penalty, -ties
penance
   penanse   penance
   penant   pennant
pence
penchant
pencil, -cilled, -cilling
pendant
pendent
pending
pendulous, -ly
pendulum
   pendulus   pendulous
penetrable, -bly
   pentrabul   penetrable
penetrate, -trated, -trating
penetration
penfriend
penguin
   pengwin   penguin
penicillin
   peniless   penniless
peninsula
penis, -nes, -nises
   penisilin   penicillin
   penitenshary   penitentiary
   penitenshul   penitential
penitent, -ly
penitential, -ly
penitentiary, -ries
penknife, -knives
pen-name
pennant
penniless
pennon
penny, pennies, pence
penny-farthing
penny-pinching
penological
penologist

penology
pen-pusher

pense	pence
penshun	pension
penshuner	pensioner
pensil	pencil

pension
pensionable

| pensionabul | pensionable |

pensioner
pensive, -ly
pentagon

| pentathalon | pentathlon |

pentathlon
penthouse

| penthowse | penthouse |

pent-up
penultimate, -ly
penumbra, -brae, -bras
penurious, -ly
penury

| penut | peanut |

peon
peony, -nies
people, -pled, -pling
pep, pepped, pepping

peper	pepper
pepermint	peppermint
pepery	peppery

pepper
peppercorn
peppermint
peppery
pep pill
pep talk
peptic
perambulate, -lated, -lating
perambulation
perambulator
perambulatory
per annum
per capita
perceivable, -bly
perceive, -ceived, -ceiving
per cent
percentage

| percentige | percentage |

percentile

| percepshun | perception |
| perceptabul | perceptible |

perceptible, -bly
perception
perceptive, -ly
perceptual, -ly

| percession | procession |

perch, perches
perch, -ed, -ing

| perchase | purchase |

percipience
percipient
percolate, -lated, -lating

| percolater | percolator |

percolation
percolator

| percushun | percussion |

percussion
percussionist
percussive

| perdishun | perdition |

perdition
peregrinate, -nated, -nating
peremptoriness
peremptory, -torily
perennial, -ly

| perfeckshun | perfection |

perfect, -ed, -ing
perfectible

| perfectibul | perfectible |

perfection
perfectionism
perfectionist
perfidious, -ly

| perfidius | perfidious |

perfidy, -dies
perforate, -rated, -rating
perforation
perforce
perform, -ed, -ing
performance

| performanse | performance |

perfume, -fumed, -fuming
perfumery, -ries
perfunctory, -torily

| perfunctry | perfunctory |

pergarey — perjury
pergative — purgative
pergatry — purgatory
perge — purge
pergola
perhaps
perhibit — prohibit
periferal — peripheral
perifery — periphery
peril, -rilled, -rilling
perilous, -ly
perilus — perilous
perimeter
period
periodic
periodical, -ly
peripatetic
peripheral, -ly
periphery, -ries
periscope
perish, -ed, -ing
perishable
perishabul — perishable
perisher
peritonitis
periwinkle
perjure, -jured, -juring
perjurer
perjury, -ries
perk, -ed, -ing
perkushun — percussion
perky, -kier, -kiest
perl — pearl (gem)
perl — purl (knit)
perloin — purloin
perloyn — purloin
perm, -ed, -ing
permananse — permanence
permanence
permanency, -cies
permanent, -ly
permanganate
permeability
permeable
permeate, -ated, -ating
permeation
permiate — permeate

permisabul — permissible
permishun — permission
permissible, -bly
permission
permissive, -ly
permissiveness
permit, -mitted, -mitting
permutation
permute, -muted, -muting
pernicious, -ly
perniciousness
pernickety
pernishus — pernicious
perokside — peroxide
peroration
peroxide, -ided, -iding
perpechual — perpetual
perpechuate — perpetuate
perpendicular, -ly
perpendicularity
perpetrate, -trated, -trating
perpetrater — perpetrator
perpetration
perpetrator
perpetual, -ly
perpetuate, -ated, -ating
perpetuation
perpetuator
perpetuity, -ties
perport — purport
perpose — purpose
perquisite (profit)
perquisite — prerequisite (necessary)
per say — per se
per se
perse — purse
persecushun — persecution
persecute, -cuted, -cuting
persecution
persecutor
persepshun — perception
perseptabul — perceptible
perseve — persevere
perseverance
persevere, -vered, -vering
Persian

persimmon
persist, -ed, -ing
persistence
person
personable, -bly
personage
personal, -ly (private)

personal	personnel (employees)

personalise, -lised, -lising
personality, -ties
persona non grata
personate, -ated, -ating

personible	personable

personification
personify, -fied, -fying
personnel (employees)

personnel	personal (private)

perspective, -ly

| perspeks | perspex |
| perspektive | perspective |

perspex
perspicacious, -ly
perspicacity
perspicuous, -ly
perspicuousness
perspiration
perspire, -spired, -spiring
persuade, -suaded, -suading
persuader

persuashun	persuasion

persuasion
persuasive, -ly

pursuit	pursuit
perswade	persuade
perswasion	persuasion

pert, -ly
pertness
pertain, -ed, -ing

pertane	pertain

pertinacious, -ly
pertinacity
pertinent, -ly
perturb, -ed, -ing
perturbable
peruse, -rused, -rusing

pervade, -vaded, -vading
pervasion
pervasive, -ly
perverse, -ly

pervershun	perversion

perversion
perversity, -ties
pervert, -ed, -ing
perverter

pervurse	perverse
pervurshun	perversion
pervurt	pervert
pesabul	peaceable
pesant	peasant
pesary	pessary
pese	peace
pesimism	pessimism
pesimist	pessimist

pessary, -ries
pessimism
pessimist
pest
pester, -ed, -ing
pesticide
pestilence

pestilense	pestilence

pestilent, -ly

pestiside	pesticide

pestle

pesul	pestle

pet, petted, petting
petal
petard

peteet	petite

peter, -ed, -ing

peticoat	petticoat
petie	petty
petishun	petition

petite
petition, -ed, -ing
petrel (bird)

petrel	petrol (fuel)

petrify, -fied, -fying
petrol (fuel)

petrol	petrel (bird)

petroleum

petrul	petrel (bird)

petrul   petrol (fuel)
petticoat
pettily
pettiness
petty, -tier, -tiest
petulance
petulant, -ly
petunia
pevish   peevish
pew
pewter
phalanger
phalanx, -anxes or -anges
phalus   phallus
phallic
phallus, phalluses, phalli
phantasm
phantasmagoria
phantom
Pharaoh
pharisaic
pharisee
pharmaceutical, -ly
pharmacist
pharmacy, -cies
pharyngitis
pharynx, pharynges, pharynxes
phase, phased, phasing
pheasant
phenacetin
phenix   phoenix
phenol
phenomenal, -ly
phenomenon, -mena
phesant   pheasant
phial (vessel)
philander, -ed, -ing
philanderer
philanthropic, -ally
philanthropist
philanthropy, -pies
philarmonic   philharmonic
philatelist
philately
philharmonic
Philippines
philosofer   philosopher

philosofical   philosophical
philosofy   philosophy
philosopher
philosophical, -ly
philosophise, -phised, -phising
philosophy, -phies
philter   philtre
philtre, -tred, -tring

> For phis- words, look
> under phys-.

phlegm
phlegmatic, -ally
phlem   phlegm
phlox
phobia
phobic
phoenix
phone
phonetic, -ally
phonograf   phonograph
phonogram
phonograph
phony, phonier, phoniest
phosfate   phosphate
phosforus   phosphorus
phosphate
phosphor
phosphorescent
phosphorus
photo, photos
photocopier
photocopy, -pies
photocopy, -copied, -copying
photoelectric
photo-finish
photogenic
photograf   photograph
photograph, -graph, -graphing
photographic, -ally
photography
photostat, -stated, -stating
photosynthesis
phrase, phrased, phrasing
phraseology
phrenetic, -ally
phylactery, -teries

pier (wharf)

physic (medicine)
physical, -ly
physician
physicist
physics
physiognomy, -mies
physiological, -ly
physiology
physiotherapist
physiotherapy
physique
pi (Greek letter)

| pi | pie (food) |

pianist
piano, pianos
pianoforte

| piatsa | piazza |

piazza

| pibald | piebald |

picador

| picancy | piquancy |
| picaniny | piccaninny |

piccaninny, -nies
piccolo, -los

| pich | pitch |
| picinic | picnic |

pick, -ed, -ing
pickaxe, -axed, -axing
picket, -ed, -ing
pickle, -led, -ling
pickpocket
pick-up
picnic, -nicked, -nicking
picnicker
pictorial, -ly
picture, -tured, -turing
picturesque
pidgin (talk)

| pidgin | pigeon (bird) |

pie (food)

| pie | pi (Greek letter) |

piebald
piece, pieced, piecing (part)

| piece | peace (calm) |

piecemeal
piecework

pier (wharf)

| pier | peer (look) |

pierce, pierced, piercing

| pierse | pierce |

piety, -ties
pig, pigged, pigging
pigeon (bird)

| pigeon | pidgin (talk) |

pigeonhole, -holed, -holing
pigeon-toed

| pigery | piggery |

piggery, -geries
piggyback
pig-headed

pigiback	piggyback
pigin	pidgin (talk)
pigin	pigeon (bird)

pig-iron
piglet
pigment
pigmentation
pigmy, -mies
pigskin
pigstick, -ed, -ing
pigsticker
pigsty, -sties
pigtail

| pigtale | pigtail |
| pijamas | pyjamas |

pikau
pike, piked, piking
pikelet
pilchard
pile, piled, piling
pile-up
pilfer, -ed, -ing
pilferage
pilferer

| pilferige | pilferage |

pilgrim
pilgrimage

pilgrimige	pilgrimage
pilige	pillage
pilion	pillion

pill
pillage, -laged, -laging
pillager

pillar
pillbox, -boxes
pillion
pillory, -ries
pillory, -ried, -rying
pillow, pillows

pilon   pylon
pilory   pillory

pilot, -ed, -ing
pilotage

pilow   pillow
pilyun   pillion

pilsener
pimp, -ed, -ing
pimple
pimply, -plier, -pliest

pimpul   pimple

pin, pinned, pinning

pinacle   pinnacle

pinafore
pinball
pince-nez
pincers
pinch, -ed, -ing
pincher
pincushion
pine, pined, pining
pineapple

pineappul   pineapple

pin-feather
ping, -ed, -ing
ping-pong
pinion, -ed, -ing
pink, -ed, -ing
pinnacle, -cled, -cling
pinpoint, -ed, -ing
pinprick

pinsers   pincers

pinstripe
pint
pintuck,-ed, -ing
pin-up

pinyun   pinion
pionear   pioneer

pioneer, -ed, -ing
pious, -ly
pip, pipped, pipping

pipe, piped, piping
pipedream
pipeline
pipi
pipit
pippin
pipsqueak
piquancy
piquant, -ly
pique, piqued, piquing
piracy

piramid   pyramid

piranha

pirasy   piracy

pirate, -rated, -rating
piratical, -ly

pire   pyre
pirooet   pirouette

pirouette, -etted, -etting
piscatorial
Pisces
pistachio, -chios
pistil (flower)
pistol (gun)
piston
pit, pitted, pitting

pitanse   pittance

pitapat, -patted, -patting
pitch, -ed, -ing
pitch-black
pitchblende
pitcher (baseball)

pitcher   picture (image)

pitchfork, -ed, -ing
pitchi
piteous, -ly

piter-pater   pitter-patter

pitfall
pith
pithead
pithy, -ier, -iest
pitiable, -ly

pitiabul   pitiable

pitiful, -fully
pitiless, -ly
pittance

pittanse   pittance

pitter-patter
pittosporum
pituitary, -taries
pituri
pity, pities
pity, pitied, pitying
   pius   pious
pivot, -ed, -ing
pivotal, -ly
pixie, pixies
pixy, pixies
pizza
pizzicato
placability
placable, -bly
   placabul   placable
placard, -ed, -ing
placate, -cated, -cating
placatory
place, placed, placing (position)
   place   plaice (fish)
placebo, -bos, -boes
placement
placenta, -tas, -tae
placental
placid, -ly
placidity
placket
   plagarism   plagiarism
   plage   plague
plagiarise, -rised, -rising
plagiarism
plagiarist
plague, plagued, plaguing
plaice (fish)
plaid (cloth)
plain, -ly (clear)
   plain   plane (flat)
plain-clothes
plain-spoken
plains wanderer
plaint
plaintiff (sue)
plaintive, -ly (sad)
plait, -ed, -ing (braid)
   plait   plate (dish)
   plaket   placket

plan, planned, planning
plane, planed, planing (flat)
   plane   plain (clear)
planet
planetarium
planetary
plank
plankton
planner
plant, -ed, -ing
plantation
planter
   plantif   plaintiff (sue)
   plantive   plaintive (sad)
plaque
   plase   place (position)
   plase   plaice (fish)
   plasenta   placenta
   plasid   placid
plasma
plaster, -ed, -ing
plasterboard
plasterer
plastic, -ally
   plasticene   plasticine
plasticine
plasticity
   plastisene   plasticine
plate, plated, plating (dish)
   plate   plait (braid)
plateau, -eaus, -eaux
platelet
   plater   platter
platform
   platichude   platitude
platinum
   platipus   platypus
platitude
platitudinous
   plato   plateau
Platonic
platoon
platter
platypus, -puses, -pi
plaudit
plausible, -bly
   plausibul   plausible

play, -ed, -ing
playback
playboy
player
playful, -ly
playground
play-off
  playrite — playwright
playwright
plaza
plea, pleas (request)
plead, -ed, -ing
  pleas — please (satisfy)
pleasant, -ly
pleasantry, -tries
please, pleased, pleasing (satisfy)
pleasurable, -bly
  pleasurabul — pleasurable
pleat, -ed, -ing
  plebean — plebeian
plebeian
plebiscite
  plebisite — plebiscite
plectrum, -tra, -trums
pledge, pledged, pledging
  plee — plea
  pleed — plead
  pleet — pleat
  plege — pledge
plenary, -rily
plenipotentiary, -ries
plenitude
plenteous, -ly
plentiful, -ly
  plentius — plenteous
plenty
  plesant — pleasant
  plese — pleas (requests)
  plese — please (satisfy)
  plesurabul — pleasurable
  plesure — pleasure
plethora
pleurisy
  pli — ply
pliable, -bly
  pliabul — pliable
pliant, -ly

pliers
plight, -ed, -ing
Plimsoll line
plinth
  plite — plight
  pliwood — plywood
plod, plodded, plodding
plodder
  ploi — ploy
plonk, -ed, -ing
  ploomage — plumage
  plootocrasy — plutocracy
  plooviul — pluvial
plop, plopped, plopping
plot, plotted, plotting
plough, -ed, -ing
ploughshare
plover
  plow — plough
ploy
pluck, -ed, -ing
plucky, -ily
plug, plugged, plugging
plum (fruit)
  plum — plumb (test)
plumage
plumb, -ed, -ing (test)
plumber
plumbline
plume, plumed, pluming
  plumige — plumage
  plumline — plumbline
  plummer — plumber
plummet, -ed, -ing
plump, -ed, -ing
plunder, -ed, -ing
plunge, plunged, plunging
plural
pluralism
plurality, -ties
  plurasy — pleurisy
plus
plus-fours
plush
plutocracy, -cies
plutocrat
plutonium

pluvial
ply, plies
ply, plied, plying
plywood
pneumatic, -ally
pneumonia
poach, -ed, -ing
poacher
poch   poach
pock
pocket, -ed, -ing
pocket-book
pocket-knife, -knives
pocket-money
pockmark
pod, podded, podding
poddy
podiatrist
podiatry
podium, -dia
poem
poet
poetess
poetic
poetical, -ly
poetry
pogrom
poignancy
poignant, -ly
poinancy   poignancy
poinant   poignant
poinsettia
point, -ed, -ing
point-blank
pointedly
pointer
pointillism
pointless, -ly
poise, poised, poising
poison, -ed, -ing
poisoner
poisonous, -ly
poke, poked, poking
poker
pokey, pokies (machine)
poky, -kier, -kiest (small)
polar (region)

polar   poler (horse)
polarise, -rised, -rising
polarity
polaroid
pole, poled, poling (stick)
pole   poll (vote)
polemic
polemical, -ly
polen   pollen
poler (horse)
poler   polar (region)
polese   police
police, -liced, -licing
policeman, -men
policewoman, -women
policy, -cies
poligamus   polygamous
poligamy   polygamy
poliglot   polyglot
poligon   polygon
polinate   pollinate
Polineshun   Polynesian
poliomyelitis
polip   polyp
polish, -ed, -ing
polisy   policy
politburo
polite, -ly
politic
polithene   polythene
political, -ly
politician
politicise, -cised, -cising
politicking
politics
politishun   politician
polka, -kaed, -kaing
poll, -ed, -ing (vote)
poll   pole (stick)
pollard
pollen
pollinate, -nated, -nating
pollination
pollster
pollutant
pollute, -luted, -luting
pollution

polo	
polo-neck	
poltegeist	poltergeist
poltergeist	
poltise	poultice
poltry	poultry
polushun	pollution
polute	pollute
polyandrous	
polyandry	
polyanthus	
polyester	
polygamist	
polygamous, -ly	
polygamy	
polyglot	
polygon	
Polyneshun	Polynesian
Polynesian	
polyp	
polysaturated	
polythene	
polyunsaturated	
pomander	
pomegranate	
pomel	pommel
Pomeranian	
pommel, -melled, -melling	
pommy, -mies	
pomp	
pompom	
pomposity	
pompous, -ly	
poncho, -chos	
ponder, -ed, -ing	
ponderous, -ly	
ponderus	ponderous
ponie	pony
pontiff	
pontifical, -ly	
pontificate, -cated, -cating	
pontoon	
pony, -nies	
ponytail	
pooch	
poodle	
poodul	poodle

pool, -ed, -ing	
poop, -ed, -ing	
poor, -ly (needy)	
poor	paw (foot)
poor	pore (skin)
poor	pour (flow)
poorhouse	
pop, popped, popping	
popcorn	
pope	
popery	
popet	poppet
popie	poppy
popish, -ly	
poplar (tree)	
poplin	
popourri	potpourri
poppet	
poppy, -pies	
poppycock	
populace	
popular, -ly (known)	
popularise, -rised, -rising	
popularitey	popularity
popularity	
populase	populace
populate, -lated, -lating	
population	
populer	popular
populous, -ly	
populus	populous
popy	poppy
por	paw (foot)
por	poor (needy)
por	pore (skin)
por	pour (flow)
porcelain	
porcelane	porcelain
porch	
porcupine	
pore (skin)	
pore	paw (foot)
pore	poor (needy)
pore	pour (flow)
porfrey	porphyry
poridge	porridge
porige	porridge

pork

porkupine	porcupine
pornografy	pornography

pornographer
pornographic
pornography
porosity
porous
porphyry, -ries
porpoise, -poises

porpus	porpoise

porridge

porselin	porcelain
porshun	portion
porslin	porcelain

port
portable
portal
portend, -ed, -ing

portenshus	portentous

portent
portentous, -ly
porter
portfolio, -lios
porthole
portico, -coes, -cos
portion, -ed, -ing
portly, -lier, -liest
portmanteau, -teaus, -teaux
portrait
portraiture
portray, -ed, -ing
portrayal

portret	portrait
portul	portal
porus	porous
poschur	posture

pose, posed, posing
poser

poseshun	possession
posess	possess
posessive	possessive
posey	posy

posh, -ly

poshun	potion
posibility	possibility
posibul	possible

posishun	position

position
positive, -ly
posse
possess, -ed, -ing
possession
possessive, -ly
possessor
possible, -bly
possibility, -ties

possibul	possible

possum
post, -ed, -ing
postage
postal
postcard
postcode
postdate, -dated, -dating
poster

posterier	posterior

posterior, -ly
posterity
postern
postgraduate
posthaste
posthumous, -ly

posthumus	posthumous
postige	postage

post-mortem
post-office
postpone, -poned, -poning
postponement
postulant
postulate, -lated, -lating

postumus	posthumous

posture, -tured, -turing
posy, -sies
pot, potted, potting
potable
potash

potasium	potassium

potassium
potato, -toes
pot-bellied
pot-belly, -lies
potency

potenshul	potential

potensy	potency	practishun	practician
potent		practishuner	practitioner
potentate		practitioner	
potential, -ly		pragmatic, -ally	
potentiality, -ties		pragmatism	
poter	potter	pragmatist	
potery	pottery	prairey	prairie
pothole		prairie	
potion		praise, praised, praising	
potluck		praiseworthy, -thily	
potpourri, -ris		pram	
pottage		prance, pranced, prancing	
potter, -ed, -ing		prandial, -ly	
pottery, -ries		prang, -ed, -ing	
potty, -ties		prank	
pouch, pouches		pranse	prance
poulterer		prarey	prairie
poultice, -ticed, -ticing		prase	praise
poultise	poultice	prate, prated, prating	
poultry		prattle, -tled, -tling	
pounce, pounced, pouncing		pratul	prattle
pound, -ed, -ing		prawn	
pour, -ed, -ing		pray, -ed, -ing (beg)	
pour	poor (needy)	pray	prey (hunt)
pour	pore (skin)	prayer	
pout, -ed, -ing		prayerbook	
poverty		preach, -ed, -ing	
poverty-stricken		preacher	
powch	pouch	preamble	
powder, -ed, -ing		preambul	preamble
powdery		prearrange, -ranged, -ranging	
power, -ed, -ing		precarious, -ly	
powerful, -ly		precaution	
powerhouse		precautionary	
powerless, -ly		precautionry	precautionary
pownce	pounce	precawshun	precaution
pownd	pound	precede, -ceded, -ceding (before)	
powt	pout	precede	proceed (ahead)
pow wow, -wowed, -wowing		precedence	
pox		precedent (law)	
practicable, -bly		precedent	president (head)
practicabul	practicable		
practical, -ly		precept	
practicality		preceptor	
practice, -ticed, -ticing		prech	preach
practician		precinct	
practise, -tised, -tising			

precious, -ly
precipatation — precipitation
precipice
precipise — precipice
precipitant, -ly
precipitate, -tated, -tating
precipitation
precipitous, -ly
precipitus — precipitous
precis (summary)
precise, -ly (exact)
precishun — precision
precision
preclude, -cluded, -cluding
precocious, -ly
precocity
preconceive, -ceived, -ceiving
preconcieve — preconceive
preconsepshun — preconception
preconception
preconseve — preconceive
precoshus — precocious
precursor
predater — predator
predator
predatory
predecessor
predesessor — predecessor
predestination
predestine, -tined, -tining
predetermination
predetermine, -mined, -mining
predicament
predicate, -cated, -cating
predicative, -ly
predict, -ed, -ing
predictable, -bly
predictabul — predictable
prediction
predictor
predilecshun — predilection
predilection
predispose, -posed, -posing
predisposition
predominance
predominant, -ly
predominate, -ated, -ating

pre-eminence
pre-eminent, -ly
pre-empt, -ed, -ing
pre-emptory
preen, -ed, -ing
prefabricate, -cated, -cating
prefabrication
preface, -faced, -facing
prefatory, -rily
prefect
prefecture
prefer, -ferred, -ferring
preferable, -bly
preference
preferense — preference
preferenshul — preferential
preferential, -ly
preferment
prefice — preface
prefiks — prefix
prefix
pregnancy, -cies
pregnansy — pregnancy
pregnant, -ly
prehensile
prehistoric, -ally
prejudge, -judged, -judging
prejudgment
prejudice, -diced, -dicing
prejudicial, -ly
prejudise — prejudice
prejudishul — prejudicial
prelate
preliminary, -aries
prelude, -luded, -luding
premarital
premature, -ly
premenstrual tension
premier (chief)
premiere (first performance)
premise, -ised, -ising
premises
premium
premonishun — premonition
premonition
premonitory
prenatal

prene   preen
preoccupation
preoccupy, -pied, -pying
preparation
preparatory, -rily
    preparatry   preparatory
prepare, -pared, -paring
preponderance
preponderant, -ly
preposition
preposterous, -ly
    prerekwisit   prerequisite
prerequisite (necessary)
    prerequisite   perquisite
                           (profit)
prerogative
    pres   press
presage, -saged, -saging
    prescripshun   prescription
prescription
prescriptive, -ly
    presede   precede
    presedence   precedence
    presedent   precedent
    presedent   president
    preseed   precede
    preseleckshun   preselection
preselect, -ed, -ing
preselection
presence
    presense   presence
present, -ed, -ing
presentable, -bly
presentation
presentiment
presently
    presept   precept
preservation
preservative
preserve, -served, -serving
    presher   pressure
    presherise   pressurise
    preshus   precious
preside, -sided, -siding
presidency
    presidenshul   presidential
    presidensy   presidency

president
presidential
    presige   presage
    presinct   precinct
    presipice   precipice
    presipis   precipice
    presipitate   precipitate
    presipitus   precipitous
    presise   precise
press, -ed, -ing
press-up
pressure, -sured, -suring
pressurisation
pressurise, -rised, -rising
    prest   priest
    prestege   prestige
    presthood   priesthood
prestige
prestigious, -ly
    prestigus   prestigious
presto
presume, -sumed, -suming
presumption
presumptuous, -ly
    presumshun   presumption
    presumtuus   presumptuous
presuppose, -posed, -posing
presupposition
pretence
pretend, -ed, -ing
pretender
    pretense   pretence
    pretenshun   pretension
    pretenshus   pretentious
pretension
pretentious, -ly
preternatural, -ly
pretext
    pretie   pretty
prettily
prettiness
pretty, -tier, -tiest
    prety   pretty
pretzel
prevail, -ed, -ing
    prevale   prevail
prevalence

prevalense	prevalence	princedom	
prevalent, -ly		princely, -lier, -liest	
prevaricate, -cated, -cating		princess	
prevarication		principal (head)	
prevenshun	prevention	principality, -ties	
prevent, -ed, -ing		principle (law)	
preventable, -bly		principul	principal (head)
preventabul	preventable		
preventative, -ly		prinse	prince
prevention		prinsess	princess
preventive, -ly		prinsipal	principal
preview, -ed, -ing		prinsipality	principality
previous, -ly		print, -ed, -ing	
prey, -ed, -ing (hunt)		printer	
prey	pray (beg)	printery, -ries	
pri	pry	print-out	
price, priced, pricing		prion	
priceless, -ly		prior	
prick, -ed, -ing		priority, -ties	
prickle, -led, -ling		priority-paid	
prickly, -lier, -liest		priory, -ries	
prickul	prickle	prise, prised, prising (move)	
pride, prided, priding		prise	price (cost)
prie	pry	prise	prize (award)
prier	prior	prism	
priery	priory	prismatic, -ally	
priest		prison	
priesthood		prisoner	
priestly, -lier, -liest		prissy, -ier, -iest	
prig		pristeen	pristine
priggish, -ly		pristine	
prim, primmer, primmest		privacy, -cies	
primacy		privasy	privacy
prima donna		privisy	privacy
prima-facie		private, -ly	
primary, -ries		privateer	
primer		privation	
primeval, -ly		privelage	privilege
primitive, -ly		privet	
primogenitor		privie	privy
primogeniture		privilege, -leged, -leging	
primordial, -ly		privy, -vies	
primrey	primary	prize, prized, prizing (award)	
primrose		prizm	prism
primula		probability, -ties	
primus		probable, -ly	
prince		probabul	probable

probate, -bated, -bating	
probation	
probationer	
probe, probed, probing	
probible	probable
probity	
problem	
problematic, -ally	
procedural, -ly	
procedure	
proceed, -ed, -ing	
proceshun	procession
process, -ed, -ing	
procession	
processional, -ly	
processor	
proclaim, -ed, -ing	
proclamation	
proclaym	proclaim
procrastinate, -nated, -nating	
procrastination	
procrastinator	
procreate, -ated, -ating	
proctor	
procurable	
procurabul	procurable
procure, -cured, -curing	
procurer	
prod, prodded, prodding	
prodigal, -ly	
prodigality, -ties	
prodigious, -ly	
prodigus	prodigious
prodigy, -gies	
prodijus	prodigious
produce, -duced, -ducing	
producer	
producible	
producshun	production
product	
production	
productive, -ly	
productivity	
produse	produce
produser	producer
profane, -faned, -faning	
profanely	

profanity, -ties	
profecy	prophecy (noun)
profecy	prophesy (verb)
profer	proffer
profeser	professor
profeshunal	professional
profesor	professor
profess, -ed, -ing	
professional, -ly	
professionalism	
professor	
professorial, -ly	
profet	profit (gain)
profet	prophet (seer)
proffer, -ed, -ing	
proficiency, -cies	
proficient, -ly	
profile, -filed, -filing	
profishency	proficiency
profishent	proficient
profit, -ed, -ing	
profitable, -bly	
profitabul	profitable
profiteer, -ed, -ing	
profitless	
profligacy	
profligate, -ly	
pro-forma	
profound, -ly	
profownd	profound
profundity, -ties	
profuse, -ly	
profushun	profusion
profusion	
progenitor	
progeny, -nies	
prognosis, -noses	
prognostic	
prognosticate, -cated, -cating	
prognostication	
program, -grammed, -gramming	
programmable	
programme	
programmer	
progreshun	progression
progress, -ed, -ing	

progression
progressive, -ly
prohibishun   prohibition
prohibit, -ed, -ing
prohibition
prohibitive, -ly
projecshun   projection
project, -ed, -ing
projectile
projection
projectionist
projector
proksimate   proximate
proksy   proxy
prolapse, -lapsed, -lapsing
proletarian
proletariat
proliferate, -rated, -rating
prolific, -ally
prolog   prologue
prologue
prolong, -ed, -ing
prolongation
prom
promenade, -naded, -nading
prominence
prominense   prominence
prominent, -ly
promiscuity, -ties
promiscuous, -ly
promiscus   promiscuous
promise, -mised, -mising
promissory
promontory, -ries
promontry   promontory
promoter
promotion
promp   prompt
prompt, -ed, -ing
prompter
promulgate, -gated, -gating
promulgation
prone
prong, -ed, -ing
pronoun
pronounce, -nounced, -nouncing
pronouncement

pronown   pronoun
pronownse   pronounce
pronto
pronunciation
prood   prude
proof, -ed, -ing
proofread, -read, -reading
proofreader
proon   prune
proove   prove
prop, propped, propping
propaganda
propagate, -gated, -gating
propagation
propagator
propane
propel, -pelled, -pelling
propellant (noun)
propellent (adjective)
propeller
propensity, -ties
proper, -ly
property, -ties
prophecy, cies
prophesy, -sied, -sying
prophet
prophetess
prophetical, -ly
prophilactic   prophylactic
prophylactic
propishiate   propitiate
propishus   propitious
propitiate, -ated, -ating
propitious, -ly
proponent
proporshunal   proportional
proportion
proportional, -ly
proportionate, -ly
proposal
propose, -posed, -posing
proposer
proposishun   proposition
proposition
propound, -ed, -ing
propownd   propound
proprietary

proprieter	proprietor
proprietor	
proprietry	proprietary
propriety, -ties	
propulsion	
pro-rata	
prorogue, -rogued, -roguing	
prosaic, -ally	
proscenium, -nia	
proscribe, -scribed, -scribing	
proscription	
prose	
prosecushun	prosecution
prosecute, -cuted, -cuting	
prosecution	
prosecutor	
prosedure	procedure
proseed	proceed
proselite	proselyte
proselyte, -lyted, -lyting	
proselytise, -tised, -tising	
prosess	process
prosicute	prosecute
prosilite	proselyte
prosilitise	proselytise
prosody	
prospect, -ed, -ing	
prospective, -ly	
prospector	
prospectus	
prosper, -ed, -ing	
prosperity, -ties	
prosperous, -ly	
prosperus	prosperous
prostate gland	
prosthesis, -ses	
prostitushen	prostitution
prostitute, -tuted, -tuting	
prostitution	
prostrate, -trated, -trating	
prostration	
protagonist	
protea	
protecshun	protection
protect, -ed, -ing	
protection	
protectionist	

protective, -ly	
protector	
protectorate	
proteen	protein
protégé	
protein	
protest, -ed, -ing	
Protestant	
Protestantism	
protestation	
protocol	
proton	
prototipe	prototype
prototype	
protract, -ed, -ing	
protractor	
protrood	protrude
protrooshun	protrusion
protrude, -ruded, -ruding	
protrusion	
protruberance	
protruberant, -ly	
proud, -ly	
provable	
prove, proved, proven, proving	
provender	
proverb	
proverbial, -ly	
provide, -vided, -viding	
providence	
providense	providence
provident, -ly	
providential, -ly	
provider	
province	
provincial, -ly	
provinshul	provincial
provishun	provision
provision	
provisional, -ly	
proviso	
provocation	
provocative, -ly	
provoke, -voked, -voking	
provost	
prow	
prowd	proud

prowess
prowl, -ed, -ing
proximate, -ly
proximity
proxy, proxies
~~prozaic~~ prosaic
prude
prudence
~~prudense~~ prudence
prudent, -ly
prudential, -ly
prudish, -ly
prune, pruned, pruning
prunus
prurience
prurient, -ly
~~Prushan~~ Prussian
Prussian
pry, pried, prying
psalm
psalmist
psaltery, -teries
pseudo
pseudonym
psyche
psychedelic
psychiatric, -ally
psychiatrist
psychiatry
psychic, -ally
psychoanalyse, -lysed, -lysing
psychoanalysis
psychoanalyst
psychological, -ly
psychologist
psychology, -gies
psychopath
psychopathy
psychosis, -ses
psychosomatic
psychotherapist
pschotherapy
psychotic

For psyco- words, look
under **psycho-**.

~~psykey~~ psyche

~~psykic~~ psychic
ptomaine
puberty
pubes
pubescence
pubescent
pubic
~~publesher~~ publisher
public, -ly
publican
publication
publicise, -cised, -cising
publicity
publish, -ed, -ing
publisher
~~publisise~~ publicise
~~publisity~~ publicity
puce
puck
pucka (genuine)
pucker, -ed, -ing (fold)
pudding
puddle, -dled, -dling
~~puddul~~ puddle
~~puding~~ pudding
puerile, -ly
puerility, -ties
puff, -ed, -ing
puffin
puffy, -fier, -fiest
~~pufy~~ puffy
pugilism
pugilist
pugilistic, -ally
pugnacious, -ly
pugnacity
~~pugnasity~~ pugnacity
pug-nosed
pukka
pulchritude
~~pulie~~ pulley
~~pulkritude~~ pulchritude
pull, -ed, -ing
pullet
pulley, -leys
pullover
pulmonary

pulmonry — pulmonary
pulp, -ed, -ing
pulpit
pulpwood
pulpy, -pier, -piest
pulsar
pulsate, -ated, -ating
pulsation
pulsator
pulse, pulsed, pulsing
pulser — pulsar
pulverise, -rised, -rising
puma
pumice
pumise — pumice
pumkin — pumpkin
pummel, -melled, -melling
pump, -ed, -ing
pumpernickel
pumpkin
pun, punned, punning
punative — punitive
punch, -ed, -ing
punch-drunk
punch-up
punctilious, -ly
puntilius — punctilious
punctual, -ly
punctuality
punctuate, -ated, -ating
punctuation
puncture, -tured, -turing
pundit
pungency
pungent, -ly
punie — puny
punish, -ed, -ing
punishable
punishment
punitive, -ly
pungensy — pungency
punjent — pungent
punk
punnet
punt, -ed, -ing
punter
puny, -nier, -niest

pup, pupped, pupping
pupet — puppet
pupie — puppy
pupil
puppet
puppeteer
puppetry
puppy, -pies
pur annum — per annum
puray — puree
purceive — perceive
purchase, -chased, -chasing
purdah
pure, purer, purest
puree, -reed, -reeing
purgative, -ly
purgatory
purgatry — purgatory
purge, purged, purging
purifie — purify
purify, -fied, -fying
purile — puerile
puritan
puritanical, -ly
puritanism
puritie — purity
purity
purje — purge
purjery — perjury
purl, -ed, -ing (knit)
purl — pearl (gem)
purloin, -ed, -ing
puroolense — purulence
purple, -pled, -pling
purport, -ed, -ing
purpose
purposeful, -ly
purpul — purple
purr, -ed, -ing
purser
pursuant, -ly
pursue, -sued, -suing
pursuit
pursute — pursuit
purulence
purulent, -ly
purvay — purvey

purvey, -ed, -ing
purveyor
pus
  puse   puce
push, -ed, -ing
pushbike
push-button
pushover
push-up
pushy
pusillanimous, -ly
pussyfoot
put, put, putting
putative, -ly
  puter   pewter
  putie   putty
putrefaction
putrefy, -fied, -fying
putrescent
putrid, -ly
  putrify   putrefy
putt, -ed, -ing
putter
putty, -ties
putty, puttied, puttying
put-upon
  puty   putty
  puzel   puzzle
puzzle, -zled, -zling
  pye   pi (Greek
                   letter)
  pye   pie (food)
pygmy, -mies
pyjamas
pylon
pyramid
pyramidal, -ly
pyre
pyrex
  pyric   pyrrhic
pyrotechnics
pyrrhic
pythagoras
python
pyx

Qq

qeue	queue
quack, -ed, -ing	
quackery, -eries	
quad (timber)	
quadrangle	
quadrangul	quadrangle
quadrant	
quadrafonic	quadraphonic
quadraphonic	
quadrasonic	
quadratic	
quadril	quadrille
quadrille	
quadrillion	
quadriplegia	
quadriplegic	
quadruped	
quadrupedal	
quadruple, -pled, -pling	
quadruplet	
quadrupul	quadruple
quaff, quaffed, quaffing	
quagmire	
quail	
quaint, -ly	
quaintness	
quake, quaked, quaking	
Quaker	
Quakerism	
qualification	
qualifi	qualify
qualified	
qualifier	
qualify, -fied, -fying	
qualitative, -ly	
quality, -ties	
qualm	
quandary, -ries	

quandong	
quandry	quandary
quango	
quantifi	quantify
quantifiable	
quantification	
quantify, -fied, -fying	
quantitative, -ly	
quantity, -ties	
quarantine, -tined, -tining	
quarel	quarrel
quarey	quarry
quark	
quarm	qualm
quarrel, -relled, -relling	
quarreller	
quarrelsome, -ly	
quarry, -ries	
quarry, -ried, -rying	
quart, quarts	
quarter	
quarterdeck	
quarterly	
quartermaster	
quartet	
quartile	
quarto, -tos	
quartz (rock)	
quartz	quarts (measures)
quash, -ed, -ing	
quasi	
quatrain	
quattrocento	
quaver, -ed, -ing	
quavery	
quay (wharf)	
que	cue (billiards)
que	queue (line)
queasy, -sier, -siest	
queasiness	
queen, -ly	
queer, -ly	
queerness	
quell, -ed, -ing	
queller	
quench, -ed, -ing	

quenchable

quenchless

querie — query

querulous, -ly

querulousness

querulus — querulous

query, -ries

query, -ried, -rying

queschun — question

quest, -ed, -ing

quester

question, -ed, -ing

questionable, -bly

questionair — questionnaire

questioner

questionnaire

questyun — question

queue, queued, queuing

quibble, -bled, -bling

quibbler

quibel — quibble

quich — quiche

quiche

quick, -ly

quicken

quickie

quicklime

quickness

quicksand

quicksilver

quickstep

quick-tempered

quick-witted

quid, quid, quids

quid pro quo

quiescence

quiescent, -ly

quiesense — quiescence

quiet, -ly (silent)

quiet — quite (rather)

quieten, -ed, -ing

quietness

quill

quilt

quilted

quince

quinella

quinine

quinse — quince

quinsy, -sies

quintesense — quintessence

quintessence

quintessential

quintet

quintette

quintuple, -pled, -pling

quintuplet

quintupul — quintuple

quip, quipped, quipping

quipster

quire (paper)

quire — choir (sing)

quirk

quish — quiche

quisine — cuisine

quit, quitted or quit, quitting

quite (rather)

quite — quiet (silent)

quits

quitter

quiver, -ed, -ing

quivery

quixotic

quixotism

quiz, quizzes

quiz, quizzed, quizzing

quizzical, -ly

quod (prison)

quod — quad (timber)

quoit

quokka

quorum

quoshent — quotient

> For other quo- words, look under **qua-**.

quota

quotation

quote, quoted, quoting

quotient

Rr

rabbi, -bis
rabbinical
rabbit, -bited, -biting
rabbiter
rabble, -bled, -bling
rabblerouser
rabi   rabbi
rabid, -ly
rabies
rabit   rabbit
rabud   rabid
rabul   rabble
raccoon
race, raced, racing
racecorse   racecourse
racecourse
racegoer
racehorse
racer
racetrack
raceway
racial, -ly
racialism
racialist
racism
racist
rack, -ed, -ing
rack-and-pinion
racket, -ed, -ing
racketeer
rackit   racket
raconter   raconteur
raconteur
racquet
racy, -cier, -ciest
radar
raddle, -led, -ling
rade   raid

radeo   radio
radial, -ly
radialogy   radiology
radial-ply
radian
radiance
radianse   radiance
radiant, -ly
radiate, -ated, -ating
radiater   radiator
radiation
radiator
radical, -ly
radicalism
radicul   radical
radii
radio, -dioed, -dioing
radioactive
radioastronomy
radiografy   radiography
radiogram
radiographer
radiography
radiologist
radiology
radiotelephone
radiotherapy
radish
radiul   radial
radium
radius, radii, radiuses
raffia
raffish, -ly
raffle, -led, -ling
raft
rafter
rag, ragged, ragging
ragamuffin
rage, raged, raging
raglan
ragout, -gouted, -gouting
ragtime
raid, -ed, -ing
rail, -ed, -ing
raillery, -ries
railroad
railway

raiment		rane	rain (water)
rain, -ed, -ing (water)		rane	reign (rule)
rain	reign (rule)	rane	rein (bridle)
rain	rein (bridle)	range, ranged, ranging	
rainbird		rangefinder	
rainbow		ranger	
raincoat		rangul	wrangle
rainfall		rank, -ed, -ing	
rainforest		rankle, -kled, -kling	
raise, raised, raising (lift)		ransack, -ed, -ing	
raise	rays (beams)	ransid	rancid
raisin		ransom, -ed, -ing	
raison d' être		ransome	ransom
raisun	raisin	ransum	ransom
raje	rage	rant, -ed, -ing	
rake, raked, raking		rap, rapped, rapping (strike)	
rakish, -ly		rap	wrap (cover)
rakket	racket	rapacious, -ly	
rale	rail	rapacity	
ralie	rally	rapashus	rapacious
rally, -lies		rapasity	rapacity
rally, -lied, -lying		rapcher	rapture
ram, rammed, ramming		rape, raped, raping	
ramble, -bled, -bling		rapid, -ly	
rambler		rapid-fire	
rambul	ramble	rapier	
ramification		rapine	
ramify, -fied, -fying		rapist	
ramp		rapport	
rampage, -paged, -paging		rapprochement	
rampageous, -ly		rapsody	rhapsody
rampagius	rampageous	rapt (engrossed)	
rampant, -ly		rapt	wrapped
rampart			(cover)
ramrod		rapture	
ramshackle		rapturous, -ly	
ramshackul	ramshackle	rapturus	rapturous
ranch		rare, rarer, rarest	
rancher		rarefacshun	rarefaction
rancid		rarefaction	
rancidity		rarefy, -fied, -fying	
rancorous, -ly		rarely	
rancour		raring	
rancur	rancour	rarity, -ties	
rancurus	rancorous	rasbery	raspberry
random, -ly		rascal	
randy		rascality, -ties	

rascally
rase, rased, rasing (destroy)
  rase   race (run)
  rase   raise (lift)
rash, -ly
  rashal   racial
  rashalist   racialist
rasher
  rashio   ratio
rashness
  rashul   racial
  rashun   ration
  rashunalise   rationalise
  rasin   raisin
  rasism   racism
  rasist   racist
  raskul   rascal
rasp, -ed, -ing
raspberry, -ries
rat, ratted, ratting
  ratabul   rateable
ratchet
rate, rated, rating
  rateo   ratio
ratepayer
  rath   wrath
rather
ratification
ratify, -fied, -fying
ratio, -tios
ration, -ed, -ing
rational, -ly (reasonable)
rationale (statement)
rationalise, -lised, -lising
rationalism
rationality, -ties
rat-race
rattan
rattle, -tled, -tling
rattlesnake
rattletrap
ratty, -tier, -tiest
  ratul   rattle
raucous, -ly
  raucus   raucous
ravage, -aged, -aging
ravager

rave, raved, raving
ravel, -elled, -elling
raven
  ravene   ravine
ravenous, -ly
  ravige   ravage
ravine
ravioli
ravish, -ed, -ing
raw (uncooked)
  raw   roar (noise)
  rawcus   raucous
rawhide
ray
rayon
rays (beams)
  rays   raise (lift)
  rays   raze (destroy)
raze, razed, razing (destroy)
  razer   razor
razoo
razor
reach, -ed, -ing
  reacktion   reaction
react, -ed, -ing
reaction
reactionary
reactive, -ly
reactor
read, read, reading (book)
  read   red (colour)
  read   reed (plant)
readable, -bly
  readabul   readable
reader
readership
readily
readiness
ready, readied, readying
ready, readier, readiest
ready-made
  reaf   reef
reafforest, -ed, -ing
reafforestation
reagent
  reak   reek (smell)
  reak   wreak (inflict)

real, -ly (true)
real — reel (wind)
realign, -ed, -ing
realisation
realise, -lised, -lising
realism
realist
realistic, -ally
reality, -ties (fact)
realm
realter — realtor
realtor
realty (real estate)
ream, reamed, reaming
reap, -ed, -ing
reaper
reappear, -ed, -ing
rear, -ed, -ing
reargard — rearguard
rearguard
rearmament
reason, -ed, -ing
reasonable, -bly
reasonabul — reasonable
reassemble, -bled, -bling
reassembul — reassemble
reassert, -ed, -ing
reassertion
reassess, -ed, -ing
reassessment
reassurance
reassure, -sured, -suring
reath — wreath
rebate, -bated, -bating
rebel, -belled, -belling
rebellion
rebellious, -ly
rebelyun — rebellion
rebild — rebuild
rebound, -ed, -ing
rebownd — rebound
rebuff, -ed, -ing
rebuild, -built, -building
rebuke, -buked, -buking
rebut, -butted, -butting
rebutal — rebuttal
rebuttal

recalcitrance
recalcitrant
recall, -ed, -ing
recant, -ed, -ing
recantation
recapitulate, -lated, -lating
recapitulation
recede, -ceded, -ceding
receipt
receit — receipt
receive, -ceived, -ceiving
receiver
receivership
recent, -ly
recepe — recipe
recepshun — reception
recepshunist — receptionist
receptacle
receptacul — receptacle
reception
receptionist
receptive, -ly
receshun — recession
recess, -ed, -ing
recessive, -ly
rech — retch (vomit)
rech — wretch (victim)
recidivism
recidivist
reciept — receipt
recieve — receive
recipe
recipient
reciprocal, -ly
reciprocate, -cated, -cating
reciprocation
reciprocity
reciprosity — reciprocity
recital
recitation
recite, -cited, -citing
reck — wreck
reckage — wreckage
reckless, -ly
reckon, -ed, -ing
reclaim, -ed, -ing
reclamation

reclassify, -fied, -fying
recline, -clined, -clining
recluse
recognisable, -bly
  recognisabul   recognisable
recognise, -nised, -nising
  recognishun   recognition
recognition
recoil, -ed, -ing
  recolecshun   recollection
recollect, -ed, -ing
recollection
recommend, -ed, -ing
recommendation
reconcile, -ciled, -ciling
reconciliation
recondite
recondition, -ed, -ing
reconnaissance
  reconnoiter   reconnoitre
reconnoitre, -tred, -tring
reconsider, -ed, -ing
  reconsile   reconcile
  reconsiliation   reconciliation
reconstruct, -ed, -ing
reconstruction
  recoop   recoup
record, -ed, -ing
recorder
  recorse   recourse
recount, -ed, -ing
recoup, -ed, -ing
recourse
recover, -ed, -ing
recovery, -eries
  recownt   recount
recreant, -ly
recreation
recriminate, -nated, -nating
recrimination
recriminatory
recruit, -ed, -ing
recruitment
  recrute   recruit
rectangle
  rectangul   rectangle
rectangular, -ly

rectification
rectifier
rectify, -fied, -fying
rectilinear, -ly
  rectilinier   rectilinear
rectitude
rector
rectory, -ries
rectum
recumbency
  recumbensy   recumbency
recumbent, -ly
recuperate, -rated, -rating
recuperation
recuperative
recur, -curred, -curring
recurrence
  recurrense   recurrence
recurrent, -ly
recyclable
  recyclabul   recyclable
recycle, -cycled, -cycling
  recycul   recycle
red, redder, reddest (colour)
  red   read (book)
redbreast
  redbrest   redbreast
redden, -ed, -ing
reddish
  reddy   ready
redeem, -ed, -ing
redeemable, -ably
redeemer
  redempshun   redemption
redemption
redemptive
  reden   redden
  redeploi   redeploy
redeploy, -ed, -ing
redeployment
redevelop, -ed, -ing
redevelopment
red-handed
  redie   ready
redistribute, -buted, -buting
redistribution
redolence

redolent, -ly
redouble, -led, -ling
redoubtable, -bly
redound, -ed, -ing
redoutabul → redoubtable
redress, -ed, -ing
redskin
reduce, -duced, -ducing
reducksun → reduction
reduction
redundancy, -cies
redundansy → redundancy
reduplicate, -cated, -cating
redwood
reed (plant)
reed → read (book)
reedwarbler
reedy, reedier, reediest
reef, -ed, -ing
reefer
reek, -ed, -ing (smell)
reek → wreak (inflict)
reel, -ed, -ing (wind)
reel → real (true)
re-elect, -ed, -ing
re-election
re-entry, -tries
refer, -ferred, -ferring
referee, -reed, -reeing
reference
referense → reference
referendum, -da, -dums
referent
referral
refill, -ed, -ing
refine, -fined, -fining
refinement
refinery, -ries
refleckshun → reflection
reflect, -ed, -ing
reflection
reflector
refleks → reflex
reflex
refloat, -ed, -ing
reform, -ed, -ing
reformation

reformatory, -ries
reformer
refrackshun → refraction
refraction
refractive, -ly
refrain, -ed, -ing
refrence → reference
refresh, -ed, -ing
refresher
refreshment
refrigerant
refrigerate, -rated, -rating
refrigerater → refrigerator
refrigeration
refrigerator
refuel, -elled, -elling
refuge
refugee
refulgence
refulgent, -ly
refund, -ed, -ing
refurbish, -ed, -ing
refusal
refuse, -fused, -fusing
refutation
refute, -futed, -futing
regain, -ed, -ing
regal, -ly (royal)
regale, -galed, -galing (feast)
regalia
regane → regain
regard, -ed, -ing
regardless, -ly
regatta
regeme → regime
regency, -cies
regenerate, -rated, -rating
regeneration
regenerative, -ly
regent
regime
regimen
regiment
regimental
regimentation
region
regional, -ly

regionalism

register, -ed, -ing

registrar

registration

registry, -tries

regon — region

regreshun — regression

regress, -ed, -ing

regression

regressive, -ly

regret, -gretted, -gretting

regretabul — regrettable

regretful, -ly

regrettable, -bly

regulalation — regulation

reguard — regard

regular, -ly

regularity

regulate, -lated, -lating

regulation

regulator

regulatory

reguler — regular

regurgitate, -tated, -tating

rehabilitate, -tated, -tating

rehabilitation

rehash, -ed, -ing

rehearsal

rehearse, -hearsed, -hearsing

reherse — rehearse

reign, -ed, -ing (king)

reign — rain (water)

reign — rein (bridle)

reimburse, -bursed, -bursing

reimbursement

rein, -ed, -ing (bridle)

rein — rain (water)

rein — reign (rule)

reincarnation

reindeer, -deer

reinforce, -forced, -forcing

reinforcement

reinstate, -stated, -stating

reiterate, -rated, -rating

reiteration

reiterative, -ly

rejeckshun — rejection

reject, -ed, -ing

rejection

rejeme — regime

rejister — register

rejoice, -joiced, -joicing

rejoin, -ed, -ing

rejoinder

rejoise — rejoice

rejoovenate — rejuvenate

rejuvenate, -nated, -nating

rejuvenation

rekord — record

> For rekw- words, look
> under requ-.

relaks — relax

relapse, -lapsed, -lapsing

relate, -lated, -lating

relation

relative, -ly

relativity

relax, -ed, -ing

relaxation

relay, -ed, -ing

release, -leased, -leasing

relegate, -gated, -gating

relegation

releif — relief

relent, -ed, -ing

relentless, -ly

relese — release

relevance

relevancy

relevanse — relevance

relevant, -ly

releve — relieve

reli — rely

reliable, -bly

reliability

reliabul — reliable

reliance

reliant

relic

relief

relieve, -lieved, -lieving

religion

religious, -ly

rel|igun religion
relig|us religious
relinkwish relinquish
relinquish, -ed, -ing
relish, -ed, -ing
reluctance
relm realm
reluctanse reluctance
reluctant, -ly
rely, relied, relying
remain, -ed, -ing
remainder
remains
remand, -ed, -ing
remark, -ed, -ing
remarkable, -bly
remedial, -ly
remedy, -dies
remedy, -died, -dying
remember, -ed, -ing
remembrance
remembranse remembrance
remind, -ed, -ing
reminder
reminisce, -nisced, -niscing
reminiscence
reminiscent, -ly
reminisense reminiscence
reminisent reminiscent
reminiss reminisce
remishun remission
remiss, -ly
remission
remit, -mitted, -mitting
remittance
remnant
remonstrate, -trated, -trating
remonstrative
remooval removal
remoove remove
remorse
remorseful, -ly
remote, remoter, remotest
remotely
removable
removalist
remove, -moved, -moving

remunerate, -rated, -rating
remuneration
remunerative, -ly
ren wren
Renaissance
renal
rench wrench
rend, rent, rending
render, -ed, -ing
rendezvous, -voused, -vousing
rendition
renegade
renege, reneged, reneging
renew, -ed, -ing
renounce, -nounced, -nouncing
renovate, -vated, -vating
renovater renovator
renovation
renovator
renown
renowned
rent, -ed, -ing
rental
rentul rental
renue renew
renunciation
reorganisation
reorganise, -nised, -nising
repair, -ed, -ing
repairer
reparable, -bly
reparation
repartee
repast
repatriate, -ated, -ating
repatriation
repay, -paid, -paying
repeal, -ed, -ing
repeat, -ed, -ing
repeatedly
repeater
repel, -pelled, -pelling
repellant repellent
repellent, -ly
repent, -ed, -ing
repentance
repentanse repentance

repentant, -ly
  repercushun   repercussion
repertoire
repertory, -ries
  repetishus   repetitious
repetition
repetitious, -ly
  repetry   repertory
  repitition   repetition
replace, -placed, -placing
replacement
replay, -played, -playing
replenish, -ed, -ing
replenishment
replete
replica
reply, -plies
reply, -plied, -plying
report, -ed, -ing
reportable
reporter
repose, -posed, -posing
repository, -tories
  repositry   repository
  reposseshun   repossession
repossess, -ed, -ing
repossession
  reprehenshun   reprehension
reprehensible, -bly
reprehension
represent, -ed, -ing
representation
representational
representative, -ly
  represhun   repression
repress, -ed, -ing
  repressabul   repressible
repressible
repression
repressive, -ly
reprieve, -prieved, -prieving
reprimand, -ed, -ing
reprint, -ed, -ing
reprisal
  reprisul   reprisal
reproach, -ed, -ing
reproachable, -bly

reprobate, -bated, -bating
reprobation
  reproch   reproach
reproduce, -duced, -ducing
  reproducshun   reproduction
reproduction
reproof, -ed, -ing
reprove, -proved, -proving
reproval
reptile
reptilian
republic
republican
republicanism
repudiate, -ated, -ating
repudiation
repugnance
  repugnanse   repugnance
repugnant, -ly
repulse, -pulsed, -pulsing
repulsion
repulsive, -ly
reputable, -bly
  reputabul   reputable
reputation
repute, -puted, -puting
request, -ed, -ing
requiem
  requierment   requirement
require, -quired, -quiring
requirement
  requisishun   requisition
requisite
requisition
  rerite   rewrite
  reritten   rewritten
  rerote   rewrote
rescind, -ed, -ing
rescue, -cued, -cuing
rescuer
research, -ed, -ing
researcher
  reseat   receipt
  resede   recede
  reseipt   receipt
resemble, -bled, -bling
  resembul   resemble

resent, -ed, -ing (hurt)
resent   recent (new)
resentful, -ly
resentment
resepshun   reception
reseptacul   receptacle
reseptive   receptive
reserch   research
reservation
reserve, -served, -serving
reservoir
resess   recess
resesshun   recession
resession   recession
reset, -set, -setting
reseve   receive
resovoir   reservoir
reside, -sided, -siding
residence
residenshul   residential
resident
residential
residivision   recidivism
residual, -ly
residuary
residue
resign, -ed, -ing
resignation
resilience
resilient, -ly
resin
resind   rescind
resinous
resinus   resinous
resipe   recipe
resipient   recipient
resiprocul   reciprocal
resiprosity   reciprocity
resist, -ed, -ing
resistance
resitation   recitation
resistor
resite   recite
resolute, -ly
resolution
resolve, -solved, -solving
resonance

resonant, -ly
resonate, -nated, -nating
resorce   resource
resort, -ed, -ing
resound, -ed, -ing
resource
resourceful, -ly
respect, -ed, -ing
respectability, -ties
respectable, -bly
respectabul   respectable
respectful, -ly
respective, -ly
respiration
respirator
respiratory
respiratry   respiratory
respite
resplendent, -ly
responce   response
respond, -ed, -ing
respondent
response
responsibility, -ties
responsible, -bly
responsive, -ly
rest, -ed, -ing (sleep)
rest   wrest (grab)
restaration   restoration
restaurant
resterant   restaurant
restful, -ly
restitushion   restitution
restitution
restive, -ly
restle   wrestle
restler   wrestler
restless, -ly
restoration
restorative
restore, -stored, -storing
restrain, -ed, -ing
restraint
restricshun   restriction
restrict, -ed, -ing
restriction
restrictive, -ly

restructure, -tured, -turing

result, -ed, -ing

resultant

resumay   résumé (review)

résumé (review)

resume, -sumed, -suming (take up)

resumption

resurgence

resurgent

resurrect, -ed, -ing

resurrection

resuscitate, -tated, -tating

resuscitation

resuscitator

resusitation   resuscitation

retail, -ed ,-ing

retain, -ed, -ing

retainer

retaliate, -ated, -ating

retaliation

retard, -ed, -ing

retardation

retch, -ed, -ing (vomit)

retch   wretch (victim)

retention

retentive, -ly

reticence

reticent, -ly

retina, -nas, -nae

retinew   retinue

retinue

retire, -tired, -tiring

retirement

retisent   reticent

retoric   rhetoric

retoricul   rhetorical

retort, -ed, -ing

retrace, -traced, -tracing

retract, -ed, -ing

retractable

retrase   retrace

retread, -treaded, -treading

retreat, -ed, -ing

retred   retread

retreive   retrieve

retrench, -ed, -ing

retrenchment

retribushun   retribution

retribution

retrieve, -trieved, -trieving

retrievable

retrieval

retriever

retroactive, -ly

retrograde, -graded, -grading

retrogreshun   retrogression

retrogress, -ed, -ing

retrogression

retrogressive, -ly

retro-rocket

retrospect

retrospective, -ly

return, -ed, -ing

reunion

reunite, -nited, -niting

rev, revved, revving

revalie   reveille

revaluation

revalue, -ued, -uing

revalueation   revaluation

reveal, -ed, -ing

reveille (bugle call)

revel, -elled, -elling

revelation

reveller (festivity)

revelry, -ries

revenew   revenue

revenge, -venged, -venging

revenue

reverberate, -rated, -rating

reverberation

reverberatory

revere, -vered, -vering (respect)

reverence

reverend

reverense   reverence

reverent, -ly

reverie (daydream)

reversal

reverse, -versed, -versing

reversion

revert, -ed, -ing

revertabul   revertible

revertible

review, -ed, -ing (survey)
review   revue (theatre)
revile, -viled, -viling
revise, -vised, -vising
revishun   revision
revision
revival
revivalism
revive, -vived, -viving
revocation
revoke, -voked, -voking
revolt, -ed, -ing
revolushun   revolution
revolution
revolutionary, -ries
revolutionise, -nised, -nising
revolutionry   revolutionary
revolve, -volved, -volving
revolver
revue (theatre)
revue   review (survey)
revulshun   revulsion
revulsion
reward, -ed, -ing
rhapsodical, -ly
rhapsodise, -dised, -dising
rhapsody, -dies
rhesus
rhetoric
rhetorical, -ly
rheumatic
rheumatism
rheumatoid arthritis
rhinestone
rhino, -nos
rhinoceros, -roses, -ros
rhododendron
rhombus, -buses, -bi
rhubarb
rhyme, rhymed, rhyming (verse)
rhythm
rhythmical, -ly
rib, ribbed, ribbing
ribald
ribaldry
ribbon
rice

rich, -ly
riches
Richter scale
rick, -ed, -ing
rickets
rickety
rickshaw
ricochet, -ed, -ing
ricshore   rickshaw
rid, rid or ridded, ridding
ridance   riddance
riddance
riddle, -dled, -dling
ride, rode, ridden, riding
rider
ridge, ridged, ridging
ridicule, -culed, -culing
ridiculous, -ly
ridiculus   ridiculous
ridul   riddle
rie   rye (grain)
rie   wry (askew)
Riesling
rife
riffraff
rifle, -fled, -fling
rift
riful   rifle
rig, rigged, rigging
right, -ed, -ing (correct)
right   rite (ceremony)
right   write (inscribe)
righteous, -ly
rightful, -ly
right-handed
right-winger
rigid, -ly
rigidity
rigmarole
rigor mortis
rigorous, -ly
rigorus   rigorous
rigour
rig-out
rigul   wriggle
rile, riled, riling
rim, rimmed, rimming (edge)

rime, rimed, riming (frost)
| rime | rhyme (verse) |

rind

ring, ringed, ringing (surround)

ring, rang, rung, ringing (bell)
| ring | wring (squeeze) |

ringbark, -ed, -ing

ringer
| ringer | wringer |

ring-in

ringleader

ringlet

ringtail possum

ringworm

rink

rinse, rinsed, rinsing

riot, -ed, -ing

riotous, -ly
| riotus | riotous |

rip, ripped, ripping

ripcord

ripe, riper, ripest

ripen, -ed, -ing

rip-off

ripper

ripple, -pled, -pling
| rippul | ripple |

> If the word is not under **ri-**
> look under **re-**.

---

rip-roaring

rip-tide

rise, rose, risen, rising

risk, -ed, -ing
| riskay | risqué |

riskily

risky, -kier, -kiest

risqué

rissole
| rist | wrist |
| rit | writ |

rite (ceremony)
rite	right (correct)
rite	write (inscribe)
riter	writer
rithe	writhe
ritten	written

ritual, -ly

rival, -valled, -valling

rivalry, -ries

river

rivergum

rivet, -ed, -ing

rivulet
| ro | roe (fish) |
| ro | row (boat) |

roach, -ches

road (street)
| road | rode (did ride) |

roadblock

roadworthiness

roadworthy

roar, -ed, -ing (noise)
| roar | raw (uncooked) |

roast, -ed, -ing

rob, robbed, robbing

robber

robbery, -ries

robe, robed, robing
| robery | robbery |

robin

robot

robust, -ly

rock, -ed, -ing

rocker

rockery, -ries

rocket, -ed, -ing

rocketry

rock'n'roll

rock-wallaby

rococo

rod
| rodayo | rodeo |

rode (did ride)
| rode | road (street) |

rodent

rodeo, -deos
| rodio | rodeo |

roe (fish)
roe	row (boat)
roge	rogue
rogish	roguish

rogue, rogued, roguing

roguery, -gueries

roguish,-ly
role (character)
roll, -ed, -ing (turn)
roll bar
rollcall
roller
roller-skate, -skated, -skating
rolling-pin
rollick, -ed, -ing
rollmop
roll-up
roly-poly
Roman Catholic
romance, -manced, -mancing
romantic, -ly
romanticise, -cised, -cising
romanticism
romanticist
Romany, -nies (gipsy)

rombus	rhombus
rome	roam

romp, -ed, -ing
rondo, -dos
roneo, -ed, -ing

rong	wrong

roo (kangaroo)

roo	rue (regret)
roodiment	rudiment

roof, roofs
roofless
roof-rack

rooful	rueful
rooge	rouge
rooin	ruin
rooinous	ruinous

rook, -ed, -ing
rookery, -ries
rookie

rool	rule
roolet	roulette

room, -ed, -ing

roomatism	rheumatism
roomer	rumour

roomy, -mier, -miest

roon	ruin
roopee	rupee
roorul	rural

roose	ruse

roost, -ed, -ing
rooster
root, -ed, -ing (plant)

root	route (way)

ropable
rope, roped, roping
ropeable
ropeway
ropey
ropy, ropier, ropiest

ror	roar (noise)
ror	raw (uncooked)

rort
rosary, -ries

rosay	rosé (wine)

rose, rosed, rosing (flower)
rosé (wine)
rosella
rosemary

rosery	rosary
roset	rosette

rosette
rosewood

rosie	rosy

rosily

rost	roast

roster
rostrum, -trums, -tra
rosy, rosier, rosiest
rot, rotted, rotting
rotary
rotate, -tated, -tating
rotation
rote (routine)

rote	wrote (did write)
roten	rotten
roter	rotor

rotisserie
rotor
rotten, -ly
rotund, -ly
rotundity

roudy	rowdy

rouge, rouged, rouging
rough, -ly

roughage	
roughen, -ed, -ing	
roughshod	
rought	wrought
roulet	roulette
roulette, -letted, -letting	
round, -ed, -ing	
roundabout	
rounders	
roundly	
round-up	
rouse, roused, rousing	
rouseabout	
rout, routed, routing (defeat)	
route (way)	
route	root (plant)
routeen	routine
routine	
rove, roved, roving	
rover	
row, -ed, -ing (boat)	
row	roe (fish)
rowdie	rowdy
rowdily	
rowdy, -dier, -diest	
rowel, -elled, -elling	
rowlock	
rownd	round
rowse	rouse
rowt	rout
royal, -ly	
royalist	
royalty, -ties	
rub, rubbed, rubbing	
rubber	
rubbish	
rubbishy	
rubble	
rubella	
ruber	rubber
rubicund	
rubie	ruby
rubish	rubbish
rubric	
rubul	rubble
ruby, -bies	
ruck, -ed, -ing	

rucksack	
ruckshun	ruction
ruction	
rudder	
ruddy, -dier, -diest	
rude, ruder, rudest (rough)	
rude	rued (regret)
rudely	
rudeness	
ruder	rudder
rudimentary	
rudiments	
rudy	ruddy
rue, rued, ruing (regret)	
rued	rude (rough)
rueful, -ly (pity)	
ruf	rough (coarse)
ruffen	roughen
ruffian	
ruffle, -fled, -fling (annoy)	
rufful	ruffle
rufian	ruffian
rufige	roughage
rufle	ruffle
ruful	rueful
rug, rugged, rugging	
rugby	
ruin, -ed, -ing (destroy)	
ruin	rune (letter)
ruination	
ruinous, -ly	
ruinus	ruinous
rule, ruled, ruling	
ruler	
rum	
rumatism	rheumatism
rumba	
rumble, -bled, -bling	
rumbul	rumble
rumen, -mina	
rumer	rumour
rumige	rummage
ruminant	
ruminate, -nated, -nating	
rummage, -maged, -maging	
rumour, -ed, -ing	
rump	

rumple, -pled, -pling
   rumpul   rumple
rumpus
run, ran, run, running
runabout
rune (letter)
   rune   ruin (destroy)
rung (did ring)
   rung   wrung (squeezed)
run-in
runner
runner-up
runny
run-off
run-of-the-mill
run-on
runt
runway
   rupcher   rupture
rupee
rupture, -tured, -turing
rural, -ly
ruse
rush, -ed, -ing
   Rushun   Russian
   rusit   russet
rusk
russet
Russian roulette
rust, -ed, -ing
rustic, -ally
rusticity, -ties
rustle, -tled, -tling
rustproof
rusty, -tier, -tiest
rut, rutted, rutting
ruthless, -ly
rye (grain)
   rye   wry (askew)
rye-grass
   ryme   rhyme
   rythm   rhythm

Ss

Sabath	Sabbath
Sabbath	
sabbatical	
sabbaticul	sabbatical
sabel	sable
saber	sabre
Sabin vaccine	
sable	
sabot	
sabotage, -taged, -taging	
saboteur	
sabre, -bred, -bring	
sabre-toothed	
sac (bag)	
sac	sack (hessian)
sacarin	saccharin
saccharin	
sacerdotal, -ly	
sachay	sachet
sachel	satchel
sachet	
sack, -ed, -ing	
sackarin	saccharin
sackcloth	
sacrament	
sacramental, -ly	
sacred, -ly	
sacredness	
sacrement	sacrament
sacrifice, -ficed, -ficing	
sacrificial, -ly	
sacrifise	sacrifice
sacrifishul	sacrificial
sacriledge	sacrilege
sacrilege	
sacrilegious, -ly	
sacrilige	sacrilege
sacriligus	sacrilegious

sacrosanct	
sad, sadder, saddest	
sadden, -ed, -ing	
saddle, saddled, saddling	
saddleback	
saddler	
saddlery, -ries	
saden	sadden
sadler	saddler
sadlery	saddlery
sadism	
sadist	
sadistic, -ally	
sadul	saddle
safari, -ris	
safe, safer, safest	
safegard	safeguard
safeguard	
safekeeping	
safely	
safety, -ties	
saffire	sapphire
saffron	
safire	sapphire
safron	saffron
saftie	safety
sag, sagged, sagging	
saga	
sagacious, -ly	
sagacity, -ties	
sagasity	sagacity
sagayshus	sagacious
sage, sager, sagest	
Sagittarius	
sago	
said	
sail (boat)	
sail	sale (sold)
sailsman	salesman
sailboard	
sailcloth	
sailor	
sailplane, -planed, -planing	
saint, -ly	
sainted	
sainthood	
saintliness	

sake		salon		
sakred	sacred	saloobrius	salubrious	
sakson	Saxon	saloon		
saksophone	saxophone	saloot	salute	
salaam		salow	sallow	
salacious, -ly		salt, -ed, -ing		
salad		saltbush		
salamander		saltcellar		
salami		saltery	psaltery	
salamy	salami	saltseller	saltcellar	
salaried		salubrious, -ly		
salary, -ries (wage)		salubrius	salubrious	
salary	celery (food)	salud	salad	
salasious	salacious	salutary		
sale (sold)		salutation		
sale	sail (boat)	salute, -luted, -luting		
saleability		salvage, -vaged, -vaging (save)		
saleable, -ly		salvage	selvedge (edge)	
saleabul	saleable	salvager		
salene	saline	salve, salved, salving		
salesgirl		salver		
saleslady, -dies		salvidge	salvage (save)	
salesman, -men		salvidge	selvedge (edge)	
salesmanship		salvo, -vos, -voes		
salesroom		sal volatile		
saleswoman, -women		samantic	semantic	
saleyard		samba		
salie	sally	same		
salience		samon	salmon	
saliense	salience	samovar		
salient, -ly		Samoyed		
saline		sampan		
salinity		sample, -pled, -pling		
saliva		sampler		
salivary		sampul	sample	
salivate, -vated, -vating		samurai		
salivation		samuri	samurai	
sallow		sanatarium	sanitarium	
sallowish		sanatorium, -toriums, -toria		
sally, -lies		sancshun	sanction	
sally, -lied, -lying		sanctification		
salm	psalm	sanctify, -fied, -fying		
		sanctimonious, -ly		
For all other sall- words, look under sal-.		sanctimonius	sanctimonious	
		sanction, -ed, -ing		
salmon		sanctity, -ties		
salmonella		sanctuary, -ries		

sanctum, -tums
sand, -ed, -ing
sandal
sandalwood
sandbag, -bagged, -bagging
sandbank
sandblast, -ed, -ing
sandfly, -flies
sandpaper, -ed, -ing
sandpiper
sandshoe
sandsoap
sandstone
sandul — sandal
sandwhich — sandwich
sandwich, -wiches
sandwitch — sandwich
sane, saner, sanest (not mad)
sane — seine (net)
sanely
saneness
sang
sangfroid
sanguinary
sanguine, -ly
sangwin — sanguine
sanitarium, -tariums, -taria
sanitary
sanitation
sanitorium — sanatorium
sanity
sank

> For all other sank- words,
> look under **sanct-**.

sanskrit
Santa Claus
Santa Klaus — Santa Claus
sap, sapped, sapping
saper — sapper
sapience
sapiency
sapient, -ly
sapling
sapper
sapphire
sappling — sapling

sapwood
sarcasm
sarcastic, -ally
sarcofagus — sarcophagus
sarcophagus, -gi, -guses
sardeen — sardine
sardine, -dines
sardonic, -ally
sargent — sergeant
sari
sarong
sarsaparilla
sartorial, -ly
sary — sari
saserdotal — sacerdotal
sash
sashay (trip)
sashay — sachet (bag)
sashiate — satiate
sassafras
Sassenach
Satan (devil)
Satanic, -ally
Satanism
Satanist
satay
satchel
sate, sated, sating
sateen (cotton)
satellite
Saten — Satan (devil)
saten — sateen (cotton)
saten — satin (silk)
Saterday — Saturday
satiabel — satiable
satiable, -ly
satiate, -ated, -ating
satiation
satin (silk)
satinwood
satire (sarcasm)
satire — satyr (a god)
satiric
satirical, -ly
satirist
satisfacshun — satisfaction
satisfaction

satisfactorily
satisfactory

satisfactry — satisfactory
satisfiabul — satisfiable

satisfy, -fied, -fying
saturate, -rated, -rating
saturation
Saturday
Saturn (planet)

saturn — sauterne (wine)
saturnine, -ly

satyr (a god)

satyr — satire (sarcasm)

sauce (liquid)

sauce — source (origin)

saucepan
saucer

saucerer — sorcerer
saucery — sorcery

saucily
sauciness
saucy, -cier, -ciest
sauerkraut
sauna
saunter, -ed, -ing
saurian
sausage

sausy — saucy

sauté, -téed, -téeing
sauterne (wine)

sauturn — sauterne

savage, savaged, savaging
savagely
savagery, -ries

savana — savanna

savanna
savant
save, saved, saving
saveloy
saver (keeper)

saver — savour (taste)
savier — saviour
savige — savage
savigery — savagery
savigry — savagery

saving
saviour

savoir-faire
savory, -vories (herb)
savour, -ed, -ing (taste)

savour — saver (keeper)

savoury, -vouries (tasty)
savoy
savvy
saw, sawed, sawing (cut)

saw — soar (rise)
saw — sore (hurt)
sawcer — saucer
sawcey — saucy
sawdid — sordid

sawdust
sawmill

sawna — sauna
sawnter — saunter

sawpit

saws — sauce (liquid)
saws — source (origin)
sawser — saucer
sawsey — saucy

saxhorn

saxofone — saxophone
saxofonist — saxophonist

Saxon
saxophone
saxophonist
say, said, saying

sayance — seance

say-so
scab, scabbed, scabbing
scabbard

scabees — scabies

scabies
scaffold
scaffolding
scalar
scald, -ed, -ing (burn)

scald — scold (chide)

scale, scaled, scaling

scaliwag — scallywag

scallop, -ed, -ing
scallywag
scalp, -ed, -ing
scalpel
scalper

scalpul scalpel
scamp
scamper, -ed, -ing
scan, scanned, scanning
scandal
scandalise, -lised, -lising
scandalmonger
scanner
scanshun scansion
scansion
scant
scantness
scanty, scantier, scantiest
scapegoat
scapula, -lae
scar, scarred, scarring
scarab
scarce, scarcer, scarcest
scarcely
scarceness
scarcity, -ties
scare, scared, scaring
scarecrow
scaremonger
scarf, scarfs, scarves
scarify, -fied, -fying
scarlet
scarp
scarper
scarsity scarcity
scary, scarier, scariest
scate skate
scathing, -ly
scatter, -ed, -ing
scatterbrain
scatty, -tier, -tiest
scavenge, -venged, -venging
scavenger
sceme scheme
scenario, -narios
scene (view)
scene seen (to see)
scenery, -neries
scenic, -ally
scent (perfume)
scent cent (coin)
scent sent (to send)

scepter sceptre
sceptic
sceptical, -ly
scepticism
sceptre
scerge scourge
scermish skirmish
schedule, -uled, -uling
schematic, -ally
scheme, schemed, scheming
schemer
schism
schismatic
schizofrenia schizophrenia
schizoid
schizophrenia
schizophrenic
schnapper
schnapps
scholar
scholarly
scholarship
scholastic, -ally
scholasticism
school, -ed, -ing
schoolboy
schoolgirl
schooner
sciatic
sciatica
science
scientific, -ally
scientist
scimitar
scintillate, -lated, -lating
sciolism
scion
scissors
scitsofrenia schizophrenia
sclerosis, -ses
scoff, -ed, -ing
scolar scholar
scolarship scholarship
scolastic scholastic
scold, -ed, -ing (chide)
scold scald (burn)
scollop

scone
  scool   school
scoop, -ed, -ing
scooter
scope
scorch, -ed, -ing
score, scored, scoring
scorer
scorn, -ed, -ing
scornful, -ly
Scorpio
scorpion
  scorpiun   scorpion
Scotch
scotch, -ed, -ing
scot-free
Scotsman, -men
Scotswoman, -women
Scottish
scoundrel
  scoundrul   scoundrel
scour, -ed, -ing (scratch)
  scour   scow (barge)
scourge, scourged, scourging
scout, -ed, -ing
scow (barge)
  scow   scour (scratch)
scowl, -ed, -ing
  scowndrel   scoundrel
  scowt   scout
scrabble, -bled, -bling
  scrabbul   scrabble
scrag, scragged, scragging
scraggly, -glier, -gliest
scraggy, -gier, -giest
scram, scrammed, scramming
scramble, -bled, -bling
  scrambul   scramble
scrap, scrapped, scrapping
scrapbook
scrape, scraped, scraping
scraper
scrappily
scrappy, -pier, -piest
  scrapy   scrappy
scratch, -ed, -ing
scrawl, -ed, -ing

scrawny, -nier, -niest
scream, -ed, -ing
screamer
scree
screech, -ed, -ing
screed
screen, -ed, -ing
screenplay
screw, -ed, -ing
screwball
screwdriver
  screwtinise   scrutinise
screwy, screwier, screwiest
scribal (writer)
scribble, -bled, -bling (write)
scribbler
  scribbul   scribble
scribe, scribed, scribing
scrim
  scrimage   scrimmage
scrimmage, -maged, -maging
scrimp, -ed, -ing
scrip (receipt)
  scripcher   scripture
script (handwriting)
scriptural, -ly
Scripture
scrofula
scrofulous, -ly
scroll
  scroo   screw
  scrotem   scrotum
scrotum
scrounge, scrounged, scrounging
scrounger
  scrownge   scrounge
scrub, scrubbed, scrubbing
scrubber
scrubby, -bier, -biest
scruff
scruffy, scruffier, scruffiest
scrum, scrummed, scrumming
  scrumage   scrummage
scrummage
  scrumpshus   scrumptious
scrumptious, -ly
scrumptiousness

scrumshus	scrumptious	scuttlebutt	
scrunch, -ed, -ing		scuttul	scuttle
scruple, -pled, -pling		scythe, scythed, scything	
scrupul	scruple	sea (ocean)	
scrupulosity		see	see (look)
scrupulous, -ly		sea-anemone	
scrupulousness		seaboard	
scrutinise, -nised, -nising		seabord	seaboard
scrutiny, -nies		seafarer	
scuba		seafaring	
scud, scudded, scudding		seafood	
scuff, -ed, -ing		seagoing	
scuffle, -fled, -fling		seagull	
scuful	scuffle	seahorse	
scul	scull (row)	seal, -ed, -ing	
scul	skull (head)	sealant	
sculery	scullery	sealer	
scull, -ed, -ing (row)		sea-level	
scull	skull (head)	sealing (close)	
scullery, -leries		sealing	ceiling (roof)
scullion		seam, -ed, -ing (join)	
scullyon	scullion	seam	seem (appear)
sculpcher	sculpture	seaman, -men (sailors)	
sculpt, -ed, -ing		seamanship	
sculpter	sculptor	seamen	semen (seed)
sculptor		seamstress	
sculptress		seamy -mier, -miest	
sculptural, -ly		sean	scene (view)
sculpture, -tured, -turing		sean	seen (to see)
scum, scummed, scumming		seance	
scummy, -mier, -miest		seanse	seance
scungie	scungy	seaplane	
scungy		sear, -ed, -ing (burn)	
scurf		sear	seer (prophet)
scurge	scourge	search, -ed, -ing	
scurie	scurry	searcher	
scurilus	scurrilous	searchlight	
scurrilous, -ly		search-warrant	
scurrulus	scurrilous	sea-scout	
scurry, -ries		sea-shell	
scurry, -ried, -rying		seashore	
scurvey	scurvy	seasickness	
scurvily		seaside	
scurvy, -vier, -viest		season, -ed, -ing	
scury	scurry	seasonable, -bly	
scuttel	scuttle	seasonabul	seasonable
scuttle, -tled, -tling		seasonal, -ly	

seat, -ed, -ing
seawards
seaweed
seaworthiness
seaworthy
sebaceous
  sebashus — sebaceous
  secaters — secateurs
secateurs
secede, -ceded, -ceding
  secesshun — secession
secession
  secetary — secretary
seclude, -cluded, -cluding
  seclushun — seclusion
seclusion
second, -ed, -ing
secondary, -arily
secondary boycott
second-class
second-degree
second-hand
secondly
second-rate
  secondry — secondary
seconds
  secratery — secretary
secrecy, -cies
  secreshun — secretion
  secresy — secrecy
secret, -ly
secretarial
secretariat
  secretariul — secretarial
secretary, -ries
secrete, -creted, -creting
secretion
secretive, -ly
  secretry — secretary
  secshun — section
sect
  sectar — sector
sectarian
sectarianism
section
sectional, -ly
  secter — sector

sector
secular, -ly
secularism
secularist
securable
  securabul — securable
secure, -cured, -curing
security, -ties
  sed — said
  sedament — sediment
sedan
sedate, -dated, -dating
sedation
sedative
sedentary
  sedentery — sedentary
  seder — cedar
sedge
sediment
sedimentary
sedimentation
  sedimentery — sedimentary
  sedishun — sedition
  sedishus — seditious
sedition
seditious, -ly
  seditive — sedative
seduce, -duced, -ducing
seducer
  seducshun — seduction
seduction
seductive, -ly
seductiveness
sedulous
  sedulus — sedulous
see, saw, seen, seeing (look)
  see — sea (ocean)
seed, seeded, seeding (plant)
  seed — cede (yield)
seediness
seedling
seedy, seedier, seediest
  seefarer — seafarer
  seefood — seafood
  seege — siege
  seegull — seagull
seek, sought, seeking

seel	seal
seelant	sealant
seeler	sealer
see-level	sea-level
seeling	ceiling (roof)
seeling	sealing (close)

seem, -ed, -ing (appear)

seem	seam (join)
seeman	seaman (sailor)

seemly, -lier, -liest

| seemstress | seamstress |
| seemy | seamy |

seen (to see)

seen	scene (view)
seenery	scenery
seenic	scenic
seenile	senile

seep, -ed, -ing

seepage

seepige	seepage
seequel	sequel

seer (prophet)

seer	sear (burn)
searsucker	seersucker

seersucker

seesaw

seese	cease
seesfire	ceasefire
seeshore	seashore
seesun	season
seet	seat

seethe, seethed, seething

seeweed	seaweed
seeze	seize
seezure	seizure
sege	sedge

segment

segmentation

segregate, -gated, -gating

segregation

segregationist

seige	siege

seine (net)

seine	sane (not mad)
seismagraf	seismograph

seismic

seismograph

seismologist

seismology

seize, seized, seizing

seizure

sekaters	secateurs
sekond	second
sekrete	secrete
seks	sex
sekshun	section
sekstant	sextant
seksual	sexual
seksy	sexy
sekt	sect
sektor	sector
sekular	secular
sekure	secure
sekwel	sequel
sekwense	sequence
sekwin	sequin
Selcius	Celsius

seldom, -ly

selebrate	celebrate
selebrity	celebrity
seleckshun	selection

select, -ed, -ing

selecter	selector

selection

selective, -ly

selectivity

selector

seler	cellar (room)
seler	seller (goods)
selerity	celerity
selery	celery (food)
selery	salary (wage)
selestial	celestial

self, selves

self-addressed

self-aggrandisement

self-assurance

self-centred

self-confessed

self-confidence

self-confident

self-conscious, -ly

self-contained

self-defence

self-denial		salvage (edge)	
self-destruct		selvedge (edge)	
self-determination		selvedge	salvage (save)
self-employed		semafor	semaphore
self-evident, -ly		semantic	
self-fertilisation		semaphore, -phored, -phoring	
self-government		semblance	
self-image		semblanse	semblance
self-imidge	self-image	semen (seed)	
self-important, -ly		semen	seamen (sailors)
self-interest			
selfish,-ly		semester	
selfishness		semibreve	
selfless, -ly		semicercul	semicircle
self-made		semicircle	
self-opinionated		semicircular	
self-pollination		semicolon	
self-possessed		semiconductor	
self-raising flour		semidetached	
self-respect		seminal, -ly	
self-righteous, -ly		seminar	
self-rule		seminary, -aries	
self-sacrifice		seminery	seminary
self-service		semiprecious	
self-sown		semipreshus	semiprecious
self-starter		semiquaver	
self-sufficient		Semite	
self-willed		semitery	cemetery
selibacy	celibacy	Semitic	
selibat	celibate	semitone	
selibrate	celebrate	semitrailer	
sell, sold, selling (goods)		semolina	
sell	cell (prison)	sena	senna
seller (goods)		senario	scenario
seller	cellar (room)	senat	senate
sellofane	cellophane	senate	
sellophane	cellophane	senater	senator
sell-out		senator	
sellullar	cellular	senatorial	
selluloid	celluloid	senatoriul	senatorial
sellulose	cellulose	send, sent, sending	
sellvage	salvage (save)	sender	
sellvedge	selvedge (edge)	senile	
Selsius	Celsius	senilitey	senility
selular	cellular	senility	
seluloid	celluloid	senior	
selulose	cellulose	seniority, -ties	

senna
   senotaf — cenotaph
   sensability — sensibility
   sensabul — sensible
sensation
sensational, -ly
sensationalise, -ised, -ising
sensationalism
sensationalist
   sensatise — sensitise
sense, sensed, sensing
   senser — censer (incense)
   senser — censor (books)
   senser — sensor (device)
   senshual — sensual
   senshur — censure (blame)
sensible, -bly
sensibility, -ties
   sensibul — sensible
sensitise, -tised, -tising
sensitivity, -ties
sensor (device)
   sensor — censer (incense)
   sensor — censor (books)
   sensorey — sensory
   sensorious — censorious
sensory, -orily
sensual, -ly
sensualist
   sensualitey — sensuality
sensuality, -ties
sensuous, -ly
   sensus — census
sent (to send)
   sent — cent (money)
   sent — scent (perfume)
   sentenary — centenary
sentence, -tenced, -tencing
   sentenchus — sententious
   sentennial — centennial
sententious, -ly
   senter — centre
sentience
sentient, -ly
   sentigrade — Centigrade
   sentigram — centigram
sentiment

sentimental, -ly
sentimentalism
sentimentalist
sentimentality, -ties
   sentimeter — centimetre
sentinel, -nelled, -nelling
   sentipede — centipede
   sentor — centaur
   sentral — central
   sentralise — centralise
   sentrey — sentry
   sentrifugal — centrifugal
   sentifuge — centrifuge
   sentripetal — centripetal
sentry, -tries
   sentupul — centuple
   senturion — centurion
   sentury — century
   senyor — senior
   senyority — seniority
sepal
separable, -bly
   separabul — separable
separate, -rated, -rating
separately
separation
separationist
separator
   seperabul — separable
   seperate — separate
   seperation — separation
   sephalitis — cephalitis
sepia
sepoy
sepsis
September
septennial, -ly
   septer — sceptre
septet
septic
septicaemia
   septisemia — septicaemia
septuagenarian
sepulchral, -ly
sepulchre
   sepulchrul — sepulchral
   sepulker — sepulchre

sequel		serimony	ceremony
sequence		serious, -ly	
sequense	sequence	seriousness	
sequenshul	sequential	serius	serious
sequential, -ly		serjent	sergeant
sequester, -ed, -ing		serloin	sirloin
sequestration		serly	surly
sequin		serman	sermon
ser	sir	sermise	surmise
seraf	seraph	sermon	
serafic	seraphic	sermount	surmount
seramic	ceramic	sername	surname
seranade	serenade	serpent	
serch	search	serpentine	
seremony	ceremony	serplice	surplice (gown)
seraph, -aphs, -aphim		serplus	surplus (extra)
seraphic, -ally		serprise	surprise
serch	search	serrate, -rated, -rating	
sere (dry)		serration	
sere	sear (burn)	serry, -ried, -rying	
serebrul	cerebral	sertain	certain
sereen	serene	sertanty	certainty
serees	series	sertax	surtax
serenade, -naded, -nading		sertifiabul	certifiable
serendipity		sertificate	certificate
serene, -ly		sertify	certify
serenitey	serenity	sertitude	certitude
serenity, -ties		serum, sera, serums	
seres	series	servant	
sereze	cerise	servay	survey
serf (slave)		servaylanse	surveillance
serf	surf (sea)	serve, served, serving	
serfdom		server	
serge (cloth)		servery, serveries	
serge	surge (rush)	servical	cervical
sergeant		service, -viced, -vicing	
serial, -ly (part)		serviceability	
serial	cereal (grain)	serviceable, -bly	
serialisation		serviceabul	serviceable
serialise, -lised, -lising		serviceman, -men	
seribelum	cerebellum	servicewoman, -women	
seribrul	cerebral	serviet	serviette
seribrum	cerebrum	serviette	
series		serviks	cervix
serif		servile, -ly	
serimonial	ceremonial	servility	
serimonius	ceremonious	servitude	

servival	survival	severely	
servive	survive	severitey	severity
serviver	survivor	severity, -ties	
servix	cervix	sew, sewed, sewn, sewing (stitch)	
sesame		sew	sow (plant)
sesayshun	cessation	sewage	
sese	cease	sewer (drain)	
seseed	secede	sewer (stitcher)	
seseshun	secession	sewer	sower (planter)
seshun	cession (yield)	sewerage	
seshun	session (period)	sewerige	sewerage
sesless	ceaseless	sewige	sewage
seson	season	sex, -ed, -ing	
sesonabul	seasonable	sexiness	
sesonal	seasonal	sexist	
sespit	cesspit	sextant	
sesquicentenary, -ries		sextet	
sesseshun	secession	sexton	
session (period)		sexual, -ly	
session	cession (yield)	sexualitey	sexuality
set, set, setting		sexuality	
setback		sexy, sexier, sexiest	
setee	settee	sezarian	caesarian
seter	setter	sfere	sphere
setul	settle	sfericul	sperical
settee		sferoid	spheroid
setter		sfincter	sphincter
settle, -tled, -tling		sfinx	sphinx
settlement		sha	shah
settler		shabbily	
settul	settle	shabbiness	
set-up		shabby, -bier, -biest	
seudo	pseudo	shaby	shabby
seudonim	pseudonym	shack	
sevear	severe	shackle, -led, -ling	
seven		shackul	shackle
seventeen		shaddow	shadow
seventeenth		shade, shaded, shading	
seventh		shadow, -ed, -ing	
Seventh-Day Adventist		shadowy	
seventieth		shady, -dier, -diest	
seventy, -ties		shaft	
sever, -ed, -ing		shag, shagged, shagging	
several, -ly		shagginess	
severance		shaggy, -gier, -giest	
severanse	severance	shagrin	chagrin
severe, -verer, -verest		shagy	shaggy

shah
  shak   shack
shake, shook, shaken, shaking
shakedown
shaker
Shakespearian
shake-up
  shakey   shaky
shakily
shakiness
shaky, shakier, shakiest
  shal   shall
  shalay   chalet
shale
  shalet   chalet
shall (will)
  shall   shell (cover)
shallot
shallow, -ly
shallowness
sham, shammed, shaming
shamble, -bled, -bling
shambles
  shambul   shamble
shame, shamed, shaming
shamefaced, -ly
shameful, -ly
shameless, -ly
  shampane   champagne
shampoo, -ed, -ing
shamrock
  shamy   chamois
  shandeleer   chandelier
  shandie   shandy
shandy, -dies
shanghai, -haied, -haiing
shank
shan't (shall not)
  shant   shan't
shantung
shanty, -ties
shape, shaped, shaping
shapeliness
shapely, -lier, -liest
  shaperon   chaperone
  sharade   charade
shard

share, shared, sharing
sharebroker
sharefarmer
shareholder
shark
sharkskin
sharp, -ly
sharpen, -ed, -ing
sharpener
sharper
sharpness
sharpshooter
sharpwitted
  shasee   chassis
shashlik
  shater   shatter
  shatow   chateau
shatter, -ed, -ing
shave, shaved, shaven, shaving
shaver
shawl
sheaf, sheaves
shear, sheared, shorn, shearing (cut)
  shear   sheer (thin)
shearer
shearwater
sheath, sheaths
sheathe, sheathed, sheathing
sheave, sheaved, sheaving
shed, shed, shedding
  shedule   schedule
  sheef   sheaf
  sheek   chic (smart)
  sheek   sheik (ruler)
sheen
sheep, sheep
sheep-dip
sheepdog
sheepish, -ly
sheepishness
sheep-run
sheepskin
sheer, -ed, -ing (swerve)
sheer (thin)
  sheer   shear (cut)
sheet, -ed, -ing
  shef   chef

sheik (ruler)	
sheik	shake (move)
sheila	
sheild	shield
shekel	
shel	shell
shelac	shellac
shelf, shelves	
shelfish	shellfish
shell, -ed, -ing (cover)	
she'll (she will)	
shell	she'll
shellac, -lacked, -lacking	
shellfish, -fishes, -fish	
shell-shocked	
shelly, -lier, -liest	
shelter, -ed, -ing	
shelve, shelved, shelving	
shemozzle	
shenanigan	
she-oak	
sheperd	shepherd
shepherd, -ed, -ing	
shepherdess	
sherbet	
sherbut	sherbet
sherie	sherry
sherif (Muslim leader)	
sheriff (law man)	
sherry, -ries	
shery	sherry
sheth	sheath
sheves	sheaves
shevron	chevron
shibboleth	
shic	chic (smart)
shic	sheik (ruler)
shicanery	chicanery
shickered	
shied	
shield, -ed, -ing	
shiffon	chiffon
shift, -ed, -ing	
shiftiness	
shiftless, -ly	
shifty, -tier, -tiest	
shiling	shilling

shillelagh	
shilling	
shimmer, -ed, -ing	
shimmery	
shimmy, -mies	
shimmy, -mied, -mying	
shin, shinned, shinning	
shindig	
shine, shone, shined, shining	
shiner	
shingel	shingle
shingle, -gled, -gling	
shingles	
shinguls	shingles
shiny, shinier, shiniest	
ship, shipped, shipping	
shipment	
shipreck	shipwreck
shipright	shipwright
shipshape	
shipwreck, -ed, -ing	
shipwright	
shiralee	
shirk, -ed, -ing	
shirker	
shirr, -ed, -ing	
shirt	
shirty	
shish-kebab	
shivalrey	chivalry
shivalrus	chivalrous
shiver, -ed, -ing	
shivery	
shnaps	schnapps
shoal, -ed, -ing	
shock, -ed, -ing	
shocker	
shod	
shoddily	
shoddiness	
shoddy, -dier, -diest	
shodie	shoddy
shody	shoddy
shoe, shoes	
shoe, shod, shoeing (footwear)	
shoe	shoo (scare)
shoehorn	

shoelace
shoemaker
shoeshine
shoestring
shofer — chauffeur
shogun
sholder — shoulder
shole — shoal
shoo, -ed, -ing (scare)
shoo — shoe (footwear)
shood — should
shook
shoot, shot, shooting (gun)
shoot — chute (channel)
shooter
shoot-out
shop, shopped, shopping
shopkeeper
shop-lift, -ed, -ing
shop-lifter
shop-soiled
shop-steward
shore, shored, shoring (sea)
shore — sure (certain)
shorely — surely
shorety — surety
shorn
short, -ly
shortage
shortbread
shortbred — shortbread
shortcake
short-change, -changed, -changing
short-circuit, -ed, -ing
shortcoming
shorten, -ed, -ing
shortfall
shorthand
shortidge — shortage
shorts
short-sighted
short-sited — short-sighted
short-wave
shot
shotgun
shot-put
shot-putter

should
shoulder, -ed, -ing
shoulder-blade
shout, -ed, -ing
shove, -ed, -ing
shovel, -ed, -ing
shoveler (bird)
shoveller (bird), (person)
shovinism — chauvinism
shovinist — chauvinist
show, showed, shown, showing
showboat
showdown
shower
showery
showily
showjumper
showjumping
showman, -men
showmanship
show-off
showt — shout
showy, showier, showiest
shrank
shrapnel
shred, shredded, shredding
shredder
shreek — shriek
shrew
shrewd, -ly
shrewish, -ly
shriek, -ed, -ing
shrift
shrike
shrill
shrimp
shrine
shrink, shrank, shrunk, shrinking
shrinkage
shrinkige — shrinkage
shrivel, -elled, -elling
shroo — shrew
shrood — shrewd
shroud
shrowd — shroud
shrub
shrubbery

shrug, shrugged, shrugging
shrunk
shudder, -ed, -ing
shuffel — shuffle
shuffle, -fled, -fling
shun, shunned, shunning
shunt, -ed, -ing
shunter
shurbet — sherbert
shurk — shirk
shurt — shirt
shush, -ed, -ing
shut, shut, shutting
shutdown
shut-eye
shut-out
shuttel — shuttle
shutter
shuttle, -tled, -tling
shuttlecock
shuttul — shuttle
shuttulcock — shuttlecock
shutul — shuttle
shuve — shove
shuvel — shovel
shy, shied, shying
shy, shyer, shyest
shyly
shyness
shyster
sianide — cyanide
siatic — sciatic
sibernetics — cybernetics
sibilant, -ly
sibling
sicamore — sycamore
sicedelic — psychedelic
siciatry — psychiatry
sicick — psychic
sick
sicken, -ed, -ing
sickie
sickle
sickliness
sickly, -lier, -liest
sickul — sickle
siclamate — cyclamate

siclamen — cyclamen
sicle — cycle
siclic — cyclic
siclist — cyclist
siclone — cyclone
siclotron — cyclotron
sicoanalise — psychoanalyse
sicological — psychological
sicology — psychology
sicophant — sycophant
sicopath — psychopath
sicosis — psychosis
sicosomatic — psychosomatic
sicotherapist — psychotherapist
sicotic — psychotic
sicul — cycle
side, sided, siding
sideboard
sidebord — sideboard
sidelight
sideline
sidelite — sidelight
sider — cider
sideshow
sidestep, -stepped, -stepping
sidetrack, -ed, -ing
sideways
sidel — sidle
sidle, -dled, -dling
sie — sigh
siege, sieged, sieging
sienna
sience — science
siense — science
sientific — scientific
sientist — scientist
sierra
siesta
sieve, sieved, sieving
sieze — seize
sifer — cypher
sifilis — syphilis
sifon — syphon
sift, -ed, -ing
sigar — cigar
sigaret — cigarette
sigh, -ed, -ing

sight, -ed, -ing (view)		silie	silly
sight	cite (quote)	silige	silage
sight	site (place)	silinder	cylinder
sightless, -ly		silindricul	cylindrical
sightly, -lier, -liest		silk	
sightseeing		silken	
sightseer		silkiness	
sigma		silk-screen	
sign, -ed, -ing (mark)		silkworm	
sign	sine (maths)	silky, -kier, -kiest	
signal, -ed, -ing		silky oak	
signatory, -ries		sill	
signatry	signatory	sillabul	syllable
signature		silliness	
signefy	signify	silly, -lier, -liest	
signet (ring)		silo, -los	
signet	cygnet (swan)	silogism	syllogism
significance		silt, -ed, -ing	
significanse	significance	siluet	silhouette
significant, -ly		silver, -ed, -ing	
signification		silverfish, -fish, -fishes	
signifie	signify	silverside	
signify, -fied, -fying		silversmith	
signpost		silvery	
signul	signal	sily	silly
sign-writer		simbiosis	symbiosis
sikedelic	psychedelic	simbiotic	symbiotic
sikey	psyche	simbol	cymbal (music)
Sikh		simbol	symbol (sign)
sikiatrist	psychiatrist	simbolicul	symbolical
sikiatry	psychiatry	simbolise	symbolise
sikick	psychic	simbolism	symbolism
siksty	sixty	siment	cement
silabul	syllable	simer	simmer
silabus	syllabus	simetry	symmetry
silage		simfoney	symphony
silence, silenced, silencing		simian	
silencer		similar, -ly	
silense	silence	similarity, -ties	
silent, -ly		simile	
silestial	celestial	similer	similar
silf	sylph	simmer, -ed, -ing	
silhouette, -etted, -etting		simmetry	symmetry
silica		simpathetic	sympathetic
silicon (element)		simpathise	sympathise
silicone (synthetic)		simpathy	sympathy
silicosis		simpel	simple

simper, -ed, -ing
simple, -pler, -plest
simple interest
simpleton
simplicity, -ties
simplification
simplify, -fied, -fying
   simplisity   simplicity
simplistic, -ally
simply
   simposium   symposium
   simptom   symptom
   simptomatic   symptomatic
   simpul   simple
   simpulton   simpleton
simulate, -lated, -lating
simulation
simulator
simultaneous, -ly
   simultaynius   simultaneous
sin, sinned, sinning
   sinagog   synagogue
   sinamon   cinnamon
since
sincere, -cerer, -cerest
sincerely
sincerity, -ties
   sinchromesh   synchromesh
   sincronise   synchronise
sine (maths)
   sine   sign (mark)
   sine camera   cine camera
sinecure
   sinema   cinema
   sinematograf   cinematograph
   sinepost   signpost
sinew
sinewy
sinful, -ly
sing, sang, sung, singing
singe, singed, singeing
   singel   single
singer
single, -gled, -gling
single-handed
single-minded
singlet

singsong
singular, -ly
singularity, -ties
   singuler   singular
   sinic   cynic
   sinical   cynical
   sinema   cinema
   sinimatograf   cinematograph
   sinisism   cynicism
sinister, -ly
sink, sank, sunk or sunken, sinking
sinker
sinkhole
   sinod   synod
   sinonim   synonym
   sinonimus   synonymous
   sinopsis   synopsis
   sinoptic   synoptic
   sinoshure   cynosure
   sinse   since
   sinsere   sincere
   sinserity   sincerity
   sintax   syntax
   sinthesis   synthesis
   sinthesise   synthesise
   sinthetic   synthetic
   sinue   sinew
sinuous, -ly
sinus, -nuses
sinusitis
   sinuus   sinuous
sip, sipped, sipping
   sipet   sippet
   sipher   cipher
siphon, -ed, -ing
sippet
   sipress   cypress
sir
   sirca   circa
   sircharge   surcharge
sire, sired, siring
siren
   siringe   syringe
sirloin
   sirosis   cirrhosis
   sirup   syrup
   sirus   cirrus

sisal		sixth, -ly		
sise	size	sixtieth		
sism	schism	sixty, -ties		
sismic	seismic	size, sized, sizing		
sismograf	seismograph	sizeable, -bly		
sismologist	seismologist	sizeabul	sizeable	
sissers	scissors	sizemic	seismic	
sissy		sizers	scissors	
sist	cyst	sizul	sizzle	
sistem	system	sizzle, -zled, -zling		
sistematic	systematic	sizzler		
sistematise	systematise	sizzul	sizzle	
sister		skane	skein	
sister-in-law, sisters-in-law		skate, skated, skating		
sisterly		skateboard		
sistern	cistern	skater		
sit, sat, sitting		skedule	schedule	
sitadel	citadel	skee	ski	
sitar		skeem	scheme	
sitation	citation	skein		
site, sited, siting (place)		skeletal		
site	cite (state)	skeleton		
site	sight (view)	skeletul	skeletal	
sitely	sightly	skematic	schematic	
siteseeing	sightseeing	skeme	scheme	
siteseer	sightseer	skeptic	sceptic	
sitey	city	skepticism	scepticism	
sithe	scythe	skepticul	sceptical	
sitie	city	skerick	skerrick	
sit-in		skermish	skirmish	
sitizen	citizen	skerrick		
sitric	citric	skert	skirt	
sitrus	citrus	sketch, -ed, -ing		
sitter		sketcher		
situate, -ated, -ating		sketchily		
situation		sketchiness		
sive	sieve	sketchy, sketchier, sketchiest		
sivere	severe	skew, -ed, -ing		
sivic	civic	skewer		
sivilian	civilian	ski, skis, ski		
sivilisation	civilisation	ski, skied, skiing		
sivilise	civilise	skid, skidded, skidding		
sivilitey	civility	skiff		
six		skil	skill	
six-shooter		skilet	skillet	
sixteen		skilful, -ly		
sixteenth		skilfulness		

skilite — skylight
skill
skilled
skillet
skillion
skillyun — skillion
skim, skimmed, skimming
skimp, -ed, -ing
skimpily
skimpiness
skimpy, skimpier, skimpiest
skin, skinned, skinning
skin-deep
skindiver
skindiving
skiney — skinny
skinflint
skinhead
skink
skinny, -nier, -niest
skip, skipped, skipping
skiper — skipper
ski-pole
skipper
skirmish
skirt, -ed, -ing
skiscraper — skyscraper
skit (making fun)
skite, skited, skiting (boast)
skitsofrenia — schizophrenia
skittel — skittle
skittish, -ly
skittle, skittled, skittling
skivvy
skol, skolled, skolling
skua
skue — skew
skulk, -ed, -ing
skull (head)
skull — scull (row)
skullcap
skunk

For all skw- words,
look under **squ-**.

sky, skied or skyed, skying
skydiver

skylark
skylight
skyline
skylite — skylight
skyrocket
skyscraper
slab
slack, -ly
slacken, -ed, -ing
slacks
slag, slagged, slagging
slain
slake, slaked, slaking
slaken — slacken
slalom
slam, slammed, slamming
slander, -ed, -ing
slanderer
slanderous, -ly
slane — slain
slang
slangy
slant, -ed, -ing
slap, slapped, slapping
slapdash
slapstick
slash, -ed, -ing
slasher
slat
slate, slated, slating
slater
slatern — slattern
slather, -ed, -ing
slattern, -ly
slaughter, -ed, -ing
slaughterhouse
Slav
slave, slaved, slaving
slaver
slavish, -ly
slavishness
Slavonic
slawter — slaughter
slay, slew, slain, slaying (kill)
slay — sleigh (sledge)
sleazy, -zier, -ziest
sled, sledded, sledding

sledge
sledge-hammer
sleek, -ly
sleekness
sleep, slept, sleeping
sleeper
sleepily
sleepiness
sleepless, -ly
sleep-out
sleepy, sleepier, sleepiest
sleet
sleeve
sleeved

slege	sledge

sleigh (sledge)
sleight (skill)

sleight	slight (small)

slender, -ly
slept
sleuth
slew

sli	sly

slice, sliced, slicing
slick, -ly
slide, slid, sliding
slight, -ly (small)

slight	sleight (skill)

slim, slimmed, slimming
slim, slimmer, slimmest
slime
slimily
sliminess
slimy, slimier, slimiest
sling, slung, slinging
slink, slunk, slinking
slinky, slinkier, slinkiest
slip, slipped, slipping

sliper	slipper

slipknot

slipnot	slipknot

slipper
slippery, -perier, -periest

sliprale	sliprail

sliprail
slipshod
slip-stitch

slipstream
slipway

slise	slice

slit, slit, slitting

slite	slight

slither, -ed, -ing
sliver

slo	sloe (fruit)
slo	slow (not fast)

slob
slobber, -ed, -ing
slobbery
sloe (fruit)

sloe	slow (not fast)

slog, slogged, slogging
slogan
sloop

sloose	sluice
slooth	sleuth

slop, slopped, slopping
slope, sloped, sloping

slopily	sloppily

sloppiness
sloppily
sloppy, -pier, -piest

slopy	sloppy

slosh, -ed, -ing
slot, slotted, slotting
sloth
slothful, -ly
slouch, -ed, -ing
slough (skin)
sloven, -ly
slovenliness
slow, -ed, -ing (not fast)

slow	sloe (fruit)
slow	slough (skin)
slowch	slouch

slowcoach
slow-motion
sludge
sludgy, sludgier, sludgiest

slue	slew
sluff	slough

sluggard
sluggardly
sluggish, -ly

sluice, sluiced, sluicing
slum, slummed, slumming
slumber, -ed, -ing
slump, -ed, -ing
slung
slunk
slur, slurred, slurring
  slurie   slurry
slurp, -ed, -ing
slurry
slush
slushy, -shier, -shiest
slut
sluttish, -ly
sly, slyer, slyest or slier, sliest
slyly
slyness
smack, -ed, -ing
small
smallgoods
smallpox
small-time
smarmy
smart, -ed, -ing
smart, smarter, smartest
smart alec
smarten, -ed, -ing
smartly
smash, -ed, -ing
smasher
smattering
smear, -ed, -ing
  smeer   smear
smell, smelled or smelt, smelling
smelly, smellier, smelliest
smelter
smidgin
smile, smiled, smiling
smirch, -ed, -ing
smirk, -ed, -ing
smite, smote, smiting
smith
smithereens
  smithey   smithy
smithy, smithies
smitten
smock, -ed, -ing

smog
smoggy, smoggier, smoggiest
  smogy   smoggy
smoke, smoked, smoking
smoke-bush
smoker
smokescreen
smokestack
smoko
smoky, smokier, smokiest
  smolder   smoulder
smooch, -ed, -ing
smoodge, smoodged, smoodging
smooth, -ed, -ing
smoothly
smoothness
smorgasbord
smother, -ed, -ing
smoulder, -ed, -ing
smudge, smudged, smudging
smug, smugger, smuggest
  smuge   smudge
smuggle, smuggled, smuggling
smuggler
  smuggul   smuggle
  smugle   smuggle
smugly
  smurch   smirch
  smurk   smirk
smut
smuttily
smuttiness
smutty, smuttier, smuttiest
  smuty   smutty
snack
snaffle, -fled, -fling
  snafful   snaffle
snag, snagged, snagging
snagger
snail
snake, snaked, snaking
snakebite
snaky, snakier, snakiest
  snale   snail
snap, snapped, snapping
snapdragon
  snaper   snapper

snapper

snappily

snappiness

snappy, -pier, -piest

snapshot

snapy — snappy

snare, snared, snaring

snarl, -ed, -ing

snatch, -ed, -ing

sneak, -ed, -ing

sneaker

sneek — sneak

sneeker — sneaker

sneer, -ed, -ing

sneeze, sneezed, sneezing

snib, snibbed, snibbing

snick, -ed, -ing

snicker, -ed, -ing

snide

snif — sniff

snifel — sniffle

sniff, -ed, -ing

sniffle, -fled, -fling

sniffui — sniffle

sniger — snigger

snigger, -ed, -ing

snip, snipped, snipping (cut)

snipe, sniped, sniping (shoot)

sniper

snipet — snippet

snippet

snitch, -ed, -ing

snivel, -elled, -elling

sniveller

snivul — snivel

snob

snobbery

snobbish, -ly

snood

snook

snooker, -ed, -ing

snoop, -ed, -ing

snoopy

snooze, snoozed, snoozing

snore, snored, snoring

snorkel

snorkle — snorkel

snorkul — snorkel

snort, -ed, -ing

snout

snow, -ed, -ing

snowball

snowey — snowy

snowflake

snow job

snowline

snowman, -men

snowplough

snowshoe, -shoed, -shoeing

snowt — snout

snowy, snowier, snowiest

snub, snubbed, snubbing

snuff, -ed, -ing

snuffle, -fled, -fling

snug, snugger, snuggest

snuggle, -gled, -gling

so (in this way)

so — sew (stitch)

so — sow (pig, plant)

soak, -ed, -ing

so-and-so

soap, -ed, -ing

soapbox

soapie

soap opera

soappy — soapy

soapstone

soapy, soapier, soapiest

soar, -ed, -ing (fly)

soar — sore (hurt)

sob, sobbed, sobbing

sober, -ed, -ing

sobriety

sobrikay — sobriquet

sobriquet

so-called

soccer

sociability

sociable, -bly

sociabul — sociable

social, -ly

socialisation

socialise, -lised, -lising

socialism

socialist	
socialistic, -ally	
socialite	
society, -ties	
socioeconomic, -ally	
sociologist	
sociology	
sociul	social
sock, -ed, -ing	
socker	soccer
socket	
sockit	socket
sockeye	
sod	
soda	
soda-water	
sodden	
soden	sodden
sodium	
sodomite	
sodomy	
sofa	
sofar	sofa
sofen	soften
sofism	sophism
sofist	sophist
sofisticate	sophisticate
sofistication	sophistication
sofistry	sophistry
soft, -ly	
softball	
soften, -ed, -ing	
soft-pedal, -alled, -alling	
soft-soap	
software	
softwear	software
soggily	
sogginess	
soggy, -gier, -giest	
sogie	soggy
sogy	soggy
soia	soya
soil, -ed, -ing	
soiray	soiree
soiree	
soiya	soya
sojern	sojourn

sojourn, -ed, -ing	
soke	soak
solace, -aced, -acing	
solar	
solareum	solarium
solarium, -laria	
solass	solace
solatude	solitude
sold	
solder, -ed, -ing	
soldier, -ed, -ing	
soldierly	
sole (shoe)	
sole	soul (spirit)
solecism	
soled	solid
soleful	soulful
solem	solemn
solemn, -ly	
solemnisation	
solemnise, -nised, -nising	
solemnitey	solemnity
solemnity, -ties	
solenoid	
soler	solar
solesism	solecism
solfa, -faed, -faing	
solger	soldier
solicit, -ed, -ing	
solicitation	
soliciter	solicitor
solicitor	
solicitous, -ly	
solicitude	
solicitus	solicitous
solid, -ly	
solidarity, -ties	
solidifi	solidify
solidification	
solidify, -fied, -fying	
solid-state	
solilokwy	soliloquy
soliloquy, -quies	
solisit	solicit
solisitor	solicitor
solisitus	solicitous
solitaire	

solitary, -taries
solitude
  soljer   soldier

> For soll- words,
> look under sol-.

solo, -los
soloist
solstice
  solstiss   solstice
solubility, -ties
soluble, -bly
  solubul   soluble
  solushun   solution
solution
solvable
solve, solved, solving
solvency
  solvensy   solvency
solvent
  somber   sombre
  sombraro   sombrero
sombre, -ly
sombrero
some (few)
  some   sum (total)
somebody, -bodies
somehow
someone
  somersalt   somersault
somersault
something
sometime
somewhat
somewhere
somnambulism
somnolence
  somnolense   somnolence
son (boy)
  son   sun (star)
sonar
sonata
  soner   sonar
song
songster
songstress
sonic

sonic boom
  sonick   sonic
son-in-law, sons-in-law
sonnet
sonny, -nies
sonorous, -ly
  sonorus   sonorous
  soo   sue
  soocher   suture
  soocrose   sucrose
  sooet   suet
  sooflay   souffle
sook
sooky
soon
  soop   soup
soot (chimney)
  soot   suit (clothes)
sooth (truth)
soothe, soothed, soothing (calm)
soothsayer
  soovenir   souvenir
sop, sopped, sopping
  sope   soap
sophism
sophist
sophisticate, -cated, -cating
sophistication
sophistry, -ries
soporific
sopping
soppy, -pier, -piest
soprano, -pranos, -prani
sorbet
  sorce   sauce (liquid)
  sorce   source (origin)
sorcerer
sorceress
sorcery, -ceries
  sord   sword
sordid, -ly
  sordust   sawdust
sore, sorer, sorest (hurt)
  sore   saw (cut)
  sore   soar (rise)
  sorel   sorrel
  sorey   sorry

sorghum		Southern Cross	
sorgum	sorghum	southward, -ly	
sorie	sorry	south-west	
sorna	sauna	south-wester	
sornter	saunter	south-western	
sorority, -ties		souvenir	
sorow	sorrow	sovereign	
sorrel		sovereignty, -ties	
sorrow		soverin	sovereign
sorrowful, -ly		soviet	
sorry, -rier, -riest		sovrenty	sovereignty
sort (type)		sow, sowed, sowing (pig, plant)	
sort	sought (looked)	sow	sew (stitch)
sortee	sortie	sown (planted)	
sortie, -tied, -tieing		sown	sewn (stitched)
soshable	sociable	sownd	sound
soshal	social	sowr	sour
soshalise	socialise	sowth	south
sosietey	society	soy	
sosige	sausage	soya	
so-so		spa	
sot		space, spaced, spacing	
soto vochay	sotto voce	spaceship	
sotto voce		spacious, -ly	
soufflé		spade, spaded, spading	
sough (rustling sound)		spadework	
sough	sow (pig)	spagetti	spaghetti
sought (looked)		spaghetti	
soul (spirit)		span, spanned, spanning	
soul	sole (shoe)	spaner	spanner
sound, -ed, -ing		spangle, -gled, -gling	
soundbox		spangul	spangle
sounding-board		Spaniard	
soundproof		spaniel	
soundtrack		spank, -ed, -ing	
soundwave		spanner	
soup		Spanyard	Spaniard
sour, -ed, -ing		spanyel	spaniel
source (origin)		spar, sparred, sparring (fight)	
source	sauce (liquid)	spare, spared, sparing (extra)	
souse, soused, sousing		spark, -ed, -ing	
south		sparkle, -kled, -kling	
south-east		sparkler	
south-easter		sparkul	sparkle
south-eastern		sparow	sparrow
southerly		sparrow	
southern		sparrowhawk	

sparse, sparser, sparsest
sparsity
Spartan
  spase   space
  spashus   spacious
spasm
spasmodic, -ally
spastic, -ally
spat (did spit)
  spatal   spatial
spate (sudden)
spatial, -ly
spatter, -ed, -ing
spatula
spawn, -ed, -ing
spay, -ed, -ing
speak, spoke, spoken, speaking
speakeasy, -easies
speaker
spear, -ed, -ing
spearmint
spec (gamble)
  spec   speck (spot)
special, -ly
specialisation
specialise, -lised, -lising
specialist
speciality, -ties
specialty, -ties
species, -cies
specific, -ly
specification
specify, -fied, -fying
specimen
specious, -ly
speck, -ed, -ing (spot)
  speck   spec (gamble)
speckle, -kled, -kling
spectacle
  spectacul   spectacle
spectacular, -ly
spectator
  specter   spectre
spectre
spectroscope
spectrum, -tra
speculate, -lated, -lating

speculation
speculator
speech
speed, sped, speeding
speedometer
speedway
  speek   speak
  speer   spear
  spekul   speckle
  spel   spell
spell, spelt or spelled, spelling
spellbound
spencer
spend, spent, spending
spendthrift
sperm
  spern   spurn
  spert   spurt
  speshal   special
  speshalist   specialist
  speshus   specious
  spesify   specify
  spesimen   specimen
spew, -ed, -ing
sphere
spherical, -ly
spheroid
sphinx
  spi   spy
spice, spiced, spicing
spick-and-span
spicy, spicier, spiciest
spider
spidery
spiel, -ed, -ing
spigot
spike, spiked, spiking
spill, spilt or spilled, spilling
spillage
  spillige   spillage
spin, spun, spinning
spina bifida
spinach
  spinaker   spinnaker
spinal
spindle, -dled, -dling
spin-dry, -dried, -drying

spine

spinifex

spinige · spinach

spinnaker

spinner

spin-off

spinster

spiny, spinier, spiniest

spiral, -ralled, -ralling

spire

spirel · spiral

spirichual · spiritual

spirichualist · spiritualist

spirit, -ed, -ing

spiritual, -ly

spiritualism

spiritualist

spirituality, -ties

spise · spice

spisy · spicy

spit, spat, spitting

spite, spited, spiting

spiteful, -ly

spitfire

spittle

spittoon

spittul · spittle

spiv

splash, -ed, -ing

splashdown

splatter, -ed, -ing

splay, -ed, -ing

spleen

splender · splendour

splendid, -ly

splendour

splice, spliced, splicing

splicer

splint

splinter, -ed, -ing

splise · splice

split, split, splitting

split-level

splurge, splurged, splurging

splutter, -ed, -ing

spoil, spoilt, spoiling

spoilage

spoilsport

spoke

spoken

spokesperson

sponge, sponged, sponging

sponger

spongy, -gier, -giest

sponser · sponsor

sponsor, -ed, -ing

sponsorship

spontaneity, -ties

spontaneous, -ly

sponteneity · spontaneity

spoof, -ed, -ing

spook, -ed, -ing

spool

spoon, -ed, -ing

spoonbill

spoonerism

spoon-feed, -fed, -feeding

spoor (trail)

spoor · spore (germ)

sporadic, -ally

spore, spored, sporing (germ)

spore · spoor (trail)

sporran

sport, -ed, -ing

sportive, -ly

sportsman, -men

sportswoman, -women

spot, spotted, spotting

spotlight, -ed, -ing

spotlite · spotlight

spouse

spout, -ed, -ing

spowse · spouse

spowt · spout

sprain, -ed, -ing

sprane · sprain

sprang

sprat

sprawl, -ed, -ing

spray, -ed, -ing

spread, spread, spreading

spread-eagle, -gled, -gling

spred · spread

spree

sprie   spry
sprightly, -lier, -liest
spring, sprang, sprung, springing
springboard
springbok, -boks
spring-clean, -ed, -ing
spring-loaded
springy, -gier, -giest
sprinkle, -kled, -kling
sprinkler
sprinkul   sprinkle
sprint, -ed, -ing
sprit (pole)
sprite, -ly (elf)
sprocket
sproose   spruce
sprout, -ed, -ing
sprowt   sprout
spruce, spruced, sprucing
spruce, sprucer, sprucest
sprung
spry, spryer, spryest
spud, spudded, spudding
spume, spumed, spuming
spun
spunge   sponge
spunk
spunky, spunkier, spunkiest
spur, spurred, spurring
spurious, -ly
spurius   spurious
spurm   sperm
spurn, -ed, -ing
spurt, -ed, -ing
sputnik
sputter, -ed, -ing
sputum, sputa
spy, spies
spy, spied, spying
squabble, -bled, -bling
squabul   squabble
squad
squadron
squalid, -ly
squall, -ed, -ing
squalor
squander, -ed, -ing

square, squared, squaring
squarely
square-rigged
squash, -ed, -ing
squat, squatted, squatting
squatter
squattocracy
squaw
squawk, -ed, -ing
squeak, -ed, -ing
squeal, -ed, -ing
squeamish, -ly
squeeze, squeezed, squeezing
squelch, -ed, -ing
squib, squibbed, squibbing
squid, squids, squid
squiggle, -gled, -gling
squiggly
squiggul   squiggle
squint, -ed, -ing
squire, squired, squiring
squirm, -ed, -ing
squirrel
squirt, -ed, -ing
squiz, -ed, -ing
squod   squad
squodron   squadron
squolid   squalid
squonder   squander
squosh   squash
squot   squat
stab, stabbed, stabbing
stabilisation
stabilise, -lised, -lising
stabiliser
stability, -ties
stable, -bled, -bling
stabul   stable
staccato
stack, -ed, -ing
stadium, -dia, -diums
staf   staff
staff, -ed, -ing
stag
stage, staged, staging
stagecoach
stager   stagger

stagflation
stagger, -ed, -ing
staghorn
stagnant, -ly
stagnate, -nated, -nating
stagnation
staid, -ly (calm)
staid   stayed
              (stopped)
staidium   stadium
stain, -ed, -ing
stainless, -ly
stair (step)
stair   stare (look at)
staircase
stairwell
stake, staked, staking (post)
stake   steak (meat)
stalactite
stalagmite
stale, staled, staling
stale, staler, stalest
stalemate, -mated, -mating
stalion   stallion
stalk, -ed, -ing (hunt)
stalk   stork (bird)
stall, -ed, -ing
stallion
stalwart, -ly
stalwert   stalwart
stamen
stamena   stamina
stamer   stammer
stamina
stammer, -ed, -ing
stamp, -ed, -ing
stampede, -peded, -peding
stance
stanchion
stanchun   stanchion
stand, stood, standing
standard
standardise, -dised, -dising
stand-by
standerd   standard
stand-in
stand-offish, -ly

standstill
stane   stain
stank
stanse   stance
stanza
staple, -pled, -pling
stapler
stapul   **staple**
star, **starred, starring**
starboard
starbord   **starboard**
starch, -ed, -ing
star-crossed
stardom
stare, stared, staring (look at)
stare   stair (step)
starfish, -fishes, -fish
stargaze, -gazed, -gazing
stargazer
stark, -ly
starkers
starling
start, -ed, -ing
startch   starch
starter
startle, -tled, -tling
starvation
starve, starved, starving
stash, -ed, -ing
stashun   station
stashunry   stationary
stashunry   stationery
state, stated, stating
stateliness
stately, -lier, -liest
statement
stateroom
statesman, -men
stateswoman, -women
static, -ally
station, -ed, -ing
stationary (still)
stationer (sells paper)
stationery (paper)
statistical, -ly
statistician
statistics

statistishun — statistician
stattic — static
statuary, -aries (statues)
statue
statuesk — statuesque
statuesque, -ly
stature
status
status quo
statute
statutory (law)
statutry — statutory
staunch, -ed, -ing
stave, staved, staving
stawk — stalk
stay, stayed, staying
stead
steadfast, -ly
steadily
steady, steadied, steadying
steady, steadier, steadiest
steak (meat)
steak — stake (post)
steal, stole, stolen, stealing (rob)
steal — steel (metal)
stealth
stealthily
stealthy, -thier, -thiest
steam, -ed, -ing
steam-engine
steamer
steamroller
sted — stead
stedfast — steadfast
stedy — steady
steed
steel, -ed, -ing (metal)
steel — steal (rob)
steely
steep, -ed, -ing
steeple
steeplechase
steepul — steeple
steer, -ed, -ing
steerage
steerige — steerage
steersman, -men

stelth — stealth
stem, stemmed, stemming
stench
stencil, -cilled, -cilling
stenografer — stenographer
stenografy — stenography
stenographer
stenography
stensil — stencil
step, stepped, stepping, (pace)
stepladder
steppe (plain)
stereo, stereos
stereogram
stereophonic
stereotype, -typed, -typing
sterile, -ly
sterilisation
sterilise, -lised, -lising
steriliser
sterio — stereo
steriofonic — stereophonic
steriotype — stereotype
sterling
stern, -ly
sternum
stethoscope
stetson
stevedore, -dored, -doring
stew, -ed, -ing
steward
stewardess
sti — sty
stich — stitch
stick, stuck, sticking
sticker
stickler
stick-up
sticky, stickier, stickiest
stickybeak
stif — stiff
stifen — stiffen
stiff
stiffen, -ed, -ing
stiffener
stifle, -fled, -fling
stiful — stifle

stigma, -mas, -mata
stigmatise, -tised, -tising

stikler — stickler
stil — still
stile (steps)

stile — style (type)
stiletto, -tos

stilish — stylish
stilist — stylist
still, -ed, -ing
stillbirth
stillborn
still-life
stilt
stilted, -ly
stilton

stilus — stylus
stimie — stymie
stimulant
stimulate, -lated, -lating
stimulation
stimulator
stimulus, -li, -luses
sting, stung, stinging
stingray
stingy, -gier, -giest
stink, stank, stunk, stinking
stinker
stinkhorn
stinkpot
stint, -ed, -ing
stipend
stipendiary, -ries
stipple, -pled, -pling

stipul — stipple
stipulate, -lated, -lating
stipulation
stir, stirred, stirring

stirling — sterling
stirrup

stirup — stirrup
stitch, -ed, -ing
stoat
stock, -ed, -ing
stockade, -aded, -ading
stockbroker
stock-car

stocking
stockman, -men
stockpile, -piled, -piling
stocktaking
stockwhip
stocky, -kier, -kiest
stodgily
stodgy, -gier, -giest

stogy — stodgy
stoical, -ly
stoicism

stoisism — stoicism
stoke, stoked, stoking
stoker
stole
stolen
stolid, -ly
stoma, stomata
stomach
stomach-ache

stomick — stomach
stone, stoned, stoning
stonefish
stonemason
stoneware
stony, stonier, stoniest
stood
stooge, stooged, stooging
stool
stoop, stooped, stooping
stop, stopped, stopping
stopcock

stope, stoped, stoping
stopgap
stoppage
stopper
stopwatch
store, stored, storing
storey (floor)

storey — story (tale)
storie — storey (floor)
storie — story (tale)
storige — storage
stork (bird)

stork — stalk (hunt)
storm, -ed, -ing
stormily

stormy, -mier, -miest

story, -ries (tale)

story   storey (floor)

stout, -ly

stove, stoved, stoving

stow, -ed, -ing

stowaway

stowt   stout

straddle, -dled, -dling

straf   strafe

strafe, strafed, strafing

straggle, -gled, -gling

straggler

straight (line)

straight   strait (passage)

straightaway

straighten, -ed, -ing

straightforward, -ly

strain, -ed, -ing

strainer

strait (passage)

strait   straight (line)

straiten

straitjacket

straitlaced

strand

strane   strain

strange, stranger, strangest

strangle, -gled, -gling

strangler

stranglehold

strangul   strangle

strangulate, -lated, -lating

strangulation

strap, strapped, strapping

strapper

strasbourg

strata

stratagem

strata title

strate   straight (line)

strate   strait (passage)

strategie   strategy

strategic, -ally

strategist

strategy, -gies

stratification

stratify, -fied, -fying

stratigem   stratagem

stratosfere   stratosphere

stratosphere

stratum, strata

straw

strawberie   strawberry

strawberry, -ries

stray, -ed, -ing

streak, -ed, -ing

streaky, streakier, streakiest

stream, -ed, -ing

streamer

streamline, -lined, -lining

streek   streak

streem   stream

street

strength

strengthen, -ed, -ing

strenuous, -ly

strenuus   strenuous

streptomycin

stress, -ed, -ing

stretch, -ed, -ing

stretcher

strew, strewed, strewn, strewing

striate, -ated, -ating

striation

strick   strict

stricken

strict, -ly

stricture

stride, strode, striding

stridence

strident, -ly

strife

strike, struck, stricken, striking

strikebound

strikebreaker

striknun   strychnine

strine

string, strung, stringing

stringency

stringensy   stringency

stringent, -ly

stringer

stringy, -gier, -giest

strip, stripped, stripping
stripe, striped, striping
stripling
stripper
striptease
strive, strove, striven, striving
strobe
stroboscope
strode
stroke, stroked, stroking
stroll, -ed, -ing
stroller
strong, -ly
stronghold
stroo   strew
strop, stropped, stropping
stroppie   stroppy
stroppy, stroppier, stroppiest
strove
struck
struckcher   structure
structure, -tured, -turing
strudel
struggle, -gled, -gling
struggler
strugul   struggle
strum, strummed, strumming
strummer
strumpet
strung
strut, strutted, strutting
strychnine
stu   stew
stuard   steward
stub, stubbed, stubbing
stubble
stubbly
stubborn, -ly
stuben   stubborn
stucco, -coes, -cos
stuck-up
stud, studded, studding
student
studie   study
studied
studio, -dios
studious, -ly

studius   studious
study, studies
study, studied, studying
stuf   stuff
stuff, -ed, -ing
stuffily
stuffy, -fier, -fiest
stufy   stuffy
stuko   stucco
stultifie   stultify
stultify, -fied, -fying
stumble, -bled, -bling
stumbul   stumble
stump, -ed, -ing
stump-jump plough
stun, stunned, stunning
stunner
stunt, -ed, -ing
stuntman, -men
stupefie   stupefy
stupefy, -fied, -fying
stupendous, -ly
stupendus   stupendous
stupid, -ly
stupidity, -ties
stupify   stupefy
stupor
sturdie   sturdy
sturdily
sturdy, -dier, -diest
sturgeon
sturgun   sturgeon
sturling   sterling
sturn   stern
stuter   stutter
stutter, -ed, -ing
stutterer
stuward   steward
St Vitus dance
sty, sties
style (type)
style   stile (steps)
stylish, -ly
stylist
stylistic, -ally
stymie, -mied, -mieing
styptic

suage   sewage
suave, -ly
suavity, -ties
sub, subbed, subbing
subaltern
subcomitee subcommittee
subcommittee
subconscious, -ly
subconshus subconscious
subcontinent
subcontract, -ed, -ing
subcontractor
subculture
subcutaneous, -ly
subdivide, -vided, -viding
subdivishun subdivision
subdivision
subdue, -dued, -duing
subeditor
suberb suburb
suberban suburban
subgigate subjugate
subgroup
subheading
subjecshun subjection
subject, -ed, -ing
subjection
subjective, -ly
subjectivity
sub judice
subjugate, -gated, -gating
subjugation
subjunctive
sublimate, -mated, -mating
sublimation
sublime, -limed, -liming
subliminal, -ly
sublimity, -ties
sublimminal subliminal
submarine
submerge, -merged, -merging
submishun submission
submission
submissive, -ly
submit, -mitted, -mitting
submurge submerge
subnormal, -ly

subordinate, -nated, -nating
subordination
suborn, -ed, -ing
subpena subpoena
subpoena, -naed, -naing
subscribe, -ribed, -ribing
subscriber
subscription
subsection
subsekwent subsequent
subsequent, -ly
subservience
subservient, -ly
subset
subside, -sided, -siding
subsidence
subsidie subsidy
subsidise, -dised, -dising
subsidy, -dies
subsist, -ed, -ing
subsistence
subsistense subsistence
subsistent, -ly
subsoil
substance
substandard
substanshul substantial
substantial, -ly
substantiate, -ated, -ating
substation
substitute, -tuted, -tuting
subtefuge subterfuge
subterfuge
subterranean
subtitle, -tled, -tling
subtitul subtitle
subtle, -tly
subtlety, -ties
subtracshun subtraction
subtraction
subtropical
suburb
suburban
suburbia
subversion
subversive
subvert, -ed, -ing

subway
succeed, -ed, -ing
success
successful, -ly
succession
successive, -ly
successor
succinct, -ly
succour, -ed, -ing (aid)
succulent, -ly
succumb, -ed, -ing
such
   suchure   suture
suck, -ed, -ing
sucker (dupe)
   suckshun   suction
   suckulent   succulent
   suckum   succumb
sucrose
   sucsede   succeed
   sucseshun   succession
   sucses   success
   sucseser   successor
   sucsesful   successful
   sucsint   succinct
suction
sudden, -ly
suds
sue, sued, suing
suede
   suer   sewer
suet (meat)
   sufer   suffer
suffer, -ed, -ing
sufferance
   sufferanse   sufferance
suffice, -ficed, -ficing
sufficiency
sufficient, -ly
   suffiks   suffix
   suffishensy   sufficiency
suffix
suffocate, -cated, -cating
suffocation
suffrage
suffragette
suffuse, -fused, -fusing

suffusion
   sufocashun   suffocation
   sufocate   suffocate
   sufrajet   suffragette
   sufrance   sufferance
   sufrige   suffrage
   sufuse   suffuse
sugar
sugary
   sugeschun   suggestion
   sugest   suggest
suggest, -ed, -ing
suggestive, -ly
suicidal
suicide, -cided, -ciding
   suiside   suicide
suit, -ed, -ing (clothes)
   suit   suet (meat)
suitability
suitable, -bly
suitcase
suite (rooms)
   suiter   suitor
suitor
sulk, -ed, -ing
sulky, sulkier, sulkiest
sullage
sullen, -ly
sully, -lied, -lying
sulphur
sulphuric
sultan
sultana
   sultrie   sultry
sultriness
sultry, -trier, -triest
sum, summed, summing (total)
   sum   some (few)
   sumbody   somebody
   sumhow   somehow
   summarine   submarine
summarise, -rised, -rising
summary, -ries (short)
   summary   summery
                      (warm)
summation
summer

summerhouse
summerise   summarise
summery (warm)
summery   summary (short)
summit
summon, -ed, -ing (call)
summons, -monses (court)
sumo
sums
sump
sumptuous, -ly
sun, sunned, sunning (star)
sun   son (boy)
sun inlaw   son-in-law
sunbake, -baked, -baking
sunburn, -ed, -ing
sundae (ice-cream)
Sunday (day)
sundeck
sunder, -ed, -ing
sundial
sundown
sundowner
sundries
sundry, -rily
sunfish, -fishes, -fish
sunflower
sung
sunglasses
sunk
sunken
sunlamp
sunny, -nier, -niest
sunshine
sunspot
sunstroke
suntan, -tanned, -tanning
sup, supped, supping
super
superannuate, -ated, -ating
superannuation
superb, -ly
supercharge, -charged, -charging
supercilious, -ly
superficial, -ly
superfishul   superficial

superfluity, -ties
superfluous, -ly
superfosfate   superphosphate
superhuman, -ly
superimpose, -posed, -posing
superintendent
superior, -ly
superiority
superlative, -ly
superman, -men
supermarket
supernatural, -ly
supernumerary, -aries
superphosphate
superpower
supersaturate, -rated, -rating
supersede, -seded, -seding
supersonic
superstructure
supervise, -vised, -vising
supervishun   supervision
supervision
supervisor
supervisory
supervisry   supervisory
supine, -ly
suple   supple
suplement   supplement
suport   support
suposition   supposition
supper
supplant, -ed, -ing
supple, -pler, -plest
supplement
supplementation
supplementary
suppliant, -ly
supplier
supply, -plied, -plying
support, -ed, -ing
supporter
supposable, -bly
supposabul   supposable
suppose, -posed, -posing
supposition
suppository, -ries
suppress, -ed, -ing

suppression
suppressive
suppurate, -rated, -rating
suppuration
supremacy

supremasy	supremacy

supreme, -ly

supres	suppress
supreshun	suppression
suprintend	superintend
supul	supple
sur	sir

surcharge, -charged, -charging
surcingle

> For other **surc-** words,
> look under **circ-**.

sure, -ly (certain)

| sure | shore (sea) |
| sureptishus | surreptitious |

surety, -ties
surf, -ed, -ing (sea)

| surf | serf (slave) |

surface, -faced, -facing
surfboard

| surfeet | surfeit |

surfeit, -ed, -ing
surfer
surfie

| surfis | surface |

surge, surged, surging

| surgen | surgeon |

surgeon
surgery, -geries
surgical, -ly
surly, -lier, -liest

| surly | surely |

surmise, -mised, -mising
surmount, -ed, -ing
surname

| surogat | surrogate |

surpass, -ed, -ing
surplice (garment)

| surplis | surplice |

surplus (extra)
surprise, -prised, -prising
surrealism

surrealist
surrender, -ed, -ing

| surreptishus | surreptitious |

surreptitious, -ly
surrogate
surround, -ed, -ing

| surtaks | surtax |

surtax
surveillance
survey, -veys
surveyor
survival
survive, -vived, -viving
survivor
susceptibility
susceptible, -bly
suspect, -ed, -ing
suspend, -ed, -ing
suspender
suspense
suspicion
suspicious, -ly

| suspishun | suspicion |

sustain, -ed, -ing

| sustayn | sustain |

sustenance

sustenanse	sustenance
sut	soot
sutable	suitable
suter	suitor
suthen	southern
sutlety	subtlety
sutul	subtle

suture, -tured, -turing
swab, swabbed, swabbing
swaddle, -dled, -dling

| swade | suede |

swag
swagger, swaggered, swaggering
swagman, -men
swain
swallow, -ed, -ing
swam
swamp, -ed, -ing
swampy, -pier, -piest
swan
swank, -ed, -ing

swap, swapped, swapping
sware — swear
swarm, -ed, -ing
swarthy, -thier, -thiest
swashbuckler
swastika
swat, swatted, swatting
swathe, swathed, swathing
sway, -ed, -ing
swear, swore, sworn, swearing
sweat, -ed, -ing
sweater
sweatshop
swede
sweep, swept, sweeping
sweeper
sweepstake
sweet, -ly (taste)
sweet — suite (rooms)
sweetbread
sweeten, -ed, -ing
sweetener
sweethart — sweetheart
sweetheart
swell, swelled, swollen, swelling
swelter, -ed, -ing
swerve, swerved, swerving
swet — sweat
sweter — sweater
swich — switch
swift, -ly
swill, -ed, -ing
swim, swam, swum, swimming
swimmer
swimsuit
swindle, -dled, -dling
swindul — swindle
swine
swing, swung, swinging
swipe, swiped, swiping
swirl, -ed, -ing
swish, -ed, -ing
switch, -ed, -ing
switchboard
swivel, -elled, -elling
swob — swab
swollen

swollow — swallow
swomp — swamp
swoon, -ed, -ing
swoop, -ed, -ing
sword
swordfish
sworm — swarm
sworn
swot, swotted, swotting
swum
swurl — swirl
swurve — swerve
syanide — cyanide
sybarite
sybaritic, -ally
sycamore
sycedelic — psychedelic
syche — psyche
syciatrist — psychiatrist
syciatry — psychiatry
sycick — psychic
syclone — cyclone
sycoanalise — psychoanalyse
sycoanalisis — psychoanalysis
sycofant — sycophant
sycological — psychological
sycologist — psychologist
sycology — psychology
sycophant
sycophantic, -ally
sycosis — psychosis
sycotherapist — psychotherapist
sycotherapy — psychotherapy
sycotic — psychotic
Sydney
Sydneysider
syfilis — syphilis
sygnet — cygnet
sylable — syllable
sylf — sylph
sylinder — cylinder
syllabic, -ally
syllable
syllabus, -buses, -bi
syllogise, -gised, -gising
syllogism
syllogistic, -ally

sylph
sylvan
  sylvun — sylvan
symbiosis
symbiotic, -ally
symbol (sign)
  symbol — cymbal (music)
symbolic, -ally
symbolise, -lised, -lising
symbolism
symbolist
  symfony — symphony
symmetrical, -ly
symmetry, -tries
sympathetic, -ally
  sympathey — sympathy
sympathise, -ised, -ising
sympathiser
symphonic
symphony, -nies
symposium, -siums, -sia
symptom
symptomatic
  synagog — synagogue
synagogue
  synanym — synonym
synchromesh
synchronisation
synchronise, -nised, -nising
synchronous, -ly
  synchronus — synchronous
syncopate, -pated, -pating
syncopation
syndical
syndicalism
syndicate, -cated, -cating
syndication
syndrome
  synic — cynic
  synical — cynical
synod
synodal
  synonimus — synonymous
synonym
synonymous, -ly
synopsis, -ses
synoptic, -ally

syntactical, -ly
  syntaks — syntax
syntax
synthesis, -ses
synthesise, -ised, -ising
synthesiser
synthetic, -ally
  sypher — cipher
syphilis
syphilitic
syphon, -ed, -ing
syringe, -ringed, -ringing
syrup
syrupy
system
systematic
systematical, -ly
systematisation
systematise, -tised, -tising
systemic, -ally
systole
  sythe — scythe
Szechuan
Szechwan

Tt

tab, tabbed, tabbing
tabacco   tobacco
tabard
tabasco
tabasko   tabasco
tabby, -bies
tabel   table
tabie   tabby
table, -bled, -bling
tableau, -leaux, -leaus
tablespoon
tablespoonful, -fuls
tablet
tablit   tablet
tablo   tableau
tabloid
tabloyd   tabloid
taboo, -boos
taboo, -booed, -booing
tabul   table
tabular
tabulate, -lated, -lating
tabulation
taby   tabby
tachometer
tacit, -ly
taciturn
tack, -ed, -ing
tackie   tacky
tackle, -led, -ling
tackler
tackometer   tachometer
tackul   tackle
tacky, -kier, -kiest
taco
tact
tactic
tactical, -ly

tactician
tactics
tactile
tactyle   tactile
tadpole
taffeta
tafita   taffeta
tag, tagged, tagging
tail (end)
tail   tale (story)
tailgate
tailor, -ed, -ing
tailor-made
taint, -ed, -ing
taipan
take, took, taken, taking
takeover
taks   tax
taksation   taxation
taksi   taxi
talc
talcum powder
tale (story)
tale   tail (end)
talent
talented
talie   tally
talisman, -mans
talk, -ed, -ing
talk   talc
talkative, -ly
talkback
tall
tallboy
tallow
tallowwood
tally, -lies (score)
tally, -lied, -lying (score)
tally   telly (T.V.)
Talmud
talon
talor   tailor
talow   tallow
tamale
tamarind
tamborine   tambourine
tambourine

tame, tamed, taming
tame, tamer, tamest
tameable
tam-o'-shanter
tamper, -ed, -ing
tampon
tan, tanned, tanning
tanbark
tandem
tang
   tangenshul   tangential
tangent
tangential, -ly
tangerine
tangible, -bly
   tangibul   tangible
tangle, -gled, -gling
tango, -gos
tango, -goed, -going
   tangul   tangle
   tanjent   tangent
tank
tankard
tanker
tannin
tantalise, -lised, -lising
tantamount
   tantamownt   tantamount
tantrum
tap, tapped, tapping
tap-dancing
tape, taped, taping
taper, -ed, -ing
tape-recorder
tapestry, -tries
tapeworm
tapioca
   tapistry   tapestry
tappet
taproot
tar, tarred, tarring
tarantella (dance)
tarantula (spider)
   tardie   tardy
tardily
tardy, -dier, -diest
tare (weight)

   tare   tear (rip)
target
   targit   target
   tarie   tarry
   tarif   tariff
tariff
tarmac
tarnation
tarnish, -ed, -ing
tarot
   tarow   tarot
tarpaulin
   tarpollun   tarpaulin
tarragon
   tarrif   tariff
tarry, ries
tarry, -ried, -rying
tartan
tartar
tartare sauce
   tarter   tartar
tartily
tarty
   tasit   tacit
   tasiturn   taciturn
task
taskmaster
tassel, tasselled, tasselling
   tassul   tassel
taste, tasted, tasting
tastebud
tasteful, -ly
tasty, -tier, -tiest
   tatoo   tattoo
tattle, -led, -ling
tattoo, -toos
tattoo, -tooed, -tooing
   tattul   tattle
tatty
   taudry   tawdry
taught (teach)
   taught   taut (tight)
   taught   tort (law)
taunt, -ed, -ing
Taurus
taut, -ly (tight)
   taut   taught (teach)

taut	tort (law)
tautological, -ly	
tautology, -gies	
taven	tavern
tavern	
tawdrily	
tawdry, -drier, -driest	
tawny, -nier, -niest	
tax, taxed, taxing	
taxable	
taxabul	taxable
taxation	
tax-deductible	
taxi, taxis	
taxi, taxied, taxiing	
taxicab	
taxidermy	
taxie	taxi
taxonomy, -mies	
tea (drink)	
tea	tee (golf)
teach, taught, teaching	
teachable, -ably	
teachabul	teachable
teacher	
tea-chest	
teacup	
teal	
team, -ed, -ing (group)	
team	teem (rain)
teamster	
teapot	
tear (crying)	
tear, tore, torn, tearing (rip)	
tear	tare (weight)
tear	tier (row)
tearful, -ly	
tearjerker	
tease, teased, teasing	
teaspoon	
teat	
teath	teeth (noun)
teathe	teethe
tea-tree	
tech	teach
techer	teacher
technical, -ly	

technicality, -ties	
technician	
technicolour	
technique	
technocracy	
technological, -ly	
technologist	
technology	
tecneek	technique
tecnical	technical
tecnicality	technicality
tecnishun	technician
tecnocrasy	technocracy
tecnology	technology
tedious, -ly	
tee, teed, teeing (golf)	
tee	tea (drink)
teech	teach
teek	teak
teel	teal
teem, -ed, -ing (rain)	
teem	team (group)
teenager	
teese	tease
tee-shirt	
teet	teat
teeter, -ed, -ing	
teeth (noun)	
teethe, teethed, teething	
teetotal, -ly	
teetotaller	
teflon	
tekneek	technique
teknical	technical
teknicality	technicality
teknicolor	technicolour
teknishun	technician
teknocrasy	technocracy
teknology	technology
tekst	text
tekstile	textile
teksture	texture
telecast, -ed, -ing	
telecommunication	
telefone	telephone
telefonist	telephonist
telefoto	telephoto

telegraf	telegraph
telegram	
telegraphic	
telegraphist	
telegraphy	
teleks	telex
telepathic	
telepathist	
telepathy	
telephone, -phoned, -phoning	
telephonic, -ally	
telephonist	
telephoto lens	
teleprinter	
telescope, -coped, -coping	
televise, -vised, -vising	
televishun	television
television	
telex	
telifone	telephone
telifonist	telephonist
teligram	telegram
teliphoto	telephoto
teliscope	telescope
telivise	televise
telivishun	television
tell, told, telling	
teller	
telltale	
telly, tellies (T.V.)	
temerity	
temper, -ed, -ing	
tempera	
temperament	
temperamental, -ly	
temperance	
temperanse	temperance
temperate, -ly	
Temperate Zone	
temperature	
tempest	
tempestuous, -ly	
tempestuus	tempestuous
template	
temple	
templut	template
tempo, -pos	

temporal, -ly	
temporarily	
temporary	
temporise, -rised, -rising	
tempory	temporary
temprament	temperament
tempratcher	temperature
tempremental	temperamental
tempt, -ed, -ing	
temptation	
tempter	
temtation	temptation
tenable, -bly	
tenabul	tenable
tenacious, -ly	
tenancy	
tenansy	tenancy
tenant	
tend, -ed, -ing	
tendency, -cies	
tendenshus	tendentious
tendentious, -ly	
tender, -ed, -ing	
tenderfoot, -foots, -feet	
tenderly	
tendon	
tendril	
tenement	
tenet	
teniment	tenement
tenis	tennis
tennis	
tenon	
tenor	
tenpin bowling	
tense, tensed, tensing	
tense, tenser, tensest	
tenshun	tension
tension	
tent	
tentacle	
tentative, -ly	
tenterhook	
tenth	
tenuous, -ly	
tenure	
tenuus	tenuous

tenyer	tenure	terribul	terrible
tepee		terrier	
tepid, -ly		terrific, -ally	
teracota	terracotta	terrify, -fied, -fying	
terain	terrain	terrine	
terarium	terrarium	territorial, -ly	
terazo	terrazzo	territory, -ries	
terban	turban	terror	
terbid	turbid	terrorise, -rised, -rising	
terbine	turbine	terrorism	
terbo	turbo	terrorist	
terbulent	turbulent	terse, terser, tersest	
terf	turf	tersely	
tergid	turgid	tertiary, -ries	
teribul	terrible	tertle	turtle
terier	terrier	terylene	
terific	terrific	teselate	tessellate
terifie	terrify	teselation	tessellation
teritry	territory	tespoon	teaspoon
terjid	turgid	tessellate, -ated, -ating	
terkey	turkey	tessellation	
terkwoise	turquoise	test, -ed, -ing	
term		testament	
termagant		testicle	
terminable, -ly		testicul	testicle
terminabul	terminable	testifie	testify
terminal, -ally		testify, -fied, -fying	
terminate, -nated, -nating		testimonial	
termination		testimony, -nies	
terminology, -gies		testis, testes	
terminus, -ni, -nuses		test-tube	
termite		testy, -tier, -tiest	
termoil	turmoil	tetanus	
tern (bird)		tete-a-tete	
tern	turn (move)	tether, -ed, -ing	
ternip	turnip	tetragon	
teror	terror	tetrahedron, -drons, -dra	
terorist	terrorist	texchur	texture
terpentine	turpentine	text	
terpitude	turpitude	textbook	
terrace, -raced, -racing		textile	
terracotta		textual, -ly	
terrain		texture, -tured, -turing	
terrarium, -rariums, -raria		thach	thatch
terrazzo		thalidomide	
terrestrial, -ly		than	
terrible, -bly		thank, -ed, -ing	

thankful, -ly	
thankless, -ly	
thanksgiving	
that, those	
that's (that is)	
thats	that's
thatch, -ed, -ing	
thaw, -ed, -ing	
thay	they
theater	theatre
theatre	
theatrical, -ly	
theft	
their (possessive)	
their	there (at that place)
theirs (possessive)	
theirs	there's (there is)
theism	
theist	
theistic, -ally	
theif	thief
theives	thieves
theiving	thieving
thematic, -ally	
theme	
themselves	
then	
thence	
thense	thence
theocracy, -cies	
theocrasy	theocracy
theocrat	
theodolite	
theological, -ly	
theologian	
theology, -gies	
theolojun	theologian
theorem	
theoretic	
theoretical, -ly	
theorise, -rised, -rising	
theorist	
theorm	theorem
theory, -ries	
theosofie	theosophy

theosophical, -ly	
theosophist	
theosophy	
therapeutic, -ally	
therapey	therapy
therapist	
therapy, -pies	
therd	third
there (at that place)	
there	their (possessive)
there	they're (they are)
thereabouts	
thereby	
therefore	
therem	theorem
therein	
thereof	
thereon	
there's (there is)	
theres	theirs (possessive)
theres	there's (there is)
theretic	theoretic
thereticul	theoretical
therey	theory
thereupon	
therewith	
therise	theorise
therist	theorist
therm	
thermal, -ly	
thermodynamic, -ally	
thermometer	
thermometrical,-ly	
thermonuclear	
thermoplastic	
thermos	
thermostat	
thermostatic, -ally	
Thersday	Thursday
therst	thirst
thersty	thirsty
therteen	thirteen
therty	thirty

thesaurus, -sauri

these

thesis, -ses

  thesorus   thesaurus

Thespian

they'd (they had)

  theyd   they'd

they'll (they will)

  theyll   they'll

they're (they are)

  theyre   they're

they've (they have)

  theyve   they've

  thi   thigh

thick, -ly

thicken, -ed, -ing

thickener

thicket

thickhead

thickness

thickset

thickskinned

thief, thieves

thieve, thieved, thieving

thievish, -ly

thigh

thimble

  thimbul   thimble

  thime   thyme

thin, thinned, thinning

thin, thinner, thinnest

thine

  thiner   thinner

thing

thingamajig

think, thought, thinking

think-tank

thinly

thinner

thinness

third, -ly

third-degree

  thirm   therm

  thiroid   thyroid

thirst, -ed, -ing

thirstily

thirsty, -tier, -tiest

thirteen

thirteenth

  thirtie   thirty

thirtieth

thirty, -ties

this, these

  thisis   thesis

  thisle   thistle

  thisorus   thesaurus

thistle

thistledown

  thisul   thistle

  thitha   thither

thither

  tho   though

thong

  thor   thaw

  thoraks   thorax

thorax, thoraces, thoraxes

thorn

thorny, -nier, -niest

thorough, -ly (absolute)

  thorough   through (pass)

thoroughbred

thoroughfare

  thort   thought

those

thou (you)

though (but)

thought (did think)

thoughtful, -ly

thoughtless, -ly

thousand

thousandth

  thowsand   thousand

thrall

thrash, -ed, -ing

thread, -ed, -ing

threat

threaten, -ed, -ing

  thred   thread

three

three-dimensional

threepence

three-quarter

threesome

thresh, -ed, -ing

threshold
  thret   threat
threw (did throw)
  threw   through
                (between)
  threwout   throughout
thrice
thrift
thrifty, -tier, -tiest
thrill, -ed, -ing
thriller
thrips, thrips
  thrise   thrice
thrive, throve, thrived, thriving
thro' (through)
throat
throb, throbbed, throbbing
throe (spasm)
  throe   throw (toss)
thrombosis, -oses
throne (chair)
  throne   thrown (tossed)
throng, -ed, -ing
  throo   threw (tossed)
  throo   through
                (between)
  throte   throat
throttle, -tled, -tling
  throttul   throttle
through (pass)
  through   thorough
                (absolute)
  through   threw (tossed)
throughout
throve
throw, threw, thrown, throwing (toss)
  throw   throe (spasm)
throwaway society
thrown (tossed)
  thrown   throne (chair)
thrum, thrummed, thrumming
thrush
thrust, thrust, thrusting
thud, thudded, thudding
thug
thuggery
thuggish, -ly

thum   thumb
thumb, -ed, -ing
thump, -ed, -ing
thunder, -ed, -ing
thunderbolt
thunderclap
thunderous, -ly
thunderstruck
thundery
  thundrus   thunderous
  thurer   thorough
  thurerbred   thoroughbred
  thurerfare   thoroughfare

> For **thurm-** words, look
> under **therm-**.

Thursday
  thurst   thirst
  thurteen   thirteen
  thurty   thirty
thus
thwart, -ed, -ing
  thwort   thwart
thyme (plant)
thyroid
tiara
tibia, tibiae, tibias
tic (twitch)
tick, -ed, -ing (sound)
ticker
ticket
tickle, -led, -ling
ticklish
  tickul   tickle
  ticoon   tycoon
tic-tac
tidal
tiddler
tiddlywinks
tide, tided, tiding (ocean)
  tide   tied (bound)
  tidie   tidy
tidily
tidings
  tidul   tidal
tidy, tidied, tidying
tidy, tidier, tidiest

tie, tied, tying

tier, (row)

tier	tear (crying)
tier	tire (weary)
tier	tyre (wheel)
tif	tiff

tiff

tiffin

tifoid	typhoid
tifoon	typhoon
tifus	typhus

tiger

tigeress	tigress

tight, -ly

tighten, -ed, -ing

tightrope

tights

tigress

tiki

tile, tiled, tiling

till, -ed, -ing

tiller

tilt, -ed, -ing

timber, -ed, -ing (wood)

timbre (sound)

timbrel

timbrul	timbrel

time, timed, timing (clock)

time	thyme (plant)

timekeeper

timeless, -ly

timely, -lier, -liest

timepiece

timetable

timid, -ly

timidity

timorous, -ly

timorus	timorous

timpano, -ni

tin, tinned, tinning

tinchur	tincture

tincture, -tured, -turing

tinder

tinderbox

tine

tinea

tinge, tinged, tingeing

tingle, tingled, tingling

tingul	tingle
tinie	tiny

tinker, -ed, -ing

tinkle, -led, -ling

tinkture	tincture
tinkul	tinkle

tinny, -nier, -niest

tin-pot

tinsel, -selled, -selling

tinselly

tinsul	tinsel

tint, -ed, -ing

tintack

tiny, tinier, tiniest

tip, tipped, tipping

tipe	type
tipewriter	typewriter
tipical	typical
tipify	typify
tipist	typist
tipografy	typography

tipple, -led, -ling

tipsily

tipsy, -sier, -siest

tiptoe, -toed, -toeing

tiptop

tipul	tipple

tirade

tiranical	tyrannical
tiranise	tyrannise
tirant	tyrant
tiranus	tyrannous
tirany	tyranny

tire, tired, tiring (weary)

tire	tier (row)
tire	tyre (wheel)

tiresome

tiresum	tiresome

'tis (it is)

tis	'tis (it is)
tis	tizz (anxiety)
tishoo	tissue

tissue, -sued, -suing

tit

titan

titanic

titavation	titivation	todstool	toadstool
titbit		todul	toddle
tite	tight	tody	toddy
titen	tighten	toe, toed, toeing (foot)	
tites	tights	toe	tow (pull)
tithe, tithed, tithing		toey	
titian		tofee	toffee
titillate, -lated, -lating		toff	
titillation		toffee (sweet)	
titivate, -vated, -vating		toffy (rich)	
titivation		tog, togged, togging	
title, -tled, -tling (name)		together	
titrate, -trated, -trating		togetherness	
titter, -ed, -ing		toggle, -gled, -gling	
tittillate	titillate	toggul	toggle
tittle (dot)		toheroa	
tittle-tattle, -tled, -tling		toi	toy
titul	title	toil, -ed, -ing	
titular		toilet	
tizz (anxiety)		toiletrain	toilet-train
to (towards)		toiletry, -tries	
to	too (also)	toilet-train	
to	two (number)	token	
toad		toksic	toxic
toadfish		toksin	tocsin (alarm)
toadstool		toksin	toxin (poison)
toady, toadies		tol	toll
toady, toadied, toadying		told	
toast, -ed, -ing		tole	toll
toaster		tolerable, -bly	
toastmaster		tolerance	
toastmistress		toleranse	tolerance
tobacco		tolerant, -ly	
tobacconist		tolerate, -rated, -rating	
tobaco	tobacco	tolerense	tolerance
tobogan	toboggan	toll, -ed, -ing	
toboggan		tolrabul	tolerable
tobogganist		tomahawk	
tocsic	toxic	tomahork	tomahawk
tocsin (alarm)		tomarto	tomato
tocsin	toxin (poison)	tomato, -toes	
today		tomb	
toddle, -dled, -dling		tomboy	
toddler		tombstone	
toddy, -dies		tome	
tode	toad	tomfoolery	
todler	toddler	tomorow	tomorrow

tomorrer	tomorrow	topografer	topographer
tomorrow		topografy	topography
ton		topper	
tonal, -ly		topple, -pled, -pling	
tongs		toppul	topple
tongue, tongued, tonguing		topsail	
tongue-tied		topside	
tongue-twister		topsoil	
tonic		topsy-turvy	
tonight		tor (hill)	
tonite	tonight	tor	tore (ripped)
tonnage		tor	tour (trip)
tonne		torch	
tonnige	tonnage	torcher	torture
tonsher	tonsure	torchlight	
tonsil		torchlite	torchlight
tonsillectomy, -mies		tore (ripped)	
tonsillitis		tore	tour (trip)
tonsure, -sured, -suring		toreador	
too (also)		torent	torrent
too	to (towards)	torid	torrid
too	two (number)	torism	tourism
took		torment, -ed, -ing	
tool, -ed, -ing		tormenter	tormentor
toom	tomb	tormentor	
toomstone	tombstone	torn	
toon	tune	tornado, -does, -dos	
toor	tour	tornament	tournament
toot, -ed, -ing		torney	tawny
tooth, teeth		tornt	taunt
toothache		torpedo, -does	
toothake	toothache	torpedo, -doed, -doing	
toothbrush, -brushes		torper	torpor
toothcomb		torpid, -ly	
toothless		torpidity	
toothpaste		torpor	
toothy, -thier, -thiest		torque	
tootle, -tled, -tling		torrenshul	torrential
tootul	tootle	torrent	
top, topped, topping		torrential, -ly	
topas	topaz	torrid, -ly	
topaz		torshun	torsion
topic		torsion, -ally	
topical, -ly		torso, -sos	
topknot		tort (law)	
topless, -ly		tort	taught (teach)
topmast		tort	taut (tight)

tortilla

tortoise

tortoiseshell

   tortology → tautology

tortuous, -ly

torture, -tured, -turing

torturer

   tortus → tortoise

   tortuus → tortuous

toss, tossed, tossing

toss-up

   tost → toast

tot, totted, totting

total, -talled, -talling

totalisator

totalitarianism

totality, -ties

totally

tote, toted, toting

totem

   toter → totter

totter, -ed, -ing

tottery

   totul → total

touch, -ed, -ing (feel)

touchdown

touché (good point)

touchily

touchline

touchstone

touch-type, -typed, -typing

touchy, -chier, -chiest

tough, -ly

toughen, -ed, -ing

toupee

tour, -ed, -ing (trip)

   tour → tor (hill)

   tour → tore (ripped)

tourer

tourism

tourist

tournament

   tournikay → tourniquet

tourniquet

tousle, -sled, -sling

tout, -ed, -ing

tow, -ed, -ing (pull)

tow

toward

towards

towel, -elled, -elling

tower, -ed, -ing

   towl → towel

town

town-planner

township

   towring → towering

   towsl → tousle

   towt → tout

toxic, -ally

toxicity

toxin (poison)

   toxin → tocsin (alarm)

toy, -ed, -ing

   toyl → toil

   toylet → toilet

trace, traced, tracing

tracer

tracery, -ries

trachea, tracheae

trachoma

track, -ed, -ing

   trackshun → traction

tracksuit

tract

tractable, -bly

   tracter → tractor

traction

tractor

trade, traded, trading

trade-in

trademark

trader

tradesman, -men

tradeswoman, -women

   tradishun → tradition

tradition

traditional, -ly

traduce, -duced, -ducing

traducer

   traduse → traduce

traffic, -ficked, -ficking

trafficable

trafficator

toe (foot)

towel

towering

tousle

tout

trafficker

trafic   traffic

tragedian

tragedienne

tragedy, -dies

tragic

tragical, -ly

tragicomedy, -dies

trail, -ed, -ing

trailblazer

trailer

train, -ed, -ing

trainee

trainer

traipse, traipsed, traipsing

trait

traiter   traitor

traitor

traitorous, -ly

traitrous   traitorous

trajectory, -ries

trajectry   trajectory

trajedy   tragedy

trakia   trachea

trakshun   traction

tram, trammed, tramming

tramcar

tramline

trammel, -melled, -melling

tramp, -ed, -ing

trample, -pled, -pling

trampoline, -lined, -lining

trampul   trample

tramul   trammel

trance, tranced, trancing

trane   train

trankwil   tranquil

trankwility   tranquillity

tranquil, -ly

tranquilliser

tranquillity

transact, -ed, -ing

transaction

transactor

transceiver

transcend, -ed, -ing

transcendent

transcendental, -ally

transcribe, -scribed, -scribing

transducer

transe   trance

transend   transcend

transept

transfer, -ferred, -ferring

transferal

transference

transfigure, -ured, -uring

transfiks   transfix

transfix, -ed, -ing

transform, -ed, -ing

transformation

transformer

transfuse, -fused, -fusing

transfusion

transgress, -ed, -ing

transgression

transgressor

transient, -ly

transishun   transition

transister   transistor

transistor

transit, -sited, -siting

transition

transitional, -ly

transitory

translate, -lated, -lating

translation

translator

translucent, -ly

transmigrate, -grated, -grating

transmigration

transmigratory

transmishun   transmission

transmission

transmit, -mitted, -mitting

transmitter

transom

transparency, -cies

transparensy   transparency

transparent, -ly

transperant   transparent

transpire, -spired, -spiring

transplant, -ed, -ing

transplantation

transport, -ed, -ing
transporter
transportation
transpose, -posed, -posing
transsexual
transversal, -ly
transverse, -versed, -versing
transvestism
transvestite
trap, trapped, trapping
trapdoor
trapeze
trapezium, -ziums, -zia
trapper
trappings
  trapse   traipse
  trase   trace
trash
trashy, trashier, trashiest
  trate   trait
  trater   traitor
  traterus   traitorous
trauma, -mata, -mas
traumatic
travail, -ed, -ing (labour)
  travale   travail
travel, -elled, -elling (tour)
traveller
  travelog   travelogue
travelogue
traverse, -versed, -versing
travesty, -ties
travesty, -tied, -tying
trawl, -ed, -ing
trawler
  trawma   trauma
  trawmatic   traumatic
treacherous, -ly
treachery, -eries
treacle
tread, trod, trodden, treading
treadle, -dled, -dling
treadmill
treason
treasonable, -bly
treasonous, -ly
  treasonus   treasonous

treasure, -ured, -uring
treasurer
treasure-trove
treasury, -uries
treat, -ed, -ing
treatable
treatise
  treatiss   treatise
treatment
treaty, -ties
treble, -bled, -bling
  trebul   treble
  trecherus   treacherous
  trechery   treachery
  tred   tread
tree
  treecul   treacle
  treet   treat
  treetis   treatise
  treetment   treatment
  treety   treaty
trefoil
trek, trekked, trekking
trekker
trellis
tremble, -bled, -bling
trembly, -blier, -bliest
  trembul   tremble
tremendous, -ly
  tremendus   tremendous
  tremer   tremor
tremolo, -los
tremor
tremulous, -ly
  tremulus   tremulous
trench, -ed, -ing
trenchant, -ly
trend
trendiness
trendy, -dier, -diest
  treo   trio
trepidation
  treshure   treasure
  treshury   treasury
  treson   treason
trespass, -ed, -ing
trespasser

tress	
tressul	trestle
trestle	
trevally	
tri	try
triad	
trial	
triangel	triangle
triangle	
triangul	triangle
triangular, -ly	
tribal, -ly	
tribalism	
tribe	
tribul	tribal
tribulation	
tribunal	
tribune	
tributary, -ries	
tribute	
tributry	tributary
trice, triced, tricing	
triceps	
trick, -ed, -ing	
trickery, -eries	
trickle, -led, -ling	
trickster	
tricky, -kier, -kiest	
tricolour	
tricycle	
trident	
tried	
triel	trial
triennial, -ly	
triennium, -enniums, -ennia	
trifecta	
trifle, trifled, trifling	
trifler	
triful	trifle
trigger, -ed, -ing	
trigonometrical, -ly	
trigonometry	
trilby, -bies	
trillion	
trilogy, -gies	
trim, trimmed, trimming	
trim, trimmer, trimmest	

trimaran	
trimester	
trimmer	
trinity, -ties	
trinket	
trio, trios	
trip, tripped, tripping	
tripartite	
tripe	
triple, -pled, -pling	
triplet	
triplicate, -cated, -cating	
tripod	
tripple	triple
triptick	triptych
triptych	
tripul	triple
trise	trice
trisicul	tricycle
trite, triter, tritest	
tritely	
triumf	triumph
triumph	
triumphal	
triumphant, -ly	
trivia	
trivial, -ly	
triviality, -ties	
trod	
trodden	
troff	trough
trofy	trophy
troglodyte	
troika	
trolie	trolley
troll, -ed, -ing	
trolley, -leys	
trollop	
trolop	trollop
troly	trolley
trombone	
trombonist	
troo	true
trooant	truant
trooly	truly
troop, -ed, -ing (soldier)	
troop	troupe (band)

trooper

troos   truce
trooth   truth
troothful   truthful
trophy, -phies
tropic
tropical, -ly

trorma   trauma
trormatic   traumatic

trot, trotted, trotting
troth
trotter
troubadour
trouble, -bled, -bling
troublemaker
troublesome, -ly
troubleshooter
trough
trounce, trounced, trouncing
troupe (band)
trousers
trousseau, -seaux, -seaus
trout
trowel, -elled, -elling

trownce   trounce
trowsers   trousers
trowt   trout

truancy

truansy   truancy

truant

trubul   trouble

truce
truck, -ed, -ing
truckie
truculence

truculense   truculence

truculent, -ly
trudge, trudged, trudging
true, truer, truest
true-blue

truf   trough

truffle

truful   truffle
truge   trudge

truism

trulie   truly

trump, -ed, -ing

trumpery, -ries
trumpet
trumpeter
truncate, -cated, -cating
truncheon

trunchon   truncheon

trundle, -dled, -dling

trundul   trundle

trunk

truseau   trousseau

truss, -ed, -ing
trust, -ed, -ing
trustee
trustful, -ly

trustwerthy   trustworthy

trustworthy
trusty, trustier, trustiest
truth
truthful, -ly
try, tries
try, tried, trying

tryce   trice
trycycle   tricycle
trype   tripe

tryst

tryte   trite
tryumph   triumph

tsar
T-shirt
tuan
tub, tubbed, tubbing
tuba, -bas, -bae (instrument)
tubby, -bier, -biest
tube, tubed, tubing
tuber (plant)
tuberculosis
tuberculous
tubular

tuch   touch
tuchy   touchy

tuck, -ed, -ing
tucker
Tuesday

tuf   tough
tuffen   toughen

tuffet
tuft, -ed, -ing

tug, tugged, tugging		turm	term
tugboat		turmeric	
tuishun	tuition	turminabul	terminable
tuition		turminal	terminal
tuk	tuck	turminate	terminate
tuksedo	tuxedo	turminus	terminus
tulip		turmite	termite
tulle		turmoil	
tumble, -bled, -bling		turn, -ed, -ing (rotate)	
tumbler		turn	tern (bird)
tumbleweed		turncoat	
tumbul	tumble	turnikay	tourniquet
tumer	tumour	turniket	tourniquet
tumescent		turnip	
tumour		turnout	
tumult		turnover	
tumultuous, -ly		turnstile	
tumultuus	tumultuous	turntable	
tuna (fish)		turpentine	
tundra		turpitude	
tune, tuned, tuning		turquoise	
tuneful, -ly		turret	
tuner (radio)		turse	terse
tung	tongue	turshury	tertiary
tungsten		turtle	
tunic		turtledove	
tunige	tonnage	turtleneck	
tunnel, -nelled, -nelling		turtul	turtle
tunnul	tunnel	Tusday	Tuesday
turban		tusk, -ed, -ing	
turbid, -ly		tussle, -sled, -sling	
turbine		tussock	
turbojet		tusul	tussle
turboprop		tutelage	
turbot, -bots, -bot		tutelige	tutelage
turbulence		tuter	tutor
turbulense	turbulence	tutor	
turbulent, -ly		tutorial	
tureen		tutoriul	tutorial
turet	turret	tutu	
turf, turfs, turves		tuxedo, -dos	
turgid, -ly		twaddle, -dled, -dling	
turgidity		twain	
turjid	turgid	twang	
turkey, -keys		twangy	
Turkish		tweak, -ed, -ing	
turkwoise	turquoise	tweed	

tweek	tweak	tyfoon	typhoon
tweet		tyfus	typhus
tweeter		tympanic	
tweezers		tympanum, -nums, -na	
twelfth		type, typed, typing	
twelth	twelfth	typecast, -cast, -casting	
twelve		typeface	
twentieth		typescript	
twenty, -ties		typeset, -set, -setting	
twice		typesetter	
twich	twitch	typewriter	
twiddle, -dled, -dling		typhoid	
twidul	twiddle	typhoon	
twig, twigged, twigging		typhus	
twiggy		typical, -ly	
twilight		typify, -fied, -fying	
twilite	twilight	typist	
twill (fabric)		typographical, -ally	
'twill (it will)		typography	
twill	'twill (it will)	tyranical	tyrannical
twin, twinned, twinning		tyrannical, -ly	
twine, twined, twining		tyrannise, -nised, -nising	
twinge, twinged, twinging		tyranny, -nies	
twinkle, -kled, -kling		tyrant	
twinkul	twinkle	tyrany	tyranny
twin-set		tyre (wheel)	
twirl, -ed, -ing		tyre	tire (weary)
twist, -ed, -ing		tyro, -ros	
twitch, -ed, -ing		tzar	
twitcher			
twitchy			
twitter, -ed, -ing			
two (number)			
two	to (towards)		
two	too (also)		
two-dimensional			
two-faced			
twopence			
twostep			
two-time, -timed, -timing			
two-tooth			
'twould (it would)			
twould	'twould		
two-up			
twurl	twirl		
tycoon			
tyfoid	typhoid		

Uu

ubikwity	ubiquity
ubiquitous, -ly	
ubiquity	
U-boat	
ubote	U-boat
uda	udder
udder	
ufologist	
ug	ugh
ug boot	
ugh	
uglee	ugly
ugliness	
ugly, -lier, -liest	
ugly duckling	
ukelele	
ukulele	
ulcer	
ulcerate, -rated, -rating	
ulceration	
ulcerous, -ly	
ullage, ullaged, ullaging	
ulsa	ulcer
ulserate	ulcerate
ulserayshun	ulceration
ulserus	ulcerous
ultamatum	ultimatum
ulteeria	ulterior
ultemo	ultimo
ulterior, -ly	
ultimate, -ly	
ultimatum, -tums, -ta	
ultimit	ultimate
ultimo	
ultra	
ultramareen	ultramarine
ultramarine	
ultrasound	

ultraviolet	
ululate, -lated, -lating	
umber	
umberella	umbrella
umbilical cord	
umbilicus, -bilici	
umbra, -brae	
umbrage	
umbrageous, -ly	
umbrella	
umbridge	umbrage
umpire, -pired, -piring	
umpyre	umpire
umpteen	
umpteenth	
unable	
unabul	unable
unaccompanied	
unaccountable, -bly	
unaccustomed	
unacustumed	unaccustomed
unakumpneed	unaccompanied
unanimity	
unanimous, -ly	
unanimus	unanimous
unapproachable, -bly	
unaprochibul	unapproachable
unassuming, -ly	
unattached	
unattended	
unatural	unnatural
unavailing, -ly	
unavaleing	unavailing
unaware	
unawares	
unawear	unaware
unbalance, -anced, -ancing	
unbecoming, -ly	
unbecuming	unbecoming
unbeknown	
unbeknownst	
unbeleif	unbelief
unbeleiver	unbeliever
unbeleiving	unbelieving
unbelief	
unbeliever	
unbelieving, -ly	

unbend, -bent or -bended, -bending	
unbenown	unbeknown
unblinking, -ly	
unblushing, -ly	
unborn	
unbosom, -ed, -ing	
unbounded, -ly	
unbownded	unbounded
unbrideld	unbridled
unbridled	
unburden, -ed, -ing	
uncalled-for	
uncanny, -nily	
unceremonious, -ly	
uncertain, -ly	
uncharitable, -ly	
uncharted	
uncircumcised	
uncle	
unclean, -ly	
uncomfortable, -ly	
unconfortibul	uncomfortable
uncommon, -ly	
uncommunicative, -ly	
uncomon	uncommon
uncompromising, -ly	
unconcerned, -ly	
uncondishunal	unconditional
unconditional, -ly	
unconnected, -ly	
unconscionable, -bly	
unconscious, -ly	
unconshunibul	unconscionable
unconshus	unconscious
unconstitutional, -ly	
unconventional, -ly	
uncooth	uncouth
uncouth, -ly	
uncover, -ed, -ing	
unction	
unctuous, -ly	
uncumftibul	uncomfortable
uncut	
uncuver	uncover
undaunted	
undecided	
undefined	

undemonstrative, -ly	
undeniable, -bly	
undeniabul	undeniable
under	
under-age	
underarm	
undercarriage	
undercarridge	undercarriage
underclose	underclothes
underclothes	
undercoat	
undercote	undercoat
undercover	
undercurent	undercurrent
undercurrent	
undercut, -cut, -cutting	
undercuver	undercover
underdeveloped	
underdeveloping	
underdevelopment	
underdevelopt	underdeveloped
underdog	
underdone	
underdun	underdone
underestamate	underestimate
underestimate, -mated, -mating	
underexpose, -exposed, -exposing	
underexposhur	underexposure
underexposure	
underexpows	underexpose
underfoot	
undergo, -went, -gone, -going	
undergraduate	
undergrajuate	undergraduate
undergroth	undergrowth
underground	
undergrowth	
underhand	
underite	underwrite
underlay, -laid, -laying	
underlie, -lay, -lain, -lying	
underlieing	underlying
underline, -lined, -lining	
underling	
underly	underlie
underlying	
undermine, -mined, -mining	

underneath
 underneeth   underneath
undernourish, -ed, -ing
 undernurish   undernourish
underpants
underpass
underpin, -pinned, -pinning
underplay, -played, -playing
underprivileged
underproof
 underprufe   underproof
 underscaw   underscore
underscore, -scored, -scoring
undersecretary, -taries
undersell, -sold, -selling
undershot
undersign
 undersine   undersign
understand, -stood, -standing
understanding
 understait   understate
understate, -stated, -stating
understatement
 understayt   understate
understood
understudy, -studied, -studying
 undertaik   undertake
 undertaiker   undertaker
undertake, -took, -taken, -taking
undertaker
under-the-counter
 undertoan   undertone
 undertoe   undertow
undertone
undertow
 underware   underwear
underwear
underworld
underwrite, -written, -writing
undesirable, -bly
 undesiribul   undesirable
undeveloped
 undevelupt   undeveloped
 undew   undue
 undewlate   undulate
 undewly   unduly
undo, -did, -done, -doing

 undoo   undo
undoubted, -ly
 undowted   undoubted
undress, -dressed, -dressing
undue
undulate, -lated, -lating
undulation
undulatory
unduly
 undur   under
undying
 undyou   undue
unearned
unearned income
unearth, -ed, -ing
unearthly
uneasily
uneasiness
uneasy, -easier, -easiest
 unecessary   unnecessary
uneducated
 uneekwell   unequal
 uneesy   uneasy
 uneeven   uneven
 unekwivacal   unequivocal
unemployed
unemployment
unequal, -ly
 uneque   unique
unequivocal, -ly
unerring, -ly
 unesesary   unnecessary
uneven, -ly
unevenness
unfailing, -ly
unfair, -ly
 unfaling   unfailing
 unfare   unfair
unfamiliar, -ly
unfamiliarity
unfeeling, -ly
 unfemilyer   unfamiliar
unfinished
unfit, -fitted, -fitting
unflagging, -ly
 unflapibul   unflappable
unflappable, -bly

unfold, -ed, -ing
   unforchinate   unfortunate
unforeseen
unforgettable
unformed
   unforsean   unforeseen
unfortunate, -ly
unfounded, -ly
   unfowld   unfold
   unfownded   unfounded
unfrock, -ed, -ing
unfurl, -ed, -ing
ungainliness
ungainly
   unganely   ungainly
   ungarded   unguarded
ungodliness
ungodly
ungracious, -ly
   ungrashus   ungracious
unguarded, -ly
unguent
ungulate
unhappily
unhappiness
unhappy, -pier, -piest
unhealthily
unhealthiness
unhealthy, -thier, -thiest
unheard-of
   unhelthy   unhealthy
   unherdoff   unheard-of
unhinge, -hinged, -hinging
   unhinj   unhinge
   unholey   unholy
unholy, -lier, -liest
   unholesum   unwholesome
uni
unicameral
unicellular
   uniceluler   unicellular
unicorn
   unidirechunal   unidirectional
   unifacation   unification
unification
uniform, -ly
uniformity, -ties

unify, -fied, -fying
   unike   unique
unilateral, -ly
   unilatrel   unilateral
unimaginable, -ably
   unimaginabul   unimaginable
unimpeachable, -ably
   unimpeechibul   unimpeachable
   unimployed   unemployed
   unimprooved   unimproved
unimproved
uninhibited
uninspired
uninspiring
union
union card
unionisation
unionise, -nised, -nising
unionist
unionistic
Union Jack
unique, -ly
uniqueness
   unirve   unnerve
unisex
unisexual, -ly
unisexuality
unison
unit
Unitarian
Unitarianism
unitary
unite, united, uniting
unit trust
unity, -ties
universal, -ly
universal suffrage
universe
university, -ties
unkempt
   unkemt   unkempt
unkind, -ly
   unkined   unkind
   unkle   uncle
unknit, -knitted, -knitting
unknown
unlawful, -ly

unlearned, -ly
unlearnt
unleash, -ed, -ing
unleavened

unleesh	unleash
unlerned	unlearned
unlernt	unlearnt
unles	unless

unless
unlettered
unlike
unlikelihood
unlikely

| unlikelyhood | unlikelihood |

unlimited
unlisted
unload, -ed, -ing

| unlode | unload |

unlooked-for
unluckily
unluckiness
unlucky

| unluckyly | unluckily |

unmake, -made, -making
unmanageable, -bly

| unmanagebul | unmanageable |

unmanliness
unmanly
unmannerliness
unmannerly

| unmenchunabul | unmentionable |

unmentionable, -bly
unmistakable, -bly

| unmistakabul | unmistakable |

unmitigated, -ly

| unmooved | unmoved |

unmoved
unnatural, -ly
unnecessary, -rily
unnerve, -nerved, -nerving

unnesesarily	unnecessarily
unnesesary	unnecessary
unobtrusif	unobtrusive

unobtrusive, -ly
unofficial, -ly

| unofishel | unofficial |

unorganised

| unorgenized | unorganised |

unpalatable, -bly

| unpalatabul | unpalatable |
| unparaleled | unparalleled |

unparalleled

| unparralleled | unparalleled |

unpicked
unplaced

| unplaised | unplaced |

unpolished
unpopular, -ly
unpopularity

| unpopuler | unpopular |

unprecedented, -ly

| unpresidented | unprecedented |

unprincipled

| unprinsipled | unprincipled |

unprintable

| unprintibul | unprintable |
| unprofeshunel | unprofessional |

unprofessional, -ly

| unproffessinal | unprofessional |
| unkwalified | unqualified |

unqualified
unquestionable, -bly

| unquestionibul | unquestionable |

unravel, -elled, -elling

| unravell | unravel |

unreal, -ly
unrealistic, -ally

| unreckonized | unrecognised |
| unredeamed | unredeemed |

unredeemed

unreel	unreal
unreelistic	unrealistic
unreesenibul	unreasonable
unrekwited	unrequited
unrelaited	unrelated

unrelated
unrelenting, -ly

| unreleived | unrelieved |

unrelieved

| unremiting | unremitting |

unrepeatable, -bly

| unrepeetibul | unrepeatable |

unrequited, -ly
unrest

unrivalled	
unriveled	unrivalled
unrooly	unruly
unruffled	
unrufled	unruffled
unruly	
unsafe, -ly	
unsaif	unsafe
unsaterated	unsaturated
unsaturated	
unsavery	unsavoury
unsavoury	
unscathed	
unschooled	
unscrew, -ed, -ing	
unscrupulous	
unskru	unscrew
unskuled	unschooled
unseasonable, -bly	
unseat, -seated, -seating	
unseesenibul	unseasonable
unseet	unseat
unsecured	
unsecurred	unsecured
unseemliness	
unseemly	
unseemlynes	unseemliness
unseen	
unselfish, -ly	
unsellfish	unselfish
unserviceable	
unservisabul	unserviceable
unsetled	unsettled
unsettled	
unshakable, -bly	
unshakeable, -bly	
unshakibul	unshakeable
unshore	unsure
unsightly	
unsitely	unsightly
unskild	unskilled
unskilled	
unsociability	
unsociable, -bly	
unsolicited	
unsolisited	unsolicited
unsoshabul	unsociable

unsound, -ly	
unsownd	unsound
unspeakable, -bly	
unspeekabul	unspeakable
unspoilt	
unspoylt	unspoilt
unstable, -bly	
unstabul	unstable
unsteady, -dily	
unstedie	unsteady
unstructured	
unstruxured	unstructured
unstudied	
unstudyed	unstudied
unsubstanshul	unsubstantial
unsubstantial, -ly	
unsung	
unsure	
unswerving, -ly	
unswurving	unswerving
untangel	untangle
untangle, -gled, -gling	
untapped	
untenable, -bly	
unthinkable, -bly	
unthinkabul	unthinkable
unthinking, -ly	
untidie	untidy
untidiness	
untidy, -dier, -diest	
untie, -tied, -tying	
until	
untill	until
untimely	
unto	
untoo	unto
untold	
untouchable	
untouchabul	untouchable
untooward	untoward
untoward, -ly	
untroo	untrue
untrooth	untruth
untrue	
untruth	
unturned	

unushual	unusual	upholster, -ed, -ing	
unusual, -ly		upholsterer	
unutterable, -bly		upholstery, -ries	
unutterabul	unutterable	upill	uphill
unvale	unveil	upkeep	
unveil, -ed, -ing		uplift	
unvoiced		up-market	
unvoised	unvoiced	upold	uphold
unwarented	unwarranted	upolster	upholster
unwarranted		upon	
unweeldy	unwieldy	upper	
unwelcome, -ly		upper case	
unwellcum	unwelcome	upper chamber	
unwholesome, -ly		uppercut	
unwieldiness		upper hand	
unwieldy		upper house	
unwiling	unwilling	uppermost	
unwilling, -ly		upright	
unwillingness		uprising	
unwind, -wound, -winding		uprite	upright
unwined	unwind	uproar	
unwitting, -ly		uproarious, -ly	
unworldliness		uproot, -ed, -ing	
unworldly		uprore	uproar
unworthily		upset, -set, -setting	
unworthiness		upshot	
unworthy		upside down	
unwritten		upstage, -staged, -staging	
up, upped, upping		upstairs	
up-and-coming		upstaje	upstage
up-beat		upstanding	
upbrade	upbraid	upsurge, -surged, -surging	
upbraid, -ed, -ing		upsurje	upsurge
upbringing		upswing, -swung, -swinging	
up-country		uptaik	uptake
updait	update	uptake	
update, -dated, -dating		up-tempo	
upeld	upheld	uptight	
uper	upper	uptite	uptight
up-end, -ended, -ending		up-to-date	
upgrade, -graded, -grading		up-too-date	up-to-date
upgraid	upgrade	upturn, -ed, -ing	
upheaval		upward, -ly	
upheevul	upheaval	upwards	
upheld		upwood	upward
uphill		uranic	
uphold, -held, -holding		uranium	

Uranus
urban (town)
urbane, -ly (civilised)
urbanity, -ties
urchin
urea
  urear — urea
ureter
urethra, -thrae, -thras
urethral
urge, urged, urging
urgency
urgent, -ly
urinal
urinary
urinate, -nated, -nating
urination
urine
  urinel — urinal
urinous
  urj — urge
  urjensy — urgency
  urjent — urgent
urn (jug)
  urn — earn (gain)
urogenital
  urojenital — urogenital
urology
  urolojy — urology
ursine
usability
usable
usableness
  usabul — usable
usage
  usaje — usage
use, used, using
useable
  useabul — useable
used
useful, -ly
usefulness
useless, -ly
uselessness
usher
usherette
usual, -ly

  ushuel — usual
  ushuelly — usually
usurp, usurped, usurping
usurpation
usurper
usury, -ries
  utalisation — utilisation
ute
utensil
  utensle — utensil
uterine
uterus, uteri
utilisation
utilise, -lised, -lising
utilitarian
utilitarianism
utility, -ties
utmost
utopia
utopian
utopianism
  utta — utter
utter, uttered, uttering
utterly
uttermost
U-turn
  uttur — utter
  uturus — uterus
uvula, -las, -lae
uxorious, -ly
uxoriousness

vacancy, -cies
  vacansy   vacancy
vacant, -ly
vacate, -cated, -cating
vacation
vaccinate, -nated, -nating
vaccination
vaccine
  vaccuum   vacuum
  vacency   vacancy
vacillate, -lated, -lating
  vacseen   vaccine
  vacsinate   vaccinate
  vacsination   vaccination
  vacsine   vaccine
vacuity, -ties
vacuous, -ly
vacuum
vacuum-packed
vacuum-sealed
  vacuus   vacuous
vagabond
vagary, -ries
vagarious
  vagarius   vagarious
  vage   vague
vagina, -nas, -nae
vaginal
vagrancy, -cies
  vagransy   vagrancy
vagrant, -ly
vague, vaguer, vaguest
vaguely
  vail   vale (valley)
  vail   veil (cover)
vain, -ly (proud)
  vain   vane (blade)
  vain   vein (blood)

vainglorious, -ly
  vainglorius   vainglorious
vainglory
  vajina   vagina
  valadation   validation
  valantine   valentine
  valay   valet
vale (valley)
  vale   veil (cover)
  valedicshun   valediction
valediction
valedictory
  valedictry   valedictory
valentine
  valer   valour
  valerus   valorous
  valese   valise
valet, -leted, -leting
valiant, -ly
valid, -ly
validate, -dated, -dating
validation
validity, -ties
valise
valley, -leys
  valor   valour
valorous, -ly
  valorus   valorous
valour
valuable, -bly
valuation
value, -ued, -uing
valuer
valve, valved, valving
valvular
  valy   valley
  valyu   value
  valyubul   valuable
  valyuless   valueless
vamoose, -moosed, -moosing
vamp, -ed, -ing
vampire
van
vandal
vandalism
  vandul   vandal
vane (blade)

vane	vain (proud)	veal	
vane	vein (blood)	vector	
vaneer	veneer	veel	veal
vangard	vanguard	veemense	vehemence
vanglorius	vainglorious	veement	vehement
vanguard		veer, -ed, -ing	
vanilla		vegatation	vegetation
vanish, -ed, -ing		vegetable	
vanity, -ties		vegetabul	vegetable
vankish	vanquish	vegetarian	
vanquish, -ed, -ing		vegetarianism	
vantage		vegetate, -tated, -tating	
vapid, -ly		vegetation	
vaporise, -rised, -rising		vegetative, -ly	
vaporiser		vegtabul	vegetable
vaporous, -ly		vehemence	
vapour		vehement, -ly	
variability		vehicle	
variable, -bly		vehicular	
variabul	variable	veicular	vehicular
variance		veil, -ed, -ing (cover)	
varianse	variance	veil	vale (valley)
variant		vein (blood)	
variation		vein	vain (proud)
varicolored	varicoloured	vein	vane (blade)
varicoloured		veks	vex
varicose		veksashus	vexatious
varied		vektor	vector
variegate, -gated, -gating		Velcro	
varietal, -ly		veldt	
variety, -ties		vellum	
various, -ly		velocipede	
varius	various	velocity, -ties	
varnish, -ed, -ing		velodrome	
vary, varied, varying		veloor	velour
vascular, -ly		velour	
vase		velum	vellum
vasectomy, -mies		velt	veldt
vaseline		velvet	
vasillate	vacillate	velveteen	
vast, -ly		velvety	
vat, vatted, vatting		venal, -ly	
Vatican		venality, -ties	
vaudavil	vaudeville	vend, -ed, -ing	
vaudeville		vender	vendor
vault, -ed, -ing		vendetta	
vaunt, -ed, -ing		vendor	

veneer		verb	
venerability		verbal, -balled, -balling	
venerable, -bly		verbalise, -lised, -lising	
venerabul	venerable	verbally	
venerate, -rated, -rating		verbatim	
veneration		verbel	verbal
venereal		verbena	
venerial	venereal	verbiage	
venetian blind		verbige	verbiage
venew	venue	verbose, -ly	
vengeance		verbosity	
vengeful, -ly		verdant, -ly	
vengense	vengeance	verdict	
venial, -ly		verdure	
venison		verdurous	
venom		verge, verged, verging	
venomous, -ly		verger	
venomus	venomous	vergin	virgin
venous (of veins)		verie	vary
venous	Venus (planet)	verifiable, -bly	
vent, -ed, -ing		verification	
ventalation	ventilation	verifie	verify
ventilate, -lated, -lating		verify, -fied, -fying	
ventilation		verily	
ventilator		verisimilitude	
ventral, -ly		veritable, -bly	
ventricle		vermicelli	
ventricul	ventricle	vermilion	
ventrilokwism	ventriloquism	vermin	
ventriloquism		verminous, -ly	
ventriloquist		vermouth	
venture, -tured, -turing		vernacular, -ly	
venturer		vernal, -ly	
venturesome, -ly		vernier	
venturous, -ly		versatile, -ly	
venturus	venturous	versatility	
venue		verse, verses (poem)	
Venus (planet)		verses	versus (against)
venus	venous (of veins)	versification	
veracious, -ly (honest)		versify, -fied, -fying	
veracious	voracious (greedy)	version	
veracity, -ties		versus (against)	
veranda		versus	verses (poems)
verashus	veracious	vertebra, -brae	
verasity	veracity	vertebrate	
		verteks	vertex
		vertex, -tices	

vertical, -ly
vertiginous, -ly
   vertiginus   vertiginous
vertigo, -goes
verve
very, -rier, -riest
   vesa   visa
vespers
vessel
vest, -ed, -ing
vestal
   vestibul   vestibule
vestibule
vestige
vestigial, -ly
vestment
   vestrie   vestry
vestry, -tries
   vestul   vestal
vesture, -tured, -turing
vet, vetted, vetting
   vetenary   veterinary
   vetenry   veterinary
veteran
veterinary, -ries
veto, -toes
veto, -toed, -toing
vex, -ed, -ing
vexation
vexatious, -ly
   veza   visa
   vi   vie
via
viability
viable, -bly
   viabul   viable
viaduct
vial (tube)
   vial   vile (bad)
   vialate   violate
   vialin   violin
viand
viaticum, -ca, -cums
vibes
vibrant, -ly
vibrate, -brated, -brating
vibration

   vibrater   vibrator
vibrator
viburnum
vicar
vicarage
   vicarige   vicarage
vicarious, -ly
   vicarius   vicarious
vice
vice-chairman, -men
vice-chancellor
vice-president
   vicer   vicar
viceregal, -ly
   viceroi   viceroy
viceroy
vice versa
vicinity, -ties
vicious, -ly (evil)
   vicious   viscous (thick)
vicissitude
   vicount   viscount
   victer   victor
victim
victimisation
victimise, -mised, -mising
victor
Victorian
victorious, -ly
   victorius   victorious
victory, -ries
victual, -ualled, -ualling
victualler
video
videophone
videotape, -taped, -taping
   vidio   video
vie, vied, vying
   vieing   vying
Vietnamese, -ese
view, -ed, -ing
viewer
viewfinder
viewpoint
   viger   vigour
vigil
vigilance

vigilanse — vigilance
vigilant, -ly (watchful)
vigilante (law enforcer)
vigneron
vignette, -gnetted, -gnetting
vigoro
vigorous, -ly
vigorus — vigorous
vigour
viksen — vixen
vilafication — vilification
vilain — villain
vile, viler, vilest (bad)
vile — vial (tube)
vilely
vilification
vilifie — vilify
vilifier
vilify, -fied, -fying
vilige — village
villa
village
villager
villain
villainous, -ly
villainy, -nies
villanus — villainous
vim
vinaigrette
vindicate, -cated, -cating
vindication
vindictive, -ly
vine
vinegar
vinegary
vineyard
vinigar — vinegar
vino
vintage, -taged, -taging
vintige — vintage
vinul — vinyl
vinyl
viola
violate, -lated, -lating
violation
violator
violence

violense — violence
violent, -ly
violet
violin
viper
viperous, -ly
viperus — viperous
virago, -goes, -gos
viral
virgin
virginal, -ly
virginity
Virgo
virile
virility, -ties
virtual, -ly
virtue
virtuoso
virtuous, -ly
virtuus — virtuous
virulence
virulense — virulence
virulent, -ly
virus, viruses
visa, -saed, -saing
visage
vis-a-vis
viscera
viscosity
viscount
viscountess
viscous, -ly, (thick)
viscous — vicious (evil)
viscuus — viscous (thick)
vise — vice
vise-chairman — vice-chairman
vise-president — vice-president
visera — viscera
viseregal — viceregal
viseversa — vice versa
vishiate — vitiate
vishun — vision
vishunry — visionary
vishus — vicious (evil)
visibility, -ties
visible, -bly
visibul — visible

visinity	vicinity
vision	
visionary, -ries	
visionry	visionary
visissitude	vicissitude
visit, -ed, -ing	
visitant	
visitation	
visiter	visitor
visitor	
viskosity	viscosity
vista	
visual, -ly	
visualise, -lised, -lising	
visuul	visual
visuulise	visualise
vital, -ly	
vitality, -ties	
vitamin	
vitel	vital
vitiate, -ated, -ating	
viticulture	
vitreous, -ly	
vitrification	
vitrifie	vitrify
vitrify, -fied, -fying	
vitriol	
vitriolic	
vituperate, -rated, -rating	
viul	vial (tube)
viul	vile (bad)
vivacious, -ly	
vivasious	vivacious
viva voce	
vivid, -ly	
vivisecshun	vivisection
vivisect, -ed, -ing	
vivisection	
vivisectionist	
vixen	
vocabulary, -ries	
vocal, -ly	
vocalisation	
vocalise, -lised, -lising	
vocalist	
vocation	
vocational, -ly	

vociferous, -ly	
vociferus	vociferous
vodka	
voge	vogue
vogue	
voice, voiced, voicing	
void, -ed, -ing	
voiige	voyage
voile	
voise	voice
volatile	
volatility	
volcanic, -ally	
volcano, -noes, -nos	
voley	volley
volishun	volition
volition	
volley, -leys	
volley, -ed, -ing	
volleyball	
volt	
voltage	
voltaic	
voltmeter	
voluble, -bly	
volubul	voluble
volume	
volumetric, -ally	
voluminous, -ly	
voluminus	voluminous
voluntarily	
voluntary, -taries	
volunteer, -ed, -ing	
voluptuous, -ly	
voluptuus	voluptuous
vomit, -ed, -ing	
voodoo, -doos	
voodoo, -dooed, -dooing	
voodooism	
voracious, -ly (greedy)	
voracious	veracious (honest)
voracity	
vorasious	voracious
vortex, -texes, -tices	
vortical, -ly	
vosiferus	vociferous

votary, -ries
vote, voted, voting
voter
votive, -ly
vouch, -ed, -ing
voucher
vouchsafe, -safed, -safing
vow, -ed, -ing

vowch	vouch
vowcher	voucher

vowel

vowul	vowel

voyage, -aged, -aging
voyager

voyd	void

voyeur
voyeurism

voyse	voice
vue	view

vulcanise, -nised, -nising
vulcanism
vulcanite

vulcher	vulture

vulgar, -ly
vulgarism
vulgarity, -ties
vulnerability
vulnerable, -bly

vulnerabul	vulnerable

vulpine
vulture
vulva, -vae, -vas

vurb	verb
vurchoo	virtue
vurchual	virtual
vurchuus	virtuous
vurgin	virgin
vurtue	virtue
vurtuous	virtuous
vye	vie

wack	whack
wad, wadded, wadding	
waddle, -dled, -dling	
waddy, -dies (club)	
waddy	wadi (channel)
wade, waded, wading	
wader	
wadi, -dies (channel)	
wadi	waddy (club)
wadle	waddle
wadul	waddle
wafe	waif
wafer	
wafery	
waffle, -fled, -fling	
waful	waffle
wag, wagged, wagging	
wage, waged, waging	
wager	
waggish, -ly	
waggle, -gled, -gling	
waggly	
wagon	
wagtail	
wagul	waggle
wahine	
waif	
wail, wailed, wailing (cry)	
wail	wale (welt)
wail	whale (mammal)
wainscot, -scotted, -scotting	
wainwright	
waipiro	
waist (body)	
waist	waste (squander)
waistband	

waistcoat	
waistline	
wait (stay)	
wait	weight (amount)
waiter	
waitey	weighty
waitress	
waive, waived, waiving (forgo)	
waive	wave (ocean)
waiver (law)	
waiver	waver (sway)
wake, woke, woken, waking	
wakeful, -ly	
waken, -ened, -ening	
waks	wax
walabey	wallaby
wale, waled, waling (welt)	
wale	wail (cry)
wale	whale (mammal)
walk, -ed, -ing	
walkabout	
walkathon	
walker	
walkie-talkie	
walkout	
walkover	
wall	
wallaby, -bies	
wallaroo	
wallet	
walleyed	
wallflower	
wallop, -ed, -ing	
wallow, -ed, -ing	
wallpaper	
wall-to-wall	
walnut	
walop	wallop
walow	wallow
walrus, -ruses	
walts	waltz
waltz, -ed, -ing	
wampum	
wan, wanner, wannest (pale)	
wan	won (win)

wand
wanda (ghost)
wander, -ed, -ing (walk)
   wander   wonder (think)
wanderer
wanderlust
wane, waned, waning
wangle, -gled, -gling
wangler
   wangul   wangle
want, -ed, -ing
wanton, -ly (lewd)
   wanton   won ton
                     (dough)
war, warred, warring
   warant   warrant
   warantee   warranty
waratah
warble, -bled, -bling
warbler
war cry
ward
warden
wardress
wardrobe
ware (goods)
   ware   wear (cover)
   ware   where (place)
warehouse
   warehowse   warehouse
   warey   wary
   warf   wharf
warfare
warhead
warily
wariness
   warior   warrior
warlike
warlock
warm, -ed, -ing
warm-blooded
warmonger
warmongering
warmth
warn, -ed, -ing (signal)
   warn   worn (tired)
warp, -ed, -ing

warrant, -ed, -ing
warrant officer
warrantor
warranty, -ties
warren
warrigal
warrior
wart (lump)
   wart   wort (plant)
wart-hog
   warves   wharves
wary, warier, wariest
was
wash, -ed, -ing
washboard
washer
washing soda
wash-out
wasn't (was not)
   wasnt   wasn't
wasp
waspish, -ly
wassail
wassailer
wastage
waste, wasted, wasting (squander)
   waste   waist (body)
wasteful, -ly
wasteland
wastrel
   wat   watt (power)
   wat   what (question)
watch, -ed, -ing
watchdog
watchful, -ly
watchman, -men
watchword
   wate   wait (stay)
   wate   weight
                    (measure)
water, -ed, -ing
waterbed
water-buffalo
water-closet
watercolour
watercolourist
water-column

watercourse
watercress
waterfall
waterfowl
waterfront
waterfrontage
watergate
waterhole
watering-can
watering hole
waterlily
waterlog, -logged, -logging
waterloo
watermark
watermelon
water-pistol
water-polo
waterproof
water-rat
water-repellent
watershed
water-ski, -ski'd or skied, -skiing
watertable
watertight
    watertite   watertight
water-tower
water-vapour
waterway
waterwheel
waterworks
watery
    watige   wattage
watt (power)
    watt   what (question)
wattage
wattle, -tled, -tling
wattlebird
wave, waved, waving (ocean)
    wave   waive (forgo)
waveband
wavefront
wavelength
waver, wavered, wavering (sway)
    waver   waiver (law)
wavily
waviness
wavy, -vier, -viest

wax, waxed or waxen, waxing
waxen
    waxflour   waxflower
waxflower
waxplant
waxwork
way (method)
    way   weigh (amount)
    way   whey (liquid)
waybill
wayfarer
waylay, -laid, -laying
way-out
wayward, -ly
    waywerd   wayward
we (us)
    we   wee (little)
weak, -ly (feeble)
    weak   week (time)
weaken, -ed,-ing
weakling
weakly, -lier, -liest (feebly)
    weakly   weekly (time)
weal (hurt)
    weal   wheel (disc)
wealth, -ily
wealth tax
wealthy, -thier, -thiest
wean, -ed, -ing
weaner
weapon
wear, wore, worn, wearing (cover)
    wear   ware (goods)
    wear   where (place)
    wearey   weary
wearisome, -ly
weary, -rier, -riest
weary, -ried, -rying
weasel
    weat   wheat
weather, -ed, -ing (rain)
    weather   wether (geld)
    weather   whether (if)
weatherboard
weathercock
weathervane
weave, wove or weaved, weaving

weave	we've (we have)	weja	ouija
web, webbed, webbing		welch, -ed, -ing	
webfoot, -feet		welcher	
webfooted		welcome, -comed, -coming	
wed, wedded or wed, wedding (join)		weld, -ed, -ing	
we'd		welder	
wed	we'd (we had)	welfare	
Wedensday	Wednesday	welfare state	
wedge, wedged, wedging		well, better, best	
wedge-tailed eagle		we'll (we will)	
wedgie		well-appointed	
wedlock		well-balanced	
Wednesday		well-being	
wee, weer, weest (small)		well-born	
weed, weeded, weeding		well-bred	
weediness		well-connected	
weedul	wheedle	well-disposed	
weedy, -dier, -diest		well-grounded	
week (time)		well-heeled	
week	weak (feeble)	well-informed	
weekday		well-known	
weeken	weaken	well-meaning	
weekend		well-off	
weekender		well-preserved	
weekling	weakling	well-read	
weekly, -lies (time)		well-rounded	
weekly	weakly (feebly)	well-to-do	
weel	weal (hurt)	welsh, -ed, -ing	
weel	wheel (disc)	welt	
weelbarow	wheelbarrow	welter	
weeld	wield	welth	wealth
ween	wean	wen (swelling)	
weep, wept, weeping		wen	when (at what time)
weeping willow		wench	
weet	wheat	wend, wended, wending	
weevil		wenever	whenever
weeze	wheeze	Wensday	Wednesday
weft		went	
wege	wedge	wepon	weapon
weigh, -ed, -ing		wept	
weight, -ily		wer	weir (dam)
weightiness		werd	weird
weightlessness		were (was)	
weighty, -tier, -tiest		were	where (place)
weild	wield	we're (we are)	
weir (dam)		were	we're (we are)
weird, -ly			

wereabouts	whereabouts
wereas	whereas
werefore	wherefore

weren't (were not)

werent	weren't
weresoever	wheresoever
wereupon	whereupon
werever	wherever
werewithal	wherewithal

werewolf, -wolves

werey	weary
werisum	wearisome
werk	work

> For other werk-words,
> look under work-.

werld	world

> For other werl-words,
> look under worl-.

werm	worm

> For other wer-words,
> look under wor-.

Wesleyan
west
West End
westerly, -lies
western
westerner
Westernise, -nised, -nising
westernmost
Westminster system
westward
westwardly
westwards
wet, wetted, wetting (soak)
wet, wetter, wettest

wet	whet (sharpen)

wether, -ed, -ing (geld)

wether	weather (rain)
wether	whether (if)
wetherboard	weatherboard
wethercock	weathercock
wethervane	weathervane

wetsuit
wettex

we've (we have)

weve	weave (cloth)
weve	we've (we have)
weevel	weevil

whack, whacked, whacking
whacko
whale, whales (mammal)
whale, whaled, whaling
whaleboat
whalebone
whaler
whaler shark
wham, whammed, whamming
wharf, wharves, wharfs

wharfey	wharfie

wharfie
what (question)

what	watt (energy)

whata
what-d'ye-call-it
whatever
whatnot
whatsoever
wheat
wheat germ
wheatmeal

whedul	wheedle

wheedle, -dled, -dling
wheel (disc)

wheel	weal (hurt)

wheelbarrow
wheelchair
wheeler-dealer

wheet	wheat

wheeze, wheezed, wheezing
wheezy, -zier, -ziest
whelk
whelp
when
whenever
where (place)

where	ware (goods)
where	wear (cover)

whereabouts
whereas
wherefore
wheresoever

whereupon

wherever

wherewithal

  wherl   whirl (spin)

  wherl   whorl (circle)

wherry, -ries

whet, whetted, whetting (sharpen)

  whet   wet (soak)

whether (if)

  whether   weather (rain)

  whether   wether (geld)

whew

whey (liquid)

  whey   way (method)

  whey   weigh
                   (measure)

which (what)

  which   witch (magic)

whichever

whiff

whiffle, -fled, -fling

while, whiled, whiling (time)

  while   wile (trick)

whilst

whim

whimper, -ed, -ing

whimsey, -sies

whimsical, -ally

whimsicality, -ties

whimsy, -sies

whine, whined, whining (complain)

  whine   wine (grape
                  juice)

whinge, whinged, whingeing

whinny, -nies

whinny, -nied, -nying

whip, whipped, whipping

whipbird

whipcord

whiplash

whippersnapper

whippet

whipping boy

whip-round

whirl (spin)

  whirl   whorl (circle)

whirligig

whirlpool

whirlwind

whirr, whirred, whirring

whisk, whisked, whisking

whisker

whiskey, -keys (U.S., Irish)

whisky, -kies (Scotch, Canadian)

whisper, -ed, -ing

whist

whistle, -tled, -tling

whistler

  whisul   whistle

whit (jot)

  whit   wit (humour)

white, whiter, whitest

whitebait, -bait

whitecap

white-collar

white-elephant

white ensign

white-eye

whitefish, -fishes, -fish

white flag

white lie

white light

white pointer

white slave

whitewash

whither (where)

  whither   wither (shrivel)

whiting

whitlow

whittle, -tled, -tling

  whitul   whittle

whiz, whizzed, whizzing

who

whoa (stop)

  whoa   woe (sorrow)

who'd (who would)

  whod   who'd

whodunit

whoever

whole (all)

  whole   hole (opening)

wholegrain

wholehearted

wholemeal

whole number

wholesale, -saled, -saling

wholesome, -ly

who'll (who will)
    wholl   who'll

wholly (entirely)
    wholly   holy (good)

whom
    whom   womb (uterus)

whoop (cry)
    whoop   hoop (ring)

whoopee

whooping cough

whoops

whoops-a-daisy

whoosh

whop, whopped, whopping

whopper

whore, whored, whoring
    whore   who're

who're (who are)

whorl (circle)
    whorl   whirl (spin)

whorled

who's (who has)
    whos   who's

whose (possessive)

whosoever
    whur   whirr
    whurl   whirl (spin)
    whurl   whorl (circle)

who've (who have)
    whove   who've

why, whys
    wich   which
                   (question)
    wich   witch (magic)

wick

wicked, -ly

wickedness

wicker

wickerwork

wicket

wicket-keeper

wide, wider, widest

wide-angle

widely

widen, -ed, -ing

widespread

widgie

widow, -ed, -ing

widower

width

wield
    wierd   weird

wife, wives

wig, wigged, wigging

wiggle, -gled, -gling

wiggly
    wiggul   wiggle

wigwam

wilco

wild, -ly

wildcat, -catted, -catting

wildcat strike

wilderness

wildfire

wild flower

wildfowl

wild-goose chase

wildlife

Wild West

wile (trick)
    wile   while (time)

wilful, -ly

wiliness

will, willed, willing

willingness

will-o'-the-wisp

willow

willowy

willpower

willy-nilly
    wilst   whilst

wilt, wilted, wilting

wily, -lier, -liest
    wim   whim
    wimen   women

> For other wi- words,
> look under **whi-**.

wimple, -pled, -pling

win, won, winning

wince, winced, wincing

winch, winched, winching
wind, -ed, -ing (air)
wind, wound, winding (turn)
windbag
windbreak
windcheater
winder
windfall
wind gauge
windjammer
windlass
windmill
window
window-dressing
window-shop, -shopped, -shopping
windpipe
windrow
windscreen
windsock
windsurf, -ed, -ing
windsurfer
wind-tunnel
windvane
windward
windy, windier, windiest
wine, wined, wining (grape juice)

  wine   whine
                   (complain)

wing, winged, winging
winger
wingspan
wingspread
wink, -ed, -ing
winkle, -kled, -kling
winnings
winnow, -ed, -ing
winnower
winsome, -ly
winsomeness
winter
wintery
wintry

  wip   whip

> For other wip- words,
> look under **whip-**.

wipe, wiped, wiping

wipe-out
wiper
wire, wired, wiring
wireless
wirrah

  wirl   whirl (spin)
  wirl   whorl (circle)
  wirr   whirr

wiry, wirier, wiriest
wisdom
wisdom tooth, -teeth
wise, wiser, wisest
wisecrack
wisecracker
wish, wished, wishing
wishbone
wishful, -ly
wishy-washy

  wisk   whisk

> For other wis- words,
> look under **whis-**.

wisp, wisped, wisping
wisteria
wistful, -ly
wistfulness
wit (humour)

  wit   whit (jot)

> For other wit- words,
> look under **whit-**.

witch (magic)

  witch   which
                 (question)

witchcraft
witchdoctor
witchetty grub
witch-hunt
witch-hunting
with
withdraw, -drew, -drawn, -drawing
withdrawal
withdrawal sympton
withdrawn

  withdroo   withdrew

wither, -ed, -ing (shrivel)

  wither   whither (where)

withers		womanly	
withhold, -held, -holding		womb	
withholder		wombat	
within		women	
withold	withhold	women's lib	
without		women's liberation	
withstand, -stood, -standing		womera	
witness, -ed, -ing		won (win)	
witticism		won	one (number)
wittisism	witticism	wonder, -ed, -ing (think)	
witty, -tier, -tiest		wonder	wander (walk)
wives		wonderful, -ly	
wiz	whiz	wonderland	
wizard		wonderment	
wizened		wondrous, -ly	
wo	whoa (stop)	wondrus	wondrous
wo	woe (sorrow)	wonky, wonkier, wonkiest	
wobbegong		wont (accustomed)	
wobble, -bled, -bling		wont	want (need)
wobble board		wont	won't (will not)
woble	wobble	won't (will not)	
wobul	wobble	won ton (dough)	
wod	wad	wonton	wanton (lewd)
wodle	waddle	woo, wooed, wooing	
wodul	waddle	wood (timber)	
woe (sorrow)		wood	would (will)
woe	whoa (stop)	woodblock	
woebegone		woodcarving	
woeful, -ly		woodchip	
woft	waft	woodchuck	
woful	woeful	woodcut	
wolet	wallet	wooden, -ly	
wok		woodenness	
wolf, wolves		woodwind	
wolfish, -ly		woodwork	
wolfhound		woody, woodier, woodiest	
wolfram		wooer	
wolf spider		woof, -ed, -ing	
wolf-whistle, -led, -ling		woofer	
wolop	wallop	wool	
wolow	wallow	wool classer	
wolves		wool classing	
wom	womb	woolclip	
woman, women		woolen	woollen
womanise, -nised, -nising		woolf	wolf
womaniser		wool-gatherer	
womanish, -ly		wool-gathering	

woolgrower
wool-growing
woollen
woollies
woolly, -lier, -liest
woolshed
wool-stapler
wool-stapling
woom   womb
wooman   woman
woomera
woond   wound
woozily
wooziness
woozy
wop   whop (hit)
wor   war
worble   warble
worbul   warble
word, worded, wording
worden   warden
wordily
wordiness
wordless, -ly
word processor
wordrobe   wardrobe
wordy, -dier, -diest
wore
worf   wharf
worfair   warfare
work, worked, working
workable
workaday
workaholic
workbench
workbox
worker
work force
workhorse
workhouse
working capital
working class, -classes
working model
working party, -parties
workman, -men
work-out
works committee

workshop
work-to-rule
worl   whirl (spin)
worl   whorl (circle)
world (earth)
world   whirled (spun)
world-class
worldliness
worldly, -lier, -liest
worm, wormed, worming
worm   warm (heat)
wormhole
wormwood
wormy, wormier, wormiest
worn (tired)
worn   warn (signal)
worn-out
worp   warp
worrier
worrisome
worry, -ries
worry, -ried, -rying
worse
worsen, -ed, -ing
worship, -shipped, -shipping
worshipper
worst
worsted
wort (plant)
wort   wart (lump)
worth
worthily
worthiness
worthless, -ly
worthwhile
worthy, -thier, -thiest
wos   was

> For other wo- words,
> look under **wa-**.

would (will)
would   wood (timber)
would-be
wouldn't (would not)
wouldnt   wouldn't
wound, wounded, wounding (injure)
wove

woven
wowser
wrack (seaweed)
wraith
wrangle, -gled, -gling
wrangler
   wrangul   wrangle
wrap, wrapped or wrapt, wrapping
wrapper
wrath
wrathful, -ly
wreak, -ed, -ing
wreath, wreaths (flowers)
wreathe, -thed, -thing (encircle)
wreck, -ed, -ing
wreckage
wrecker
   wrek   wreck
wren
wrench, -ed, -ing
wrest, wrested, wresting
wrestle, -tled, -tling
wrestler
wretch
wretched, -ly
   wri   wry
wrick, wricked, wricking
wriggle, -gled, -gling
wriggler
wriggly
   wrigul   wriggle
wright (worker)
wring, wrung, wringing
wringer
wrinkle, -kled, -kling
wrinkly
   wrinkul   wrinkle
wrist
wristpin
wristwatch
writ
write, wrote, written, writing
   write   right (true)
   write   rite (ceremony)
   write   wright (worker)
write-off, written-off, writing-off
writer

writhe, writhed, writhing
written
wrong
wrongdoing
wroth
wrought
wrought iron
wrung
wry, wrier, wriest
   wun   one (number)
   wun   won (win)
   wunce   once
   wunder   wonder
   wunse   once
   wur   whirr
   wurl   whirl (spin)
   wurl   whorl (circle)
wurley
wurlitzer
wurrung
wurrup
wye, wyes

X-axis
X chromosome
  X cromosome   X chromosome
  xenofobia   xenophobia
xenophobe
xenophobia
xenophobic
  xerograf   xerograph
  xerografic   xerographic
  xerografy   xerography
xerograph
xerographic
xerography
  xeroks   xerox
xerox
Xmas
X-ray
X-ray tube
xylocarp
  xylofone   xylophone
  xylograf   xylograph
  xylografer   xylographer
  xylografic   xylographic
  xylografy   xylography
xylograph
xylographer
xylographic
xylography
xyloid
xylophagous
xylophone
xylophonic
xylophonist

Yy

y   why
yabber
  yabbie   yabby
yabby, yabbies
yacht
yachting
  yack   yak
yahoo
yahweh
yak, yakked, yakking
yakka
yam
  yandie   yandy
yandy
Yang
yank, yanked, yanking (pull)
Yank (American)
yap, yapped, yapping
yard
yardarm
yardstick
yarmelke
yarmulke
yarn, -ed, -ing
yarran
yaw, -ed, -ing
  yaw   yore (long ago)
  yaw   your
  yaw   you're (you are)
yawl
yawn, -ed, -ing
yaws (disease)
  yaws   yours
Y-axis
  yay   yea
Y chromosome
  Y cromosome   Y chromosome
ye

yea
yeah
  yeald   yield
year
yearbook
yearling
yearly, -lies
yearn, -ed, -ing
yeast
yeasty, yeastier, yeastiest
  yeeld   yield
  yeer   year
  veest   yeast
yell, -ed, -ing
yellow
yellowcake
yellowish
yellow pages
yellow peril
  yelosih   yellowish
  yelow   yellow
yelp, -ed, -ing
yen, yenned, yenning
yeoman, -men
  yern   yearn
yes, yeses
yes-man, -men
yesterday
yesteryear
yet
yeti
  yety   yeti
yew (tree)
  yew   ewe (sheep)
  yew   you (person)
  yewse   use
  yewshual   usual
  yewshuul   usual
  yewsual   usual
  yewsuul   usual
  ┌─────────────────────────────┐
  │ For other ye- words,   │
  │   look under u-.   │
  └─────────────────────────────┘
Yiddish
yield, yielded, yielding
Yin
yippee

yob
yodel, -delled, -delling
yodeller

yodle	yodel
yodul	yodel

yoga

yogert	yoghourt
yogert	yoghurt
yogert	yogurt

yoghourt
yoghurt
yogurt
yogi, -gis
yogism
yoicks
yoke, yoked, yoking (frame)

yoke	yolk (egg)

yokel

yokle	yokel
yokul	yokel

yolk (egg)

yoman	yeoman

Yom Kippur
yonder
yoo-hoo
yore (long ago)

yore	yaw (move)
yore	your
yore	you're (you are)
yors	yours

yorker
Yorkshire pudding

yot	yacht

you (person)

you	ewe (sheep)
you	yew (tree)

you'd (you would)

youd	you'd

you'll (you will)

youll	you'll

young
youngster
your (possessive)

your	yaw (move)
your	yore (long ago)
your	you're (you are)

you're (you are)

youre	you're

yours
yourself, -selves
youth, youths
youthful, -ly
you've (you have)

youve	you've
yowey	yowie

yowie
yowl, yowled, yowling
yoyo, -yos
yuan

yuckey	yucky, yukky
yuckie	yucky, yukky

yucky, yuckier, yuckiest
yuk
yukky, yukkier, yukkiest
yule (Christmas)

yule	you'll (you will)

yummy, yummier, yummiest

yung	young
yungster	youngster
yurn	yearn
yuse	use
yuseful	useful
yusual	usual
yusuul	usual
yutensle	utensil
yutensul	utensil
yuterine	uterine
yuteris	uterus
yuterus	uterus
yuth	youth
yutilise	utilise
yutopia	utopia

> For other yu- words,
> look under u-.

Zz

zabaglione
zany, -nier, -niest
zap, zapped, zapping
   zar   tsar
zeal
zealot
zealotry
zealous, -ly
zebra
zebra crossing
zebu
   zeel   zeal
   zefer   zephyr
   zelot   zealot
   zelous   zealous
Zen
zenith
zenithal
   zenofobia   xenophobia
   zenophobia   xenophobia
   zepher   zephyr
zephyr
   zeplen   zeppelin
zeppelin
   zercon   zircon
zero, -ros
zero, -roed, -roing
   zeroks   xerox
zero population growth
   zerox   xerox
zest
zestful, -ly
   zigote   zygote
zigzag, -zagged, -zagging
zilch
zillion
   zilofone   xylophone
   zilophone   xylophone

zinc
zing
   zink   zinc
zinnia
Zion
Zionism
Zionist
Zionistic
zip, zipped, zipping
zip-fastener
zipper
zippy, -pier, -piest
zircon
zirconium
zither
zodiac
zodiacal
zombie, -bies
zombiism
   zomby   zombie
zone, zoned, zoning
zonk, zonked, zonking
zoo
   zoochiney   zucchini
   zoochini   zucchini
   zoologey   zoology
zoological, -ly
zoologist
zoology, -gies
zoom, zoomed, zooming
zot, zotted, zotting
zucchini, zucchini, zucchinis
Zulu, -lus, -lu
Zuni, -nis, -ni
zwieback
zygote

HARRAP'S ENGLISH STUDY AIDS

In the same series:

ENGLISH GRAMMAR
★ Comprehensive grammar of modern English
★ Ideal reference for all users of English
★ Lively examples to illustrate grammatical points
★ Special treatment of 'problem' areas

142mm × 96mm/256pp/plastic cover
ISBN 0 245-54746-0

ENGLISH VERBS
★ 1,000 phrasal verbs with definitions and examples
★ Verb formation
★ Tense usage
★ Index to verb patterns and forms

142mm × 96mm/256pp/plastic cover
ISBN 0 245-54745-2

BASIC ENGLISH VOCABULARY
★ 2,000 frequently used words
★ Thousands of other words formed from the main words
★ Many examples to show how each word is used
★ Short notes to explain language problems
★ Exercises and key

142mm × 96mm/331pp/plastic cover
ISBN 0 245-54747-9

ENGLISH SYNONYMS
★ 8,000 key words alphabetically listed
★ Synonyms grouped according to meaning
★ Parts of speech specified for each key word
★ Clear distinction between literal and figurative meanings

142mm × 96mm/abt 400pp/plastic cover
ISBN 0 245-54831-9

ENGLISH USAGE
★ Over 4,000 alphabetical entries
★ Practical guidance on all aspects of usage
★ Clear examples to illustrate spelling and grammar rules
★ Coverage of foreign and scientific terms

142mm × 96mm/abt 400pp/plastic cover
ISBN 0 245-54830-0

MINI ENGLISH DICTIONARY
★ 125,000 words and meanings
★ Totally modern vocabulary
★ Definitions for every word
★ Phonetic transcriptions

142mm × 96mm/633pp/plastic cover
ISBN 0 245-54587-5